# BY WHAT RIGHT?

## A Commentary on the Supreme Court's Power to Revise the Constitution

BY
**LOUIS LUSKY**

THE MICHIE COMPANY
*Law Publishers*
CHARLOTTESVILLE, VIRGINIA

COPYRIGHT 1975

BY

THE MICHIE COMPANY

A portion of Chapter I and all of Chapter II were published November 6, 7, and 8, 1974, and an excerpt from Chapter XVI was published March 31, 1975, by the New York Law Journal, all under the copyright of Louis Lusky.

Library of Congress Catalog Card No. 75-32387

To Grenville Clark, Private Citizen (1882-1967)
Defender of the Court and
the Constitution

# TABLE OF CONTENTS

|  | PAGE |
|---|---|
| Preface | vii |
| Acknowledgments | ix |
| Apologia | 1 |

### Part One. The Task and the Tools

| | | |
|---|---|---|
| I | The Thesis | 9 |
| II | Why Judicial Review? | 27 |
| III | Terms and Concepts | 44 |
| IV | Lawmaking and Constitution-making | 59 |
| V | Constitutional Interpretation | 68 |
| VI | Implied Power | 85 |

### Part Two. The Observational Data

| | | |
|---|---|---|
| VII | The 1937 Crossroads | 97 |
| VIII | Peace...the Presence of Justice | 115 |
| IX | Freedom of Expression and Electoral Rights | 124 |
| X | Protection of the Suspect and the Accused | 145 |
| XI | Church-State Separation | 167 |
| XII | Equality: Race—The Post-Reconstruction Heritage | 179 |
| XIII | Equality: Race—The Post-World War II Development | 211 |
| XIV | Equality: Beyond Race | 243 |

### Part Three. A Modest Proposal

| | | |
|---|---|---|
| XV | The Court's New Role | 273 |
| XVI | What Difference It All Makes | 311 |
| XVII | *Quo Vadimus?* | 349 |

| | |
|---|---|
| Numbered Notes | 369 |
| Table of Cases | 407 |
| Subject Index | 419 |

# Preface

This has been a very hard book to write. Ever since I became a lawyer I have revered the United States Supreme Court as the finest of our institutions — and I still do. The book was begun as an effort to justify virtually everything the Court had done since its 1937 rebirth as the citadel of American freedom, equality, and justice. As I studied and wrote, however, I found that I could not do what I had planned. Gradually I became convinced that the Court's record of stunning achievement is significantly flawed. In the past few years particularly, the Justices have given serious cause for suspicion that they have come to consider the Court to be above the law. Like a son who is just discovering his father to be less than perfect, I was shaken by the deepening suspicion that my Galahad was a Lancelot.

My difficulty would not have been so great if the only consequence of erroneous analysis were damage to my professional reputation; but the potential for harm is more extensive. Exploratory surgery is a hazardous procedure. When one applies the logical scalpel to get inside the body politic and examine close-up the functioning and interrelationship of its major organs, there is a chance of infecting the patient. People whose interest is not to improve its health but to kill it (their most effective weapon being cultivation of cynicism about the society's vaunted ideals) will get the same close-up look as everyone else who reads these pages.

More worrisome than such anarchists are the totalitarians. Their program is not to kill government but to focus its whole power on a single objective, the regimentation of thought and action in pursuit of submissive conformity. They will doubtless take advantage of the close-up look for the purpose of maiming the body politic rather than improving its health. They will adduce the marshaled evidence in support of their own prediction that congenital disorders ("internal contradictions," the Leninists call them) *must* kill it unless radical surgery is performed. Exploiting the universal yearning for simple solutions, they will profess despair at the complexity of the organism (and of its function and dysfunction) and bewail the time and sustained effort that conservative therapy demands, saying: "The illness is too acute for temporizing expedients. Better to cut away whatever is nonessential to life, though it leave the organism crippled, than to attempt salvage of valuable organs whose present malfunction is revealed to lie at the root of the trouble. The state can *live* without freedom of expression, equality of opportunity, and other civil liberties; and life without them — bleak as it may be — is more tolerable than relapse into anarchic barbarism, which is societal death."

Thus there are two dangers. The exploratory surgeon runs the personal risk that he will be seen as the coadjutor of all who seek to make use of his observations. He also runs the much graver risk that his observations will be used destructively. What makes these risks acceptable is the faith that constructive use is also possible, and the blind hope that most Americans have the patience and wisdom it demands.

That faith and hope have driven me to complete the book.

Louis Lusky

Columbia Law School
New York, New York
May 16, 1975

## Acknowledgments

It is customary for an author to make known his indebtedness to those who have helped him on his manuscript. I must start further back by acknowledging the inspiration and encouragement I received from Grenville Clark, without which there might never have been a manuscript.

From the very beginning of my career at the bar and for the first three decades of this book's long gestation, Mr. Clark showed me — as he coped with one severe challenge after another, year after year — that labors in the public interest are compatible with the effective practice of law, even in a big, hardnosed law firm. Today this may seem obvious, but 37 years ago it was not; the tithing practice now followed by many enlightened firms, which detach junior associates for as much as a day a week to work for the poor in neighborhood law offices, would have been ridiculed as an idealistic dream.

In the milieu of a pre-World War II Wall Street law office, a young lawyer could easily fear that time spent in unpaid representation of dissenters or alleged criminals (other than prosperous white-collar offenders such as tax evaders and anti-trust violators) would impair his chances for eventual accession to partnership in his firm — the conventional hallmark of professional success. Consider what it meant for him to see a founding partner champion justice for the nonconformer, the outcast, or the accused. Mr. Clark had won his spurs in the arena of Big Business during the proud halcyon days before 1929. He had helped to organize one of the half-dozen greatest legal engines of New York City. He commanded the respect of even that citadel of conservatism, as it then was, the American Bar Association. And still he acknowledged the duty to resist oppression wherever he saw it. His courage was not only a mighty reassurance for the novice; it also endowed Root, Clark, Buckner & Ballantine with a distinction enjoyed by few of its fellow-Titans; and it nourished the public careers of a whole generation of younger associates of whom John

M. Harlan and Henry J. Friendly, though perhaps the best known, have been by no means the only exemplars.

To provide a few specifics that will sharpen the picture of this remarkable man, let me refer to some of the public work Mr. Clark did while I was privileged to serve as one of his helpers. In the spring of 1938, a few months before I joined his firm as the most junior of associates, he had made history with an address to the American Bar Association in which he advanced the then outlandish thesis that defense of constitutional rights is a fundamentally conservative line of work and that the venerable Association ought no longer suffer it to be virtually monopolized by liberal and left-wing organizations. Responding to his challenge, the Association established its Bill of Rights Committee and appointed Mr. Clark chairman. And it so happened that, having assembled a group of distinguished lawyers and law teachers to serve with him, Mr. Clark was ready for action at just about the time when I came to his firm.

This is how it came to pass that he invited me to assist him and his committee in writing the first two of the great briefs they filed in the United States Supreme Court. One of them successfully opposed the claim of Mayor Frank Hague of Jersey City to dictatorial control over speeches and demonstrations in the city streets and parks, and his "deportation" of Norman Thomas to prevent the Socialist leader from addressing a public meeting. The other opposed, vainly at first but successfully three years later, the expulsion from public school of young Jehovah's Witnesses who refused to join in a flag salute ceremony which they and their parents considered a violation of the Second Commandment's injunction against bowing down to graven images.

World War II took both Mr. Clark and me away from his law firm. In 1944 he retired from active legal practice and moved to Dublin, New Hampshire, where for the rest of his life he devoted most of his formidable strength to the quest for world peace. Most, but not all; he still found time to intervene in major civil liberties issues, and was instrumental in persuading the Ford Foundation to establish the Fund for the Republic (now the Center for the Study of Democratic Institutions) to resist erosion of citizen liberties. With the help of other lawyers, of whom I was one, he also participated in a number of broadly significant cases. For example, in 1960 he retained me to request reconsideration by the Supreme Court of its 1959 ruling which bade fair to result in life imprisonment for Dr. Willard Uphaus by reason of his refusal to cooperate in an investigation of alleged subversives by Louis C. Wyman, then Attorney General of New Hampshire. The next year he retained me on a "watching brief" to report on the Freedom Rider cases in Montgomery, Alabama, and Jackson, Mississippi (and, with no publicity at all, advanced $20,000 of his own money to help meet extortionate bail requirements in the Jackson cases).

Enough has been said to show why it is right to dedicate a book about constitutional law to Grenville Clark. But I must add one more thing which, perhaps more than all the others, makes it appropriate to dedicate *this* book to him. While I was still in my last year of law school, President Franklin D. Roosevelt attempted to bring the Supreme Court under his control by means of his so-called "Court-packing" program. Mr. Clark, a friend of F.D.R. since their days at school together and a sympathetic though not undiscriminating supporter of his legislative objectives which the Court had been stubbornly frustrating, led the winning fight against subjection of the Court to the executive's will. This determination to defend the Court as an institution while insisting upon the right and duty to call upon it to correct its mistakes (as we did in the *Uphaus* case) is my own central theme.

It is to Grenville Clark that I owe the sense of obligation which has led me to offer the observations and appraisals of which the book consists.

\* \* \* \* \*

Now for brief thanks to the people who helped me get going on the manuscript and then shape it into this book. They are more than ordinarily numerous; I know what the astronauts mean when they acknowledge, as they always do, the vital part played by their co-workers back in Houston. I simply cannot name every one of my valued helpers without expanding this prefatory note beyond reasonable bounds. On the other hand, it is equally impossible for me to leave unmentioned those who have made major contributions.

Most of them fall into two categories: those who helped me find the time for research and the initial writing, and those who helped me shape the first draft into this book. I can do no more than name them here. In the first category are my Dean, Michael I. Sovern (who enabled me to take a year off from teaching by locating a replacement on very short notice) and those who, in various ways, aided me in financing the twelve-month salary interruption: Henry J. Friendly, Millard L. Midonick, Maury L. Spanier and the Dextra Baldwin McGonagle Foundation, Sanford M. Jaffe and the Ford Foundation, and Bernard H. Goldstein. In the second category are those who read my several drafts and criticized, scolded, ridiculed, and stormed at them until my pride of authorship yielded to their words of pure gold. They include my wife Ruth, my daughter Mary and her fiancé Michael H. Friedman, Priscilla Robertson, George D. Braden, Shana Conron, Herbert A. Deane, Sigmund Diamond, Ferrie Feldbrugge, Tim Koopmans, Herman J. Kornreich, Robert B. Wrege, my constitutional law students, and a full quota of my colleagues on the Columbia Law School Faculty — Walter Gellhorn, Milton Handler, Herbert Wechsler (three who were also my teachers, forty years ago), Harvey J. Goldschmid, Ruth B. Ginsburg, R. Kent Greenawalt, Louis Henkin, Alfred E. Hill, Michael Meltsner, Walter E. Oberer, Maurice Rosenberg, Peter L. Strauss, H. Richard Uviller, and William F. Young, Jr. I am the more grateful because most of them had reservations about some of the things I say in the book.

There are a few whose contributions were critically important for special reasons. It was Priscilla Robertson who drove me to realize that the Court's post-1969 decisions had trapped me between my desire to appraise its work fully and honestly and my hope of justifying virtually everything it had done since 1937, a predicament explained below in my Apologia. It was Harold Leventhal who gave me a decisive push at a moment when I was ready to give the project up. And it was Rose and Bill Martin whose spontaneous generosity buoyed me in a way known only to us.

ACKNOWLEDGMENTS

The earlier drafts would have been delayed for months, except for the stenographic and administrative skills of Anne Lupo who shepherded them to completion. The later drafts achieved timely birth only through the patient and painstaking eagerness of my secretary Betty Kopple. Fred Santillan and his tireless crew in the Columbia Law School machine room responded uncomplainingly to my endless requests for rapid xerox and multilith work. And, by no means least, that redoubtable lawyer-cum-librarian Sam Cohen and his staff of Columbia reference librarians nosed out dozens of obscure publications for indispensable documentation, verification, or correction of my aging memory.

With such support, how could one fail?

## *Apologia*

I am irretrievably prejudiced in favor of substituting law for self-help as a means of resolving social conflict. The reader is entitled to know this basic personal bias of mine, which doubtless pervades the whole ensuing discussion of the question whether the United States Supreme Court is still the law's servant or has become its master.

I do not deny all moral justification of civil disobedience, or the inevitability of other crime, in the world as it is. I have done my share of advocacy on behalf of those who have defied the law in the name of conscience or engaged in criminal activity for less altruistic reasons.[1] Yet, so far as writing and teaching are concerned, my guiding hope is to seek ways of making civil disobedience *unnecessary* and of relieving the social pressures that conduce to criminal behavior of the headstrong or selfish variety.

Like others of my generation, I grew up admiring the exploits of Robin Hood. But a glance at my writings [2] will reveal consistent and repeated efforts to put the twentieth-century Robin Hoods out of business. I have not proposed that they be cowed into submission (which all history shows to be impossible in the long run). Instead, I have worked at civilizing the Sheriff of Nottingham and those he seeks to protect — who, nowadays, are collectively described as The Establishment. With full recognition of the possible paradox, I affirm (a) that justice is as real, as objectively definable and recognizable, *and as natural,* as is physical and mental health; *

---

* At pages 47-48 of my brief for the petitioner in Thompson v. City of Louisville, 362 U.S. 199 (1960), I said:

> We hold that justice is a real thing having an objective existence and knowable attributes. It is the solvent which converts raw power into morally binding law. The courts are privileged to seek it and to define its meaning in particular contexts, but they are powerless to alter its substance.
>
> There are cases where the pursuit of justice is a complex matter, and reasonable judgments may differ as to where it leads. But there are also cases — and this is one of them — where even a simple man can know that justice has been denied him. And that knowledge is a grievous hurt.
>
> The hurt done by a denial of justice is not easy to describe, but it is nonetheless real. A man's sense of innate dignity, his conception of himself as a person unique yet part of a community, his feeling of proud security in the impartiality of the law — impairment or destruction of these values cannot be

but (b) that, nevertheless, "Man has hence this cause of pride: that he has bethought himself of justice in a world without justice, and has put justice there."[3] I disagree with those who hold that ability to achieve emancipation from unyielding standards of right and wrong is a measure of maturity.*

My preference for law is a preference for objectively understandable rules that lead to similar results on similar facts, regardless of the identity of the parties or the adjudicator.[4] Occasionally I have wondered how it came to pass that my sense of personal security depends importantly on the existence of knowable rules. Perhaps it results partly from the fact that I belong to what Justice Frankfurter once called "the most vilified and persecuted minority in history."[5] Knowable rules of conduct are the midwives of cultural assimilation, which in this land of more or less recent immigrant families has come to be taken for granted, and is familiarly referred to as the American melting pot. Any Italian-American, Polish-American, or other hyphenated American who can learn the rules of the social game possesses the keys to the kingdom.** He can make himself and his children full participants in the general community.[6] If there are no knowable rules, however, so that admission to the mainstream depends upon the personal favor of those who have already entered it, assimilation is slow and difficult. That was why four of the Justices

---

measured in money. Yet such a hurt can shatter a man. And that is the hurt which is done when justice is denied.

* A scintillating disquisition upon the nature of justice — a subject that has baffled many great minds — has been published since the above words were written. It is Ronald P. Sokol's *Justice After Darwin* (1975). I recommend it to those who wish to probe more deeply into that subject.

** I do not think this is an overstatement. True, it is *logically* conceivable for a rule to be knowable but nevertheless unfairly discriminatory. For example, a rule that only white males could be lawyers or jurors or river-boat pilots would be entirely knowable. In fact, however, revelation of the substance of such a rule exposes it to constitutional attack if official discrimination is involved, and exposes it to severe social disapproval and possible legislative prohibition if the discrimination is purely private. That is why the most stubborn strongholds of privileged personal status are defended through concealment rather than through candid avowal of discriminatory purpose. *See* Lusky, *Racial Discrimination and the Federal Law: A Problem in Nullification,* 63 COLUM. L. REV. 1163, 1167-71 (1963).

(whose view would probably prevail today, at least with the aid of Title VII of the 1964 Civil Rights Act [7]) dissented in *Kotch v. Board of River Pilot Commissioners* (1947).[8]

In that case the Court upheld Louisiana pilotage laws which required (a) that state pilots guide all ships going through the Mississippi River approaches to New Orleans, (b) that certification by a board composed of pilots was a prerequisite to appointment as a new pilot, and (c) that only those with six months apprenticeship under an incumbent pilot were eligible for certification. The incumbent pilots' choice of apprentices was left unregulated. In practice, no one except a relative or friend of an incumbent was taken on as an apprentice so that Negroes and members of other minority groups could never become eligible for appointment as pilots, an honored calling. In the absence of knowable rules and acceptable, objective standards of eligibility, the melting pot did not work for them.

It is largely because of a fear of similar consequences that many law teachers, including me, have regretted the coarsening of law school grading systems and the abolition of class rank designations, which have attended the egalitarian surge that has swept over the universities in recent years. Enforcement of present laws against employment discrimination is far easier if the relative potential of law graduates can be quantified; and even before such laws were enacted some Jews, Negroes, and women were able to penetrate the WASP citadel of elite law firms by reason of their distinguished records of personal achievement in law school, "elitist" records they would be unable to obtain today. There is cause to fear that egalitarianism in the law schools may facilitate discrimination in the law offices.

Membership in an out-group can therefore easily breed devotion to knowable rules, as I think it did for me. It must not be supposed, however, that this is the only possible, or even the only rational, reaction. It is probably the more likely one if assimilation into the general mainstream is not too remote a hope, as it is not in the case of hyphenated Americans and most religious minorities. If the odds seem too long, however, the more likely reaction is a drive toward minority group solidarity (as by Malcolm X and by the Black

Panthers [9]), or even toward individual guerrilla warfare against the dominant classes (as by the self-styled Symbionese Liberation Army [10]). The century-long delay in making good the promise of the Emancipation Proclamation and the Civil War Amendments has understandably led a number of black Americans to these latter alternatives. Doubtless some of them, like some whites, have even descended to the bestial egocentrism depicted in Anthony Burgess' *The Clockwork Orange.*[11] But some of them, very probably the majority, aspire to such assimilation as has been achieved by Martin Luther King, Jr., Thurgood Marshall, and the many other Negroes who have won distinction and honor not as Negroes but as Americans.

That has been the achievement of many Jews as well. Justice Brandeis, Louis Marshall, Julius Rosenwald, and Samuel Gompers, for example (to name only the dead), made their way in the general community, the "big pond," though without ever renouncing the faith of their fathers. My own yearning is to follow in their footsteps. That probably accounts in part for my belief in the value of knowable rules, and for my decision to become a lawyer.

It also accounts for my almost instinctive preference for the position taken by Herbert Wechsler in his historic debate with the late Alexander Bickel. In 1959 Wechsler propounded the view that all actions of the Court, including decisions as to whether to speak at all on issues respecting the validity of action by the states or by the political organs of the Federal Government, should be governed by "neutral principles." "[T]he main constituent of the judicial process," he said in his 1959 Holmes Lectures at Harvard Law School, "is precisely that it must be genuinely principled, resting with respect to every step that is involved in reaching judgment on *analysis and reasons quite transcending the immediate result that is achieved."* [12] (Emphasis added)

In 1961, and then again more elaborately in 1962 in an enormously influential book (*The Least Dangerous Branch* [13]), Bickel took issue with Wechsler's blanket disapproval of result-oriented adjudication. Bickel denied that the Wechsler proposition, however appealing it might be as a statement of the ideal, did in fact describe the practice of the Court *in deciding whether and when to adjudicate constitutional questions on the merits.* Here, Bickel said, the Court acted on no principle susceptible of verbal formulation; rather, it acted on the "prudential" — one might say, more bluntly, opportunistic — basis of deciding questions if and when it thought the public welfare (as discerned by the Justices themselves) would be furthered.

Bickel went further. He affirmed the wholesomeness and utility of this prudential approach, and the unwisdom of attempting to formulate what may be called the principles of judicial activism. He agreed with Wechsler that, when the Court did take jurisdiction of a case, it should decide the case on a principled basis — that is, on a rationale to be applied also to other cases in the same field. But Bickel contended that in deciding *whether* to take jurisdiction the Court should and did act on a "prudential" basis. Bickel did *not* say, but the experience of the past dozen years has shown, that the "prudential" approach in the selection and mode of adjudication of cases — given the tremendous range of choice available to a Court which has time to decide only about a tenth of the cases that are tendered to it [14] — is by no means a trivial assumption of power. It is a very large assumption of power indeed; and, coupled with the Court's accelerating tendency to reconsider and modify accepted constitutional doctrine, it raises a serious question as to whether the Court has shaken itself free from all external restraint and begun to function as a continuing constitutional convention.

Such a possibility must be repellent to one who considers the existence of knowable rules to be supremely important. I recoiled from the Bickel position; and I was not alone.[15] To be sure, my experience as law clerk to Justice Stone at the 1937-1938 term left me quite unable to demonstrate that the Court adheres undeviatingly to the Wechsler view that even the grant or denial of certiorari should be governed by neutral principles. Nevertheless, for reasons to be stated later (in Chapter XVI), this did not trouble me then and does not trouble me now. The broad discretion exercised by the Court in accepting or rejecting appellate jurisdiction is, I think, reconcilable with the proposition that the Court is guided by neutral principles. The neutrality imperative is satisfied if (as I believe to be true) the Justices consider themselves obligated to vote on the grant or denial of full-dress review in accordance with articulable (even if largely unarticulated) standards, and if those standards could bear public inspection. For my immediate purposes the dominant fact is that, at least for the time being, the Court's summary actions on certiorari petitions and dismissal motions (usually without explanatory opinion) have not aroused substantial public skepticism as to the Court's adherence to neutral principles. The doubts that exist on this score result from what the Court says and does in adjudicating constitutional cases on their merits (usually *with* opinion).

As will appear, I am reluctantly compelled to conclude that a small but significant number of the Court's recent decisions must be disapproved not as casual aberrations but as usurpations of power. I regret the necessity of such disapproval, because of the danger that it may be misunderstood as disapproval of the Court as an institution and of the tremendously valuable work it has done in the past third of a century. Therefore let me affirm my belief that, of all our governmental organs — the three Federal branches, and the states with their subordinate municipalities — the Supreme Court is the only one which in recent years has performed splendidly. Untouched by scandal, alive to human need, ready to look through form to substance, and unafraid to translate into living law our noblest ideals of liberty, equality, and compassion for individual weakness, it has proved itself the citadel of the republic — the main instrument for societal self-perfection. I wish its course in the last few years had permitted the present commentary to remain unwritten.

Finally, I must acknowledge that, in a sense, this book is incomplete. It emphasizes the ideas that I believe to be primary, and de-emphasizes (perhaps to the point of neglect) finer nuances and shadings which — though valuable for the testing and refinement of the thesis, and therefore interesting to the constitutional law specialist — are less important to the general reader.

My election to address the general reader, not the specialist alone, is deliberate. It results from two considerations, one of which is a matter of principle and the other a matter of practical need. In the first place, American constitutional law contains such a large component of political science and pragmatic statesmanship that lawyers cannot rightly claim a monopoly upon it. Though I do not go as far as the late Justice Hugo L. Black, who thought it quite acceptable for nonlawyers to be seated on the Supreme Court,[16] I agree that basic constitutional choices (as distinguished from their implementation in specific cases) are well within the competence of intelligent people regardless of their professional status or the lack of it. In the second place, I believe that we are fast approaching — indeed, we may have reached, and conceivably even have passed — a moment of decision which may determine (if it has not already done so) the future of the Court for a long time to come. Therefore I consider it more useful to offer the relatively unadorned thesis now, and thus to invite critical comment that may help me and others improve and refine it, than to take the additional years which full elaboration would require.

I do hope to undertake that elaboration later on. At a minimum, I would like to expand the present documentation (which has been held to a respectable minimum) so as to explore the scholarly byways in a manner more satisfying to practitioners and teachers of constitutional law. Perhaps I can go further eventually, and offer something closer to a full-dress treatise. But in order to speak now rather than in 1984 or thereabouts, I have contented myself with enough footnotes to show that I am aware of the fine structure of this protean subject matter even though I have not dealt exhaustively with it. That is to say, I do not ignore the fact that there are responsible opinions contrary to mine on a number of points; I only defer my own rejoinder until there is time for full discussion of those opinions and of my reasons for taking a different path.

# Part One
# The Task and the Tools

CHAPTER I

## The Thesis

Since 1954 and especially since 1962, and *most* especially since 1969, the Court has engaged in constitutional innovation on a large and expanding scale;* the uneasy feeling has grown that neutral principles are being flouted; and rumbles of discontent have begun to be noticeable. Demand for impeachment of Chief Justice Warren, on the ground that the Court under his leadership had usurped the Article V amending power, was more than a murmur;[1] and in 1970 Congressman Gerald R. Ford spearheaded an actual attempt to impeach Justice Douglas (though ostensibly on grounds other than his readiness to revise the Constitution).[2]

Believing that nearly everything the Court had actually done was consistent with neutral principles that could survive public inspection, but that the Court itself had failed to make that important truth clear enough, I resolved to attempt the task myself. That was the genesis of this book.

What actually set me in motion was the appointment of four new

---

* The dates are based on observed changes in the Justices' apparent conception of their role, as revealed by a study of their opinions. It is interesting, though for present purposes unimportant, to speculate on the reasons for the changes. In this connection it may be noted (a) that 1962 was when Justice Goldberg succeeded Justice Frankfurter and added a fifth vote to the so-called liberal bloc comprised of Chief Justice Warren and Justices Black, Douglas, and Brennan, and (b) that 1969 was when President Nixon, having been elected partly because of a "law and order" backlash, took office and gained the power to appoint new Justices — a circumstance that incumbent Justices *may* have thought to add urgency to the need to nail down recent innovations in protection of individual rights, and if possible extend them. On the question whether the changes were *post hoc* or *propter hoc*, no opinion is expressed.

Justices by President Nixon within a space of little more than two years (1969 to 1971),\* each of them seemingly chosen partly because of his willingness to push the Court in a new direction — coupled with the President's obviously impending reelection in 1972 which made it likely that additional Justices of the same persuasion would soon join the first four. The time seemed right for (a) a public recommendation that the Court clarify the principles which I thought had controlled it, supported by (b) a demonstration that such an articulation of principles could be accomplished without repudiation of very much that the Court had done in the previous two decades, and without repudiation of *any* precedents of major public value. So I took advantage of my 1970 sabbatical leave and went to work on the necessary research.

In 1972, recognizing that the Court's situation might be volatile, that rapid change might occur very soon, and that a book would take a long time to complete, I was rash enough to publish a short article in the *New York Law Journal* (entitled, "The Unwritten U.S. Constitution") offering a preview of the book I was trying to write.[3] Even as I worked on the book, however, the thesis became hopelessly obsolete. It might well have been adequate to account for virtually all the Court had *done* down to 1969, and the truly valuable part of what it had *done* from then until 1971 (as distinguished from what it had said). A spate of fresh innovations, however, the most remarkable of which were the 1973 abortion rulings,[4] made it quite clear that neither the senior Justices nor the four Nixon appointees would accept my intended rationalization. Thus a return to the drawing board was indicated.

Although I have moved beyond the 1972 article, I pause to restate its central thesis; a number of my students have found it

---

\* Chief Justice Warren retired June 23, 1969, and Chief Justice Burger was sworn in the same day. Justice Fortas resigned on May 14, 1969, and Justice Blackmun was sworn in June 9, 1970, as his successor. Justice Black, having retired September 17, 1971 (and having died eight days later) was succeeded by Justice Powell on January 7, 1972. Justice Harlan, having retired September 23, 1971 (and having died on December 29) was succeeded by Justice Rehnquist on January 7, 1972. (Both Justice Powell and Justice Rehnquist had been appointed and confirmed late in 1971.)

helpful as a ground-breaker for the more elaborate analysis that here supersedes it. The following paragraphs, taken from "The Unwritten U.S. Constitution," should suffice for that purpose:

> The basic hypothesis is that the Court, in its constitutional decisions, is driven by a single dominating objective: the perfection and preservation of a society that is "open" in the sense that personal liberty is maximized and officials are the servants rather than the masters of the people, and yet is "self-governing" in the sense that rules of conduct — laws — are determined by electoral majorities which can and often do limit personal liberty in order to serve collective needs. The Court's unique and indispensable role is to formulate and enforce, through its power to grant or deny the imprimatur of legitimacy to any official act or omission, constitutional rules that reconcile (and blend together in a mutually reinforcing relationship) the opposing but equally important needs for (a) a society that is open, and (b) a society that is self-governing.
>
> The guiding principle is therefore to intervene against the other organs of government *if, but only if,* the conventional political processes of opinion formation, election, and legislative experimentation and compromise are (a) hampered or ignored by other organs of government, or (b) cannot be expected to yield an acceptable mix of liberty and authority (authority of the majority over the individual). It is a rule of necessity.
>
> I think I can demonstrate that, even during the last ten years, the stated principle has been at work in the Court — largely without regard for the election returns.
>
> Without attempting here to set forth an exhaustive enumeration of the principles — I shall call them "theorems" — that I think have been guiding the Court, and ought to guide it, I state the basic ones, *which, it will be noted, provide principled support for some of the decisions in which the Court itself gave no adequate justification in terms of "neutral principles"*:
>
> (1) The Court has primary responsibility for keeping the corrective political processes — the processes whereby the electorate ordinarily changes or repeals laws that are found to work badly — in effective working condition. This means, among other things, that the Court intervenes to prevent official interference with political expression, deprivation or degradation of the franchise, and denial of access to the ballot.

(2) The Court will accord plenary reexamination, in the mode of legislative action, to laws directed against discrete and insular minorities — groups with which so little kinship is felt by the politically dominant majority that the corrective political processes cannot be counted upon to afford relief from unjust laws. Racial and religious minorities are examples of such groups.

(3) The Court will require adherence to procedural standards that minimize the risk of convicting the innocent. Here the corrective political processes cannot be counted upon because the very fact of conviction (and perhaps even the fact of formal accusation) brands the accused as an enemy of society, and thus freezes off the public support that is required to activate the remedial political processes.

(4) The Court will do what it can, through such measures as the exclusionary rule, rendering illegally obtained evidence inadmissible in court, to discourage illegal action by the police; and it will hold prosecutors to their duty to conduct themselves as seekers after justice rather than as advocates privileged to win their cases by any means available.

Necessarily, a final theorem is to be added: That, unless one of the foregoing theorems (or a like theorem — the foregoing enumeration is not offered as being exhaustive) is applicable, the Court will *not* intervene.

It must not be supposed that the above theorems, or "neutral principles," purport to say what the Court *declares* it has been doing. The very reason for undertaking to describe the unwritten constitution is that the Court has not yet articulated, even for itself, a comprehensive rationale for its intervention in some cases and not in others.

The foregoing extracts from "The Unwritten U.S. Constitution" reveal the reason why, like Robert Louis Stevenson, I have had to continue on through Dieppe to Paris.* My five "theorems" were premised on an unduly mechanistic conception of the Court's function. They suggest that the Justices are more completely dominated by forces beyond their full comprehension and control than they probably are. Moreover, I accorded insufficient

---

\* Stevenson, *Crabbed Age and Youth,* Virginibus Puerisque 40, 54 (1897):

Because I have reached Paris, I am not ashamed of having passed through Newhaven and Dieppe.

recognition to the special constitutional status of problems inherited from black slavery, and the extent to which early interpretations (from 1873 to 1896) of the Civil War Amendments hobble rational attack on those problems in the manner probably contemplated by the Amendments' makers.

The 1972 article did, however, establish a useful level of generality for appraisal of the Court's position in the governmental scheme. It did undertake to strip away the worshipful attitude toward the Court that has beclouded perception of the basic issues on which its future status will mainly depend. It did identify most of the major national interests which the Court has been protecting through revision of the Constitution — neglecting to mention only the interest in church-state separation. And (though not in the above extract) it did describe fairly accurately the reasons why effective judicial review is a precious aspect of our governmental system; point out the true nature of the hazard involved in abuse of judicial review; and reflect the important relationship between the Court's caseload and the development of substantive constitutional doctrine.

What convinced me of the need to revise the thesis were a number of rulings in which the Justices — including, be it noted, at least three of the four Nixon appointees — made it quite clear that their conception of judicial review was fundamentally different from the conception underlying the article just quoted. I had posited a set of *unwritten* constitutional rules which I thought the Court was applying (and rightly so) in the same manner as it was applying the *written* Constitution and its formal Amendments. On January 22, 1973, however, when the Court announced its decisions in *Roe v. Wade* and *Doe v. Bolton* (the bellwether abortion cases), it became clear that no member of the Court (with the possible exception of Justice Rehnquist) would submit to any such canalization of judicial review. There had been premonitory rumblings, strongly suggesting that the Justices considered themselves free agents both in deciding whether a case was justiciable [5] and in promulgating substantively new constitutional rules;[6] but this was the convincer. At least eight of the nine showed themselves ready to engage in freehand constitution-making in order to combat what they viewed as basic injustice, in any field where they thought the Court's intervention would be helpful and effective. And, Justices Black and Harlan having died in 1971, there was no member of the Court highly sensitive to its failure to make clear the basis of its own authority to revise the Constitution — again, with the possible but not certain exception of Justice Rehnquist. A review of some representative cases will suffice to show that Nixon appointees (Chief Justice Burger and Justices Blackmun and Powell, if not Rehnquist) were no less willing than their senior colleagues to engage in constitution-making well outside the boundaries suggested by my five "theorems."

They did dissent from the assorted opinions that prevailed in *Furman v. Georgia* (1972).[7] There the other five Justices held on various grounds that the death penalty is unconstitutional as a cruel and unusual punishment if inflicted, as it then was, at a jury's unlimited discretion. But the Nixon appointees concurred with Justice White in *Apodaca v. Oregon* (1972)[8] to hold that, although the Sixth Amendment right to a jury trial in criminal cases is incorporated into the Fourteenth (and therefore applies to state as well as Federal prosecutions), the states are not bound by the settled Federal requirement that verdicts of guilt be unanimous. (Except for Justice Powell, the new appointees were ready to dispense with unanimous verdicts in Federal trials as well.[9]) *Wisconsin v. Yoder* (1972)[10] invalidated a compulsory education law as applied to Amish children whose parents, on religious grounds, objected to their attending high school. The Court's opinion, written by the Chief Justice and joined by Justice Blackmun (Justices Powell and Rehnquist taking no part), did not deny the state's power to compel attendance through elementary school, but held that the individual parent's decision must prevail with respect to high school. And in *Roe v. Wade* (1973)[11] Justice Blackmun, writing for a seven-man majority that included the Chief Justice and Justice Powell but not Justice Rehnquist, laid down a set of rules governing a newly created constitutional right of abortion.

This abortion opinion is a spectacular display of constitution-making. A Texas statute [12] prohibited abortion except "by medical advice for the purpose of saving the life of the mother." An unmarried woman who was pregnant at the commencement of the action (though not when the case was decided) was held to have standing to maintain a class action attacking the statute as an invasion of privacy. Justice Blackmun prefaced his discussion of the merits with a historical review of abortion, beginning with the ancient Persian Empire, possibly for the purpose of showing that abortion has not always been condemned. He pointed out that the Constitution had been held to guarantee some aspects of personal privacy, which he said "has some extension" to activities relating to marriage, procreation, contraception, family relationships, and child rearing and education.[13] He declared that "the right of personal privacy includes the abortion decision" [14] and characterized the right as "fundamental" [15] so that the case was governed by the "compelling governmental interest" test (to be discussed later on [16]) rather than by a presumption of constitutionality. Then, on the basis of this unconvincing attempt at justification of the Court's authority to do so, he embarked upon a delicate balancing of opposing interests.

The Justice recognized two state interests to be worthy of recognition, namely, protection of the woman's health and protection of the unborn child. The former, he said, is negligible during the first trimester of pregnancy, provided that an attending physician is in the picture:

> With respect to the State's important and legitimate interest in the health of the mother, the "compelling" point, in the light of present medical knowledge, is at approximately the end of the first trimester. This is so because of the now established medical fact . . . that until the end of the first trimester mortality in abortion may be less than mortality in normal childbirth. It follows that, from and after this point, a State may regulate the abortion procedure to the extent that the regulation reasonably relates to the preservation and

> protection of maternal health. Examples of permissible state regulation in this area are requirements as to the qualifications of the person who is to perform the abortion; as to the licensure of that person; as to the facility in which the procedure is to be performed, that is, whether it must be a hospital or may be a clinic or some other place of less-than-hospital status; as to the licensing of the facility; and the like.
>
> This means, on the other hand, that for the period of pregnancy prior to this "compelling" point, the attending physician, in consultation with his patient, is free to determine, without regulation by the State, that, in his medical judgment, the patient's pregnancy should be terminated. If that decision is reached, the judgment may be effectuated by an abortion free of interference by the State.[17]

During the first three months, the woman thus has the right to a curiously qualified "privacy." She can have her abortion without official permission, but she must have a physician who approves. This very probably makes good sense from a health standpoint, but the result is more aptly described as judicial regulation than as privacy.

As for the state's interest in protection of the unborn child, Justice Blackmun held it negligible until pregnancy has proceeded so far that the child may be capable of being born alive:

> With respect to the State's important and legitimate interest in potential life, the "compelling" point is at viability. This is so because the fetus then presumably has the capability of meaningful life outside the mother's womb. State regulation protective of fetal life after viability thus has both logical and biological justifications. If the State is interested in protecting fetal life after viability, it may go so far as to proscribe abortion during that period, except when it is necessary to preserve the life or health of the mother.[18]

These finely articulated rules bear all the earmarks of legislation — enlightened legislation no doubt, but legislation nevertheless. The factual assumption as to the state of the medical art may or may not be accurate for all areas, rural and urban. The value judgment that viability marks the tipping point where the unborn child becomes protectible is appealing but not indisputable. The reliance on physicians to guard against unsafe abortions, like the reliance on lawyers as observers at custodial interrogations and identification line-ups,[19] is a practical expedient hard to trace to any constitutional principle. And the underlying proposition that the Court rather than the state legislature bears primary responsibility for balancing the interests involved, is not rendered self-evident by intoning the term "fundamental."

The most extreme invasion of legislative prerogative, however, is one that has not received much public attention. It relates to what might be called the unborn child's right to death. Recall the Court's rule for abortions in late pregnancy:

> For the stage subsequent to viability, the State *in promoting its interest in the potentiality of human life* may, if it chooses, regulate, and even proscribe, abortion *except where it is necessary,* in appropriate medical judgment, *for the preservation of the life or health of the mother.*[20] (Emphasis added)

The Court thus strongly implied that an abortion must be permitted at *any* time, even during the ninth month of gestation, if necessary to preserve the mother's "health"; and the Court had already held that, as a matter of interpretation, "health" includes mental as well as physical health.[21] It has not yet expressly passed on the question whether, upon termination of pregnancy after viability, the mother (together with her physician) has a constitutional right to insist that the viable fetus be killed; but the above quotation, by its reference to the state's "interest in the potentiality of human life," strongly suggests that she does not. Certainly, the Court has not denied her the right to insist that the viable fetus be kept alive.

Now, the usual method of accomplishing an abortion late in pregnancy is by Caesarean section, which is calculated to result in the birth of a premature child. And there is no doubt that prematurely born babies are exposed to greater hazard of incomplete fetal development, and of post-natal catastrophe, than are babies carried to term. For example, prematurely born babies are very often incubator babies, and an incubator baby runs such risks as the danger of permanent blindness if, by reason of human or mechanical failure, it happens to be supplied with an excess of oxygen.* The net of it is that the Court appears to make the

---

\* Note well that I make no judgment as to *how many* premature babies suffer

judgment that in such a situation preservation of the mother's mental health is more important than protection of the child from abnormal risk of a life spent in darkness, or degraded by such deformities as cleft palate, harelip, or still more serious congenital defects such as brain damage.

This judgment involves considerations which, unlike the question whether life begins at conception or at viability, are based not on religious dogma (which principles of church-state separation would arguably entitle the Court to disregard [22]) but on purely secular, humanistic interests. If the issue must be resolved by a flat and rigid rule of constitutional law, as seven of the Justices appear to believe, there would seem to be only two humane ways of resolving it: (1) to forbid the abortion of a viable fetus, or (2) to require that the fetus be killed. If these are the only alternatives, there is no discernible reason why legislatures should not be permitted to make the choice between them. Yet the Court, in its wisdom, seems to deny the legislatures that power.

Of course, if the legislatures were free to perform their normal function of effecting fair compromise between competing interests, additional alternatives would be open. For example, a court or administrative tribunal might be authorized to hear and adjudicate applications for abortion after viability, plus feticide,

---

from defects of this kind. I rest my case upon two propositions that bypass this question: (a) If the risk is *at all* greater for premature babies, it is for the voters and not the judges or the physicians to decide how much is too much; if the voters believe that mercy to one potentially blind or brain-damaged child in ten million is enough to justify acceptance of heavy social costs, there is no self-evident reason why their judgment should not prevail. (b) Nothing in the statistics disproves the plausible assumption that premature babies are to *some* extent more exposed to the risk of blasted lives than are babies carried to term. Indeed, the assumption is more than merely plausible; its *prima facie* soundness is supported by accepted Darwinian views on natural selection, for there was most probably some survival-related reason why the human gestation period settled at about 280 days rather than a longer or shorter period as in the case of other animals.

Moreover, there may be social as well as physical consequences of premature birth. It has been found that a disproportionately large number of premature children turn out to be "battered children," or to suffer from the so-called "failure to thrive syndrome" in which no organic cause is found. *See* A. Fanaroff, J. Kennell & M. Klaus, *Follow-up of Low Birthweight Infants — The Predictive Value of Maternal Visiting Patterns,* 49 PEDIATRICS 287-90 (1972).

and to authorize them if the mother's need were found to be very substantial. It would be expected that such an application would be granted if, say, the mother had been impregnated incestuously and had concealed her pregnancy for seven months until it could be concealed no longer; or if the mother had been kidnaped, held hostage until her parents should give two million dollars worth of free groceries to the poor, raped and impregnated by the kidnaper, and not liberated until eight months thereafter. Contrariwise, it would be expected that the application would be denied if supported only by a borderline showing, made in the seventh month, that delivery of the child would afflict the mother with an anxiety neurosis.

It might also be possible to devise a different plan whereby, in the event of abortion after viability, the child would be immediately examined and, if found to be seriously defective, would be put to death by order of a court or administrative tribunal. The adequacy of such a plan would depend on the degree of accuracy with which an examination immediately after birth can be expected to reveal serious defects.

The Court, without demonstrating in any convincing way that it possesses lawful authority to do it, appears to have forbidden alternatives of this sort. It has forbidden them in a fully considered opinion that cannot be discounted as casual error, but rather betokens the deliberate determination to impose on the nation the will of seven men who have not been elected by the people. It is therefore necessary to ask the question to which this book is addressed: Is the Supreme Court still the law's servant, or has it now set itself above the law? *By what right* does it revise the Constitution?

It is the same question that is asked by the high prerogative writ *quo warranto* which has come down to us from early English law. *Black's Law Dictionary* (4th ed. 1951), at page 1417, defines *quo warranto* as

> a writ, in the nature of a writ of right for the king, against him who claimed or usurped any office, franchise, or liberty, to inquire *by what authority* he supported his claim, in order to determine the right. (Emphasis in original)

The question is a particularly fair one to ask the United States Supreme Court. The Court spends more and more of its time asking that same question of other governmental organs — Congress, the President, the states and their municipalities — and sternly limiting their authority where the right cannot be demonstrated. Sauce for the goose should be sauce for the gander, bitter though it be.

This nation has proudly proved that even a president cannot set himself above the law. Richard M. Nixon's landslide victory in the 1972 election did not license him to neglect his constitutional obligation "to take Care that the Laws be faithfully executed." It is necessary and right that the nine Justices be held to a like standard.

The more one studies the opinion of the seven-man majority in *Roe v. Wade,* the more he is tempted to conclude that the Justices have not only turned their backs upon the Wechsler plea for neutral principles, but have out-Bickeled Bickel in their zeal for "prudential" decision. One is tempted to conclude that the Court has indeed set itself above the Constitution, and is traveling its reformist way by dint of what Justice Byron R. White has called "raw judicial power." * One is tempted to conclude that the Justices have adopted a new conception of their role, of the meaning of their oath — prescribed by Article VI — "to support this Constitution." In short, one is tempted to conclude that there is no longer any problem on which the Court will defer to another organ of government if five or more of the Justices are confident (a) that their own solution is better and (b) that they can, as a practical matter, impose their solution upon the society.

Then, however, one considers the grave peril attendant upon such a course, peril both to the Court and to this nation that needs it to remain strong — a peril to be examined searchingly in Chapter

---

* Dissenting in Roe v. Wade, 410 U.S. 113, 222 (1973). The term "raw judicial power" is used, here and elsewhere, to denote the Court's ability to effectuate its will as a practical matter, regardless of the legitimacy of its command or prohibition. (It does *not* denote a power to enforce its will by physical means, as through marshals or other court personnel.) The term "power" *simpliciter* is used to mean "authority," or "legitimate power."

II. And so one cannot permit himself to abandon the hope of a government of laws, without casting about for a new explanation of the Court's behavior as *principled,* in Wechsler's sense, even if it is not principled in the exact way he envisaged.

Hence the thesis of the present book: The Court does revise the Constitution from time to time (exercising, to that extent, the prerogatives of a continuing constitutional convention) — *and this is legitimate* if, but only if, the Court submits to the restraint imposed by overriding principles and does not proceed on an *ad hoc* basis to implement the Justices' personal views of national policy. The overriding principles, and the limits upon them, are prescribed by the concept of implied judicial power.

The concept of implied power is familiar to American lawyers. Since *McCulloch v. Maryland* (1819)[23] it has been applied in determining the scope of Congressional power, and its use in determining the scope of Presidential power is almost as venerable.[24] Until now, however, it has not been explicitly recognized as a yardstick for Federal *judicial* power. That recognition should now be extended; it will be found to account for all the Court's constitutional rulings that (in my opinion) are worth preserving, and will serve to identify the ones that are not.

One perpetrates no violence upon logic or known historical fact by assuming that the Founding Fathers *intended* (a) to create a government; (b) to prescribe certain essential characteristics of that government, both by allocating powers among its component organs and by stipulating the general form of the relationship between it and its people; and (c) to empower the Court to serve as the Founders' surrogate for the indefinite future — interpreting the Constitution not as they themselves would have directed if they had been consulted in 1787, but as is thought right *by men who accept the Founders' political philosophy — their commitment to self-government and the open society — and consider themselves obligated to effectuate that philosophy in the America of their own day.* Can that principle serve as a basis for formulation of standards of adjudication which (1) will satisfy the substance of Wechsler's demand for neutrality, and (2) will forestall public condemnation of judicial usurpation, with consequent erosion of the Court's vitally important power of judicial review?

There is a great difference between interpretation of the constitutional *text* and exercise of implied judicial power to make new constitutional rules. The difference can best be made clear by a concrete example. The public accommodations title of the Civil Rights Act of 1964, upheld in *Heart of Atlanta Motel, Inc. v. United States* (1964)[25] and *Katzenbach v. McClung* (1964)[26] as a valid exercise of the Congressional power to regulate interstate commerce, forbade racial discrimination or segregation in all hotels and in those restaurants having the remotest connection with interstate commerce. If James Madison, Benjamin Franklin, and other Founders had been asked *in 1787* whether the Commerce Clause should be interpreted to authorize such a statute, it is entirely likely that they would have said no. Therefore the text of the Constitution, which they wrote, cannot fairly be said to empower Congress to enact the statute. But *if they had survived until 1964* — after the national market had become an integrated and interdependent whole, after the Civil War Amendments had undertaken to extirpate black slavery, and after the poisonous nationwide consequences of racial discrimination in privately-owned places of public accommodation had become known — their political philosophy would very probably have prompted an affirmative answer. At least, the Justices could reasonably believe so. That is enough to make the *Heart of Atlanta Motel* and *McClung* decisions consistent with the Founders' intent, if one accepts the implied power principle now under scrutiny.

It is not entirely clear whether Herbert Wechsler would have considered the *Heart of Atlanta* and *McClung* decisions to be conformable to "neutral principle" on this line of reasoning. What is clear, however, is that the *substance* of his position permits justification of the two decisions on the more latitudinarian basis if — and it is an important "if" — the implied power principle is not so vague as to be illusory. *That is the question on which the validity of the thesis set forth in this book must stand or fall.*

The danger that *any* power to interpret the constitutional text in such a way as to go beyond the plain meaning of the Founders' words might open the way to usurpation was very soon recognized by critics of strict constructionism as well as its proponents. Thomas Jefferson, for example, commenting on a bill to grant a Federal charter to a mining company, shortly before he was elected President in 1800, wrote:

> Congress are authorized to defend the nation. Ships are necessary for defence; copper is necessary for ships; mines, necessary for copper; a company necessary to work the mines; and who can doubt this reasoning who has ever played at "This is the House that Jack Built"? [27]

And Chief Justice Marshall, in his pseudonymous rejoinder to Judge Spencer Roane's attack on the 1819 *McCulloch* decision, wrote:

> It is not pretended that this [Congressional] right of selection [of means] may be fraudulently used to the destruction of the fair land marks of the constitution. Congress certainly may not under the pretext of collecting taxes, or of guaranteeing to each state a republican form of government, alter the law of descents; but if the means have a plain relation to the end — if they be direct, natural and appropriate,[28]

they are constitutional.[29]

Jefferson and Marshall were both commenting on implied *Congressional* power. As is well known, the Marshall position on Congressional power has won acceptance in the court of history. But may there not be greater force to Jefferson's warning when it is not the implied power of Congress that the Court legitimates, but its own? Does not the fact that it is judging its own case justify a rigid self-denying rule, just as a trustee's purchase of trust property is deemed illegal regardless of its fairness in fact? The trustee is held liable without proof of wrongdoing because a prophylactic rule is justified by (1) the known probability that one who is torn by conflicting interests will serve his own and neglect the other, and (2) the difficulty of proving that a price is unfair. Why do not similar considerations apply when the Court applies judicial review to legitimate its own implied power?

This is by no means a trivial or captious question. Justice Black, because of his inability to answer it, insisted that the Court flatly eschew implied lawmaking and constitution-making power.[30] I prefer to answer it as best I can, rather than contend that it is a pointless inquiry — as Justice Black did, because he thought the Founding Fathers and the makers of the Amendments were so wise and farseeing that their words cover all contingencies for which judicial review is sorely needed. I wish I could agree with him on this but I cannot.

Certainly the danger of judicial usurpation would make it desirable to avoid the implication of judicial power if there were any way to do it without incurring still less tolerable risks; were we drafting a new Constitution, we would surely try to find a way to preclude the implication of judicial power — which probably could only be accomplished by precluding the *need* for it. But we deal with an existing constitution, and so our opinion as to the legitimacy of implied judicial power must turn on the single question whether it is less hazardous to societal welfare than any visible alternative.

Moreover, even if we conclude that the Court is right in answering that question in the affirmative, we are still entitled to insist that the power ought to be exercised in a *manner* that will make any usurpation readily detectable, and thus expose a usurping Court to the weight of public obloquy and the threat of condemnation by posterity. The lesson of the *Dred Scott* decision is not forgotten.

It will be argued here (1) that the Court *has* been correct in answering the question in the affirmative, thus grasping implied power for itself, but (2) that the Court deserves criticism for the *manner* in which it has done so, and (3) that the methodological flaw has led to unwarranted assumption of judicial power in some cases.

Upon reading the statement of my thesis, many readers will feel their hackles rising. The thesis calls for accepting a novel conception of the Court and the Constitution — one that differs quite radically from what I was taught at Columbia Law School and, more recently, have myself taught there. I know from the reaction of some of my most perceptive Columbia colleagues, who have read drafts of this manuscript, that thoughtful constitutional law scholars find it difficult to embrace the concept of implied judicial power. For two good reasons they receive it skeptically, as an artifact that may be more ingenious than sound. The reasons are: (1) It affirms the legitimacy of constitutional rules not rooted in the constitutional text. (2) It supersedes the classic theory of judicial review, established in *Marbury v. Madison* (1803), which no member of the Court has ever overtly repudiated; for it suggests (a) that the Court need not adopt a passive posture and wait for a constitutional issue to be presented in a "justiciable case or controversy" and (b) that the Court is not limited to interposition of a negative veto against measures initiated by other organs of government, but can itself initiate changes in the law and even require the creation of administrative structures to implement them.

I think it wise to spell out these two aspects of my thesis, and to do it at the very outset. Otherwise, thoughtful readers are likely to generate emotional resistance, intensifying with each new chapter as they read on; for they will tend to scrutinize the ensuing discussion with the same suspicion of quackery that astronomers schooled in the Ptolemaic conception of the solar system must have entertained toward the Copernican theory. Therefore I say that, just as it is *possible* — by use of epicycles and equants and such refinements — to account for observed celestial phenomena on the theory that the sun circles the earth, so it is *possible* — by interjection of enough exceptions and special rules — to account for the Court's performance, and the people's acceptance of it, on the basis of orthodox constitutional theory.* But I also say that the observed phenomena can be accounted for much more simply, and in a manner that requires less straining of the meaning of words

---

* The Copernican analogy is closer than might at first appear. What Copernicus did was to shift the focus of attention from the earth to the sun, as the center of the planetary system. *See* T. KUHN, THE COPERNICAN REVOLUTION (1959). What I am trying to do is to shift the focus of attention from the text of the Constitution (and its Amendments) to the observed phenomena — the decisions of the Supreme Court, rendered as so-called "interpretations" of that text.

and is truer to the Justices' own conception of their role, and on premises more consonant with the ideal of rational government, if one accepts the thesis propounded here.

Of course it would be presumptuous of me to ask the reader to take my word for this. What I do beg is suspension of judgment until the discussion is complete. By then, I hope to have shown that there is a *way of looking* at constitutional phenomena that is different from the way of orthodox theory — a new way that ought to be approved, not because it is more nearly "correct" but because it is more *useful.*

CHAPTER II
# Why Judicial Review?

To latter-day Americans it seems entirely natural that the United States Supreme Court possesses a very broad veto power over the rest of our Government. This has not always been so, however,* and recent developments suggest that it may not always remain so. I propose to examine those developments and to peer into the Court's future as far as understanding of its past and present enables me.

The obvious first step is to trace the Court's power to its source. What is it that now prevents elected officials, from the President on down, from ignoring the Court's interpretations of the

---
* *See, e.g.,* the dissent of Justice (later Chief Justice) Gibson of Pennsylvania in Eakin v. Raub, 12 S. & R. 330 (Pa. 1825), saying in part:

> I am aware, that a right to declare all unconstitutional acts void, without distinction as to either constitution, is generally held as a professional dogma; but I apprehend rather as a matter of faith than of reason. . . . [I]t is not a little remarkable, that although the right in question has all along been claimed by the judiciary, no judge has ventured to discuss it, except Chief Justice Marshall . . . , and if the argument of a jurist so distinguished for the strength of his ratiocinative powers be found inconclusive, it may fairly be set down to the weakness of the position which he attempts to defend. . . .
>
>  . . . [T]he constitution is said to be a law of superior obligation; and consequently, that if it were to come into collision with an act of the legislature, the latter would have to give way. This is conceded. But it is a fallacy, to suppose that they can come into collision *before the judiciary.* . . .
>
> The constitution and the *right* of the legislature to pass the act, may be in collision. But is that a legitimate subject for judicial determination? If it be, the judiciary must be a peculiar organ, to revise the proceedings of the legislature, and to correct its mistakes; and in what part of the constitution are we to look for this proud preeminence? . . . [I]t is by no means clear, that to declare a law void which has been enacted according to the forms prescribed in the constitution, is not a usurpation of legislative power. It is an act of sovereignty; and sovereignty and legislative power are said by Sir William *Blackstone* to be convertible terms. It is the business of the judiciary, to interpret the laws, not scan the authority of the lawgiver; and without the latter, it cannot take cognizance of a collision between a law and the constitution. So that to affirm that the judiciary has a right to judge of the existence of such collision, is to take for granted the very thing to be proved . . . .

A reading of the full opinion would be worth the effort; it brings back a mode of thought that has almost completely disappeared today. The nearest modern approach to it was in 1936, when President Franklin D. Roosevelt proposed his "Court-packing" plan; but that approach was not very close, since there was no overt attack on judicial review as such.

Constitution — as President Thomas Jefferson was ready to do on at least one occasion,[1] and as President Andrew Jackson once openly threatened to do?\*[2] Why would Abraham Lincoln, campaigning for the Senate in 1858, refuse to counsel disobedience even of the despised *Dred Scott* decision which the Court had handed down the year before?[3] Why would Richard M. Nixon shrink from defying the Court's order to surrender tape recordings of his office and telephone conversations, even though compliance would plainly weaken his chance of remaining in the White House?[4]

The reason is that defiance of the Court has usually been thought tantamount to political suicide, because of the electorate's remarkable reverence for law and its near-unanimous recognition of the Court's ultimate authority to say what the law is. That is why it has been possible for the Court to make good its mandates in many fields which in other countries belong entirely to the executive or the legislature. Few foreign courts would presume to take charge of such matters as legislative reapportionment, executive impoundment of appropriated funds, political party structure, regulation of pornography and abortion, or any one of dozens of other subject matters which are conceded to be grist for the mill of our highest Court. Alexis de Tocqueville's observation that "Scarcely any political question arises in the United States that is not resolved, sooner or later, into a judicial question" is even truer today than in 1835 when it appeared in the first volume of his *Democracy in America*.[5]

---

\* An interesting controversy has arisen among historians as to whether Jackson actually defied the Court, or whether he merely declared his unwillingness to lend the aid of the executive branch in enforcing the Court's mandate in Worcester v. Georgia, 31 U.S. (6 Pet.) 515 (1832), if it were to request such aid — which it did not. The divergent views of the historians are set out in Burke's "The Cherokee Cases: A Study in Law, Politics, and Morality," in *Stanford Law Review* (1969), vol. 21, at pp. 500, 524-25; and see Leonard Baker's *John Marshall: A Life in Law* (1974), at pp. 744-46. Arthur Schlesinger, Jr., shows by his letter to the editor of the *New York Times* published July 25, 1974 (p. 32, col. 4) that he still adheres to the view that no defiance occurred.

This controversy, of course, does not relate to the question whether Jackson was *ready* to defy the Court and revealed his readiness to all who would listen. The authorities just cited show there is little reason to doubt that the answer to *this* question is yes.

Interesting as it would be to study the growth of the Court's overwhelming prestige, I must leave that task to the social historian; instead, accepting the undoubted fact that the prestige does exist, I shall ask where its roots lie and how vulnerable to canker they may be. Part of the answer, but only a part, resides in the Court's strategic position in our governmental system. We rely heavily upon the judiciary for enforcement of official commands and prohibitions, and therefore the Court's supreme appellate jurisdiction carries with it the *raw power* to decide which of those commands and prohibitions deserve enforcement and which do not. If a state legislature elects to use the judicial process to enforce prohibitions against disorderly assembly or pornography or abortion, or if the House of Representatives elects to use the judicial process against contumacious refusals to testify before its committees, the legislative body automatically exposes its policies to the Court's disapproval.

There are two reasons, one substantive and one conventional, why the Court's strategic position provides only part of the answer to the question whether and where the Court is vulnerable: (1) Our heavy reliance on judicial process, in preference to other means of controlling conduct, is a matter of policy rather than necessity. (2) The Constitution expressly authorizes Congress to limit (perhaps even to abolish) the Court's appellate jurisdiction.

On the first point, it is perhaps enough to point out that police with tear gas and nightsticks can break up disorderly assemblies;[6] that states can effectively mobilize public opinion against pornography, at least in communities where private ostracism is a formidable coercive device;[7] that abortions can be suppressed through revocation of licenses to practice medicine (with the consequent exclusion of doctors from hospital staffs);[8] and that the House of Representatives can send its own Sergeant-at-Arms to arrest and imprison recalcitrant witnesses for the duration of the legislative session[9] — all without resort to the courts. (This is to say only that such methods *can* be used, not that all of them are constitutionally permissible.) As for the second point, the Constitution provides (Article III, Section 2, paragraph 2) that "the supreme Court shall have appellate Jurisdiction, both as to Law and Fact, with such Exceptions, and under such Regulations as the Congress shall make." \* In short, the Court holds its strategic position largely because the electorate, through its chosen legislative representatives, has consented and continues to consent.\*\*

---

\* Doubts have been expressed as to whether the authority of Congress to carve out exceptions to the Supreme Court's appellate jurisdiction extends so far as to include the power to abrogate it entirely. These doubts, which emanate both from Justices and scholars, are reviewed in Gunther and Dowling's *Cases and Materials on Constitutional Law* (8th ed. 1970), at pp. 52-55. As will be seen, the thesis of the present book provides a basis for similar doubts — but *not* on the ground that the text of Article III calls for such a result. On that question — whether the power to make exceptions includes the power to make a "100% exception" — it seems to me that the cases upholding Congressional power to prescribe the times, places, and manner of holding Congressional elections, provide cogent authority for an affirmative answer. Article I, Section 4 says:

> The Times, Places and Manner of holding Elections for Senators and Representatives, shall be prescribed in each State by the Legislature thereof; but the Congress may at any time by Law make or alter such Regulations, except as to the Places of chusing Senators.

Yet the Court has placed no limit on the power of Congress to take over control of Federal elections; in South Carolina v. Katzenbach, 383 U.S. 301 (1966), it even upheld a Federal statute providing for Federal voting registrars.

\*\* Compare John Stuart Mill's observations in *Considerations on Representative Government* (1861), at pp. 242-43, published four years after the *Dred Scott* decision:

> There must be a Supreme Court of Justice, and a system of subordinate courts in every State of the Union, before whom such questions shall be carried, and whose judgment on them, in the last stage of appeal, shall be final. Every State of the Union, and the federal Government itself, as well as every functionary of each, must be liable to be sued in those courts for exceeding their powers, or for nonperformance of their federal duties, and must in general be obliged to employ those courts as the instrument for enforcing their federal rights. This involves the remarkable consequence, actually realized in the United States, that a Court of Justice, the highest federal tribunal, is supreme over the various governments, both state and federal; having the right to declare that any law made, or act done by them, exceeds the powers assigned to them by the federal Constitution and, in consequence, has no legal validity. It was natural to feel strong doubts, before trial had been made, how such a provision would work — whether the tribunal would have the courage to exercise its constitutional power; if it did, whether it would exercise it wisely and whether the governments would consent to submit peaceably to its decision. The discussions on the American Constitution, before its final adoption, give evidence that these natural apprehensions were strongly felt; but they are now entirely quieted, since, during the two generations and more which have subsequently elapsed, nothing has occurred to verify them, though there have at times been disputes of considerable acrimony, and which became the badges of parties, respecting the limits of the authority of the federal and state governments. The eminently beneficial working of so singular a provision is probably, as M. de Tocqueville remarks, in a great measure attributable to the peculiarity inherent in a Court of Justice acting as such — namely, that it does not declare the law *eo nomine*

To be sure, by-passing the courts in enforcing prohibitions against disapproved behavior, or in coercing testimony before Congressional committees, would involve collateral disadvantages. There would probably be a loss in efficiency, and public confidence in the fairness of the process would probably be impaired. Therefore reliance on the courts cannot be ascribed *solely* to blind faith in law and the Court, and not at all to practical considerations. It is nevertheless true that, if the electorate were to become sufficiently disenchanted with "government by judiciary," there would be no difficulty in stripping the Court of most of its power. It maintains its strategic position because the voters do not object.

But, *why* do they not object? In a nation dedicated to government by consent of the governed, how is it that the people acquiesce in the exercise of broad veto power over acts of their elected representatives by the vote of a majority of nine Justices who are almost completely insulated from electoral control? Here we reach the heart of the matter. They acquiesce mainly because most of them cling to the conception of the Court limned by Alexander Hamilton in the 78th *Federalist,* in support of judicial review. After declaring that "the judiciary, *from the nature of its functions,* will

---

and in the abstract, but waits until a case between man and man is brought before it judicially involving the point in dispute; from which arises the happy effect that its declarations are not made in a very early stage of the controversy, that much popular discussion usually precedes them; that the Court decides after hearing the point fully argued on both sides by lawyers of reputation; decides only as much of the question at a time as is required by the case before it, and its decision, instead of being volunteered for political purposes, is drawn from it by the duty which it cannot refuse to fulfill, of dispensing justice impartially between adverse litigants. Even these grounds of confidence would not have sufficed to produce the respectful submission with which all authorities have yielded to the decisions of the Supreme Court on the interpretation of the Constitution were it not that complete reliance has been felt, not only on the intellectual pre-eminence of the judges composing that exalted tribunal, but on their entire superiority over either private or sectional partialities. This reliance has been in the main justified; but there is nothing which more vitally imports the American people than to guard with the most watchful solicitude against everything which has the remotest tendency to produce deterioration in the quality of this great national institution. *The confidence on which depends the stability of federal institutions* was for the first time impaired by the judgment declaring slavery to be of common right and, consequently, lawful in the Territories while not yet constituted as States, even against the will of a majority of their inhabitants. This memorable decision has probably done more than anything else to bring the sectional division to the crisis which has issued in civil war. The main pillar of the American Constitution is scarcely strong enough to bear many more such shocks. (Emphasis added)

always be the least dangerous to the political rights of the constitution," (emphasis added) he went on to explain the nature of those functions:

> The judiciary . . . has no influence over either the sword or the purse; no direction either of the strength or of the wealth of the society; and can take no active resolution whatever. It may truly be said to have neither FORCE nor WILL, but merely judgment. . . .[10]

The conception is that the Justices, constrained by the tradition of their profession and their office, do not consider themselves free to make or remake the law according to their own notions of what is best for the society; they interpret and apply the law as it is given to them from outside sources, such as Congress and the state legislatures. One such outside source of law is the Constitution, which expresses the will of those who made it; and to the extent that the Court does no more than ascertain their will and apply it to the case at hand, it acts out the role that Hamilton assigned to it — a role that does not trench upon popular sovereignty because the Constitution itself is an expression of *the popular will.*

Another question must be raised. It is historically true that the Constitution and its Amendments reflect a high degree of popular consensus, but for the most part it is the consensus of people long dead. The original Constitution and the first ten Amendments date from the eighteenth century; the most basic of the later Amendments are more than a century old; and only the Twenty-second and three later Amendments (perhaps a fourth, on sex equality, will have been ratified by the time this is published) can confidently be said to reflect the will of *living* Americans. It is necessary to account for the people's willingness to let the will of dead supermajorities (three fourths or two thirds) override the will of live majorities.

This, of course, is the central mystery of constitutional government. Volumes have been written about it, and more remain to be written. But for present purposes we can skirt the profundities of political theory and forgo exhaustive analysis of the necessary and sufficient conditions of general submission to the injunctions of an ancient constitution. For present purposes it is enough to take note of the special contribution made by judicial review to the feasibility of constitutional government.

Plainly, constitutional government can exist without judicial review as we know it in this country — determination of constitutionality *by adjudication.* In Great Britain, for example, where constitutional government existed long before 1776, no court claims authority to annul statutes by declaring them to be void because they conflict with the British constitution. Yet any British lawyer will assure you that his nation's constitution is a living force. What does he mean? If a current Parliamentary majority legislates in violation of that constitution, what difference does it make? Indeed, how can one be sure that the British constitution *has* been violated, if the law courts stand ready to enforce an Act of Parliament regardless of its constitutionality? And, since the British constitution is not embodied in any single document, but is evidenced by an untidy succession of writings from Magna Carta on, how can one know its precise substance?

All these queries can be met by an explanation of the Britisher's conception of his constitution. For him it is a set of political principles and practices (a) which the people understand about as precisely as we understand our own Constitution; (b) which is defended in the political arena and is not used by the courts to invalidate political action; and (c) the breach of which would be widely thought to justify civil disobedience and even rebellion if necessary.\* For example, if a Parliamentary majority by statute were to suppress the "loyal opposition" and institute one-party rule, no law court would presume to invalidate the unconstitutional statute; but sooner or later the populace would rise.\*\* Unconstitutionality thus is pragmatically defined as violation of

---

\* *Changes* in the British constitution, such as virtual elimination of the power of the House of Lords — supported, as it was, by a large popular consensus — are not "breaches."

\*\* This proposition has not been tested recently in Great Britain but a test appears imminent in India, where the British tradition of tolerating the "loyal opposition" has been thought to be firmly entrenched. In June, 1975, mounting protest against Prime Minister Indira Gandhi — stimulated by a lower court

some principle, or departure from some practice, that is so widely accepted and so intensely believed in that its violation leads to major civil disobedience or rebellion. Of course, no one can be quite sure beforehand whether a particular bill would, if enacted, touch off such a result. But then, there is also uncertainty in this country about the constitutionality of proposed legislation.

Our system of judicial review does appear to have one clear advantage: It permits the resolution of constitutional controversy without defiance of the government. (There is a huge difference between *breaking* the law and *defying* it.) *A priori,* one might suppose that internal factional struggles during the two centuries since our two nations went their separate ways would have been markedly more bloody in Great Britain than here. It has not been so. This might mean that the advantage of judicial rather than political resolution of deep social conflict is more theoretical than real.* But a different explanation seems more plausible.

The ability of the British to get along quite well without judicial review may be attributable to *the greater homogeneity of their population.* By "homogeneity" is meant the feeling of common kinship throughout a society, a kinship based simply on a sense of belonging to a single community perfused by a common culture. In a body politic that enjoys a high degree of homogeneity, a legislature whose membership reflects a cross-section of the constituent population will ordinarily bridge factional differences by accomplishing fair compromise between the competing needs and desires of different groups.** In a body politic not thus blessed,

---

decision declaring her election invalid because of corrupt practices — led to the arrest of a large number of opposition leaders. Rioting ensued, followed by declaration of a state of emergency with suspension of basic personal liberties and the bludgeoning or arrest of many demonstrators chanting such slogans as, "Indira Gandhi, get off your throne!" See, *e.g., New York Times,* June 30, 1975, p. 1, col. 8. It remains to be seen whether a full-scale rebellion will ensue.

* My colleague William F. Young, Jr., comments: "The content of the British constitution is determined by the sensibilities of a current establishment, both to traditions and to principles. The development of comparable sensibilities and loyalties may actually be *stunted* in America by our reliance on judicial review."

** Commenting on this sentence, Professor F.J.M. Feldbrugge of the University of Leiden writes me:

only a *constitutional* bridge, buttressed by judicial review, can effectively span the gap between potentially warring factions, because majoritarian legislation is not adequate to the need. Thus, judicial review can be more easily dispensed with in Great Britain than in our nation — which, as I have written elsewhere,[11] is more far-flung, polyglot, and generally heterogeneous than that tight little island. For self-government and the open society can co-exist without judicial review only if a relatively high degree of homogeneity has been achieved.

The subtlety of the concept of homogeneity, and its key significance in any appraisal of the Court's work, justifies brief elaboration. I pray permission to quote a few paragraphs from a paper I published in 1957:

> At this point a new concept must be introduced: the "homogeneous" population and its alternative, the "heterogeneous" population. A homogeneous population is one that satisfies Solon's definition of a model state:
>
>> "... being asked what city was best modelled, 'That,' said he, 'where those that are not injured try and punish the unjust as much as those that are.'"
>
> In such a city, Solon thought, "the citizens, like members of the same body, [would] resent and be sensible of one another's injuries." Or, in more modern terms, a fully homogeneous population is one in which each member experiences a high degree of empathy for every other.
>
> A heterogeneous population, on the other hand, is one in which this high degree of mutual empathy does not exist. A population in which each person was wholly self-centered would satisfy this definition, but in fact this is not true of any national population. Instead, there exist groups within the population which are fairly homogeneous internally, but which are more or less hostile to each other, or at least estranged. Typically, one or more of these groups will dominate the government; and the others, which the sociologist would call "out-groups" and the political scientist would call "minorities," cannot expect the legislature to give their needs and desires full weight in the process of compromise which is

---

Let me just add the point that societies based on more homogeneous cultures are better able to resolve their conflicts not only through legislative compromise, as opposed to adjudication, but also through a multitude of other, more informal procedures. I remember that this was one of the most vivid experiences of my year in the United States.

legislation. In other words, there is a tendency to deny them legislative justice.

. . . .

The art of constitution-making knows devices whereby some of the more acute problems of heterogeneity can be mitigated. These devices fall into two main categories. First, the mechanics of legislation can be so arranged that a simple majority cannot prevail. This can be done directly, by providing for special majorities — two thirds or three fourths, for example — on certain types of question. Or it can be done indirectly, as by provision for a bicameral legislature with the two houses elected on different bases — a device originally adopted in our own Constitution for the protection of the smaller states, and later for a time used for the protection of Southern states against the rise of abolitionist feeling.

Second, the constitution can forbid the central government to act at all on specified issues, or in specified ways. For example, as a protection to the Southern states, whose exports were the life-blood of their economy, our Constitution prohibited [Federal] export duties; and it forbade Federal interference with the slave trade until 1808. Congress was denied power to make any "Regulation of Commerce or Revenue" which gave preference to the ports of one state over those of another. The richer states were afforded some protection against being taxed for the benefit of their poorer neighbors, by a provision requiring that direct taxes be imposed in proportion to population.

. . . .

It may be thought that the difficulty of the problem has been overstated. Even though there is little empathy between the people of the various component states, why cannot they all feel safe if the central government is simply required to afford to all persons the equal protection of the laws — that is, to enact no statute which does not apply in the same way to all persons similarly situated? We have such a provision in the Fourteenth Amendment to our own Constitution, and it has been a useful means of enabling the courts to control the grosser forms of discrimination. But it is entirely possible for a statute which is undiscriminatory on its face to impose quite unequal burdens on different segments of the population, and so to give rise to claims of legislative injustice. A classic example is the protective tariff. On its face it deals with all persons alike. In its application, it has historically helped the North and hurt the South; and for over a century it has been the object of bitter attack on the ground that it is designed to milk one part of the country for the benefit of the other, and thus is legislatively unjust.[12]

Alexander Bickel has taken note of the Constitution's function as a symbol of national unity, and the Court's unique place as its official keeper:

> But the Supreme Court as a legitimating force in society also casts a less palpable yet larger spell. With us the symbol of nationhood, of continuity, of unity and common purpose, is, of course, the Constitution, without particular reference to what exactly it means in this or that application. The utility of such a symbol is a commonplace. Britain — the United Kingdom, and perhaps even the Commonwealth — is the most potent historical demonstration of the efficaciousness of a symbol, made concrete in the person of the Crown. The President in our system serves the function somewhat, but only very marginally, because the personification of unity must be above the political battle, and no President can fulfill his office while remaining above the battle. The effective Presidents have of necessity been men of power, and so it has in large part been left to the Supreme Court to concretize the symbol of the Constitution. Keeping in mind that this is offered as an observation, not as justification, it is surely true that the Court has been able to play the role partly — but only partly — by virtue of its power of judicial review.
>
> . . . .
>
> The Framers were moved . . . by considerations looking beyond the immediate objective of ratification. They knew, and this was perhaps their greatest wisdom, that in order to last and be stable and thus affect the behavior of posterity in any degree, a constitution must make it possible for future battles to be fought out by men who, on both sides of contested issues, can in good faith profess allegiance to the organic law and to the regime established by it. They were aware, in other words, of the function of the Constitution as the symbol of nationhood, meant to transcend and to endure beyond the fiercest political differences. It is possible to have an institution such as the Supreme Court, especially clothed with the constitutional mystique, which will intervene in special ways on special issues — rarely, subtly, mindful that the rule of principle has limits. But both Constitution and Court must remain above the day-to-day battle, and the Constitution itself, for the most part, above the battle altogether. The constitutional generalities must be capable of containing most differences and of embracing either result of most trials of political strength. Hence, as Marshall said in *McCulloch v. Maryland,* a constitution — or to quote him more precisely, a *constitution* — must not "partake of the prolixity of a legal code" and so seem false and alien to the people, who are

expected to pour into it and draw from it the sense of union and common purpose, past and future. If a constitution purports to settle, in detail and for all time, most of the issues that are likely to be the grist of the political mill, it invites either abandonment or frequent amendment. The familiarity of amendment will breed a species of contempt and incapacitate the document for symbolic service.[13]

When judicial review is seen as a means of keeping potentially hostile factions from each others' throats — whites and blacks, the rich and the poor, Roman Catholics and Protestants, Christians and Jews, "100% Americans" and hyphenated Americans, and so on — it is readily recognizable as a vital national resource. And when it is understood that judicial review exists by sufferance of the electorate, and can be truncated or abolished if the voters come to regard it as a straitjacket upon popular sovereignty, the importance of detecting quickly any danger of that eventuality is clear. This is the task we are about to undertake.

Let us resume the thread of the argument. We have observed that judicial review exists by sufferance of the electorate, and have suggested that the electoral consent has been yielded because of a general belief that judicial review, being an expression of the people's will as declared in the written Constitution and its Amendments, is consistent with popular sovereignty. We have also raised the question why popular sovereignty is not thought to be impaired when the will of dead supermajorities is allowed to prevail over the will of live majorities. Let us now approach that question.

The people correctly perceive that legislation is the primary bridge between potentially warring factions and that judicial review under the Constitution is a valuable backstop for settling those few types of conflict that cannot easily be resolved by majoritarian legislation. However deeply the contending parties disagree on the merits of a controversy, they agree that it is better for them to accept official arbitrament of their competing claims than for each of them to insist upon full and immediate satisfaction of his own needs and desires — *provided* that legislative compromise is available under conditions which can be expected to accomplish fair reconciliation of competing interests, and provided further that the Constitution (a) requires maintenance of those conditions to the extent permitted by the heterogeneity of the population and (b) affords *judicial* arbitrament of those controversies for which the prerequisites of fair *legislative* compromise do not exist.

We have observed further that, *at the present time,* the Supreme Court possesses the "raw power" to go further: to veto *any* legislative settlement that it considers unwise. Such a course would indeed impair popular sovereignty — the will of live majorities — more heavily than can be justified on the basis of demonstrable necessity. What then?

This question must be dealt with by considering whether the Court's actions do, or do not, reflect the *actual* majority will more truly than the legislatures themselves have been able to do. A confident affirmative answer cannot often be given, since legislators are more directly in touch with electoral opinion than are the Justices. Yet an affirmative answer *is* warranted occasionally, particularly when the legislative process is cramped by taboo-laden social attitudes (often rooted in religious dogma) that make it politically dangerous for legislators to do what most of their constituents really want. Such attitudes, for example, have very probably retarded legislative reconsideration of laws restricting abortion and the use of contraceptives (in which connection it must be remembered that, on a given issue, one dedicated partisan may outweigh two apathetic opponents). In that event, popular disenchantment with judicial review is unlikely to reach a significant level.

It is also possible, however, that Justices intoxicated with the raw power they currently possess — I refrain from following Lord Acton in charging them with *corruption* — may utilize judicial review in ways which do frustrate the actual popular will and which cannot be justified on the basis of legislative incapacity. The Justices may be moved to such lengths by a sense of obligation to bring to fruition certain basic principles of humanity (sometimes called "natural law"), and — as we shall see — they may be driven to adopt patently artificial interpretations of the constitutional text in order to justify their decisions. What are the probable consequences of such a course?

The least troublesome consequence would be an effort at further amendment of the Constitution. It is a difficult remedy; in nearly two centuries only a few Amendments have been adopted for the purpose of overruling Supreme Court decisions — the Eleventh (suability of states),[14] the first sentence of the Fourteenth (eligibility of Negroes for national citizenship),[15] the Sixteenth (income tax),[16] the Twenty-sixth (voting age),[17] and arguably the Twenty-fourth (poll tax).[18] Other measures, not calling for such a high degree of consensus, or involving such protracted and cumbersome procedures, are more likely to be taken. For example, efforts may be made to narrow the Court's jurisdiction, or change its position through new appointments (or even through impeachment). If the electorate were to see the Court as a *usurper* of the ultimate lawmaking power, murmurs against a nine-man oligarchy insulated almost completely from electoral control would swell, popular sovereignty being thought lost or endangered.[19] To a greater or lesser extent, respect for the law as declared by the Court would be eroded, and many people would feel morally justified in evading that law by technical stratagem or passive resistance, or even in defying it through affirmative acts of civil disobedience. The society would be polarized between legitimists, supporting the Court because they would fear anarchic consequences if its authority were defied, and rebels, acting in the name of patriotic obligation to a higher ideal — government by the people.

Even if the rebellious element were a minority, its repudiation of moral obligation to obey the law would jeopardize the open society.* Coercive police measures — curfews, internments,

---

* Chief Justice Vinson was probably making the same point in Dennis v. United States, 341 U.S. 494, 509 (1951), where the Court upheld the Smith Act convictions of Communist Party leaders:

> The argument that there is no need for Government to concern itself, for Government is strong, it possesses ample powers to put down a rebellion, it may defeat the revolution with ease[,] needs no answer. For that is not the question. Certainly an attempt to overthrow the Government by force, even though doomed from the outset because of inadequate numbers or power of the revolutionists, is a sufficient evil for Congress to prevent. The damage which such attempts create both physically *and politically* to a nation makes it impossible to measure the validity [of the Smith Act] in terms of the

official eavesdropping, searches and arrests on mere suspicion of lawbreaking, imputation of guilt by association, and so on — would be instituted to provide elementary security of person and property. Or, if some state or local governments were mobilized in support of the rebels, they would employ similar intrusive police measures to suppress the legitimists.[20]

The Court must look down this dark road whenever it utilizes judicial review beyond the boundaries of demonstrable necessity. This does not mean that imminent danger resides in every such action. Respect for the Court, confidence in its wisdom, and reluctance to suspect it of self-aggrandizement are deeply ingrained in the people. They give the Court the benefit of every reasonable doubt. But it should not be supposed that their tolerance is boundless. To be sure, it is conceivable that in this eighth decade of the twentieth century they have become indifferent to the loss of self-government, or have lost the ability to recognize usurpation when they see it (so long as it is cloaked in reassuring slogans). More probably, however, their tolerance is attributable to a generous readiness to allow the Court some leeway for good-faith mistakes in its decisions or in its opinions supporting them. If this is the explanation, the people's tolerance will not be unlimited. If they still care about self-government, and if it is impossible to fool them "all of the time," the Court must beware of convincing them that they must choose between judicial review and popular sovereignty. If they are pressed too far, they will opt for popular sovereignty; and the result will be either impairment of the open society, for reasons already noted (if judicial review is preserved in form but defied in fact), or (if judicial review is crippled or abolished) the danger of still greater disaster — for reasons now to be mentioned.

At the risk of belaboring the obvious, let us glance about us for examples of the chaos that threatens the nation whose people have lost faith in the capacity of its legislature to render them justice, and whose constitutional system lacks judicial review (or confines it within too-narrow limits) so that deep social schisms cannot be

---

probability of success, or the immediacy of a successful attempt. (Emphasis added)

transferred from the political to the judicial arena. We need look no further than contemporary Ulster. We have already referred to the homogeneity of the British population, which has enabled it to avoid major civil disobedience and civil war in recent centuries. No such homogeneity exists across the Irish Sea in Ulster, or between Ulster and Great Britain, and the bombings and assassinations go on and on. It was comparable heterogeneity that led to partition of the Indian subcontinent between Hindus and Moslems, which has already spawned war between India and Pakistan — a conflict marked by some of the special horror of *civil* war. South Africa and Rhodesia live in dread of racial uprising. Cyprus hung in precarious tension between Greek and Turk for decades until war exploded in 1974. The list could be lengthened.

One cannot be sure that judicial review on as broad a scale as ours could have bridged the national, racial, and religious schisms that divide Ulster, India-Pakistan, South Africa, Rhodesia, and Cyprus. Some schisms are too broad to be bridged in that way, as our Civil War showed. What is clear, however, is that in those countries broad judicial review remains an untried resource that *might* have averted bloodshed if it had been available.

Thus far, the United States has remained sufficiently united to avoid such a breakdown, or the serious threat of it, with the one monumental exception of the Civil War. No one can say that judicial review has been the sole reason, but it has surely been one of the reasons. In this connection it is instructive to note that the Civil War was sparked by the only first-magnitude issue that the original Constitution failed to resolve through acceptable compromise, the issue of slavery. To be sure, the issue was recognized and a compromise was attempted. The slave-holding states were given representation in Congress that was partly based on the number of their slaves [21] and were guaranteed autonomy on the issue of abolishing or retaining slavery;[22] in return, Congress was empowered to abolish the slave *trade* after twenty years.[23] It was hoped that slavery would wither away for economic reasons if the importation of slaves were brought to a halt, but the hope was frustrated by Eli Whitney's gin and the ascendancy of

King Cotton.[24] The Supreme Court made one desperate effort to ward off Southern secession — to *settle* the slavery controversy through the medium of judicial review, in the *Dred Scott* case.[25] The Court's prescription was too drastically inhumane, and its prestige was then too limited, to permit success.[26] Four years of war ensued, followed by the Thirteenth, Fourteenth, and Fifteenth Amendments which formalized what was settled on the battlefield. Except for this one dreadful episode, however, the Constitution has been found to provide enough flexibility through the amendment process and through judicial reinterpretation to permit the resolution of dangerous social tensions without major civil disobedience or civil war.

CHAPTER III

## Terms and Concepts

Unfortunately we must put off our investigation and evaluation of the Court's work while we fashion some convenient, perhaps even necessary, analytical tools — terms and concepts designed to facilitate the main task. This and the next three chapters are devoted to that rather exacting preliminary.

At the outset I freely acknowledge that I shall use a few terms in a sense that varies somewhat from the commonly accepted meaning of the words. As for concepts, we shall be using some that are familiar and others that I have invented. Any reader who is inclined to be critical is asked to reserve judgment until the end of the book, so as to permit appraisal of my terms and concepts on the basis of their *utility*. Subject only to that stern criterion, the analyst is entitled to complete freedom in shaping his analytical tools.

We ordinarily think of the Constitution as a set of allocations of, and limitations upon, governmental power. And so it is; but it is more. Underlying the allocations and limitations, and infusing them with life and meaning, is a pattern — a pattern of national objectives which the Constitution authenticates and confirms.

Sometimes we think of a national objective as a "commitment," sometimes as a "goal," depending on whether it involves acceptance of a national obligation (such as the extirpation of slavery) or attainment of some social good (such as equality of opportunity). Analytically, however, commitments and goals are equivalents; they both involve identification of an objective which the American people, acting with the high degree of consensus required for adoption of constitutional provisions, have claimed as their own.

Again and again we shall refer to the objective of the persons who have performed the constitution-making act of identifying a national objective. It will be convenient for this purpose to coin a collective term describing those persons, since no such term exists.

A term does exist for the somewhat analogous purpose of describing the objective of a legislative enactment. In resolving uncertainty as to whether or how a statute applies to a particular situation that it does not plainly provide for, we ask what was the "legislative intent." This term, of course, is a trope — a figure of speech. An "intent" is entertained by a *person,* or perhaps by a group of persons who must act unanimously if at all. As applied to a group of persons who act by majority rule, as do legislators, the word "intent" does not carry its usual meaning. What courts and lawyers do understand it to mean, when they use it as a guide to statutory interpretation, is the answer to the question: "If the legislators had been called on for explicit directions for handling the very situation now under consideration, what would a majority of them have said?"

A familiar technique for determining legislative intent is to examine the "legislative history" — reflected by committee hearings, committee reports, and floor debates — which often speaks more directly than the words of the statute to the particular situation at issue.

We might coin the term "constitutive intent" to denote the answer that would have been given to an inquiry as to whether or how most of the adopters of the constitutional provision would (if asked) have said it applies to the particular situation at issue. There is the difficulty, however, that those adopters, unlike legislators who enact a statute, did not comprise a single organized group of persons who deliberated together and spoke to each other. The original Constitution was adopted by the Founding Fathers who convened at Philadelphia in 1787, *and* by the several state ratifying conventions. Likewise, each Amendment was adopted by the Congress that proposed it *and* by the several state legislatures that ratified it. These various bodies may have been moved by widely divergent considerations. For example, the Fourteenth Amendment, which did more than any other to reshape national objectives, was proposed by the Thirty-ninth Congress for the primary purpose of solidifying the emancipation of black slaves; but Southern legislatures whose ratification was indispensable to its adoption yielded their assent as the price of restored Congressional representation, a price stipulated by the Reconstruction Act of March 2, 1867.[1] Examination of the Congressional debates on the proposal of the Amendment thus provides only an uncertain guide to "constitutive intent."

It seems preferable to avoid this term because "intent" has no simple and understandable referent, and to adopt instead a term that refers directly to those scattered and varied groups, acting at different times from 1787 down to the present time, who adopted the Constitution and its Amendments. With full recognition of the awkwardness, I shall refer to them as "the Constitutors." The implied parallelism with "legislators" is deliberate; both are makers of rules.

I shall also refer frequently to the Supreme Court in the same figurative way that I refer to a legislature (*i.e.,* as if it were a single person), speaking of its "intent," its "purpose," and so on. Care will be taken, however, to attribute a state of mind to the Court only if a majority of its sitting members are known to have that state of mind. This comports with current usage.

The reader should be put on notice of the somewhat special sense in which the term "legislature" will be used. In ordinary parlance it refers to Congress and the representative lawmaking assemblies of the several states. It will be convenient, however, to use the term in a slightly broader sense, as meaning *those who participate in the formal lawmaking process.* Thus it includes the President and the state governors, to the extent that they participate in the process by exercising their functions of initiative and veto. "Legislative" will also be used in this broader sense.

Another term that will be given a special meaning is "elected officials." In ordinary speech it means simply officials chosen by popular vote, but I shall use it in a sense that is both broader and narrower. On the one hand, it will mean Congress, the President, state and local legislatures, state governors, and elected local executives, *and* officials whom they appoint and continuously control (which includes policemen, for example, but not the personnel of independent administrative agencies). On the other hand, judges and independent administrative personnel are not "elected officials" in my terminology, even though most state judges are chosen by popular election and most *independent* administrators are appointed by elected officials, because these judges and administrators are supposed to be controlled by *the law* rather than the current desires of the voters or their elected delegates. The purpose of this partly artificial definition is to identify the class of public servants who are directly or indirectly subject to continuing control by popular majorities through the electoral process.

Further, the arrogant but thrifty ellipsis involved in shortening "United States of America" to "America" will be indulged here — with appropriate apologies to Canada and nations to the south of the United States. By an equally thrifty ellipsis, as will already have been noticed, "the Supreme Court of the United States" is called "the Court." And, contrary to the Court's usage, "lower courts" means state as well as lower Federal courts.

It remains to define four additional terms that require a bit more explanation: tentative judicial review; definitive judicial review; governmental powers; and limitations on governmental powers.

Judicial review has two forms: tentative and definitive. Tentative judicial review occurs when the Court does not claim the last word. As we shall see, there are various situations in which the Court is justified in declaring some official action to be unconstitutional but subsequently yielding to a contrary determination by another organ of government. Perhaps the most familiar of these situations arises when official action is held invalid not because it is forbidden by the Constitution but (1) because the Constitution empowers *Congress* to forbid it; (2) because Congress has not spoken; and (3) because the Court "interprets" Congressional silence to imply an intent to forbid. It is probably a fiction to call this process "interpretation" of the silence, since the fact is, ordinarily, that Congress has not crystallized any position at all (if indeed the question has even been brought to its attention). What the Court actually does is to declare national policy on the basis of its own conception of the national interest and invoke the Constitution to justify its decision — explaining that the policy declared by the Court is called for by the Constitutors' objectives (though not by their express language).

Thus, the Commerce Clause is phrased as a grant of power to Congress, not the Court. The *objective* of the Clause is achievement of an integrated national market, unembarrassed by local trade barriers. The Court can only be invoking that objective to justify its own action when, in the absence of an applicable Federal statute, it invalidates state taxes and regulations that impede interstate commerce. Similarly, the Court invokes the *objective* of the Supremacy Clause — ability of the Federal Government to function without state interference — to justify its own action when, unaided by Federal legislation, it invalidates state taxes on Federal agencies, activities, or property. On its face the Supremacy Clause, by declaring Federal *law* to be supreme, is seemingly intended to reinforce the power of Congress as the *maker* of Federal law; yet the Court invokes the Clause (actually, invokes the objective of the Constitutors in adopting the Clause) as a basis for its own power to invalidate the state taxes.

The rationale for this type of judicial review ("tentative") is this: "The Constitutors gave Congress a certain power in order to enable (but not require) Congress to work toward an objective the Constitutors considered desirable. We, the Court, assume that Congress wants to do what the Constitutors hoped; but Congress has not thus far noticed the state tax or regulation (attacked in this lawsuit), probably because in itself the state measure is not very important, or has not been widely enforced. However, if the measure were upheld and emulated it would probably produce a cumulative effect that we think would disappoint the hope of the Constitutors (which we *assume* Congress wants to fulfill). Therefore we hold the state tax or regulation invalid. But we do not question the primary authority of *Congress* to decide whether to do what the Constitutors hoped it would, and also to decide whether state measures of this type do in fact have the harmful potential that *we* think they have. Therefore, if Congress disagrees with our decision and directs us to uphold the state tax or regulation, we will do it."

The net effect of tentative judicial review is to shift the burden of legislative initiative. Ordinarily, Congress must take affirmative action in order to exercise a power granted to it by the Constitution.* Tentative judicial review is a sort of fail-safe procedure. It requires Congress to take affirmative action not to exercise a power but to *avoid* its exercise. The difference is significant, because of the built-in friction in the legislative process — a process which is deliberately designed to make Congressional action somewhat difficult. The bicameral structure and the executive veto call for something more than simple majority approval, and additional obstacles are set up by such practices as respect for filibusters and committee screening of bills. Therefore the Court's willingness to "interpret" the silence of Congress has great practical importance. But if the Court's action is disapproved by the electorate (speaking through Congress), it can be changed by statute.

Tentative judicial review thus involves no departure from the relationship between legislature and judiciary that is familiar in the Anglo-American system of lawmaking. For centuries common law courts have been making law quite freely, in situations where rules of conduct have not been laid down by statute. They do this by deciding the case for one party or another, and explaining the result on the basis of one or more legal propositions which they affirm to be valid. But (unless prevented by an overriding constitutional imperative) the courts are always ready to defer to a later statute adopting different legal propositions to be used in future, in lieu of those initially adopted by the courts. The only way in which tentative judicial review differs from common law adjudication is that — to the extent that the Court claims to be guided by the Constitutors' policy objectives rather than its own — it escapes much of the public responsibility for the results

---

\* I here refer to Congress because tentative judicial review has until now been applied only to Federal legislation. Later on I shall argue, however, that it should also be applied to some types of state legislation.

reached. But this is unlikely to arouse fears of judicial usurpation, so long as the *ultimate* authority and responsibility are left with Congress.

The ultimate authority of the legislature to decide what the law shall be is *the normal thing*. It exists in all nonconstitutional cases, as well as in constitutional cases decided through tentative judicial review. Where it does not exist is in cases decided through what we shall call "definitive" judicial review. There the Court explains its decisions on the basis of legal propositions which it denies the power of legislatures to change. These are the cases that attract most public attention and are ordinarily thought of when the term "constitutional decision" is heard. These are the cases in which the Court thwarts the will of electoral majorities, expressed through their elected spokesmen.* These are the cases in which the Court asserts its own ultimate authority to declare the legal propositions on which it must base its decision.

In Chapter II we have pinpointed the peril inherent in employing judicial review "beyond the boundaries of demonstrable necessity" (leaving open for the time being the question as to how necessity can be demonstrated) — peril to the open society, and even to domestic tranquillity. For a long time the Court manifested its recognition of that peril through a whole panoply of practices designed to avoid judicial review whenever reasonably possible, and to minimize its scope when it could not be wholly avoided. Justice Brandeis's concurring opinion in *Ashwander v. TVA* (1936)[2] enumerated seven such practices:

---

* I recognize that "electoral majority" is not a self-defining term. There are national majorities, state majorities, and local majorities; and much of the Court's business has consisted of deciding whether the will of a national majority should prevail over that of a state or local majority. Justice Holmes said it in a 1913 address to the Harvard Law School Association (O.W. Holmes, *Collected Legal Papers* (1920), at pp. 295-96):

> I do not think the United States would come to an end if we lost our power to declare an Act of Congress void. I do think the Union would be imperiled if we could not make that declaration as to the laws of the several States. For one in my place sees how often a local policy prevails with those who are not trained to national views and how often action is taken that embodies what the Commerce Clause was meant to end.

For present purposes, however, the indefiniteness of the term "electoral majority" will not be troublesome.

The fact that it would be convenient for the parties and the public to have promptly decided whether the legislation assailed is invalid, cannot justify a departure from these settled rules of corporate law and established principles of equity practice.... "It must be evident to any one that the power to declare a legislative enactment void is one which the judge, conscious of the fallibility of the human judgment, will shrink from exercising in any case where he can conscientiously and with due regard to duty and official oath decline the responsibility." 1 Cooley, Constitutional Limitations (8th ed.), p. 332.

The Court has frequently called attention to the "great gravity and delicacy" of its function in passing upon the validity of an act of Congress; and has restricted exercise of this function by rigid insistence that the jurisdiction of federal courts is limited to actual cases and controversies; and that they have no power to give advisory opinions. On this ground it has in recent years ordered the dismissal of several suits challenging the constitutionality of important acts of Congress. [Citing cases] . . .

The Court developed, for its own governance in the cases confessedly within its jurisdiction, a series of rules under which it has avoided passing upon a large part of all the constitutional questions pressed upon it for decision. They are:

1. The Court will not pass upon the constitutionality of legislation in a friendly, non-adversary, proceeding, declining because to decide such questions "is legitimate only in the last resort, and as a necessity in the determination of real, earnest and vital controversy between individuals. It was never the thought that, by means of a friendly suit, a party beaten in the legislature could transfer to the courts an inquiry as to the constitutionality of the legislative act." [Citing cases]

2. The Court will not "anticipate a question of constitutional law in advance of the necessity of deciding it." [Citing cases] "It is not the habit of the court to decide questions of a constitutional nature unless absolutely necessary to a decision of the case." [Citing case]

3. The Court will not "formulate a rule of constitutional law broader than is required by the precise facts to which it is to be applied." [Citing cases]

4. The Court will not pass upon a constitutional question although properly presented by the record, if there is also present some other ground upon which the case may be disposed of. This rule has found most varied application. Thus, if a case can be decided on either of two grounds, one involving

a constitutional question, the other a question of statutory construction or general law, the Court will decide only the latter. [Citing cases] Appeals from the highest court of a state challenging its decision of a question under the Federal Constitution are frequently dismissed because the judgment can be sustained on an independent state ground. [Citing case]

5. The Court will not pass upon the validity of a statute upon complaint of one who fails to show that he is injured by its operation. [Citing cases] Among the many applications of this rule, none is more striking than the denial of the right of challenge to one who lacks a personal or property right. Thus, the challenge by a public official interested only in the performance of his official duty will not be entertained. [Citing cases] In Massachusetts v. Mellon, 262 U.S. 447, the challenge of the federal Maternity Act was not entertained although made by the commonwealth on behalf of all its citizens.

6. The Court will not pass upon the constitutionality of a statute at the instance of one who has availed himself of its benefits. [Citing cases]

7. "When the validity of an act of the Congress is drawn in question, and even if a serious doubt of constitutionality is raised, it is a cardinal principle that this Court will first ascertain whether a construction of the statute is fairly possible by which the question may be avoided." [Citing case][3]

The thread that runs through the cases cited by Justice Brandeis is respect for the judgment of other governmental organs — respect, that is, for positions taken by elected Federal and state officials. The "great gravity and delicacy" of overriding their wishes (and the presumed wishes of their constituents) result from the peril mentioned above, and it is fair to assume that the Court had that peril in mind when it established the seven enumerated practices. (Later on we shall see how far Justice Brandeis's successors have modified those practices.)

Plainly, the peril reaches its maximum in cases of *definitive* judicial review, and therefore counsels against resort to that type of judicial review unless necessary to avoid some even greater peril. Of course, it is hard to imagine a disaster less tolerable than a police state or rebellion, but the *peril* of a lesser misfortune might be greater because of a much greater likelihood that it would materialize.

There are other techniques for avoiding conflict with other

governmental organs, not included in the Brandeis list because the Court does not acknowledge the use it makes of them: (1) Under the pretense that it is interpreting a constitutional provision in accordance with the intent of the Constitutors, the Court sometimes attributes to the constitutional text a meaning wholly at variance with that intent. (This technique is most frequently used to avoid an adjudication of *un*constitutionality,[4] though it can be and has been used to the opposite effect.[5]) (2) Not only does the Court adopt any "fairly possible" construction of a statute that will avoid "serious doubt of constitutionality" (the seventh Brandeis category); it also sometimes adopts, for that purpose, a construction that is *not* "fairly possible" *in logic,* though the Court solemnly says it is.[6]

Incidentally, this last practice reveals even more clearly than the others a strong desire to avoid judicial review. On its face, "construction" to avoid constitutional doubt is a mystifying practice. It assumes that there is no single "correct" interpretation of the statute — "correct" in the sense that it calls for the result that a majority of the legislators would have wanted if they had been asked. No court *ever* admits taking such a position in a nonconstitutional case; it always manages to declare the *most probable* "legislative intent" in some way, however uncertain the indicia, unless the statute is so indefinite that no one can really divine what the legislature wanted to accomplish — in which event it is *constitutionally* void for vagueness, on due process grounds. Given the fact that the Court does not disclaim its complete competence to interpret and apply the Constitution, in difficult as well as in easy cases, its practice of "construing" statutes to avoid "constitutional doubt" can only be explained by a strong aversion to judicial review in those cases where the practice is followed.

At this point we should list the broad categories of "constitutional cases" — *i.e.,* cases in which a party calls on the Court to engage in judicial review. For this purpose it is useful to distinguish between (a) governmental *powers* and (b) *limitations* on governmental powers. The Constitution regulates both of them. A governmental power is authority to deal with some type of social problem through application of official force, usually by formulation of rules of conduct — definition of conduct that is forbidden, discouraged, permitted, encouraged, or required. A limitation on governmental power is a prohibition upon exercise of such a power in a particular manner.

It may seem odd to make a distinction between "governmental powers" and "limitations on governmental powers," since it is logically and semantically possible to delineate the scope of a power in such a way as to take account of any limitations upon it. For example, if the Federal Government possesses the power to regulate interstate commerce but is limited by a prohibition against exercising the power in such a way as to abridge freedom of the press, we could simply say that it possesses a power to regulate interstate commerce in a manner that does not result in abridgment of freedom of the press.

There are solid reasons, however, for recognizing the distinction between the power and limitations upon the power. For one thing, it permits simpler and less repetitive expression. If each power were subject to no more than one or two limitations, as in the above oversimplified example, there would be no danger of undue complexity. But if (as is actually the case) each power is subject to a dozen or more limitations, the power would have to be described with a large set of qualifications, at least some of which would be interdependent and interlocking; and the problem of intelligible draftsmanship would be formidable. Moreover, if (as is also actually the case), a dozen or more powers are all subject to the same limitations, the whole set of qualifications would have to be repeated in the description of each power.

There is also a second reason. The question whether government should possess a power involves considerations quite different from those involved in deciding whether a particular limitation upon it is desirable. The former question depends on whether there is a collective interest — or, in the case of a *Federal* power, a *national* collective interest — in the subject matter. The latter question depends on whether, granted the existence of the requisite collective interest, restrictions on the way the power can be exercised are necessary for protection of a *further* interest such as the interest in preservation of an open and self-governing society (which, as I wrote in 1972,[7] is among the most basic of the national objectives embodied in the Constitution).

The Constitutors therefore separated the two questions in their own thinking; and probably this circumstance (rather than convenience in drafting) mainly accounts for the fact that powers and limitations are dealt with in different provisions of the Constitution. The same habit of thought has persisted in the Supreme Court's opinions. That in itself justifies our use of terminology that reflects the distinction between the two questions, in our appraisal of the Court's work.

Constitutional cases involving claims that some official act is invalid *because of lack of governmental power* most commonly raise the question whether the power is possessed by the particular governmental organ that has undertaken to exercise it — not the contention that *no* governmental organ has authority to deal with some societal conflict. The claim may be that the power is possessed by the Federal Government and not by the state government which has undertaken to exercise it; or vice versa.[8] Or the claim may be that the power is possessed by Congress and not by the President who has undertaken to exercise it; or vice versa.[9] There are also some cases, however, in which the claim is that the power is beyond the authority of *any* governmental organ. After 1937, when the Court abandoned the view that prices, wages, and hours must ordinarily be fixed by impersonal market forces and not by governmental action, such cases became quite rare. For a time it seemed that religious principle was the only field that was barred to all government intervention; except for that field, the Court appeared unwilling to hold that any societal conflict was completely exempt from government control. In the past decade, however, the Court has taken that position in a small but growing category of so-called "privacy" cases, where individual autonomy has been declared supreme — for example, use of contraceptives by married couples, enjoyment of pornography in one's home, and a woman's decision to have an abortion in the first trimester of pregnancy.[10] Yet, even today, most claims that governmental power is lacking involve the allocation of power to one governmental organ rather than another, not the claim that the relevant societal conflict is totally exempt from governmental control.

For example, in *United States v. South-Eastern Underwriters Ass'n* (1944) [11] the Court held that interstate insurance is interstate commerce, thus abandoning a position it had taken in 1868 [12] and had adhered to for 76 years, so that (a) insurance companies became regulable by Congress under the Commerce Power, and (b) the states lost the power to burden interstate insurance by regulating or taxing it. Congress quickly enacted the McCarran Act of 1945,[13] which declared that

> the continued regulation and taxation by the several States of the business of insurance is in the public interest, and . . . silence on the part of Congress shall not be construed to impose any barrier to the regulation or taxation of such business by the several States.

Thereafter *Prudential Insurance Co. v. Benjamin* (1946) [14] held the McCarran Act to be valid legislation, effective to sustain a South Carolina tax of 3% of the insurance premiums received by out-of-state corporations on business done in that state, even though the Court assumed that the tax (not being imposed on South Carolina corporations) was a discriminatory burden on interstate commerce.

*Tentative* judicial review is adequate in any governmental power case where the question is whether a power belonging to Congress can nevertheless be exercised by the states unless and until Congress acts. These are the *typical* "silence of Congress" cases. If the Court holds the state action invalid, it will yield to a later Congressional determination to the contrary.

*Definitive* judicial review is necessary in governmental power cases where the question is whether or not the Federal Government possesses a particular power. This question has arisen in the *rare* "silence of Congress" case where the state has contended that Congressional silence is meaningless because Congress lacks power to act.[15] It has also arisen in so-called "Tenth Amendment" cases where *Congressional* action has been questioned on the ground that the relevant power resides in the states rather than the Federal Government.[16] Today this category of cases has become a virtual empty set, because the Court has almost completely abandoned the use of judicial review to protect states' rights; it appears to be satisfied that the centrifugal political forces which control Congress provide a sufficient safeguard for states' rights, [17] and that judicial intervention — which would necessarily be definitive rather than tentative, since it would be pointless to deny Congressional power but then defer to a contrary determination by Congress — is unnecessary. The only recent case of this type is the five to four decision in *Oregon v. Mitchell* (1970),[18] denying Congressional power to lower the voting age to 18 in state elections; and that decision was overruled by the Twenty-sixth Amendment half a year after it was made.[19] In the few cases where Presidential action has been challenged on the ground that Presidential power was lacking — mostly in connection with foreign relations — the Court has either upheld the power,[20] or (as in *Youngstown Sheet and Tube Co. v. Sawyer*[21]) has declared the President to possess the challenged power only if Congress says so (and this is the equivalent of tentative judicial review).

Thus it appears that definitive judicial review is no longer a factor in the governmental power cases. Quite the contrary is true in the other type of constitutional cases, which involve *limitations* on governmental power. Here the Court has applied definitive judicial review almost exclusively. At least, it has spoken in those terms; only occasionally has Congress even attempted to relax limitations imposed by the Court in the name of the Constitution.[22]

There are some power limitation cases which necessarily involve definitive judicial review or none at all. This is often true of challenges to the manner in which Congress has exercised its powers; for, except in cases which call only for a shift of the burden of legislative inertia, it would be pointless (as has already been mentioned in another connection) to hold a Federal statute invalid but then defer to a contrary determination by Congress. That consideration does not apply, however, to cases involving constitutional limitations on the President's power (mainly, limitations on powers exercised by Federal law enforcement personnel who are ultimately responsible to him), and on state power. In many such cases there may be reason for the Court to defer to a contrary Congressional determination.

In Chapter XVII we shall canvass the types of cases in which more extensive resort to tentative judicial review would be advisable. For the present, it is enough to note (a) that in view of the dangers attendant upon definitive judicial review, and the Court's routine use of tentative judicial review in some types of cases, it seems anomalous that definitive judicial review should be the preferred mode of adjudication for all power limitation cases; and (b) that these cases are the main source of current fears that the Court is now overstepping the bounds of its authority in a large way — that the Justices may have come to consider themselves to be masters of the Constitution rather than its servants.

## CHAPTER IV
## Lawmaking and Constitution-making

It is essential to draw a distinction between judicial *law*making power and judicial *constitution*-making power. I define lawmaking, somewhat restrictively,* as the formulation of standards of conduct (the paying of taxes being considered a form of such conduct) which the government will somehow enforce. I define constitution-making as the allocation or limitation of governmental power.

One principal governmental power is the power to make law. It is not the *only* governmental power; when the government delivers the mail, or builds and operates a hydroelectric plant, or wages war, it exercises powers other than the lawmaking power (though it may be, and usually is, acting *pursuant* to law); but, as already noted, the lawmaking power is the most important power possessed by the Federal Government because law is the strongly preferred medium of contact between it and the American people.

Exercise of the lawmaking power — or, more simply, lawmaking — means establishment of rules regulating the conduct of the people, including private persons, *i.e.,* rules that are not limited to the regulation of relationships within and among the several governmental organs. (Rules thus limited amount really to allocation or limitation of governmental power, which I classify as

---

* I do not equate "lawmaking" with "legislation" (meaning the making of laws by legislatures). "Lawmaking" is both broader and narrower than "legislation." It includes the making of rules of conduct by courts and by the executive, and it excludes a very important aspect of the work of legislatures, namely, exercise of their authority (granted or reserved to them by the Constitution) to allocate or limit the power of other governmental organs (*e.g.,* Federal statutes prescribing jurisdiction of Federal courts or limiting the President's foreign affairs power). This special definition of "lawmaking" is useful for present purposes but cannot be employed in other contexts without grave risk of confusion.

As will be seen, I classify as "constitution-making" the exercise by legislatures of their constitutionally granted or reserved authority to allocate or limit the power of other governmental organs, the conception being that they are thus fleshing out the structure of government along lines laid down by the Constitutors, as the Constitutors intended them to do.

constitution-making.) Thus, for example, it is constitution-making to provide that the House of Representatives cannot lawfully exclude an elected member on any grounds except lack of the requisite age, residency, and citizenship.[1] Such a rule affects the allocation of power between the House and the electorate, which — when it speaks by voting — is rightly characterized as an organ of government. It would be lawmaking to provide that conviction of embezzlement of Federal funds constitutes a disqualification for election to Congress; such a rule prescribes additional punishment for a crime, and any effect it may have on the electorate's choice of legislative representatives is incidental.

A constitutional control of lawmaking power may consist of a prohibition against making any law at all in certain fields (such as religious principle); or a restriction on the *substance* of laws made in certain fields, such as taxation (the Constitution permits Federal taxes on imports but not on exports [2]); or the specification of *methods* that are required or forbidden in the making or enforcement of laws (such as requiring origination of revenue bills in the House of Representatives,[3] or forbidding the bill of attainder process,[4] or requiring warrants for searches,[5] or forbidding compulsory self-incrimination [6]). The specification by the Constitution of required or forbidden methods does not preclude the making of laws adding other requirements or restrictions, so long as they are consistent with the ones specified by the Constitution — which in criminal cases usually means they must operate in favor of defendants rather than the prosecution. A constitution may also *contain* laws (*i.e.,* it may directly prescribe standards of conduct for the whole population including private individuals), but our Federal Constitution does this most sparingly; only the Thirteenth Amendment and the now repealed Eighteenth Amendment (respectively forbidding slavery and traffic in intoxicating liquors) have established standards of conduct for private individuals.

A constitution usually makes allocations of lawmaking power in quite general terms, leaving the further detailed allocation to be filled in, and to be changed from time to time, by some governmental organ which the constitution authorizes to do it. For example, the legislature is usually authorized to grant to municipal corporations and to administrative agencies as much lawmaking power, or as little, as it thinks desirable.

Legislatures thus possess primary authority not only to make law (formulate standards of nongovernmental conduct) but also to engage in the constitution-making function by making further grants of lawmaking power. This authority accompanies the legislative powers granted to Congress by Article I, Section 1 of the Constitution: "All legislative Powers herein granted shall be vested in a Congress of the United States, which shall consist of a Senate and a House of Representatives." Observe, however, that this provision does not grant to Congress *all* Federal lawmaking power or *all* authority to make further grants of lawmaking power. It covers only "Powers *herein granted*," that is, powers granted by the Constitution. In order to learn the substantive scope of Congressional power one must therefore look to the rest of the Constitution (mainly, but not solely, Article I, Section 8). In this respect Article I, Section 1 contrasts with Article II, Section 1 ("The executive Power shall be vested in a President of the United States of America") and Article III, Section 1 ("The judicial Power of the United States, shall be vested in one supreme Court, and in such inferior Courts as the Congress may from time to time ordain and establish").

The reason for pinpointing the nonexclusivity of the grant of lawmaking power to Congress is that, in a common law system such as ours, courts also exercise lawmaking power as a matter of course. The Constitutors surely knew this, and intended the "judicial Power of the United States" to include lawmaking power. (They would not have spontaneously said so in those words, since they were steeped in the Blackstonian tradition that courts discover the law and do not make it; but a careful cross-examiner could have extracted an admission.) This is not to say that they would necessarily have conceded to courts the authority to override law made by Congress, unless the Congressional statute conflicted with a higher law prescribed by the Constitutors themselves; they would have insisted that the *primary* lawmaking power belongs to

Congress if it resides anywhere in the Federal Government. But they would have agreed (a) that whenever a case is decided (at least if the court states the reasons for its decision), the court articulates the legal propositions that form the basis of its judgment, and affirms the validity of those legal propositions; and (b) that if such a legal proposition has not been previously declared by statute — and there are many cases involving such propositions — the court *makes law*. Judicial opinions are studded with lawmaking, *but this is not the same as judicial review*. There is a great deal of lawmaking in opinions of the British courts, for example; did they not formulate the Rule against Perpetuities [7] and absorb much of the law merchant into the common law? [8] Yet they do not engage in judicial review as we know it in this country.

As has been pointed out, there is a formal similarity between statutory interpretation and *tentative* judicial review. The latter involves "interpretation" of the silence of Congress — or, at least, that is how the process has often been characterized.[9] It is, however, a type of interpretation quite different from the interpretation of a statute, since it is based not on the words of Constitutors or legislators but on the objectives of the Constitutors and the assumption that Congress shares them. As for *definitive* judicial review, it lacks even formal similarity to statutory interpretation since it involves the overriding of legislative intent rather than its enforcement.

The question remains whether definitive judicial review consists of genuine interpretation of the intent of the *Constitutors*. The ancient litany of judicial review speaks in those terms. Yet it has probably never been entirely true, and today it is not true at all. A fairly recent recitation of the litany is the assertion by Justice Roberts in *United States v. Butler* (1936),[10] where the first Agricultural Adjustment Act was held invalid:

> When an act of Congress is appropriately challenged in the courts as not conforming to the constitutional mandate the judicial branch of the Government has only one duty, — to lay the article of the Constitution which is invoked beside the statute which is challenged and to decide whether the latter squares with the former. All the court does, or can do, is to announce its considered judgment upon the question.[11]

It would be interesting to discuss this classic oversimplification (which even Justice Roberts would probably have admitted it to be) in its aspect as a self-defensive tactic of an embattled Court; for present purposes, however, what is significant is that the Court is said to look no further than the *text* of the Constitution in adjudicating its effect. Now this is not the practice even with statutes; legislative intent is an accepted guide to statutory interpretation. And for more than a century and a half, the Court has adhered to the view that the words of a constitution can and should be interpreted with *greater* latitude than those of a statute. In *McCulloch v. Maryland* (1819),[12] Chief Justice Marshall put it this way:

> A constitution, to contain an accurate detail of all the subdivisions of which its great powers will admit, and of all the means by which they may be carried into execution, would partake of the prolixity of a legal code, and could scarcely be embraced by the human mind. It would probably never be understood by the public. Its nature therefore, requires, that only its great outlines should be marked, its important objects designated, and the minor ingredients which compose those objects be deduced from the nature of the objects themselves. . . . we must never forget, that it is *a constitution* we are expounding.[13] (Marshall's emphasis)

As we shall see later in this chapter, the basis for a still more latitudinarian technique of "interpretation" appears elsewhere in the *McCulloch* opinion. But this quotation shows clearly enough that the Great Chief Justice was willing to go outside the text of the Constitution even more readily than the text of a statute, in determining the intent of those who had made it. His successors — not excluding Justice Roberts — have followed him at least this far, however vehemently they may have denied that they were doing so.

Before examining this latitudinarian technique of constitutional "interpretation," we shall explore some aspects of judicial lawmaking.

*First:* It is not much of an overstatement to say that every case which reaches an appellate court and evokes an opinion of that court involves some judicial lawmaking. If the pre-existing law were entirely clear on every legal proposition involved in the case, the only objective of appeal (other than delay for its own sake) would be reconsideration of the facts; and appellate courts generally decline to reconsider facts, except for lower appellate courts in which a trial *de novo* is available.* (They do, of course, entertain a claim that the trial court's factual determination is against the great weight of the evidence or was premised on a faulty jury instruction, but such a claim raises a question of law — the correctness of the trial judge's instructions to the jury or his denial of a motion for directed verdict, for new trial, for judgment notwithstanding the jury's verdict, or in arrest of judgment.)

Consequently, it is by no means uncommon for an appellate opinion to involve at least the "interstitial" lawmaking of which Judge (later Justice) Cardozo wrote in *The Nature of the Judicial Process*.** It formulates rules to cover situations for which the legislature has not prescribed unambiguously (or has not prescribed at all), or — if either of two pre-existing rules of law is arguably applicable — it states a third rule saying which of the two should prevail in the circumstances of the particular case.

---

* In many states the decision of a trial court of limited jurisdiction, such as a magistrate's court or police court, can be appealed to a higher court such as a circuit court where an entirely new trial is available. Such a trial is called a trial *de novo*, since the earlier adjudication has no effect. Often it is even possible to plead guilty in a magistrate's court, take an appeal, and win an acquittal after trial *de novo* on the appeal.

** CARDOZO, THE NATURE OF THE JUDICIAL PROCESS 113-14 (1921) (reprinted by permission of Yale University Press):

> The social interest served by symmetry or certainty must . . . be balanced against the social interest served by equity and fairness or other elements of social welfare. These may enjoin upon the judge the duty of drawing the line at another angle, of staking the path along new courses, of marking a new point of departure from which others who come after him will set out upon their journey.
>
> If you ask how he is to know when one interest outweighs another, I can only answer that he must get his knowledge just as the legislator gets it, from experience and study and reflection; in brief, from life itself. Here, indeed, is the point of contact between the legislator's work and his. The choice of methods, the appraisement of values, must in the end be guided by like considerations for the one as for the other. Each indeed is legislating within the limits of his competence. No doubt the limits for the judge are narrower. He legislates only between gaps. He fills the open spaces in the law. How far he may go without traveling beyond the walls of the interstices cannot be

LAWMAKING AND CONSTITUTION-MAKING 65

*Second:* A court may find that either of two valid legal premises is available to dispose of a case, one broader than the other. Ordinarily it will prefer the narrower one, so as to leave its position more flexible in later cases, but there can be a sound reason to elect the broader. If the court has no doubt that the broader one should be applied even in other fact situations, it rightly clarifies the law and avoids the need for much future litigation by saying so. For example, the particular school segregation involved in *Brown v. Board of Education* (1954) [14] could probably have been held unconstitutional on the narrow ground that the black and white schools in Topeka, Kansas, were not in fact "equal" within the meaning of the "separate but *equal* " doctrine. Prior decisions provided ample basis for such a ruling, and the fact that the eminent counsel for Brown (led by Justice-to-be Thurgood Marshall) deliberately waived that point would not have prevented the Court from relying on it, had it so desired. But every one of the Justices was ready to announce that *no* legally required racial segregation in the public schools would pass constitutional muster, and they elected to attempt the forestalling of future litigation involving other school districts by resting their decision on that broader ground. The attempt did not succeed, of course, but that was very probably because of the unfortunate announcement of the "deliberate speed" doctrine a year later [15] — which stimulated unfounded hopes that the Court did not intend the *Brown* decision to mean everything the opinion said.

*Third:* Somewhat similar, but analytically distinct, is what may be called judicial lawmaking by dictum. A court's opinion may affirm the validity of a legal proposition that is related to the subject matter of the case but is not necessary for its decision. A

---

staked out for him upon a chart. He must learn it for himself as he gains the sense of fitness and proportion that comes with years of habitude in the practice of an art.

Cardozo reserved the term "interstitial lawmaking" for cases "where a decision one way or another, will count for the future, will advance or retard, sometimes much, sometimes little, the development of the law." *Id.* at 165. This seems somewhat narrower than "judicial lawmaking" as I use the term here.

good example is *Wolf v. Colorado* (1949) [16] where the Court asserted for the first time, by way of dictum, that

> security of one's privacy against arbitrary intrusion by the police — which is at the core of the Fourth Amendment — is basic to a free society. It is therefore implicit in "the concept of ordered liberty" and as such enforceable against the States through the Due Process Clause.[17]

Wolf's conviction was nevertheless affirmed, on the ground that the Fourteenth Amendment's Due Process Clause does not require the states to exclude illegally seized evidence from consideration by the jury (a position abandoned twelve years later [18]). Thus, the Court's actual decision — affirming Wolf's conviction — was the same as if the dictum had not been included in the opinion. Nevertheless, the dictum had a tremendously influential effect on later decisions.[19]

*Fourth:* If a legal proposition asserted by a court is derived from common law precedent, it can be changed by statute. The same is true if the legal proposition results from statutory interpretation properly so called, that is, the court's determination as to how a majority of the legislators would have wanted the instant case decided.

One qualification is necessary. The Constitution may forbid certain changes by the legislature. There is a constitutional barrier, for example, to complete abrogation of parents' common law right to control their minor children.[20] If the Constitution forbids *any* change in the common law or statutory rule, then it is really a constitutional rule also and falls outside the scope of the present point.

*Fifth:* A legal proposition consists of two elements, only one of which may be explicit: (a) It seeks to achieve one or more objectives thought to be socially beneficial, and (b) it defines conduct that is required, encouraged, permitted, discouraged, or forbidden in order to accomplish its objective(s). If a statutory or common law rule states only a standard of conduct and is silent as to social objective, the objective is inferred from the rule (or from legislative history); but it is always considered to be present, and available as a guide to interpretation if the standard of conduct is ambiguous as applied to the instant case.

If the rule states an objective but no standard of conduct, or only an incomplete one (*i.e.,* inadequate for the objective), the court commonly declares an appropriate standard of conduct. For example, where a Federal statute declared that railway employees should be free to organize themselves for collective bargaining purposes, but provided no remedies against employer interference, the Court laid down standards of employer conduct.[21] It will be noted that in such cases the Court, though it makes law, does not act without constraint. It exercises an *implied judicial power* to help the legislature reach its objective, and — considering itself limited by the scope of that objective — it does not act as a free agent. Presently we shall be saying a great deal about implied judicial power.

*Sixth:* The five foregoing points apply to nonconstitutional as well as constitutional cases. We now move closer to the heart of our inquiry. If a textual provision of the Constitution (including its preamble and its Amendments) sets forth in explicit terms neither an objective of the Constitutors relevant to the case in hand, nor an applicable standard of conduct, but the Court — on a ground yet to be discussed — articulates a constitutional objective or prescribes a constitutional standard of conduct, we have a case not of judicial lawmaking but of judicial constitution-making. The present Court undoubtedly engages in constitution-making.

Our central question is whether, in such cases, the Court considers itself to be a free agent or whether it acts (and ought to act) pursuant to a principle of implied judicial power. The answer to that question is crucial to the assessment of whether the Justices do or do not consider themselves, as a continuing constitutional convention, to be above the Constitution and the law. We have already seen that they do not, so far as tentative judicial review is concerned. In the "silence of Congress" cases, decision is guided by the Justices' understanding of the Constitutors' objectives and by an assumption as to the probable wishes of Congress. But as to definitive judicial review, a large question is raised by recent cases. It will therefore be useful to explore the concept of implied judicial power and see how far it can explain what the Court has been doing in the area of definitive judicial review.

CHAPTER V
# Constitutional Interpretation

Upon examining the Court's conception of its role as "interpreter" of the Constitution, we are immediately struck by a discrepancy between its words and its actions. As recently as 1971 the late Justice Black, speaking for a majority of the Court in *Younger v. Harris*,[1] proclaimed:

> The power and duty of the judiciary to declare laws unconstitutional is [sic] in the final analysis derived from its responsibility for resolving concrete disputes brought before the courts for decision; a statute apparently governing a dispute cannot be applied by judges, consistently with their obligations under the Supremacy Clause, when such an application of the statute would conflict with the Constitution. *Marbury v. Madison,* 1 Cranch 137 (1803).[2]

Though the decision was not unanimous, no member of the Court took issue with this statement. It is not to be supposed, however, that any single one of Justice Black's colleagues shared his belief as to what it means to "conflict with the Constitution." The year before, when he spelled out his belief on this point in *Coleman v. Alabama*,[3] he spoke for himself alone.

The *Coleman* case dealt with an Alabama conviction for murderous assault. The Court held that the defendant had a constitutional right to assistance of counsel at his preliminary hearing. There was no majority opinion. Justice Brennan, for himself and three others, stood on the proposition that, as declared in one of the Scottsboro cases, "the accused is guaranteed that he need not stand alone . . . at any stage of the prosecution . . . where counsel's absence might derogate from the accused's right to a fair trial."[4] Justice Black approved his four colleagues' conclusion but rejected their reasoning:

> I fear that the prevailing opinion seems at times to proceed on the premise that the constitutional principle ultimately at stake here is not the defendant's right to counsel as guaranteed by the Sixth and Fourteenth Amendments but rather a right to a "fair trial" as conceived by judges. While that phrase is an appealing one, neither the Bill of Rights nor

68

any other part of the Constitution contains it. The pragmatic, government-fearing authors of our Constitution and Bill of Rights did not, and I think wisely did not, use any such vague, indefinite, and elastic *language*. Instead, they provided the defendant with clear, emphatic guarantees: counsel for his defense, a speedy trial, trial by jury, confrontation with the witnesses against him, and other such unequivocal and definite rights. The explicit commands of the Constitution provide a full description of the kind of "fair trial" the Constitution guarantees, and in my judgment *that document* leaves no room for judges either to add to or detract from these commands. I can have no part in unauthorized judicial toying with the carefully selected *language of our Constitution,* which I think is the wisest and best charter of government in existence.[5] (Emphasis added)

This was by no means the first time Justice Black had stood alone in maintaining that conflict with "the Constitution" means conflict with the "language" of "that document." In 1967, for example, he dissented from the ruling in *Katz v. United States* [6] that the Fourth Amendment's prohibition against "unreasonable searches and seizures" applies to electronic eavesdropping on a public telephone booth. "If I could agree with the Court," he said, "that eavesdropping carried on by electronic means (equivalent to wiretapping) constitutes a 'search' or 'seizure,' I would be happy to join the Court's opinion." [7] Then he explained why he could not agree:

My basic objection is twofold: (1) I do not believe that the words of the Amendment will bear the meaning given them by today's decision, and (2) I do not believe that it is the proper role of this Court to rewrite the Amendment in order "to bring it in harmony with the times" and thus reach a result that many people believe to be desirable.

While I realize that an argument based on the meaning of words lacks the scope, and no doubt the appeal, of broad policy discussions and philosophical discourses on such nebulous subjects as privacy, for me the language of the Amendment is the crucial place to look in construing a written document such as our Constitution.[8]

At the close of the opinion, after accusing his colleagues of "clever word juggling" in treating the proscription of unreasonable searches and seizures as a "vehicle for holding all laws violative of the Constitution which offend the Court's broadest concept of privacy," [9] he declared:

> No general right is created by the Amendment so as to give this Court the unlimited power to hold unconstitutional everything which affects privacy. Certainly the Framers, well acquainted as they were with the excesses of *governmental power,* did not intend to grant this Court such omnipotent *lawmaking authority* as that. The history of governments proves that it is dangerous to freedom to repose such powers in courts.[10] (Emphasis added)

The references to "governmental power" and "lawmaking authority" very probably provide the key to Justice Black's disagreement with the rest of the Court. In his later years, at least, he conceived of judicial review as a power no broader than the duty to decide cases as directed by the words of the Constitutors. Judicial review did indeed have its genesis in that conception. Chief Justice Marshall, in *Marbury v. Madison* (1803),[11] examined Article III and concluded that "the plain import of the words" [12] is to deny to Congress the power to enlarge the Court's original jurisdiction beyond the grant made by the Article itself. To him it was significant that the Constitution is a written one. For courts to "close their eyes on the constitution, and see only the law [*i.e.,* the statute] ... would subvert the very foundation of all written constitutions." [13] Further:

> That it thus reduces to nothing, what we have deemed the greatest improvement on political institutions, a written constitution, would, of itself be sufficient, in America, where written constitutions have been viewed with so much reverence, for rejecting the construction.[14]

Not only Black's insistence on the necessity of explicit constitutional language, but also his assumption as to the nature of judicial review, traces back to the *Marbury* opinion. In that case, the first in which the Court asserted the power to hold an Act of Congress (namely, a statute defining the Court's original jurisdiction) unconstitutional, Marshall spoke in terms of the Court's duty, not its power. He made no claim that the Court should pass on the validity of the jurisdictional statute simply because William Marbury's suit (to compel President Jefferson's Secretary of State to deliver his commission as Justice of the Peace for the

CONSTITUTIONAL INTERPRETATION 71

District of Columbia) gave it a welcome *opportunity* to do so. Nor did he claim that the Court possesses higher authority than Congress to interpret the Constitution. Marshall's posture was wholly passive. He said that the Court is obligated to decide cases brought before it for adjudication of *legal rights* and that its decision must be governed by the most authoritative law that applies (or purports to apply). Before reaching the constitutional question, he first showed that Marbury had a "legal right" to the delivery of his commission and that mandamus, which he sued for, was the appropriate form of remedy.[15] Thus there was *no escape* from deciding whether the Supreme Court had authority to issue a writ of mandamus in such a case. The jurisdictional statute (as interpreted) said yes; Article III (again, as interpreted) said no. From there on, the issue was simple:

> The question, whether an act, repugnant to the constitution, can become the law of the land, is a question deeply interesting to the United States; but, happily, not of an intricacy proportioned to its interest.
>
> . . . .
>
> It is, emphatically, the province and duty of the judicial department, to say what the law is. . . . If two laws conflict with each other, the courts must decide on the operation of each.
>
> . . . .
>
> If then, the courts are to regard the constitution, and the constitution is superior to any ordinary act of the legislature, the constitution, and not such ordinary act, must govern the case to which they both apply.[16]

We leave for historians the question whether Marshall was right in his *fundamental* point, which he passed over lightly and without intensive analysis: that the Constitutors intended the Constitution to create legal limitations cognizable in courts — not merely to memorialize the limits of political legitimacy, transgression of which might lead to electoral repudiation or possibly to rebellion, but not to judicial review.[17] Since the issue has never divided the Court, it can safely be bypassed in this inquiry into the Court's authority, or lack of authority, for a number of its recent decisions. Had the issue been deemed to be a close one, at least a few Justices would surely have voiced their dissent at some time since 1803.

Also off our beat is the intriguing question whether Marshall's passive posture was attributable to political prudence. Doubtless, so long as Jeffersonian resentment still fulminated against John Adams' "midnight appointments" to make the judiciary safe for the Federalist Party, it might have been reckless to invite impeachment by claiming a power nowhere described in the written Constitution; it was *safer* to be driven by duty.[18] On the other hand, the safer way may also have been the only obvious one, given the jurisprudential antecedents. For example, we have observed that Hamilton in the 78th *Federalist* — asserting that judicial review would and should be a feature of the then proposed Constitution — called the judiciary "the least dangerous" of the three departments because it

> has no influence over either the sword or the purse; no direction either of the strength or of the wealth of the society; *and can take no active resolution whatever.*[19] (Emphasis added)

His scornful rejection of the thought "that the courts on the pretense of a repugnancy, may substitute their own pleasure to the constitutional intentions of the legislature," [20] is hard to square with anticipation of judicial constitution-making power. As already indicated, however, speculation as to whether Marshall's passivity stemmed from prudence or conviction must also be left for historians. Our concern is not with birth but with growth and growing pains.

Marshall's opinion in *Marbury v. Madison* is based on the idea that the decision was controlled by two distinct bodies of pre-existing law. First, there was the question whether the law imposed on Madison some judicially enforceable duty to Marbury, which Madison had violated — whether Marbury had what may be called a "legal right" to the delivery of his commission. That depended on the law prescribing the duties owed by one party to another, which is found not in the Constitution but in the common law (as modified by any applicable statutes). Second, there was the question whether the Supreme Court, rather than a lower court, had jurisdiction to decide the case in the first instance. That depended on the allocation of official power made by the

Constitution — specifically, whether the Constitution set fixed boundaries to the Court's original jurisdiction or whether it empowered Congress to enlarge that jurisdiction. In deciding this second question the Court declared what may be called a "constitutional rule," that is to say, a rule defining the limits of authority possessed by an organ of government. Here the source of law was the written Constitution.

Marshall made no claim that the Court had authority to create new legal rights or new constitutional rules. His position was that pre-existing law required the result, and that the Court did nothing but interpret that law and apply it to the facts of the case.

The *Marbury v. Madison* conception no longer adequately describes judicial review. This is not to say the original conception has been discarded. It is still available to enforce the Constitutors' prescriptions and proscriptions with respect to contingencies for which they sought to provide. A Federal statute taxing exports,[21] or suspending habeas corpus in the absence of rebellion or invasion,[22] would be dealt with today in the same terms as in 1803. However, modern constitutional adjudication also includes constitution-making — announcement of rules plainly (and sometimes admittedly) not derived from constitutional text, and creation of new legal rights whose adjudication provides an occasion for promulgation of new constitutional rules. In short, the *power* of judicial review is now broader than the *duty* to enforce the expressed will of the Constitutors.

It is easier to demonstrate the existence of this constitution-making power than to show exactly when it originated. In particular cases there is often room for reasonable doubt as to whether the Justices are interpreting or constitution-making — deciding as they think the Constitutors, if asked, would have instructed them to decide or deciding on some other basis. For example, Justice Black's dissenting strictures in *Katz v. United States* (1967)[23] may or may not have stated the true nature of his disagreement with the rest of the Court. Maybe his colleagues did use the Fourth Amendment as window dressing to hide their own exercise of power, being as doubtful as he was that the Amendment's term "searches and seizures" reaches electronic eavesdropping. But perhaps not. Perhaps they believed the Amendment was actually intended to cover all forms of official intrusion on privacy. Such an interpretation would not require the capriciousness of a Humpty Dumpty, though Justice Black's reading hews more closely to customary verbal usage. Reasonable doubt does exist.

Justice Black's use of the term "lawmaking authority" in his *Katz* dissent is worth noting. To the end of his long career, he professed strong antipathy toward what he called judicial lawmaking; and he did not expressly draw a distinction between judicial lawmaking and judicial constitution-making.[24] Of course he engaged freely in what *we* have called judicial *law*making; no Justice has ever done otherwise, or could. But he also did his full share of judicial *constitution*-making, stoutly maintaining all the while that he was merely following directions set forth in the text of the Constitution and its Amendments.[25] The only difficulty in accepting his own characterization of his approach to constitutional issues is that he seemed able to find meaning in the words of the Constitutors which none of his colleagues (or anyone else) could find there.[26] Only by utterly remarkable stretching of the words of his Holy Writ (a copy of which he always carried with him, for inspiration and ready consultation) did he arrive at the humane and enlightened judgments for which he is and will be mainly remembered.

Justice Black's vitriolic eloquence may well have been a principal reason why the Court, to this day, refuses to acknowledge that it engages in *constitution*-making, and admits to *law*making only with traces of a diffidence that lingers from the Blackstone era. So eloquent were his diatribes against judicial lawmaking, so bitter his jeremiads against a return to the pre-1937 heyday of substantive due process,[27] that he often succeeded in making judicial lawmaking *vel non* the issue between him and his Brethren. That is unfortunate, since it obscures the real bone of contention: whether it is right to bring implied judicial constitution-making power to bear on the process of judicial review, and especially definitive judicial review. Upon reading the myriad debates on judicial activism between Justice Black and other Justices, contained in their opinions, one senses a failure to isolate and focus upon the actual difference between them. Instead of examining the similarities and differences between judicial lawmaking and judicial constitution-making and between tentative and definitive judicial review, the Justices struggle with the unreal question whether it is *ever* proper for the Court to declare and apply rules of law that have not been given them by state or Federal constitution, by statute, by treaty, or by the common law. We have already seen that the answer to that question must be yes; but there remains the question, to which the Justices have rarely addressed themselves, whether it is *always* proper for the Court to exert its undoubted raw power to do that — and, if not, when is it not proper?

The fact that the Justices adopt divergent positions as to the meaning of Constitutional verbiage in one single case, such as *Katz v. United States,* does not occasion a suspicion that any of them are engaging in anything more than a good-faith effort to interpret the Constitutional text as the Constitutors would have wished. But when cases by the dozen hold that the words of the Constitutors mean more or less than they seem, at first blush, to say or imply, it gradually becomes more difficult to escape the conclusion that something more than interpretation is taking place. As constitutional rules of greater and greater complexity are spun out, it becomes gradually harder to attribute them to the Constitution's laconic phrases. As more and more judgments are announced by a divided Court (not uncommonly without majority opinion, because no five of the Justices can agree on any single position), it becomes gradually less plausible that a joint effort, focused only upon ascertaining the Constitutors' intention, has led to such wide and such frequent divergence. As dissenting Justices complain ever more often that the Court has revised rather than followed the Constitution, one's readiness to discount their charges as disgruntled polemic becomes gradually less confident. As new constitutional rules proliferate without benefit of the formal amendment process, it becomes gradually more difficult to believe that they all reflect fresh insight into the original understanding. And so, when in 1965 the Court finally announces that some of the new constitutional rules have indeed been its own, the effect is not to *inaugurate* a new and broader conception of judicial review as a power to initiate constitutional rules. The effect is, rather, to remove any lingering doubt that the broader conception is and has been in operation. Only the time of its actual birth remains uncertain.

The advent of candor, at least to a limited degree, came with official endorsement of the doctrine of "prospectivity." Until then, any meaning newly attributed to the Constitution was given retroactive effect, in the sense that the Court automatically held it applicable to past acts and transactions as if it had been the law ever since adoption of the constitutional provision from which it was deemed to flow.* For example, the holding in *Gideon v. Wainwright* (1963) [28] that any person accused of serious crime is entitled to representation by counsel, whether or not he can afford an attorney fee, opened the way to new trial or release for every felony prisoner whose poverty had led to his trial without defense counsel. By 1965 the expansion of constitutional protections for

---

* This is not to say that the result in every case was the same as if the new meaning of the Constitution had been accepted from the beginning. In order to do justice between the parties, it is sometimes necessary to recognize that the former acceptance of a different meaning is a historical fact calling for application of such rules as *res judicata* (preserving the finality of judgments) and the requirement of fair notice of criminality.

Thus, cases such as Chicot County Drainage Dist. v. Baxter State Bank, 308 U.S. 371 (1940), often cited as precedents against the principle stated in the text, actually involve a different point. The question in the *Chicot County* case was whether an unappealed decision applying a Federal municipal bankruptcy statute was *res judicata* despite a subsequent Supreme Court ruling in another case that the statute was unconstitutional. The Court held that the unappealed decision was indeed *res judicata,* and remained effective. The opinion, by Chief Justice Hughes, stressed the injustice that would result if property rights that had vested in reliance on the earlier decision were upset — which, of course, is a main basis of the *res judicata* principle. This rationale has little if any force in criminal cases, since the state and Federal governments cannot ordinarily claim vested rights in convictions obtained by unconstitutional means. It is in the criminal process field that the prospectivity doctrine has had its main application, and the Court does protect such "vested" rights in convictions as the prosecuting authority *can* fairly claim, by limiting prospectivity in cases where the defendant's guilt is not to be seriously doubted and where a new trial may be difficult or impossible. *See, e.g.,* Stovall v. Denno, 388 U.S. 293 (1967).

accused persons was getting into high gear,[29] and it had become clear that retroactive application of the tightened requirements for investigation, arrest, and prosecution would lead to the reopening of numberless cases once thought closed. Moreover, prisoners who had been incarcerated for many years, usually because they had been convicted of the most serious offenses, would be the most difficult to convict on retrial; witnesses die and disappear, memories fade, evidence deteriorates. And yet, if their convictions had been unconstitutionally obtained, a new trial was no more than their due.

The exigency of this situation drove the Court to disclose its hand. No longer was it a mere matter of artful phraseology to attribute constitutional decisions to the intent of the Constitutors. If the Constitutors indeed had made the constitutional rules, those rules had been in effect when the convictions were obtained and provided the measure of their constitutionality. Only if the *Court* had made the new rules could it restrict their effect by declaring them to be "prospective" and so inapplicable to past cases whether or not some other rule required such a result. Prospectivity on any other basis would be an assertion of power not to revise the Constitution but to disregard it at will.

There was of course a last alternative: to stop making new constitutional rules, or anyway to make only rules for which retroactive application was tolerable. But that meant the Court would have to resist the pressures which were moving it to Herculean exertions to improve the brand of justice available to accused persons. Freedom to respond adequately to public needs that to it seemed overwhelming necessitated an overt claim of power to make constitutional law. Candor was the price of continuing and expanding effectiveness, and the Court's willingness to pay that price suggests that the pressures were formidable.

The case in which the price was paid was *Linkletter v. Walker* (1965),[30] the first of a long line of prospectivity rulings that now routinely accompany new Court-made rules. In 1959 Linkletter had been convicted of burglary through the use of illegally seized evidence and had received a nine-year sentence. The Louisiana

78  BY WHAT RIGHT?

Supreme Court affirmed the conviction in 1960, and no review by the United States Supreme Court was sought — presumably because there was no visible ground for it. That Court had never abandoned the rule laid down in *Wolf v. Colorado* (1949),[31] holding that the Fourteenth Amendment does not require state courts to exclude illegal evidence. Linkletter went to prison.

The following year *Mapp v. Ohio* (1961)[32] overruled the *Wolf* case. Thereupon Linkletter petitioned for habeas corpus, claiming his imprisonment was unconstitutional. The Supreme Court decided against him.

To read Justice Clark's opinion for a seven-member majority, one might not suspect that a new conception of judicial review is making its public debut. He notes the jurisprudential controversy between Sir William Blackstone (who maintained that courts discover law from external sources — their duty being not to "pronounce a new law, but to maintain and expound the old one") and John Austin (who maintained that they *make* law). Clark accepts the Austinian position. He concedes that "heretofore, without discussion, we have applied new constitutional rules to cases finalized before the promulgation of the rule."[33] (Note the legislative term "promulgation.") But, he continues, "the Constitution neither prohibits nor requires retrospective effect."[34] (He does not mention the requirement implicit in the reasoning of *Marbury v. Madison.*) *Consequently the Court is free to determine the applicability of its new rules for itself.* And so it will "weigh the merits and demerits in each case by looking to the prior history of the rule in question, its purpose and effect, and whether retrospective application will further or retard its operation."[35] On this basis, retroactive application can be denied.

The Clark opinion thus doubly affirms the Court's power to make new constitutional law. First, it declares that replacement of the *Wolf* rule with the *Mapp* rule was indeed the Court's own doing. "It was the judgment of this Court that changed the rule," says the opinion.[36] Second, it takes the position that the Constitutors' silence on a particular question, far from limiting judicial review, leaves the Court free to formulate its own principle of decision. The result is the same as if the *Mapp* rule had been laid down not in a judicial opinion but in a constitutional amendment ratified in 1961.

Justice Black, in dissent, likewise takes no notice that the official conception of judicial review is being broadened. He does make an offhand remark that one aspect of the Court's action "sounds more like law-making than construing the Constitution"[37] but his arguments are pitched on the level of statesmanship rather than jurisprudential theory. For example, his fear of the practical consequences of prospectivity is reflected in reiteration of a warning he had uttered in an earlier case:

> In our judgment one of the great inherent restraints upon this Court's departure from the field of interpretation to enter that of lawmaking has been the fact that its judgments could not be limited to prospective application.[38]

Incidentally, this was the only suggestion in either opinion that prospectivity may have been the price of freedom on the Court's part to respond fully to felt pressures for constitutional change — probably the basic reason for the decision.

In evaluating the broadened conception of judicial review, we too shall deal in practicalities rather than pure jurisprudential theory. The first of these practicalities, however, implicates a question that might seem purely theoretical: Is the *Marbury* conception of judicial review inherent in the very nature of our governmental system and the accepted role of the Supreme Court as a part of that system? More specifically, does establishment of new constitutional rules by the Court offend Article V of the Constitution which prescribes the amendment process? Does it outrage the principle of separation of powers? Does it permit evasion of specific safeguards against oppressive legislation, such as the prohibition of bills of attainder and other provisions of Article I, Section 9? In short, is the Court guilty of plain usurpation?

This is a practical inquiry because the limitation period on usurpation is very long indeed. Generations must pass before usurped power becomes secure. Thus the result bears on the stability of the Court's work. If it has accomplished a *coup d'état*, gathering dictatorial power to itself — believing, to be sure, as dictators are prone to profess, that the welfare of the people allows no other course — its power may prove to be short-lived. Future Justices may feel duty-bound to effect a Restoration. Congress may find it politically safe to strip away much or all of the Court's appellate jurisdiction — and, if the Court should resist on the basis of some new-found constitutional principle (as Justice Douglas once hinted is possible [39]), to respond with impeachment and removal. The President may find it politically expedient to revive Andrew Jackson's scornful cry: "John Marshall has made his decision; now let him enforce it"; [40] and, shorn of Presidential and Congressional support, the Court may find itself incapable of enforcing its mandates.

We have already discussed this question. We have seen that, in the last analysis, the Court's capacity for effective judicial review depends upon acquiescence of the electorate in the *legitimacy* of its function. That is what enabled it to weather President Franklin D. Roosevelt's Court-packing effort in 1936-37. The landslide victory won by his party in the 1936 elections evidenced utter disenchantment with the Court's evisceration of the New Deal legislative program; yet Congress accurately concluded that the voters were strongly disinclined to believe that the Court had defied the limits of legitimate power.[41]

Once the faith in the legitimacy of judicial review is blasted, however, dissolution of the Court's power is just a matter of time — and not a very long time at that. And so it is *practical* to inquire whether the conception of judicial review as a constitution-making power constitutes, in itself, an overstepping of established boundaries.

I believe it does not. The conception of judicial review as a power to formulate new constitutional rules possesses credentials almost as ancient as *Marbury v. Madison* itself, emanating indeed from the same source as that venerated decision. In the 1803 opinion Chief Justice Marshall did speak of duty rather than power, but he did not say that duty is the only legitimate basis for judicial review. And although he never did address himself to that specific question, sixteen years later in *McCulloch v. Maryland* (1819) [42] (again for a unanimous Court) he laid the foundation for an extension.

The case itself involved a challenge to Congressional rather than judicial power. The question was whether Congress has power to charter a banking corporation even though the Constitution says nothing of banks or corporations. The answer was yes, because a banking corporation is a useful instrumentality for exercise of the taxing power, the borrowing power, the commerce power, and other powers that *are* expressly granted to Congress. In support of his decision the Great Chief Justice unfolded the doctrine of implied powers. And though the case dealt with *legislative* power, he spoke more broadly. He spoke of *governmental* power:

> The sword and the purse, all the external relations, and no inconsiderable portion of the industry of the nation, are entrusted to [the Federal] government. It can never be pretended that these vast powers draw after them others of inferior importance, merely because they are inferior. Such an idea can never be advanced. But it may with great reason be contended, that a government, entrusted with such ample powers, on the due execution of which the happiness and prosperity of the nation so vitally depends, must also be entrusted with ample means for their execution. The power being given, it is the interest of the nation to facilitate its execution. It can never be their interest, and cannot be presumed to have been their intention, to clog and embarrass its execution by withholding the appropriate means.[43]

Here is a line of thought that relates to the judicial (and the executive) power as well as the legislative. Indeed, as noted above, Article III grants "the judicial Power" with no definitional restriction, unlike Article I which gives Congress only "legislative Powers herein granted" and then (mainly in Article I, Section 8) goes on to specify those powers. Hence there is some basis for believing that the Constitutors not only thought of judicial authority as a "power," the same term used to denote the authority of the two other branches, but might have embraced the idea of implied judicial power even more readily than the idea of implied legislative power.

If implied power can repose in the Supreme Court as well as in Congress, the question becomes: What would the Constitutors have expected and intended the Court to do as an "appropriate means" of serving "the interest of the nation"? Can the power to make law by announcing new constitutional principles on which decisions are based, and modifying or abandoning previously accepted principles to accommodate perceived changes in social conditions, ever be regarded as an "appropriate means" of exercising "the judicial power"? If so, would the Constitutors have gone so far as to expect and intend the Court's authority to encompass revision or supplementation of their own original allocations and limitations of governmental powers, as spelled out in the text of the Constitution? No answer is to be found in Chief Justice Marshall's opinions.

We do know, however, that the Constitutors sought to create a government for the ages. They wanted it to endure and prosper through whatever exigencies might beset it, some of them so remote in time that no mortal man could foresee them even dimly. As Justice Holmes wrote long ago, they

> called into life a being the development of which could not have been foreseen completely by the most gifted of its begetters. It was enough for them to realize or to hope that they had created an organism; it has taken a century and has cost their successors much sweat and blood to prove that they created a nation.[44]

From this viewpoint the Constitution was the womb of a nascent organism. The government that issued from it was stamped with the qualities its creators treasured, as a child is stamped with its genetic endowment. Like the child too, its general form and features were and are almost unalterably fixed. Also like the child, however, it must go forth to meet its own problems; even the most foresighted parent can do no more than instill habits and attitudes and objectives that will help his son or daughter to live, grow, and flourish. Hence, said Justice Stone for the Court in *United States v. Classic* (1941),[45] the Justices read the Constitution

> not as we read legislative codes which are subject to continuous revision with the changing course of events, but as the revelation of the great purposes which were intended to be achieved by the Constitution as a continuing instrument of government.\*[46]

---

\* Chief Justice Hughes had suggested the same idea, somewhat less pointedly,

CONSTITUTIONAL INTERPRETATION 83

Justice Stone does not use the term "implied judicial power." And yet does he not continue where the teaching of *McCulloch v. Maryland* leaves off? Chief Justice Marshall made clear the Court's capacity to hold implied powers. Justice Stone — soon to become Chief Justice himself — added the thought that power is a function of social need; new institutions undreamed of by the Constitutors — in the *Classic* case, the party primary election — can awaken new powers, so long as they are consistent with loyalty to "the great purposes which were intended to be achieved by the Constitution as a continuing instrument of government."

Justice Stone was no rabid proponent of expanded judicial power. To be sure, he never denied that the Court does bear responsibility for fulfillment of "the great purposes," and he stood as a rock — alone when necessary — in defense of judicial power which he thought the responsibility entailed.[47] If "the great purposes" could best be served by formulation of a new constitutional rule, he was ready to do it. But he remained true until death to the philosophy of self-restraint that pervaded his great dissent in the 1936 *AAA* case:

> Courts are not the only agency of government that must be assumed to have capacity to govern.[48]

In short, he believed the Supreme Court to hold a share of ultimate governmental power but not all of it.

The American people have embraced that belief. Had they not, removal of the veil in *Linkletter v. Walker* would have set off a shock-wave of indignation — strengthened year by year as the Court has ever more explicitly declared that formulation of new constitutional rules is its proper business. Constitutional change without constitutional amendment is now an accepted feature of the American governmental system. Danger that the Court's promulgation of new constitutional rules, *in and of itself,* will provoke significant charges of usurpation, is to be dismissed as remote.

---

in Monaco v. Mississippi, 292 U.S. 313, 322 (1934): "Behind the words of the constitutional provisions are postulates which limit and control."

But the doctrine of implied judicial power does not teach that the Court is a free agent. The Justices cannot expect to be indulged in an assertion of power simply because they possess the tactical ability to seize it. The people must not be allowed to lose the faith that new constitutional rules are designed, *and tolerably well designed,* as "the most appropriate means" to serve "the interest of the nation." Those phrases of Chief Justice Marshall have not lost their bite. And they imply that the legitimacy of any judicial action taken in the name of the Constitution must satisfy a pragmatic test: Can the Court, by taking the action, serve the "great purposes" more effectively than elected officials are likely to do?

On this score the Court is in difficulty. To an understanding of the nature and source of the difficulty, and to a search for the direction in which a remedy is to be found, the rest of this commentary is devoted.

CHAPTER VI

## Implied Power

In the last chapter we identified the genesis of the concept of implied power and quoted from the opinion of Chief Justice Marshall in *McCulloch v. Maryland* (1819), the seminal case on that subject. There the question was whether the Constitution makes implied as well as express grants of power to Congress. The *McCulloch* opinion is generally thought of as a complete if unadorned statement of implied power doctrine; but it cannot fairly be regarded as complete. As has been noted,[1] the far-seeing Chief Justice did take care to leave an open end, by speaking of implied *governmental* rather than implied *Congressional* power; the focus of his opinion, however, is upon implied Congressional power, which was the particular type of implied power there in question. In an oft-rehearsed passage, Marshall said:

> We admit, as all must admit, that the powers of the government are limited, and that its limits are not to be transcended. But we think the sound construction of the constitution must allow to *the national legislature* that discretion, with respect to the means by which the powers it confers are to be carried into execution, which will enable *that body* to perform the high duties assigned to it, in the manner most beneficial to the people. Let the end be legitimate, let it be within the scope of the constitution, and all means which are appropriate, which are plainly adapted to that end, which are not prohibited, but consist with the letter and spirit of the constitution, are constitutional.[2] (Emphasis added)

Parenthetically, we may note in the last sentence the distinction that Marshall draws between a power and limitations upon it.[3]

It has long since been established that the doctrine of implied power applies (a) to the President and the Court, as well as to Congress and (b) to the Federal Government as a whole, as well as to its particular branches. The most striking illustration is to be found in the cases affirming the power of the Federal Government as a whole, and of the President in particular, in the field of foreign affairs.

86	BY WHAT RIGHT?

The text of the Constitution enumerates only a few fragments of such Federal and Presidential power: (1) With the advice and consent of the Senate, the President is authorized to make treaties and to "appoint Ambassadors, other public Ministers and Consuls,"[4] and to receive foreign ambassadors.[5] (2) Congress is authorized[6] to "regulate Commerce with foreign Nations"; "establish an uniform Rule of Naturalization"; "declare War, grant letters of Marque and Reprisal, and make Rules concerning Captures on Land and Water"; "provide for calling forth the Militia to ... repel Invasions"; "define and punish Piracies and Felonies committed on the high Seas, and Offences against the Law of Nations"; and

> To make all Laws which shall be necessary and proper for carrying into Execution the foregoing Powers, *and* all other Powers vested by this Constitution in the Government of the United States, or in any Department or Officer thereof. (Emphasis added)

This last clause, the so-called "Necessary and Proper Clause," is a grant of power to Congress only. It cannot reasonably be construed as a grant of implied power to the President and the Court. And still, as we have said, the Federal Government has been held to possess power in the field of foreign affairs that far outruns the fragmentary explicit authorizations found in the text of the Constitution. Louis Henkin has described, better than I can hope to do, the Court's position with respect to that power; omitting his rich documentation, I quote him:

> The attempt to build all the foreign affairs powers of the federal government with the few bricks provided by the Constitution has not been accepted as successful. It requires considerable stretching of language, much reading between lines, and bold extrapolation from "the Constitution as a whole," and that still does not plausibly add up to all the power which the federal government in fact exercises. Some of the lacunae were filled when the Supreme Court decided that in addition to the enumerated powers and their derivatives the federal government enjoys some powers inherent in the nationhood and sovereignty of the United States. In *The Chinese Exclusion Case,* for example, the Court found that Congress could legislate to exclude aliens because:

Jurisdiction over its own territory to that extent is an incident of every independent nation. It is a part of its independence.... [T]he United States, in their relation to foreign countries and their subjects or citizens are one nation, invested with powers which belong to independent nations, the exercise of which can be invoked for the maintenance of its absolute independence and security throughout its entire territory.

We are not told where in the Constitution the Court found this grant of power, how it is to be justified in the face of the provision that the powers not delegated to the federal government are reserved to the States, which are the powers that "belong to independent nations" or how are they to be determined, by whom they can be exercised, how they relate to the powers expressly conferred upon one branch or another of the Federal Government.

Some of these difficulties, the anomalous, "spotty" treatment of foreign relations in the Constitution, and perhaps an impression that the Constitution assumes rather than confers foreign relations powers, probably inspired a singular constitutional theory: the powers of the United States to conduct relations with other nations do not derive from the Constitution! Although this theory did not spring new and full blown from the mind of Mr. Justice Sutherland, it finds authoritative expression, almost 150 years after the Constitution was adopted, in his opinion for the Court in *United States v. Curtiss-Wright Export Corp.* In that case, a Joint Resolution of Congress had authorized the President to embargo arms to the countries at war in the Chaco, and imposed criminal penalties for violating such an embargo. President Franklin Roosevelt proclaimed an embargo and the defendant company, indicted for violating it, challenged the Resolution and the Proclamation as entailing an improper delegation of legislative power to the President. Sustaining the indictment, the Supreme Court held that the principles which limit delegation in domestic affairs do not apply equally in foreign affairs. Justice Sutherland's opinion includes the following essay:

> It will contribute to the elucidation of the question if we first consider the differences between the powers of the federal government in respect of foreign or external affairs and those in respect of domestic or internal affairs. That there are differences between them, and that these differences are fundamental, may not be doubted.
>
> The two classes of powers are different, both in respect of their origin and their nature. The broad statement that the federal government can exercise no powers except

those specifically enumerated in the Constitution, and such implied powers as are necessary and proper to carry into effect the enumerated powers, is categorically true only in respect of our internal affairs. In that field, the primary purpose of the Constitution was to carve from the general mass of legislative powers *then possessed by the states* such portions as it was thought desirable to vest in the federal government, leaving those not included in the enumeration still in the states.... That this doctrine applies only to powers which the states had, is self evident. And since the states severally never possessed international powers, such powers could not have been carved from the mass of state powers but obviously were transmitted to the United States from some other source. During the colonial period, those powers were possessed exclusively by and were entirely under the control of the Crown. By the Declaration of Independence, "the Representatives of the United States of America" declared the United [not the several] Colonies to be free and independent states, and as such to have "full Power to levy War, conclude Peace, contract Alliances, establish Commerce and to do all other Acts and Things which Independent States may of right do."

As a result of the separation from Great Britain by the colonies acting as a unit, the powers of external sovereignty passed from the Crown not to the colonies severally, but to the colonies in their collective and corporate capacity as the United States of America. Even before the Declaration, the colonies were a unit in foreign affairs, acting through a common agency — namely the Continental Congress, composed of delegates from the thirteen colonies. That agency exercised the powers of war and peace, raised an army, created a navy, and finally adopted the Declaration of Independence. Rulers come and go; governments end and forms of government change; but sovereignty survives. A political society cannot endure without a supreme will somewhere. Sovereignty is never held in suspense. When, therefore, the external sovereignty of Great Britain in respect of the colonies ceased, it immediately passed to the Union....

The Union existed before the Constitution, which was ordained and established among other things to form "a more perfect Union." Prior to that event, it is clear that the Union, declared by the Articles of Confederation to be "perpetual," was the sole possessor of external sovereignty and in the Union it remained without change save in so far as the Constitution in express terms qualified its exercise. The Framers' Convention was called and exerted its powers upon the irrefutable postulate that though the states were several their people in respect of foreign affairs were one. Compare *The Chinese Exclusion Case,* 130 U.S. 581, 604, 606. . . .

. . . .

It results that the investment of the federal government with the powers of external sovereignty did not depend upon the affirmative grants of the Constitution. The powers to declare and wage war, to conclude peace, to make treaties, to maintain diplomatic relations with other sovereignties, if they had never been mentioned in the Constitution, would have vested in the federal government as necessary concomitants of nationality. . . . As a member of the family of nations, the right and power of the United States in that field are equal to the right and power of the other members of the international family. Otherwise, the United States is not completely sovereign. The power to acquire territory by discovery and occupation . . . , the power to expel undesirable aliens . . . , the power to make such international agreements as do not constitute treaties in the constitutional sense . . . , none of which is expressly affirmed by the Constitution, nevertheless exist as inherently inseparable from the conception of nationality. This the court recognized, and . . . found the warrant for its conclusions not in the provisions of the Constitution, but in the law of nations.

Although Sutherland invoked *The Chinese Exclusion Case* and others, his theory seems different from and more embracing than theirs. The earlier cases found powers inherent in sovereignty to be vested in the federal government "by the Constitution"; Sutherland apparently believed they are extra-constitutional. The earlier cases seemed to consider that sovereignty provided powers supplementary to those granted; Sutherland apparently considered sovereignty the principal source of foreign affairs power. While the earlier cases said nothing on the matter, Sutherland insisted that these powers were not delegated by the States in the making of the Constitution.

For clarity, I summarize and restate his theory as I understand it, supplying occasional gloss:

—With independence the former colonies became a sovereign nation. The powers of "internal sovereignty" lay with the individual States, but those of "external sovereignty" were with the Union of States acting together.

—The Constitution created a better union and conferred upon it some of the internal powers previously enjoyed by the individual States. It did not confer upon the new union the powers of external sovereignty, for these had already belonged to the Union before the Constitution. The Constitution did not enumerate them; it assumed them, and, in general, dealt with some of them only where there was some reason for doing it: where the locus of the power within the new federal government reflected change from the Articles or had been the subject of controversy or compromise, for example, which among the branches of the new government shall make treaties.

—Since the powers of the United States to conduct its foreign relations, and other powers inherent in national sovereignty, do not derive from the Constitution, one cannot identify them exclusively, or even principally, by construction of or inference and extrapolation from constitutional language. In particular, although some of them are mentioned, foreign affairs powers are not "enumerated powers" and are not denied (or reserved to the States) if they are not enumerated; but one must look elsewhere — to political philosophy, to international law and the practices of nations — to determine their full array. And these powers are not subject to doctrines of interpretation and limitation applicable to powers granted by the Constitution, for example those implied in principles of "separation of powers" or "federalism."[7]

Not only is it held that plenary *Federal* power exists in the field of foreign affairs. It is also held that this Federal power belongs primarily to the President, whose enumerated powers are even scantier than those of Congress.[8] Only Justice McReynolds dissented from Justice Sutherland's opinion for the Court in *United States v. Curtiss-Wright Export Corp.* (1936),[9] including the following affirmation of Presidential power (which can only be characterized as implied power, since no basis for it is to be found in the text of the Constitution):

Not only, as we have shown, is the federal power over external affairs in origin and essential character different from that over internal affairs, but participation in the exercise of the power is significantly limited. In this vast external realm, with its important, complicated, delicate and manifold problems, the President alone has the power to speak or listen as a representative of the nation. He *makes* treaties with the advice and consent of the Senate; but he alone negotiates. Into the field of negotiation the Senate cannot intrude; and Congress itself is powerless to invade it. . . .

It is important to bear in mind that we are here dealing not alone with an authority vested in the President by an exertion of legislative power, but with such an authority plus the very delicate, plenary and exclusive power of the President as the sole organ of the federal government in the field of international relations — a power which does not require as a basis for its exercise an act of Congress, but which, of course, like every other governmental power, must be exercised in subordination to the applicable provisions of the Constitution.[10] (Sutherland's emphasis)

It may be that this is something of an overstatement of the President's foreign affairs power. At this writing, the Court has not yet held whether the power extends to warrantless wiretapping or housebreaking, or broadens executive privilege against testimonial or documentary disclosure.[11] There is no doubt at all, however, that the President does possess more power in the field of foreign affairs than is expressly granted to him by the text of the Constitution and its Amendments.

It is instructive to note that the implication of lawmaking power is not limited to the *expansion* of explicit power grants contained in the constitutional text. That is indeed the most common application of the doctrine. In *McCulloch v. Maryland,* for example, Congressional power to incorporate a bank was held to be implied from the expressly granted currency power, war power, commerce power, and others. The Necessary and Proper Clause is sufficient to carry the Court that far (given its expansive interpretation of the word "necessary" in Marshall's *McCulloch* opinion [12]) if the only question is whether one or more explicit grants to Congress imply another. But the implied power doctrine is not limited to that situation.

For example, the Constitution creates Federal *judicial* power in admiralty, saying: "The judicial Power shall extend . . . to all Cases of admiralty and maritime jurisdiction" (Article V, Section 2, Paragraph 1). Congress, however, is given no express lawmaking power in that field; the Necessary and Proper Clause authorizes legislation in aid of the admiralty jurisdiction of the Federal courts — their "judicial power" — but does not literally authorize

Congress to make substantive changes in the admiralty law that the courts apply. Nevertheless in *In re Garnett* (1892) [13] the Court held that Congress does have power to enact substantive admiralty legislation, such as the 1886 Federal Limited Liability Act there upheld. The reason the Court gave was that the Constitutors — who were attempting to provide for the long centuries during which they hoped and expected their handiwork to endure — could not have intended to freeze admiralty law in the *status quo* as of 1787; that legislation was the only way the law could be changed; and that they must therefore have wanted Congress to possess the power to make new admiralty law.

To be sure, there was a conceivable alternative: The Court might have held *itself* to have lawmaking power in admiralty, implied from the jurisdictional grant. For two reasons, however, its failure to mention that possibility in the *Garnett* case cannot be taken as an across-the-board disclaimer of implied judicial lawmaking power. First: In 1892, when the case was decided, the jurisprudential outlook of Blackstone was still in vogue; and it would have been a breach of etiquette for any court to acknowledge or claim power to make the law rather than discover it — though the Justices were certainly aware, even then, that such power was being exercised routinely (as in the "silence of Congress" cases [14]). Second: The Court could not reasonably claim superior competence to make *the particular type of law* that Congress had undertaken to make when it enacted the 1886 statute. Revision of the rules of shipowners' liability was a matter more sensibly handled through legislative fact-finding and compromise than through the more rigid and precedent-ridden judicial process. It is this second line of thought that will provide the starting point for our inquiry whether implied *judicial* Constitution-making power does not exist, and rightly exist, *for matters in which the Court's competence is superior to that of Congress.*

Before turning to that question, however, let us have a look at one more case showing that implication of lawmaking power is not

IMPLIED POWER 93

limited to the expansion of lawmaking powers expressly granted. The case is *Prigg v. Pennsylvania* (1842),[15] which held a grant of Congressional power to be implied by Article IV, Section 2, Paragraph 3:

> No Person held to Service or Labour in one State, under the laws thereof, escaping into another, shall, in consequence of any Law or Regulation therein, be discharged from such Service or Labour, but shall be delivered up on Claim of the Party to whom such Service or Labour may be due.

In *The Petitioners,* Loren Miller summarizes the implied power point in the *Prigg* case (footnote omitted):

> Margaret Morgan, a Maryland slave, escaped to Pennsylvania with her child in 1832. Another child was born in Pennsylvania after her escape. In 1837, Edward Prigg, a slave catcher, arrived in Pennsylvania with affidavits proving that she was the escaped slave of Margaret Ashmore and secured a warrant for Margaret Morgan's arrest, but when he took her before a magistrate, that official refused to sign a removal order. Prigg then spirited Margaret Morgan and her two children out of the state and was indicted and charged with kidnapping because the magistrate had not ordered the removal. Maryland cooperated by returning him for trial. The jury found that Margaret Morgan was born a slave, that she had escaped from Maryland, and that she and her two children were slaves since the children followed the condition of the mother. Upon that finding, the trial court held Prigg guilty of kidnapping for failure to secure the magistrate's removal order. The Pennsylvania Supreme Court affirmed the conviction in such a perfunctory manner that Justice McLean was later led to remark that he supposed the "case had been made up to bring the question" to the Supreme Court.
> 
> When the case — *Prigg v. Commonwealth* — got to the Supreme Court, Pennsylvania justified the conviction on the ground that return of fugitives was a matter of state comity and that state law must be followed to the letter. It pointed out that the Constitution did not give Congress express power to legislate on the matter, and it asserted that the federal Fugitive Slave Law of 1793 was invalid as an invasion of states' rights. "The obligation" to return fugitives "is on the states, and for the states," Pennsylvania's attorney general told the Court: "The states' power is left perfectly free and untrammeled." Prigg's lawyers were properly shocked at this enunciation of states' rights and countered with the argument that the Fugitive Slave Law had been enacted in 1793 when

constitutional meanings were fresh in the minds of congressmen. They found it perfectly in order that Congress had passed a statute setting up procedures for the reclaiming of fugitives. Congress, they said, was supreme in the field, and neither Pennsylvania nor any other state could enact laws on the subject.

Justice Story, chosen to write the opinion for the Court, ... refuted the claim that Congress lacked power to legislate on the subject, despite the absence of an express grant of such power in the Constitution, because, he said, "where an end is required, means are given, and where duty is enjoined, ability to perform it is contemplated to exist on the part of the functionaries to whom it is entrusted." [16]

The Court reversed Prigg's conviction, holding that the Federal Fugitive Slave Law was constitutional and that it overrode the Pennsylvania kidnaping statute.

In order to appreciate the full significance of the foregoing decisions, particularly those recognizing plenary Federal power over foreign affairs, one must keep in mind the provisions of the Tenth Amendment:

> The powers not delegated to the United States by the Constitution, nor prohibited by it to the States, are reserved to the States respectively, or to the people.

The Tenth Amendment is an unequivocal, formal affirmation of the proposition that the Federal Government possesses only delegated powers — those conferred upon it by the Constitution. This is not to say that it possesses only *expressly* delegated powers; indeed, the contrast between the Tenth Amendment and the corresponding provision of the 1778 Articles of Confederation clearly indicates that the Constitutors intended the contrary. Article 2 of the 1778 Articles provided:

> Each state retains its sovereignty, freedom, and independence, and every power, jurisdiction, and right, which is not by this Confederation *expressly* delegated to the United States in Congress assembled. (Emphasis added)

But the Tenth Amendment does say — in words too clear for reasonable difference of opinion — that the Federal Government possesses only those powers which the Constitution confers upon it (expressly or by implication).

Therefore, unless we are to suppose that successive generations of Justices have unanimously thumbed their official noses at their oaths to support the Constitution (including the Tenth Amendment), one must accept a definition of implied power which is broad enough to include the existence of at least some legitimate Federal power which is not rooted in the text of the Constitution or its Amendments. On the other hand, the Tenth Amendment is empty of meaning unless the implication of such power is governed by some knowable principle against which assertions of implied power can be objectively measured.

I have postulated such a principle in Chapter I: (a) preservation of the open and self-governing society to which the Constitutors intended to commit this nation, (b) by formulation of new constitutional rules which they would approve as consistent with their own political philosophy if they were alive at the time of such formulation.[17] I have acknowledged, further, that one's ability to defend the Justices against the accusation that they have set themselves above the law depends on whether this principle is sufficiently knowable to permit detection of judicial usurpation, if any has occurred, or whether it is so vague as to be illusory.[18] One way (perhaps the only way) to test that question is to review the Court's recent work in controversial constitutional areas and attempt evaluation of it on the basis of postulated principle. To that task we now turn.

# Part Two
# The Observational Data

## CHAPTER VII
## The 1937 Crossroads

In our appraisal of implied judicial constitution-making and lawmaking power, we have succeeded in reducing our inquiry to two principal questions: (1) What harm would have resulted if the Court had refused to exercise such power? In other words, what were the pressures that led the Court to exercise it? (2) Has the Court exercised the power in an appropriate manner? Part Two will consider the first of these questions. Part Three will deal with the second.

To approach the first question, let us set up a working hypothesis. Let us suppose that, in the two decades after World War II, the Court became convinced that there were major flaws in our society which had not yielded to legislative remedies and probably would not ever be corrected by political action — or at least not quickly enough to prevent such a breakdown of respect for law and government, and such intergroup hostility, as to jeopardize self-government and the open society. Let us suppose also that the Constitutors intended to commit the nation to self-government and preservation of the open society; that they intended the Court to have authority, in case some particular governmental power turned out to be necessary to those ends but they had not foreseen the need for it, to legitimize the exercise of that power by whichever organ of government was most competent to exercise it — this being the doctrine of implied power; and that the doctrine of implied power, though most commonly used to legitimize Congressional action (as in *McCulloch v. Maryland*), has also been used to uphold Presidential power (as in the field of foreign affairs), and also in fact — though not avowedly — has been used to justify constitution-making by the Court through tentative judicial review (as in the "silence of Congress" cases) as well as through definitive judicial review (as in *Lochner v. New York* (1905) [1] and other substantive due process cases).

Further, let us suppose that the Court, though it has been candid in explaining the basis of implied power on the basis of "the great purposes" of the Constitution when *Congress* or *the President* has been held to possess it, has traditionally explained *its own* assumptions of implied power through strained and unreal "interpretations" of the constitutional text, in order to shield itself from suspicion of self-aggrandizement; and that, in dealing with the major flaws mentioned above (fully perceived only after World War II) which it *was* more competent to cope with than the other organs of government, it has elected to follow this same practice.

Finally, let us describe these major flaws:

(1) Effective criticism of government in fundamental ways had become difficult because of widespread fear that such criticism (for example, by Communists) was made with destructive rather than constructive purpose.

(2) The criminal law system, which affects the people more directly and momentously (both repressively and protectively) than any other aspect of government, was antique, over-technical, and prone to convict the innocent.

(3) The police, in the detection and investigation of crime, resorted to unlawful intrusions upon personal privacy as a matter of common practice.

(4) There was danger of political organization along religious lines, particularly because of the increasing hardship imposed on Roman Catholics by the increasing cost of maintaining their separate parochial schools.

(5) The huge black minority was obviously impervious to the melting pot, and was on the verge of utter disaffection.

Our society suffered from other imperfections too, but these five were peculiarly resistant to statutory remedy; for a variety of reasons, the majoritarian political process held out little hope of relief. Laws hindering criticism of government are unlikely to be repudiated by the electorate because they smother the very processes whereby public dissatisfaction is articulated and made effective. Miscarriages of criminal "justice" are unlikely to stimulate a public outcry because the public, being unable to assess guilt or innocence for itself, assumes from the very fact of conviction that a convicted defendant is an enemy to society; therefore any procedural abuses in the course of prosecution tend to be dismissed as mere irregularities, regrettable but trivial detours on the road to a just result. Unlawful intrusions upon privacy rarely come to public attention unless they yield incriminating evidence used in a subsequent prosecution; and, again, most people believe that substantial justice has been done — that "[t]he criminal [should not] go free because the constable has blundered." [2] Political fragmentation along religious lines is intrinsically uncontrollable by the political process since such fragmentation would affect the shape of the very building blocks — political parties — which underpin the process itself.

As for the plight of the black minority, it had a special dimension. Not only did the cultural residue of slavery form a uniquely strong barrier to homogeneity, but the Court itself — in the last three decades of the nineteenth century — had crippled the political processes that might conceivably have surmounted the barrier. We shall reserve that special situation for consideration in Chapters XII and XIII.

* * * * *

Having set up a working hypothesis, let us proceed to review the recent work of the Court to ascertain whether and to what extent it is consistent with that hypothesis. At the outset we must acknowledge an inherent obstacle to objectivity. Objective evaluation of the Court's work is difficult because, despite its own strictures against use of unworthy means to achieve worthy ends, there is a persistent hesitation to criticize the methods the Court has employed to arrive at decisions that seem socially beneficial. Government is a practical affair, and the performance of a governmental organ ought to be appraised in terms of its good or bad effect on the health of the social organism. If one believes, for example, that the rules the Court laid down for abortions in *Roe v. Wade* (1973)[3] and *Doe v. Bolton* (1973)[4] are enlightened and humane, is it sensible to complain that its opinions contain no convincing justification of its own authority to prescribe those rules? Given the fact that the Court possesses unquestioned raw power to enforce its will by reversing criminal convictions for abortions which it declares to be lawful, does a denial of its authority serve any practical purpose? Is the denial not better left unspoken, since it will aid and comfort the effort to reestablish state power in a field where most of the states, one believes, have performed poorly?

The reluctant answer is that, even in pragmatic terms, there is reason to voice the denial if the methodological defect itself involves substantial harm to the society. The substantiality of that harm depends to some extent on whether the defect appears only in one or a few cases, or whether it is part of a general pattern. If it is only in isolated cases that the Court fails to explain the source of its authority, the consequences will probably be trivial. All human institutions err occasionally. Taken alone, the abortion cases show no more than that the Court either *could* not justify its authority, or *neglected* to do so. Either way, there was a mistake; but by itself it was a small one, with little potentiality for harm. If, on the other hand, the Court makes new constitutional rules in case after case without adequate explanation of the source of its authority, the possibility of harm cannot be so lightly dismissed. It becomes harder to credit the possibility that the omission results from careless opinion writing rather than the unavailability of an adequate explanation. And the conviction grows that the Court has intentionally and unjustifiably accomplished a significant shift of lawmaking power from elected representatives of the people to its own nine Justices. This calls for a wholly different calculus of social benefit and social harm. What is to be weighed against the benefit derived from an improved set of legal rules (on, say, abortion) is not the momentary uneasiness resulting from an occasional judicial mistake, but attrition of the electorate's power

THE 1937 CROSSROADS 101

to deal with a large and expanding set of problems — with no visible limit on either the attrition or the expansion.

Possibly, all things considered, there is a net benefit because the Court's rules are so much better than what Congress and the state legislatures can produce. A net harm is also possible, however. Therefore we dare not remain silent about the Court's failure to justify its authority to make new abortion rules, unless further investigation shows the abortion cases to be an isolated phenomenon.

In point of fact, further investigation reveals that they are by no means an isolated phenomenon. Presently we shall review the recent growth of constitution-making by the Court in a number of different fields, and shall note its failure to explain adequately the source of its constitution-making authority. Then we shall inquire whether, in some or all of these cases, an adequate explanation could have been made. In the course of that inquiry we shall hypothesize the premises which, if accepted, would justify the Court's constitution-making activity; and, having laid those premises bare, we shall consider whether the Court is the governmental organ best qualified to decide that they do or do not embody wise national policy. That is the basis on which the Court's constitution-making ought to be approved or condemned.

There is a temptation to give assurance of our own purity of heart by proclaiming at the outset that certain of the premises which *may* emerge from our analysis are intrinsically unacceptable because offensive to democratic axioms. For example, we might find ourselves unable to account for one or more of the Court's decisions except on the premise that the Justices *consider themselves to be above the law* — to be wholly unconstrained by pre-existing principle. Admittedly, this would be hard to swallow. It would be particularly nauseating at a time when the Justices are doing their utmost to subject every other organ of government to the law as they declare it. Yet we should reserve judgment even here, until we see what alternatives exist — hoping always that we will not be driven to the stark choice between misgovernment by law and enlightened government by decree. Even though the hope may be vain, reason requires us to proceed.

We need not reach back to the very beginning of judicial review, because the Court made a fresh start at its 1937-1938 Term, (a) reexamining freely all the earlier precedents bearing on the scope of its authority and (b) commencing a rapid and almost complete withdrawal from the business of economic regulation.

For half a century, more or less, the Court had increasingly become the protector of free business enterprise. It had limited the Federal Government's power over manufacturing, mining, farming, and labor relations, and had limited the power of Federal and state governments alike to establish terms for the sale of goods and services.[5] As a related sideline, it had curbed taxation that impaired business freedom or interfered with transmission of accumulated wealth (typically the fruit of free business).[6]

The abyssal depth of the Great Depression was widely attributed to the Court's intervention against legislation alleviating constriction of purchasing power and its failure to appreciate sufficiently the nationwide interdependence of the economy. The Court became a primary target of political criticism.[7] Whether in response to that criticism (culminating in President Roosevelt's 1936 Court-packing proposal) or in belated recognition of its own unfitness to prescribe for the nation's economic health, it unshackled the legislatures.

There had been a tentative and limited easing of constitutional shackles as early as 1934. *Home Building & Loan Association v. Blaisdell*[8] upheld the Minnesota Mortgage Moratorium Law as a temporary emergency measure, and *Nebbia v. New York*[9] upheld a New York milk price law because of the uniquely distressed condition of the milk industry. In 1935 and 1936 the continued hold of the shackles was reaffirmed, however, by the invalidation of statutes embodying several major aspects of the New Deal economic program,[10] as well as a New York minimum wage law.[11] Then, in the spring of 1937, the restraints began rapidly to fall away. Minimum wage laws were held constitutional,[12] then the National Labor Relations Act[13] and the Federal Social Security

Act.[14] Later that year the core of the old regime commenced to crumble when Justice Black was appointed to succeed Justice Van Devanter. For the next several years, the Court's main constitutional business consisted of clearing away vestiges of decayed doctrine.

The particulars of this oft-told tale [15] need not be rehearsed. The nub of our interest is not the abandoned judicial controls or the drama of their abandonment, but the aftermath. Those Justices who had deplored most vigorously the frustration of legislative efforts reflecting the will of electoral majorities were quick to sense a danger of overkill.

The libertarian diatribes against government by judiciary that accompanied the great withdrawal were premised on a broad majoritarian philosophy. The sovereign people and their elected representatives know what is best for them, so runs the dogma. If they believe the public interest demands that individual autonomy be narrowed by governmental action to cope with a collective problem, *their* will ought to prevail. *They* are the ones to say whether the problem is in fact a collective one, and to choose the remedy. If they find that they have miscalculated, *they* are the ones to correct the error. A persistent yearning to maximize their own freedom will prevent hypertrophy of official power.*

It is a useful model, but somewhat oversimplified. It does fit the reality of economic relationships fairly well; but getting and spending are not the whole of life and had not been the only objects of the Court's attention in its zeal to protect individual autonomy. Even as it solidified the right of each person to decide for himself the terms on which he would buy or sell goods or services, it made

---

* This majoritarian philosophy was reflected mainly in cases overruling the substantive due process decisions which had limited governmental power over the market system and protected individual autonomy with respect to wages, hours, prices, labor relations, and the right to engage in business. It was also reflected, however, in cases overruling the decisions which had interpreted the Tenth Amendment as reserving certain areas for regulation by the states rather than the Federal Government — and thus, as a practical matter, had created a power vacuum because political considerations precluded effective regulation by the states. *See, e.g.,* United States v. Darby, 312 U.S. 100 (1941), overruling Hammer v. Dagenhart, 247 U.S. 251 (1918) (child labor regulation).

a beginning at erection of defenses for his nonmaterial concerns — his religion,[16] his access to knowledge,[17] his security against unfounded prosecution,[18] his ability to speak his mind.[19] The body of Federal case law that had built up around these concerns was meager in comparison with the elaborate *corpus juris* of vested property rights and liberty of contract, but the Court's fitness to preserve and enlarge it had not been attacked as had its fitness to oversee the economic system. Yet Justices who valued it as a precious heritage feared it might be swept away in the tidal wave of majoritarian sentiment. The problem, as they saw it, has been well stated by Alpheus Thomas Mason:

> Having surrendered the heavy obligation of passing on the wisdom of social and economic policy, did it follow that judicial self-restraint was equally applicable to the review of legislation infringing those freedoms that constitute "the very essence of ordered liberty"? Must the Court defer to political restraints in this area, as well as in cases concerning regulation of our social and economic life? [20]

Faced with this problem, the Court now began to make clear its determination to continue denying the legitimacy of some types of official action. That is to say, its disagreement with the pre-1937 majority turned out to be not on the question whether the Court can rightly override legislative choices and executive actions, but only on the types of legislative choices and executive actions it should override.

In December, 1937, Justice Cardozo wrote the Court's opinion in *Palko v. Connecticut*.[21] Palko was convicted of second-degree murder and sentenced to life imprisonment. The state appealed to the highest state court, as permitted by Connecticut law, and that court reversed because of trial court errors in Palko's favor. At a new trial, Palko was convicted of first-degree murder and sentenced to death. The Fifth Amendment Double Jeopardy Clause would have prevented that result in a *Federal* prosecution. Palko contended that this Clause, though originally designed to cover Federal but not state prosecutions, had been rendered applicable to the states — along with all other provisions of the Bill of Rights (the first eight Amendments) — by the Fourteenth Amendment, adopted in 1868.

Years before, the Court had held that freedom of speech and press, though also originally protected by the First Amendment against Congressional action only, was part of the "liberty" safeguarded against state action by the Due Process Clause of the Fourteenth.[22] This was not a startling proposition at a time when the Court was interpreting the protected "liberty" expansively — so expansively as to include liberty to contract for goods and services. Now that the Court was renouncing such expansive interpretation, however, the only obvious basis for preserving protection of speech and press against state action was that the Fourteenth Amendment was *intended* to "incorporate" the First, subjecting the states to its limitations. And, Palko asked, if that was how the Fourteenth Amendment was intended to affect the First, on what basis could it be held that a similar effect was not intended with respect to the whole Bill of Rights including the Double Jeopardy Clause?

The Court had already held that the Fourteenth Amendment was not intended to incorporate the whole Bill of Rights,[23] and it still adheres to that position. The Court was thus faced with the need to choose between (1) repudiation of its decisions protecting speech and press from state action, (2) reversal of Palko's conviction, and (3) attribution of some meaning to the Fourteenth Amendment which justifies the Court in protecting freedom of expression but not in preventing double jeopardy. It chose the third alternative. It declared that the Fourteenth Amendment empowers it to repel state incursions upon "ordered liberty."

"Ordered liberty" is not a self-defining term. It is a vehicle for whatever meaning the Court gives it, and thus enables the Court to apply its own conceptions of public policy in deciding when state action will or will not be overridden. In Justice Cardozo's words,

> [Some] immunities that are valid as against the federal government by force of the specific pledges of particular amendments have been found to be implicit in the concept of ordered liberty, and thus, through the Fourteenth Amendment, become valid as against the states.[24]

In criminal cases, he said, the material inquiry is whether the defendant has been subjected to "a hardship so acute and shocking that our polity will not endure it." [25] So far as double jeopardy is concerned, there might be such a hardship if the state were "attempting to wear the accused out by a multitude of cases with accumulated trials"; but here it was merely insisting "that the case against him shall go on until there shall be a trial free from the corrosion of substantial legal error." [26] Thus the command of the Fifth Amendment, "nor shall any person be subject for the same offence to be twice put in jeopardy of life or limb" (interpreted as the Court had previously held it should be [27]) was not *as such* deemed incorporated into the Fourteenth. However:

> We reach a different plane of social and moral values when we pass to the privileges and immunities that have been taken over from the earlier articles of the federal bill of rights and brought within the Fourteenth Amendment by a process of absorption. These in their origin were effective against the federal government alone. If the Fourteenth Amendment has absorbed them, the process of absorption has had its source in the belief that neither liberty nor justice would exist if they were sacrificed. . . . This is true, for illustration, of freedom of thought, and speech. Of that freedom one may say that it is the matrix, the indispensable condition, of nearly every other form of freedom.[28]

Here the particularistic approach of the criminal cases is replaced by a broad affirmation that *absorption* has taken place. The Fourteenth Amendment is to be read as if it repeated specific language of the First. The difference in approach is hard to account for in terms of constitutional phraseology; rather, it reflects special solicitude for guaranties Justice Cardozo regarded as the bedrock foundation for liberty and justice.

The *Palko* opinion showed that the written Constitution would not be the sole basis of judicial review in the future, any more than it had been in the past. The Court had changed its views as to what personal immunities should have its protection; immunity from economic controls was no longer guaranteed. So far as appeared, however, nothing but its own views of sound public policy restrained the Court from giving the amorphous term "ordered liberty" any content it wished. If there was to be no resumption of unbounded power to invalidate any official action the Court thought unwise, a limiting principle was needed. Moreover, experience had shown that the Justices are not endowed with divine insight into the needs of a healthy society. To be sure, their detachment from the political scene does enhance their objectivity in effectuating policies embodied in existing law, but it also impairs their ability to appraise the need for new law. Only through the principle of implied power — based on the Court's superior competence to handle certain issues — can it claim legitimate authority to make constitutional rules not fairly derivable from the words of the written Constitution.

Implication of power in the Court to make constitutional rules involves two elements. The *first* is a national objective which is either spelled out in the written Constitution (notably in the preamble), or inferable from its underlying pattern or the known purposes of the Constitution. The *second* is a comprehensible reason why the Court is better fitted than other organs of government to effectuate that objective. If either of these elements is lacking, the Court's rule is an exercise of raw power. It does not deserve the name of law, because it does not evoke the voluntary compliance engendered by respect for legitimate authority. Instead of resolving conflicts and easing tensions within the society, which is the function of law properly so called, it aggravates them. It provokes evasion by those whom the Court has undertaken to bind, countered by angry claims of legal right on the part of those whom the Court has undertaken to benefit.

The *Palko* formulation did not satisfy the two requirements. The term "ordered liberty" is too vague to describe a national objective. It says that order and liberty are both to be sought, but provides no standard for reconciling the eternal conflict between them. Nor did the *Palko* opinion give any reason why the Court possesses special qualifications for effecting the reconciliation — why, for example, the Court can rightly override legislators who think that freedom of speech is less important at the moment than something else.

About four months later Justice Stone, writing for the Court in *United States v. Carolene Products Co.,*[29] undertook to articulate a more satisfactory justification. The body of his opinion disclaimed in explicit and emphatic terms the Court's competence to thwart Congress on a matter of business regulation — prohibition against interstate shipment of "filled milk" (milk whose butterfat has been replaced with vegetable fat). A footnote, however, warned that the Court might not be so deferential in every type of case. As first circulated among the Justices,* the footnote confined itself to relative judicial and legislative fitness to deal with certain lawmaking problems:

> It is unnecessary to consider now whether legislation which restricts those political processes which can ordinarily be expected to bring about repeal of undesirable legislation, is to be subjected to more exacting judicial scrutiny under the general prohibitions of the Fourteenth Amendment than are most other types of legislation. On restrictions upon the right to vote, see *Nixon* v. *Herndon,* 273 U.S. 536; *Nixon* v. *Condon,* 286 U.S. 73; on restraints upon the dissemination of information, see *Near* v. *Minnesota ex rel. Olson,* 283 U.S. 697, 713-714, 718-720, 722; *Grosjean* v. *American Press Co.,* 297 U.S. 233; *Lovell* v. *Griffin,* 303 U.S. 444; on interferences with political organizations, see *Stromberg* v. *California,* 283 U.S. 359, 369; *Fiske* v. *Kansas,* 274 U.S. 380; *Whitney* v. *California* [,] 274 U.S. 357, 373-378; *Herndon* v. *Lowry,* 301 U.S. 242; and see Holmes, J., in *Gitlow* v. *New York,* 268 U.S. 652, 673; as to prohibition of peaceable assembly, see *De Jonge* v. *Oregon,* 299 U.S. 353, 365.
>
> Nor need we enquire whether similar considerations enter into the review of statutes directed at particular religious, *Pierce* v. *Society of Sisters,* 268 U.S. 510, or national, *Meyer* v. *Nebraska,* 262 U.S. 390; *Bartels* v. *Iowa,* 262 U.S. 404; *Farrington* v. *Tokushige,* 273 U.S. [284], or racial minorities, *Nixon* v. *Herndon, supra*[;] *Nixon* v. *Condon, supra*: whether prejudice against discrete and insular minorities may be a special condition, which tends seriously to curtail the operation of those political processes ordinarily to be relied upon to

---

* The genesis and development of the footnote are described by Alpheus Thomas Mason in *Harlan Fiske Stone: Pillar of the Law* (1956), ch. 31, especially at pp. 513-14. See also Mason's *The Supreme Court: Palladium of Freedom* (1962), at pp. 151-59. Scholarly comments are collected in Ball's "Judicial Protection of Powerless Minorities," in *Iowa Law Review* (1974), vol. 59, p. 1059, at pp. 1060-64.

protect minorities, and which may call for a correspondingly more searching judicial inquiry. Compare *McCulloch* v. *Maryland,* 4 Wheat. 316, 428; *South Carolina* v. *Barnwell Bros.* [,] 303 U.S. 177, 184, n.2, and cases cited.[30]

These paragraphs make no reference to the words or the intentions of the Constitutors. They speak, rather, of the dynamics of government. They do not purport to map the entire area of judicial hegemony. For example, there is no mention of the criminal process or of privacy. But they plainly assume the existence of two national objectives — government by the people, and government for the whole people — and focus attention on the Court's special ability to effectuate them.

Both objectives are fairly ascribable to the Constitutors and are accepted throughout the society. No one denies that legislatures are supposed to be controlled by the people, in the sense that legislative work is subject to approval or disapproval at periodic elections. The Constitution so requires by providing for Congressional elections [31] and prescribing the republican form of government for the states.[32] And though there is no constitutional provision concerning the attitude with which legislators are to approach their task, there is broad consensus on the proposition that they should make a genuine effort to weigh impartially the competing needs of all segments of the population and seek fair compromise among such needs.[33]

Justice Stone's position is that the political processes are ordinarily adequate to achieve these objectives and that, when this is so, the wisdom of legislation — its consonance with the public welfare — is no concern of the Court. Therefore, the Court accepts the Congressional determination that natural milk is more nutritious than the cheaper filled milk and that it is more important to protect consumers from ignorance of that fact than to allow them access to the less expensive product, because the voters can make Congress repeal the Filled Milk Act if they disagree. But Justice Stone points to two situations in which legislative miscalculations of the public welfare are likely to remain uncorrected unless the Court steps in. One is where a legislature insulates itself from demands for change in the law by hampering political expression, political organization, or voting. The other is where, although the political processes are fully operative, prejudice against socially isolated minorities may render the legislature unresponsive to their grievances. In the former case, Justice Stone says, the Court is entitled to make its own judgment as to the wisdom of the statute because the electorate is unable to bring its power to bear. In the latter case, the Court is entitled to decide whether the statute reflects a fair attempt to serve the interests of all the people, because there is reason to doubt that the legislature has made the attempt.

This approach rests on the principle of implied power. It assigns to the Court a role that depends not on its ingenuity in devising new and unintended meanings for constitutional phrases but on its special aptitude for particular governmental tasks. By providing an objective measure for the Court's authority, it quiets doubts as to the legitimacy of interventions not based on the written Constitution — so long as they are within the Court's limited field of primary responsibility — and, on the other hand, emboldens the Court to shoulder full responsibility within the defined field. That was the sense of the *Carolene Products* footnote as contained in the draft opinion that Justice Stone distributed to his colleagues for their consideration.

Upon receiving the opinion, Chief Justice Hughes raised a question. "Are the 'considerations' different, or does the difference lie not in the *test* but in the nature of the right invoked?" he asked.[34] To accommodate this thought that some rights are more *important* than others, that (to use the term that later became current) they occupy a "preferred position"[35] — a thought not found in the footnote as first circulated — Justice Stone added another paragraph at the beginning, and won the Chief Justice's concurrence:

> There may be narrower scope for operation of the presumption of constitutionality when legislation appears on its face to be within a specific prohibition of the Constitution, such as those of the first ten amendments, which are deemed equally specific when held to be embraced within the Fourteenth. See *Stromberg* v. *California,* 283 U.S. 359, 369-370; *Lovell* v. *Griffin,* 303 U.S. 444, 452.

The citations are to two Hughes opinions on freedom of expression.

This is a different idea, quite foreign to the principle of implied judicial power. The Court's authority to override policies approved by legislatures depends, says this paragraph, not on its special fitness for particular tasks, but on two other circumstances: the words of the Constitution, and the Court's election to apply them in a way the Constitutors did not expect. If the Constitution contains a "specific prohibition" against Federal action, such as the First Amendment ban on restriction of speech and press, that prohibition will also be enforced against state action if it is "held to be embraced within the Fourteenth." For all that appears, the Court claims unrestrained authority to decide whether or not it is to be so held; no objective standard is prescribed for the Court's guidance. In effect, the position is that the Court is licensed to disregard the fundamental principle of interpretation (which is to give words the meaning their authors would have given them in the context of the instant case) whenever the Court thinks a different meaning would better serve the public welfare.

Superficially, this conception seems to confine the Court more closely than does the implied power approach. Instead of declaring that the Court is entitled to intervene whenever political correctives are unavailable or inadequate, it declares a verbal connection with the text of the Constitution to be necessary. In fact, however, the Court is left entirely at large. There is virtually no limit to its ability to attribute new meaning to the "specific prohibitions," once it is liberated from the need to interpret them as the Constitutors expected.

The *Carolene Products* footnote thus contained the germs of two distinct theories for expanding the Court's protection of individual freedoms and immunities. One is the implied power theory, which accepts the necessity of justification in terms of the Court's special fitness to reach definable goals. It is a rational theory, in the sense that it calls for measurement of the Court's performance against objective standards. The other has come to be known as the "preferred position" theory, which affirms that certain rights are in some sense more important than others — so important that the Court should protect them against impairment by any governmental organ — and that the Court's power to select them is limited only by its ability to manipulate words contained in the Constitution. It dispenses with the need for justification in terms of explained necessity, and assumes that any meaning the Court chooses to ascribe to the sacred text will be accepted as authentic revelation. Faith, not reason, is to be the foundation of public acquiescence.

Many decisions of the Court can be explained on the basis of either approach. For example, a state statute restricting speech can be held invalid on the declared ground that the First Amendment gives preferred status to freedom of speech, or the Court can explain its action on the basis of implied power. The difference is in the self-imposed discipline required for the latter course. The Court must take the responsibility for proclaiming its own superior fitness to attain the objective. That is a tolerable (though not a complete) substitute for responsibility to the electorate, on which legitimate lawmaking power usually depends. If the Court exposes the premises of its actions to public view, there is little danger that it will frustrate the people's power to govern themselves, as it did before 1937. Such danger does exist if the Court invests the words of the Constitutors with unintended meaning, pretends to be enforcing their explicit command, and thus avoids any responsibility at all for its own exercise of power.

In the years since 1937, the Court has proclaimed a great many new constitutional rules. It has often neglected to justify them in terms of implied power, but at least the great majority of them *can* be so justified. To determine whether the Court has exceeded its legitimate authority (and, if so, to what extent) it is necessary to inquire which constitutional innovations satisfy the implied power test and which, if any, do not.

First, however, we should take notice of a general characteristic of the Court's application of judicial review during this period.

Though it formulated a great many new constitutional rules, it long adhered to the *Marbury v. Madison* conception that constitutional pronouncements are only incidental to the adjudication of pre-existing legal rights.

During the era of judicial control over economic regulation this conception of judicial review did not cramp the Court. There was no need to go beyond the notion that its duty was to apply the most authoritative law available in determining the legal rights of contending parties. (The term "legal rights" is used not in the strict Hohfeldian sense* but as including duties, liabilities, and other legal relationships.)

That remained true after 1937. The Court's concern was still for the legal rights of the litigants before it. All that had changed was its view as to what official incursions upon those rights are tolerable. The time was to come when the Court would see its mission more broadly, transferring much if not most of its attention from the rights of particular plaintiffs and defendants to the interests of the nation at large. That time, however, was still far in the future.

The change that did take place in the first years after 1937, however, was by no means trivial. Claims to political and religious freedom, racial equality, and fair criminal procedure were entertained with suddenly heightened sensitivity. Very probably Adolf Hitler deserves much of the credit. As he and his fellow dictators revealed the ghastly consequence of drowning those values in a sea of conformist fervor, American practices tinged with the same hue were seen as symptoms of the same killing disease. The outbreak of World War II in 1939, followed by our entry into it two years later, lent added impetus to the drive against

---

* Wesley Newcomb Hohfeld, in his seminal monograph *Fundamental Legal Conceptions* (1923), sets up the following eight categories which have become an accepted part of analytic jurisprudence: right, no-right, privilege, duty, power, disability, immunity, and liability. For our present purposes it is unnecessary to distinguish between these eight conceptions, and therefore the term "right" is here used to include them all.

totalitarian abuses here at home. The *Palko* concept of the Court's responsibility for ordered liberty, and the *Carolene Products* justifications of the Court's special role, facilitated liberation from the hobbles of precedent. And the Court made full use of its newfound freedom.

## CHAPTER VIII
## Peace . . . the Presence of Justice

Before reviewing the Court's response to the totalitarian challenge I pause to explain a beautiful mystery that underpins our law of civil liberties. Herbert Agar has captured the point in a brief but sufficient aphorism: "Peace," he says, "is not the absence of war. Peace is the presence of justice."

For nearly two decades I have been trying to demonstrate the application of this concept to the problem of *international* peacekeeping.[1] Long before that, however — in fact, as early as 1942 — I explored the crucial relevance of the same concept to the problem of *internal* peacekeeping.[2]

To an outsider, our solicitude for protection of political dissidents, minority groups, and accused persons may seem to betray an ambivalent sloppiness — an untidy and intrinsically impossible effort to carry water on both shoulders, a lazy willingness to blink the conflict between the need for civil order and the yearning for freedom, equality, and justice, a complaisant acceptance of continuing discrepancy between our ideals and our practice. In fact, however, it betokens the exact opposite.

Centuries of experience in the art of free government have taught us and our British forbears that a certain amount of disorder in the expression of political views, and restraint of the majority will with respect to official treatment of minority groups and accused persons, are essential to an open and self-governing society. As I have said elsewhere,[3] the dynamics are describable as the interplay between our competing ideals of (1) freedom, (2) equality, and (3) security of person, property, and such intangible values as privacy and reputation — which, for brevity, can be called "order." These three first-magnitude stars in our constitutional firmament can hold each other in place to form a constellation of enduring beauty. But if any one of them crumbles, the others will take off on destructive courses.

In the field of freedom of speech and press, which Justice Cardozo rightly called "the matrix, the indispensable condition, of nearly every other kind of freedom,"[4] there is a helpful analogy to the basic proposition of *laissez-faire* economics which, despite heavy modification, still provides the foundation of our competitive market system. As Adam Smith perceived, it is not only possible but usual for a host of individuals, each pursuing his own interests as he understands them, to serve unwittingly the whole society's interest in a larger objective. In the economic field, the larger interest is maximum satisfaction of the need for goods and services. In the political field, the larger interest is the need for orderly and constructive change.

That is why we do not automatically apply to street demonstrations, with uncompromising rigor, the laws against obstruction of traffic.[5] That is why we tolerate unintentional defamation of political opponents, in the teeth of the strict common law rules on libel and slander, proclaiming that the *public interest* requires political debate to be "uninhibited, robust, and wide-open."[6] That is why we have gone so far — too far, in my opinion, for reasons to be detailed in later chapters — in erecting constitutional safeguards for uncivil and pornographic expression.[7]

We have learned that domestic tranquillity is to be found not in enforced conformity to the *status quo* but in nurturing and preserving the sense of justice on the part of those who believe the *status quo* to be unfair and oppressive. We have learned also that abrasive dissent may have much to teach us. Martin Luther King, Jr., was by no means the first of our dissidents to earn, even in his own lifetime, the grateful thanks of his compatriots. The roll of honor goes back at least as far as Thomas Jefferson.

A concrete example will be helpful. In April of 1968, for what seemed to me to be trivial reasons, a massive student rebellion paralyzed Columbia University for a week. After the dust had settled I decided that the event deserved careful description and analysis; and in collaboration with my daughter (who, as a college junior, could provide insights denied to my generation) I published a detailed account in the *Political Science Quarterly* under the title "Columbia 1968: The Wound Unhealed."[8]

One of the more astonishing aspects of the rebellion was that it triggered a surge of support for the rebels by the University's immediate neighbors, many of whom were tenants of Columbia-owned apartments on Morningside Heights (the high ground overlooking Harlem where the campus is located). Neighbors saw the rebellion as a holy war against a common enemy. They picketed, demonstrated, published bitter attacks on Columbia's insensitivity to neighborhood needs, and otherwise provided all possible aid and comfort to the occupants of the five illegally occupied campus buildings. *Something* had galvanized these normally docile middle-class tenants to vigorous and sometimes illegal action.

Our investigation revealed what that something was, and prompted one of our four concluding recommendations:

> The third of our four points is a simpler one. So long as the University does remain where it is, it should recognize the utmost gravity of any failure on its part to fulfill its obligations to its neighbors, and particularly its legal obligations to the tenants of the buildings it owns near the campus. As has been said, much of their anger has arisen from causes beyond Columbia's control. But there are far too many reports that they have not been given what the rent control law says they are entitled to have. There are too many reports that plumbing and plastering and elevator repairs have been neglected, that legally required redecoration has been deferred, that building superintendents have been incompetent and unwarrantably rude, that groundless eviction notices have been served, that (in furnished single-room lodgings) clothing has been removed to the halls and keyholes plugged. Such irritants may well have accounted, as much as anything else, for the zeal with which neighborhood groups rallied to the aid of the student rebels last April, marshaling supplies of food and blankets for the occupied buildings (and delivering them to the sealed campus by use of counterfeit identification cards which were forged, in substantial numbers, with the same righteous fervor felt by those who forge enemy passports for spies).[9]

The present point is that, though my daughter and I thought the student rebellion was a disproportionate and frightfully destructive response to Columbia's shortcomings such as they were, we were compelled to sympathize with the tenants' plight. We could not see them as criminals or fanatics.

Our appraisal of the tenants' behavior would have been different if we had thought it motivated solely by a desire for revenge upon their landlord for failure to provide services legally owed to them. Breach of duty on one side does not in itself justify illegality on the other. We believed, however, that the driving force was an outraged sense of justice — the tenants' not unreasonable belief that redress for their grievances was unavailable (a) because public officials, including judges, were arbitrarily denying them enjoyment of rights the state and city legislatures had created for their protection, and (b) because Columbia — taking advantage of this breakdown in law enforcement — was deliberately defaulting in its known duties as landlord. Against that background, the aid and comfort they gave to the student rebels is rightly characterized as support for a protest movement calculated to change Columbia's policies and practices vis-à-vis its tenant-neighbors as well as its students and thereby obtain through pressure the benefits that statutes and ordinances promised but did not provide. So far as the tenants were concerned, responsibility for the breakdown of civil order rested squarely on Columbia University; they were doing no more than defending their homes against lawless aggression, through the only effective means available to them.

The tenant uprising reproduced, in small, the whole paradox of the open society. In this conflict it was, astonishingly, *the tenants* who were preserving the principles of constitutional conservatism. They were the ones who, convinced by overwhelming evidence that the courts would not protect their legal rights against evasion and even direct infringement by their self-righteous landlord, and that the corrective political processes promised no relief, had undertaken limited self-help as the sole alternative route to justice (rather than angry destruction — such vandalism, arson, homicide, and mindless riot as had marked the earlier Watts incident [10] and similar central-city outbreaks). That, and not prosecutorial lethargy, was the probable reason why no tenant was punished for his seemingly lawless behavior. The tenants had followed the honored path that traces back to the Boston Tea Party.

Undeniably there is tension between the need for civil order and the need for freedom, equality, and justice. It does not follow, however, that the needs are at war with each other in the sense that one can be most fully satisfied if the other is completely neglected. The interrelationship is more complex. To describe it as I believe it appeared to the Court at least as early as 1942 (and, I think, still does), I can do no better than repeat what I wrote in that year: [11]

The people must be given a reason for obeying even unwise or apparently unwise laws. There was a time, as Ferrero has pointed out,[12] when this need could be satisfied by the general acceptance of a hereditary sovereign ruling by divine right. The Western world, however, has now advanced beyond the point where such a justification of power can be widely accepted; and the only available substitute is a faith that the government is doing its best to accommodate the needs and desires of the whole community. Given that faith, the people can be induced to obey even laws which are, or seem to be, unwise. For if the lawmaking agency is organized to serve the whole community, and if it is honestly striving to do so, the people find it more practical to obey than to resist or disregard its laws — which, if really unwise, can be fairly assumed to be temporary.* The price of obedience by the people at the enforcement level is obedience by the government at the legislative level. The key to the problem, then, is (1) a workable governmental mechanism through which everyone of whom obedience is desired — that is, everyone in the community — can effectively demand attention to his needs and desires, plus (2) a known disposition on the part of the lawmakers to seek a fair compromise between competing interests. These are the

---

\* "Prudence, indeed, will dictate that Governments long established should not be changed for light and transient causes; and accordingly all experience hath shown, that mankind are more disposed to suffer, while evils are sufferable, than to right themselves by abolishing the forms to which they are accustomed. But . . . ." THE DECLARATION OF INDEPENDENCE.

fundamental conditions of what may be called "just" legislation, legislation *for the purpose* of serving the whole community.

Having assumed responsibility for protection of the corrective political processes, the Court has evolved a consistent pattern of decisions which gives specific form to the Delphian provisions of the First and Fourteenth Amendments. First, as the Espionage Act cases [13] show, it is axiomatic that there should be no toleration of opposition having a real tendency to aid an external enemy; for defeat in war would endanger the whole structure of the state.[14] Moreover, a main purpose of the allowance of peaceful opposition being to prevent attempts at *violent* change, the permission to oppose cannot be so broad as to include toleration of violent opposition. The principle has been confirmed by the Supreme Court in the cases upholding the state criminal syndicalism statutes, when applied to forbid advocacy of the violent overthrow of government.[15] No member of the Court has ever questioned either of these propositions.\*

It is a necessary corollary, however, that political activity should not be interfered with *unless* it seeks to bypass, or threatens the existence of, the regular corrective processes. One main purpose of recognizing the right of political opposition is to avoid violence by creating and preserving the possibility of peaceful change.\*\* The

---

\* This was true in 1942, when these lines were first published. As will appear below, it requires some qualification today.

\*\* The 1842 insurrection in Rhode Island, as described in Luther v. Borden, 48 U.S. (7 How.) 1 (1849), provides a perfect illustration. The Rhode Island Charter of 1663 established a freehold qualification for voting. As the State turned from agriculture to commerce and manufacturing, this requirement denied the franchise to many "adult males of personal worth and possessed of intelligence and wealth, though not of land, and . . . made the ancient apportionment of the number of representatives, founded on real estate, very disproportionate . . . ." (Mr. Justice Woodbury, dissenting, at 48.) A constitutional convention was convened and a constitution drafted by it was submitted for ratification through universal male suffrage, all without the consent of the established government. Officials chosen under this constitution attempted a military coup but abandoned the attempt when President Tyler declared in favor of the incumbent regime, promising military aid if necessary. The Supreme Court held that the question whether the irregular government was entitled to recognition was a political question, and refused to consider it. Mr. Justice Woodbury, though concurring in this holding, expressly

duty thus devolves upon the political branches of the government in the first instance, and upon the courts ultimately, to decide whether there is sufficient danger of either to justify particular interferences with political activity; and in deciding this question in particular cases the Court cannot "play safe." Whether it errs on the side of repression or on the side of toleration, it hurts the cause of regular and peaceful adjustment of official policies to the needs of the people.

Construction and preservation of the formal corrective mechanism, however, is wholly inadequate to the purpose in hand. The machinery must work, must reconcile the competing demands of the various groups within the population and translate these demands into law. By and large, the machinery has worked well; but, as the *Carolene Products* footnote suggests, the widespread prejudice against certain groups has been a persistent obstacle to its complete effectiveness. And since this is a substantial problem for a nation whose population includes so many and such large minorities, the same reasons which led the Supreme Court to assume the position of guardian of the corrective political processes have also brought about an attack upon the cognate problem of eliminating a major obstacle to their effective operation.

As the Court has gradually clarified the content of the constitutional restrictions on state action directed against the members of minorities, there has emerged a constantly clearer picture of the governmental technique to which the Court has held us to be committed. As decision follows decision it becomes increasingly plain that an important source of the Court's concern with the so-called "civil liberties" cases is the public interest in the maintenance of certain great principles of statecraft. The aid of the Court can be most readily enlisted, in a case of this kind, by a showing that the questioned state action would contravene the

---

recognized the rightness of revolution where the corrective political processes are futile. See 48 U.S. (7 How.) at 54-55.

rules which the Court is formulating for the preservation and perfection of popular government.

Until the Court itself speaks more explicitly, there can be no confident enumeration of these principles of government which the Constitution has so recently been found to embody, or of the considerations of public policy which require them. But given the points so far fixed, we can perhaps spell out the more important ones. The main propositions can be stated rather simply.

*First:* The cardinal duty of the government is to preserve civil order, and violent opposition to lawful authority cannot be tolerated.

*Second:* Violent opposition to the government is to be prevented, where possible, not through coercion but through encouragement of voluntary cooperation. Such cooperation can ordinarily be obtained by facilitating the expression of peaceable criticism and by protecting the regular channels for bringing effective pressure to bear upon governmental officials and policies.

*Third:* Since the many minority groups in this country are by definition viewed with an irrational suspicion and disfavor by the majority and therefore cannot so effectively use the regular channels of group pressure, the need to secure their obedience and support presents a special problem. In order to confirm the faith of minority groups that the laws — however unwise they may be — are just, the government must refrain from taking any action, either by legislation or through its prosecutors and courts, which is or seems to be based on dislike of any minority as a group.

*Fourth:* The most satisfactory long-range solution of the minorities problem is to *eliminate minorities* by doing away with irrational private prejudice against particular groups. To this end, the government should refrain from erecting official barriers to association between majority and minority groups, and at least in some circumstances can properly penalize the incitation of group prejudice on the part of private individuals.

\* \* \* \* \*

So much for the political insights that have informed the Court's work in responding to the totalitarian challenge. Now let us examine that response.

CHAPTER IX
## Freedom of Expression and Electoral Rights

Major movement in response to the totalitarian challenge first appeared in the law of freedom of expression. Prior to 1937 *Near v. Minnesota* (1931)[1] and *Grosjean v. American Press Co.* (1936)[2] had already established the immunity of newspapers from official censorship and oppressive taxation by state governments, but little had been done to open the so-called "forum of the streets" to the little man, with no access to the mass media. Then *Lovell v. Griffin* (1938)[3] struck down an ordinance giving the city manager of a Georgia city arbitrary power to decide what literature should be distributed there. A Jehovah's Witness convicted of distributing a religious pamphlet without asking or receiving official permission was set free, the ordinance being held void on its face as an abridgment of press freedom.

The following year *Hague v. C.I.O.* (1939)[4] broke new ground, invalidating a Jersey City licensing requirement for meetings on city property. For the first time, the rights of land ownership were subordinated to the rights of speech and assembly. Long before, the Court had refused to take that step; in *Davis v. Massachusetts* (1897)[5] a similar licensing provision had withstood constitutional challenge. Justice Holmes, then on the state court, had said:

> For the Legislature absolutely or conditionally to forbid public speaking in a highway or public park is no more an infringement of the rights of a member of the public than for the owner of a private house to forbid it in his house.[6]

Now, in 1939, a theory was announced (actually a theory of trust law, which is traditionally for state and not Federal determination) that led to the contrary result:

> Wherever the title of streets and parks may rest, they have immemorially been held in trust for the use of the public and, time out of mind, have been used for purposes of assembly, communicating thoughts between citizens, and discussing public questions. Such use of the streets and public places has, from ancient times, been a part of the privileges, immunities, rights, and liberties of citizens.[7]

Later cases did make it clear that parades and public meetings can be regulated to accommodate the use of streets for travel and of parks for recreation, which came as no surprise; but the basic point has remained firm.[8] Public meetings and demonstrations have become a constitutionally protected feature of American life.

Already in 1939 the Court was prepared to assert that in dealing with the freedoms of speech and press it would itself decide which of two legitimate but conflicting public objectives should prevail — a function normally performed by a legislature. *Schneider v. New Jersey* (1939) and its companion cases [9] struck down city ordinances which had been applied to forbid distribution on the public streets of handbills discussing, among other things, the Spanish Civil War and the administration of unemployment insurance. It was urged in support of the ordinances that they were means of accomplishing the permissible, indeed laudable, purpose of keeping the streets clear of litter. Justice Roberts did not question the genuineness of the asserted legislative purpose or deny that the ordinances were the best (perhaps the only administratively feasible) means of achieving it fully. He simply said that clean streets are less important than freedom of expression:

> Mere legislative preferences or beliefs respecting matters of public convenience may well support regulation directed at other personal activities, but be insufficient to justify such as diminishes the exercise of rights so vital to the maintenance of democratic institutions. And so, as cases arise, the delicate and difficult task falls upon the courts to weigh the circumstances and to appraise the substantiality of the reasons advanced in support of the regulation of the free enjoyment of the rights.[10]

This is an example of the "preferred position" approach. The Court asserts the superior importance of the right of expression without explaining the basis of its own power to make that determination.

Thereafter the Court settled down to the business of extending its protection of the street forum, prescribing limits of such protection, and working out legal doctrine to support the results. In dozens of cases it struggled with special problems presented by religious evangelism, picketing, criticism of judicial performance, offensive language, commercial handbills, sound trucks, and hostile audiences. By 1951 an elaborate set of rules had evolved, which with some modifications (many of them relating to racial considerations and discussed in later chapters [11]) are still in effect.[12]

A second large development in the law of freedom of expression concerned dissident political organizations. The closest the Constitutors came to mentioning freedom of association for the pursuit of common objectives was their First Amendment prohibition upon Congressional abridgment of "the right of the people peaceably to assemble." However, inasmuch as the effectiveness of political speech depends heavily upon private organizations capable of disseminating information and opinions, consolidating varied viewpoints into concrete action proposals, mobilizing votes, and raising funds necessary to accomplish these things, the Court had no trouble treating freedom of association as implicit in the freedoms of speech and press. Not only political parties, which deal in across-the-board governmental programs, but narrower-spectrum opinion organizations concerned with particular problems such as civil liberties, penal reform, racial equality, and international peace, easily gained recognition as indispensable instrumentalities of "government by the people" — of "the corrective political processes" referred to in the *Carolene Products* footnote.[13]

Where difficulty did arise was in the widespread fear, much exaggerated but not entirely without foundation, that some organizations would not limit their efforts to conventional political channels but were bent upon sabotage, assassination, and other violent crime up to and including armed revolt. After World War II the group most widely feared was the Communist Party, along with a host of organizations sympathetic with some or all of its aims. The fear led to myriad official restraints which, when they eventually came before the Court, led to some of the bitterest divisions within it. There were state and Federal prosecutions for advocacy of criminal syndicalism or violent revolution.[14] There were wholesale denials of public employment to those who were or had been members or financial supporters of suspect organizations or distributors of their literature.[15] Such official boycotts were supplemented by legislative investigation and exposure, designed to stimulate private, as well as official, boycotts — denials of employment, tax benefits, bank credit, electoral support, office in opinion organizations such as the League of Women Voters and the American Civil Liberties Union.[16] Denaturalization and deportation proceedings were instituted.[17] Test oaths were prescribed for public employees and even candidates for elective office.[18] The right to practice law or medicine was denied for refusal to disclose organizational membership or produce organizational records.[19] In 1954 the Communist Party was formally outlawed by Congress.[20]

The Court's response to these divers restraints upon political expression and association fluctuated with changes in ambient public opinion and in the Court's membership. In *United States v. Lovett* (1946)[21] it took a firm line, holding without dissent that a rider attached to a Federal appropriation statute terminating the pay of named agency employees whose conduct had been the subject of a committee investigation, was unconstitutional as a bill of attainder. Denials of public employment, of professional licenses, and of tax benefits later became the subject of delicate distinctions (not always consistently applied) between present and past membership,[22] between innocent and knowing membership,[23] between knowing and active membership,[24] between abstract and action-oriented advocacy.[25] Several decisions turned on a distinction too fine for comprehension by anyone but a medieval scholiast, between (a) dismissal from employment or exclusion from the bar for the *impermissible* reason that a constitutional privilege against disclosure had been claimed, and (b) dismissal or exclusion for the *permissible* reason that the claim of privilege prevented disclosure of facts that might bear upon fitness for employment or admission.[26]

In *Dennis v. United States* (1951)[27] the Court upheld criminal convictions of the organizers who had reestablished the Communist Party of the United States of America in 1945 (after its hibernation during the wartime alliance with the Soviet Union). In *Yates v. United States* (1957)[28] convictions of second-string Party leaders were reversed.

Generous scope was accorded to claims of the Fifth Amendment privilege against self-incrimination by witnesses before the House Un-American Activities Committee and other Congressional committees;[29] but broader *First* Amendment claims — broader because they could be invoked for protection of others as well as the witness himself — were rejected: In *Watkins v. United States* (1957)[30] the Court accompanied a relatively narrow decision (reversing a contempt of Congress conviction) with a sweeping dictum denying Congressional power "to expose for the sake of exposure." Two years later it stripped the dictum of practical force by holding that "the Judiciary lacks authority to intervene on the basis of the motives which spurred the exercise" of Congressional investigatory power.[31] (Two witnesses, one a former client of mine, who had meanwhile relied on the misleading *Watkins* dictum, were convicted of contempt, and their convictions were affirmed in 1961.[32] As it turned out, they were the last of the few refractory witnesses who actually suffered imprisonment in the course of the anti-Communist crusade; for the Court, although holding in effect that exposure was a permissible safeguard against an organization whose power, if any, depended heavily upon its secrecy, repeatedly devised unprecedented and astonishingly strict procedural requirements for Congressional contempt prosecutions.[33]) In 1961 the Court nominally held constitutional the Subversive Activities Control Act of 1950, and sustained an order of the Subversive Activities Control Board directing the Communist Party to register as a Communist action organization.[34] In 1965, however, it held that the privilege against self-incrimination rendered the registration order unenforceable.[35]

From the above highlights of constitutional protection for dissident political organizations it can be seen that the Court has assumed primary responsibility in this field as unreservedly as for the forum of the streets. Its vacillations and fine distinctions, and an almost routine absence of unanimity, reflect the fact that the

Court was making policy — was continually appraising and reappraising the reality of the fear that organized dissent would turn violent. There was never a doubt, however, that the establishment of national policy on this question had become and would remain a part of the Court's business. On the validity of restraints upon dissident political organizations it still has the last word, and does not shrink from uttering it.

We have purposely deferred reference to protection of speech, press, and association in aid of racial equality, because that vitally important subject involves special factors and requires independent consideration.[36] For a somewhat similar reason we have taken no note of developments in the law of obscenity, which has received a free ride on the amplification of free press doctrine because of a semantic accident: the publication of words and pictures is "press" activity whether they convey political ideas or depict sexual activity. We shall postpone our glance at the weird predicament that has resulted from this verbal trap.[37] But this is the place to review the Court's work in protecting electoral activities, a field closely related to the freedoms of speech, press, assembly, and petition.

What gives freedom of political expression its practical value is the inevitability of election day. The prospective moment of reckoning sensitizes elected officials to current public opinion, which the pollsters now enable them to read with greater precision than ever before. Only occasionally does the election provide a direct mandate, as when a proposition is submitted to referendum, or a single dominating issue divides opposing candidates. Usually, voters simply favor the candidates they expect, on the basis of past official performance or otherwise, to be most understanding of their needs. But it is because elected lawmakers know that disregard of public opinion is inconsistent with political longevity, that public opinion often affects the making and administration of laws even before the election takes place.

Therefore it was not unnatural for the Court to look upon political expression and elections as two parts of the same process, and to consider its job only half done if it were to protect freedom of expression but not the effectiveness of the franchise. For a long time it had redressed racially discriminatory denial of the vote.[38] It had also sustained Federal convictions for frustration of votes by falsification of returns and for dilution of their legally prescribed effect by ballot-box stuffing.[39] But it had not undertaken the task of deciding what the legally prescribed effect of a vote should be. In a series of cases beginning with *Colegrove v. Green* (1946)[40] it had held that question to be nonjusticiable. Justice Frankfurter, speaking for three of the seven Justices who participated in the case, denied the existence of judicial power. "Courts," he said, "ought not to enter this political thicket." [41] Justice Rutledge added a fourth vote, not on the ground that judicial power was lacking but on the ground that it should not be exercised because "the cure sought may be worse than the disease." [42] For these reasons the Court refused to entertain an action for declaratory and injunctive relief to adjudicate the constitutionality, under the Equal Protection Clause and other Federal constitutional and statutory provisions, of an Illinois statute establishing Congressional districts of unequal population.

The difficulty referred to by Justices Frankfurter and Rutledge arises basically from the fact that the practical effect of a vote does not depend solely, and perhaps not even primarily, on the number of votes in the district. It also depends on such factors as the choice between single-member and multi-member districts, and the location of the district lines.

The location of district lines is particularly hard to establish on the basis of articulated principle. A geographical area from which a given number of representatives are to be elected can be divided into equally populous single-member districts in various ways, which may affect the fortunes of political parties quite differently. For example, suppose that three representatives are to be elected from an area inhabited by 60,000 voters, of whom 33,000 are Democrats and 27,000 are Republicans. If three single-member districts are established, it is easy to formulate a rule saying that each should have a population of 20,000. But unless the proportion of Democrats to Republicans is 33:27 in every small neighborhood, these electoral results may be possible:

|  | District A | District B | District C |
|---|---|---|---|
| Plan 1: | 11,000 Democrats<br>9,000 Republicans | 11,000 Democrats<br>9,000 Republicans | 11,000 Democrats<br>9,000 Republicans |
| Plan 2: | 15,000 Democrats<br>5,000 Republicans | 15,000 Democrats<br>5,000 Republicans | 3,000 Democrats<br>17,000 Republicans |
| Plan 3: | 19,000 Democrats<br>1,000 Republicans | 7,000 Democrats<br>13,000 Republicans | 7,000 Democrats<br>13,000 Republicans |

Plan 1 would give the Democrats all three representatives, Plan 2 two of them, and Plan 3 only one.

For this reason the drawing of district lines is quite important to the political parties. It is accomplished through bargain and compromise between them, or through some other process uncontrolled by legal principle, which equalization of district populations does not prevent. The *Colegrove* decision reflected a fear that courts would inevitably become embroiled in partisan politics if called upon to draw the district lines,[43] and probably recognition that judicial equalization of district populations without control of other variables determining the effect of individual votes would constitute an illusory promise of equality among voters. Moreover, it was not at all clear that equalization of district populations was the only system rational enough to satisfy the Equal Protection Clause, or that — given variations in population density between urban and rural areas — it was even the *most* reasonable system.[44] Unless the Court adopted a rule of flat population equality and refrained from dealing with other variables, the formulation of a permissible standard would be a very sticky problem. And, beyond all this, the concept of equal voting power was itself cloudy: Does a voter have more power if he casts three votes in a three-member district or if he casts one vote in a single-member district? If the parties are closely balanced, or if one of them has a large majority?

In *Baker v. Carr* (1962)[45] the Court declared itself ready for a plunge into the thicket.* The case involved legislative districts in Tennessee. The state constitution prescribed a rule of population equality with reapportionment every ten years pursuant to the decennial Federal census. Down to 1901 this mandate had been obeyed fairly well. Since that time there had been no general reapportionment, and population shifts to the cities had resulted in wide deviations from equality: One legislative district had more than eighteen times as many voters (per representative) as did one of the others. Political efforts to induce the legislature to reapportion itself were futile because the legislators were reluctant to alter the districts that had elected them. Relief through a state constitutional amendment was unavailable for the same reason, since only the legislature could initiate an amendment. The Tennessee Supreme Court had declared itself powerless to intervene.

Voters sued in the Federal district court for declaratory and injunctive relief. The three-judge tribunal dismissed the complaint for lack of Federal jurisdiction and for failure to state a claim on which relief could be granted, citing *Colegrove v. Green* and cases following it. The Supreme Court reversed.

Justice Brennan's majority opinion quietly broadened the coverage of the Equal Protection Clause. The Tennessee legislature had stubbornly declined to alter a comfortable *status quo*, but that does not necessarily mean it had been motivated by a *conscious desire* to keep the urban vote weak. The Court had previously adhered to the view that official discrimination denies equal protection only if it is "invidious," by which the Court meant a *purposive* effort to place a disfavored person or class at a

---

* As noted *supra* in the footnote on page 9, 1962 was the year in which the Court became suddenly bolder in demanding reforms that involved modification of widespread usages, and was also the year in which Justice Goldberg replaced Justice Frankfurter and added a fifth vote to the so-called "liberal wing" of the Court. The fact that *Baker v. Carr,* one of the very boldest innovations, was decided before Justice Frankfurter's retirement suggests that the change in the Court's membership was not the sole reason for its new activism.

disadvantage.⁴⁶ Justice Brennan now held that equal protection is denied if "a discrimination reflects *no* policy, but simply arbitrary and capricious action." ⁴⁷ (Brennan's emphasis)

Just as importantly, the Court's opinion was a declaration of self-emanicipation from restraints formerly imposed by the interrelated requirements of justiciability and standing, both of which are rooted in the notion that Federal judicial power is limited to the resolution of "cases and controversies." * According to the orthodox view, Article III empowers Federal courts to entertain only claims for vindication of legal rights. The fact that the defendant has harmed the plaintiff is not enough. The plaintiff must claim a *legal right* not to be harmed in the way he alleges the defendant has harmed him. For example: Where (as in most cases of competitive injury) the common law gives the injured person no legal right, he can obtain legal redress only if a right has been conferred upon him by valid statute; if there is no such statute, the door to the Federal as well as the state courthouse is closed to him.⁴⁸

So long as the creation of legal rights was left to the legislatures, the result was a real limitation on judicial review. If a claim was not founded upon a recognized common law right, such as a right of contract or property or a right against defamation, or upon a statutory right, it was rejected as "nonjusticiable." If existing law declared the defendant's conduct illegal but gave to persons in the plaintiff's situation no legal right to complain of it, the plaintiff was held to lack "standing to sue." But in *Baker v. Carr* the Court, which the year before in *Mapp v. Ohio* ⁴⁹ had autonomously made

---

\* *See* Article III, Section 2, of the Constitution:

> The judicial Power shall extend to all *Cases*, in Law and Equity, arising under this Constitution, the Laws of the United States, and Treaties made, or which shall be made, under their Authority; — to all *Cases* affecting Ambassadors, other public Ministers and Consuls; — to all *Cases* of admiralty and maritime Jurisdiction; — to *Controversies* to which the United States shall be a party; — to *Controversies* between two or more States; — between a State and Citizens of another State; — between Citizens of different States; — between Citizens of the same State claiming Lands under Grants of different States, and between a State, or the Citizens thereof, and foreign States, Citizens or Subjects. (Emphasis added)

a new *constitutional rule* — a rule limiting governmental power — took the further step of creating the *legal rights* private parties needed as the basis for "cases and controversies" in which new constitutional rules could be declared. Therefore the lower courts could no longer determine at the *beginning* of a litigation whether the plaintiff did or did not have a justiciable claim and standing to sue upon it. That would depend on the final outcome of the lawsuit.

The plaintiffs in *Baker v. Carr* claimed a legal right previously unknown to the law. They claimed a legal right that their votes have greater weight than was prescribed by the statutes governing elections. Justice Brennan, with ingenuity equal to the occasion, translated the justiciability and standing requirements into loose-jointed guidelines based upon the Court's ability to adjudicate efficiently, effectively, and without undue encroachment on the powers of Congress and the President. As to standing, he said the question was whether the plaintiffs had "alleged such a personal stake in the outcome of the controversy as to assure that concrete adverseness upon which the Court so largely depends for illumination of difficult constitutional questions." [50] As to justiciability, his position was that any inequality of treatment by a state government gives rise to a justiciable equal protection claim unless the Court considers the claim frivolous or unless a "political question" is involved; [51] and he defined "political question" as a question having one or more of the following six characteristics:

> [1] a textually demonstrable constitutional commitment of the issue to a coordinate political department; or [2] a lack of judicially discoverable and manageable standards for resolving it; or [3] the impossibility of deciding without an initial policy determination of a kind clearly for nonjudicial discretion; or [4] the impossibility of a court's undertaking independent resolution without expressing lack of the respect due coordinate branches of government; or [5] an unusual need for unquestioning adherence to a political decision already made; or [6] the potentiality of embarrassment from multifarious pronouncements by various departments on one question.[52]

Thus, justiciability and standing no longer depend solely upon the formal qualities of the litigation and the pre-existing state of the law. As for standing, the question is whether the plaintiffs can be expected to contend vigorously for their position so that the issues will be fully illuminated for the Court's benefit. It is immaterial whether the vigor is expected to result from violation of an existing legal right of the plaintiff, or from his zeal for judicial creation of a new one. Justice Brennan said:

> It would not be necessary to decide whether appellants' allegations of impairment of their votes by the 1901 apportionment will, ultimately, entitle them to any relief, in order to hold that they have standing to seek it. If such impairment does produce a legally cognizable injury, they are among those who have sustained it.[53]

As for justiciability, this too depended upon the Court's own appraisal of practicalities, specifically the six practical considerations quoted above. Of the six, all but the second involve separation of powers within the Federal Government and have no bearing on review of state action. The second — "a lack of judicially discoverable and manageable standards for resolving" the dispute — involves only the extent to which the Court is willing to exert itself. It is always *possible* for the Court to "discover" (*i.e.,* establish) a standard. If the standard is indefinite in meaning, as the next chapter will show the rule against "involuntary" confessions to be,[54] it may be hard to "manage" because its application may call for decision of many individual cases; but the Court can shoulder that burden, and it has done so when it has deemed the objective sufficiently important. It can also move to a simple, blunt, prophylactic standard, as it did in *Miranda v. Arizona*,[55] if the burden of managing an indefinite rule becomes too great. In short, *Baker v. Carr* held that the justiciability and standing requirements limit the Court only when it wants to be limited; as operative external restrictions, the decision rendered them illusory.*

---

* Since 1962 the law of justiciability has become a doctrinal morass. *See, e.g.,* Sedler, *Standing, Justiciability, and All That: A Behavioral Analysis,* 25 VAND. L. REV. 479 (1972); Scott, *Standing in the Supreme Court — A Functional Analysis,* 86 HARV. L. REV. 645 (1973). Perhaps the low point has been reached in the field of foreign affairs; a devastating but accurate analysis of Banco Nacional de Cuba v. Sabbatino, 376 U.S. 398 (1964), and First National City Bank v. Banco Nacional

In one respect the majority opinion was so obscure as to mislead one of the Justices. Justice Stewart's concurring opinion reveals the belief that the Court had left open the question whether the Equal Protection Clause had been violated:

> ... the Court today decides only: (1) that the District Court possessed jurisdiction of the subject matter; (2) that the complaint presents a justiciable controversy; (3) that the appellants have standing. ... But the merits of this case are not before us now.[56]

It is true that Justice Brennan discussed only these three questions. On the merits, he said only that equal protection can be denied by a discrimination that "reflects *no* policy."[57] But the scope of the decision is revealed at the end of his opinion:

> We conclude that the complaint's allegations of a denial of equal protection present a justiciable constitutional cause of action upon which appellants are entitled to a trial and a decision.[58]

This must mean that by proving their allegations the plaintiffs would establish an equal protection violation. For the Court to require a trial which could result in a judgment against the plaintiffs even if all their allegations were proved, and to do so in the face of a motion to dismiss the complaint for failure to state a valid claim, would constitute unthinkable disregard of the function of that motion.

What Justice Brennan did leave undone was definition of equal protection standards (important for *future* malapportionment cases) and formulation of a remedy. On the former question he asserted: "Judicial standards under the Equal Protection Clause are well developed and familiar."[59] (Although this was undoubtedly an overstatement, it was an assurance that manageable standards could and would somehow be devised.) He treated the question of remedy as premature, saying that "we have no cause at this stage to doubt that the District Court will be able to fashion relief if violations of constitutional rights are found."[60]

---

de Cuba, 406 U.S. 759 (1972), is presented by John G. Laylin in his article "Justiciable Disputes Involving Acts of State," in *The International Lawyer* (1973), vol. 7, at p. 513.

It was technically correct to leave open the possibility that violations might not be found, since the plaintiffs' allegations had not yet been proved or formally admitted. Since, however, they were in fact undisputed (as Justice Clark's concurrence pointed out [61]), it is understandable that Justice Stewart thought the Court was reserving decision on the merits.

The Court quickly dispelled any doubt that it was prepared to hold unconstitutional any avoidable inequality in the numerical weight of votes. In *Gray v. Sanders* (1963) [62] it held invalid the Georgia county unit system in primary elections for statewide offices, which had the effect of weighting votes in some counties, particularly the populous urban counties, more lightly than votes in others. Justice Douglas, for a majority of eight, declared:

> The conception of political equality from the Declaration of Independence, to Lincoln's Gettysburg address, to the Fifteenth, Seventeenth [sic], and Nineteenth Amendments can mean only one thing — one person, one vote.[63]

In *Wesberry v. Sanders* (1964) [64] Justice Black arrived at the utterly remarkable conclusion, not fairly derivable from the text of the Constitution, that,

> construed in its historical context, the command of Art. I, § 2, that Representatives be chosen "by the People of the several States" means that as nearly as practicable one man's vote in a congressional election is to be worth as much as another's.[65]

Congressional districts of unequal population were therefore held unconstitutional. And in *Reynolds v. Sims* (1964) [66] the Court declared through Chief Justice Warren:

> We hold that, as a basic constitutional standard, the Equal Protection Clause requires that the seats in both houses of a bicameral state legislature must be apportioned on a population basis. Simply stated, an individual's right to vote for state legislators is unconstitutionally impaired when its weight is in a substantial fashion diluted when compared with votes of citizens living in other parts of the State.[67]

Within nine months after *Baker v. Carr* was decided, litigation challenging the constitutionality of state legislative apportionment was instituted in at least 34 states,[68] and many attacks were made on Congressional districting.[69] The Court applied the equality rule with extreme strictness. For example, a plan was set aside in which district populations varied only from 2.84% above the average to 3.13% below it.[70] Moreover, the district courts were given great latitude in the matter of remedies; New York was ordered to elect 165 members to the lower house of its legislature in 1965, in disregard of the 150 maximum fixed by the state constitution, and the Court declined to interfere.[71] The equality rule was also extended to local government elections, including elections in special-purpose units such as junior college districts.[72]

Legislative reapportionment was not the only area in which the Court regulated voting power. By applying an unprecedentedly strict equal protection standard, it prohibited limitation of the franchise in school board elections to (1) property taxpayers, (2) tenants, and (3) parents of children attending public schools in the district.[73] It forbade restriction of the vote to property taxpayers on approval of municipal bond issues.[74] It held valid a Federal statute prohibiting an English-language literacy test for Puerto Ricans.[75] It forbade denial of the vote for nonpayment of poll tax.[76] It upheld a Federal statute fixing the voting age at 18 for Federal elections.[77] And in its most sweeping decision on the franchise, it invalidated durational residence requirements which nearly every state had imposed.[78]

The Court's concern with the political process extended beyond dilution or denial of the vote. Political expression was given additional protection by decisions which (a) provided constitutional immunity for membership in an organization dedicated to violent revolution, with knowledge of its illegal purpose but without active participation in furthering that purpose; [79] (b) invalidated loyalty oaths going beyond simple affirmations of allegiance; [80] (c) extended to juveniles the constitutional right of free expression; [81] (d) narrowly limited the exclusion of student organizations from state college campuses; [82] and (e) denied governmental power to enjoin unauthorized publicization of official documents, at least in the absence of overwhelming public danger.[83]

The Court also began to protect political parties against burdensome restrictions on access to the ballot.[84] This was a most difficult task because the imminence of an election inevitably necessitated very quick adjudication; yet the Court intervened. The time element did finally lead it to decline, by a six to three vote, to adjudicate the credentials of delegates to national party conventions.[85]

The most striking evidence of the Court's unflinching determination to guarantee the efficacy of the political process was *Powell v. McCormack* (1969).[86] When the 90th Congress convened early in 1967, the House of Representatives refused to seat Negro Congressman Adam Clayton Powell, Jr., a longtime incumbent, on the basis of committee findings that he had perpetrated large frauds on the Government by padding expense accounts, taking kickbacks from his office personnel, and other illegal practices. He and thirteen of his Harlem constituents sued Speaker John W. McCormack, all other Congressmen as a class, and the Clerk, Sergeant-at-Arms, and Doorkeeper of the House. His claim was that the House had no authority to exclude him for any reason except failure to satisfy the requirements of age, citizenship, and residence which are specified in Article I, Section 2 of the Constitution * — all of which he admittedly did satisfy. The judicial relief he and his constituents sought was an injunction requiring the Doorkeeper to admit him to the House Chamber, the Speaker to administer the oath, the Clerk to render him the services due a Congressman, and the Sergeant-at-Arms to pay him his salary. He also requested a declaratory judgment that his exclusion by the House was unconstitutional.

While the case was making its way through the lower Federal courts, which ruled against him on various grounds,[87] the 90th Congress expired and Congressman Powell, having been reelected in 1968, was seated in the 91st Congress. The question therefore arose whether any justiciable case or controversy that had originally existed had disappeared, so that the litigation was moot.

---

\* The second paragraph of Article I, Section 2, provides:

No Person shall be a Representative who shall not have attained to the Age of twenty-five Years, and been seven Years a Citizen of the United States, and who shall not, when elected, be an Inhabitant of that State in which he shall be chosen.

Chief Justice Warren held it was not, on the ground that the Congressman still had a legal claim for his withheld salary. This was a remarkable ruling. The Sergeant-at-Arms had lost control of salary funds for the 90th Congress when that Congress came to an end and undisbursed salary money reverted to the Treasury by law.[88] The defendant Representatives were held to be immune from suit under the Speech or Debate Clause of Article I, Section 6, and the case against them was dismissed on the merits.[89] The Clerk and the Doorkeeper had nothing to do with payment of Congressional salaries. Justice Stewart, dissenting, pointed out that the salary claim was against the United States, which was not a party defendant; but he dissented alone.[90] Like the Cheshire Cat, the case against the defendants had simply faded away, but the disembodied after-image was held sufficiently real to serve as a predicate for decision.

The decision on justiciability was equally remarkable. In *Baker v. Carr* the Court had listed six indicia of political questions, the existence of any one of which was said to bar judicial decision. The first was "a textually demonstrable constitutional commitment of the issue to a coordinate political department." Article I, Section 5 of the Constitution provides: "Each House shall be the Judge of the Elections, Returns and Qualifications of its own Members...." Chief Justice Warren surmounted this obstacle by declaring that if Article I, Section 2 was intended to make age, citizenship, and residence the *only* permissible qualifications for admission, the effect of accepting as final the House determination that an additional qualification can be added would be to preclude judicial review and thus let the erroneous House determination stand;[91] and he considered this unthinkable because the Court is "ultimate interpreter of the Constitution."[92] In other words, the case was justiciable because the Court needed to decide it in order to fulfill its responsibility as "ultimate interpreter."

On this premise any constitutional claim is justiciable; the justiciability requirement is even more clearly illusory as a limitation on judicial power than *Baker v. Carr* said it was.

FREEDOM OF EXPRESSION AND ELECTORAL RIGHTS 141

Incidentally, Chief Justice Warren brushed aside the fourth *Baker v. Carr* criterion ("the impossibility of a court's undertaking independent resolution without expressing lack of the respect due coordinate branches of government") and the sixth ("the potentiality of embarrassment from multifarious pronouncements by various departments on one question") with the remark that conflict with the House "cannot justify the courts' avoiding their constitutional responsibility ... as the ultimate interpreter of the Constitution." [93]

One other facet of the justiciability question, though it broke no new ground, deserves mention because it serves as a reminder of the extent to which the advent of the declaratory judgment has lengthened the Court's arm. Chief Justice Warren said that "even if . . . [Powell's] averments as to injunctive relief are not sufficiently definite, it does not follow that this litigation must be dismissed as moot.... Declaratory relief has been requested...." [94] In other words, the fact that the Court might be unable or unwilling to enter a coercive judgment did not mean that it was unable to declare the law.

There was a time, long ago, when the soundness of that proposition was seriously doubted. The first Court of Claims Act was held unconstitutional in *Gordon v. United States* (1864).[95] Chief Justice Taney drafted an opinion asserting that an award of execution is an essential part of any judgment, and that the Court lacked jurisdiction to review a Court of Claims judgment — partly because Congress could frustrate an award of damages against the Government by failing to make the necessary appropriation. Taney died before the Court had approved or disapproved his opinion (which was not officially published until long after his death), and the case was decided without opinion. Then Congress enacted a new Court of Claims Act, which eliminated a second objection Taney had made but still left the payment of damage awards subject to the availability of appropriated funds. In *United States v. Jones* (1886) [96] the Court upheld the statute, silently repudiating the Taney objection on that score — doubtless because the Court of Claims provided a procedure far preferable to the private bill procedure that it superseded.

That was sufficient to establish the principle that the Court need not stay its hand simply because it is unable to enter a coercive judgment. But a long road was still to be traveled before the justiciability of declaratory judgments was fully established. In *Willing v. Chicago Auditorium Association* (1928)[97] Justice Brandeis, for the Court, uttered a dictum which for a time was understood to bar the Federal courts from entering declaratory judgments:

> What the plaintiff seeks is simply a declaratory judgment. To grant that relief is beyond the power conferred upon the federal judiciary.[98]

Then Congress threw its weight into the scales by enacting the Declaratory Judgment Act of 1934,[99] authorizing a Federal declaratory judgment "[i]n a case of actual controversy." Persuaded of the practical utility of the procedure, the Court upheld the statute — with no dissent by Justice Brandeis — in *Aetna Life Insurance Co. v. Haworth* (1937).[100] However, Chief Justice Hughes's opinion for the Court emphasized that no general relaxation of the justiciability requirement was intended:

> A "controversy" in this sense must be one that is appropriate for judicial determination.... Where there is ... a concrete case admitting of an immediate and definitive determination of the *legal rights of the parties* in an adversary proceeding upon the facts alleged, the judicial function may be appropriately exercised although the adjudication of the rights of the litigants may not require the award of process or the payment of damages.[101] (Emphasis added)

Thus, if it be granted that Congressman Powell had a *legal right* to be admitted to membership in the House, the Court's inability to enforce its will upon the House did not stand in the way of a declaratory judgment.

On the merits, the decision was that age, citizenship, and residence are the only constitutionally permissible qualifications. The Chief Justice acknowledged that a few supporters of the secessionist cause had been excluded from the House and Senate shortly after the Civil War on the ground of disloyalty (and one for selling appointments to the military and naval academies), but he dismissed these exclusions as "among the casualties of the general upheaval produced in war's wake."[102] He dwelt at length on the fact that *the House* had rejected a number of other exclusion proposals on the ground that Article I, Section 2 forbids the adding of other qualifications to age, citizenship, and residence,[103] ignoring however the immateriality of these actions to the question whether the House or the Court has the final authority to decide.

The Chief Justice thus stated reasons for holding that the House had violated its constitutional duty to seat Congressman Powell. He never adverted, however, to the analytically separate question whether by so doing it had violated a legal right of his. According to the older conception of judicial review, violation of a legal right was essential to the existence of a "case or controversy" justiciable in the Federal courts. It will be recalled from Chapter V that, in *Marbury v. Madison,* Chief Justice Marshall did not approach the constitutional question whether Congress could broaden the Court's original jurisdiction until he had shown that a duly appointed official such as Marbury had a legal right to delivery of his commission — a common law right suitable for enforcement by a court through the established judicial remedy of mandamus.[104] But Chief Justice Warren held, by implication, that the constitutional violation was *ipso facto* a violation of legal right — a position consistent with his conception of the Court's role as ultimate interpreter of the Constitution, but inconsistent with the older and more restrictive conception of its function.*

---

* Similar indifference to the existence of a legal right had been manifested earlier in Katzenbach v. McClung, 379 U.S. 294 (1964). Shortly after enactment of the Civil Rights Act of 1964, forbidding racial discrimination in restaurants serving food that had moved in interstate commerce, the owner of Ollie's Barbecue (an Alabama restaurant) sued in a Federal district court to enjoin Federal officials from enforcing the statute, which was attacked as unconstitutional. Since no Federal official had threatened to enforce the Act against the plaintiff, there was no cause of action for injunction — and perhaps, indeed, no case or controversy between the parties. (See Public Service Comm'n v. Wycoff Co., 344 U.S. 237, 245 (1952); *cf.* Black, J., concurring in Epperson v. Arkansas, 393 U.S. 97, 109 (1968).) Justice Clark, for the Court, brushed the difficulty aside. He said the case would be treated as an action for declaratory judgment and that the Court had discretion to take jurisdiction of it — discretion which it elected to exercise because: "It is important that a decision

This virtuoso exercise in judicial review was motivated by the Court's inflexible conviction that effectuation of electoral decisions is a matter of paramount importance. Chief Justice Warren declared:

> A fundamental principle of our representative democracy is, in Hamilton's words, "that the people should choose whom they please to govern them." [105]

Special urgency was added by the fact that the case involved a Negro Congressman at a time when Negro disillusionment with electoral and legal processes was fueling the black separatist movement as never before.[106] But the decision was of a piece with the whole series of developments, mostly nonracial in motivation, which have been described in this chapter. The Court had simply taken general charge of the electoral process.

It is now time to go back for a survey of the Court's awakening vigor, after 1937, in fields other than freedom of expression and electoral rights.

---

on the constitutionality of the Act as applied in these cases be announced as quickly as possible." (379 U.S. at 296.) The jurisdictional ruling did not attract much attention, partly because the Act was sustained on the merits and partly because Justice Clark did not elaborate his reasoning on the point (as Chief Justice Warren did later in *Powell v. McCormack*) so that there was less reason to believe that the ruling presaged general broadening of the Court's conception of its role.

Further flowering of the idea that breach of constitutional duty necessarily connotes violation of legal right will be seen in Flast v. Cohen, 392 U.S. 83 (1968), to be discussed in Chapter XI, and Bivens v. Six Unknown Named Agents, 403 U.S. 388 (1971), to be discussed in Chapter XVI.

CHAPTER X
# Protection of the Suspect and the Accused

The next major object of the Court's heightened concern was conviction of the innocent, a problem more acute for state court convictions than for Federal. The Court had long kept watch for possible miscarriage of justice in Federal prosecutions, resorting when necessary to its "supervisory power" over the Federal judiciary, and had intervened against Federal trial procedures that led to substantial risk of undeserved punishment.[1] For example, in *Berger v. United States* (1935)[2] Justice Sutherland declared for the Court that the interest of the United States in a criminal prosecution "is not that it shall win a case, but that justice shall be done." Though the prosecutor "may strike hard blows, he is not at liberty to strike foul ones." He may not employ "improper suggestions, insinuations and, especially, assertions of personal knowledge," which "are apt to carry much weight against the accused when they should properly carry none," and thereby "to produce a wrongful conviction."[3]

Beyond this, the supervisory power had been used to maintain comparatively high standards of Federal *police* conduct. For example, confessions obtained during an unnecessary delay between arrest and appearance before a judicial officer were held inadmissible regardless of their voluntariness.[4]

The insistence that Federal agents function with full respect for the dignity and privacy of suspects inevitably led to acquittal of a number of plainly guilty defendants, but the adverse effect on deterrence of such offences as murder and robbery was relatively slight because (except in the District of Columbia and the territories) Federal law is not the basic protection against crimes of violence. As Justice Robert H. Jackson once observed, the state and local governments carry the main burden of protecting society from most crimes against persons and property.[5]

Once this is understood, one understands also Justice Cardozo's reluctance in the *Palko* case to measure state prosecutions against the strict double jeopardy standard established by the Sixth

Amendment for Federal prosecutions.[6] More fundamentally, one understands that there was no inconsistency on the part of the eighteenth-century Constitutors in limiting the Federal Government by the tight criminal process safeguards of the Fourth, Fifth, Sixth, and Eighth Amendments while imposing upon the states only the rule against bills of attainder and *ex post facto* laws.[7] From their viewpoint, no great harm would be done if the dread power of criminal prosecution were withheld almost entirely from the new and remote Federal Government, so long as the states were left free to pursue and punish miscreants.

That was why the Court was slow to intrude upon the state criminal process (even in the case of Sacco and Vanzetti, neither Justice Holmes nor Justice Stone could find any hope of Supreme Court reversal that would justify a stay of execution [8]) and had intervened only in the most extreme cases. In *Moore v. Dempsey* (1923) [9] it voided five death sentences imposed on Negro defendants after an Arkansas murder trial which was so thoroughly dominated by an angry mob that it was a mere substitute for the lynching that the mob was ready to perpetrate. Justice Holmes, for the Court, characterized the trial as a "mask," saying that "counsel, jury and judge were swept to the fatal end by an irresistible wave of public passion." [10] *Powell v. Alabama* (1932) [11] reversed the convictions of Negroes sentenced to death for the rape of two white women, because the defendants had been denied the effective aid of counsel. In *Mooney v. Holohan* (1935) [12] the Court held that the prosecutor's use of evidence he knows to be perjured denies due process of law. In *Brown v. Mississippi* (1936) [13] it reversed the murder convictions and death sentences of Negroes where the only evidence against them had admittedly been tortured out of them by deputy sheriffs.

It is worth while recalling in some detail the evidence in the *Brown* case. It shows vividly the need for Federal intervention to prevent conviction of the innocent, because of the callous formalism which then dominated criminal law administration. The Mississippi Supreme Court rejected the defendants' claim that their confessions should be excluded from evidence.[14] It rejected the claim not because it thought the confessions were voluntary, but because the defendants' trial counsel, though he had objected to reception of the confessions in evidence, had neglected to take a further step required in Mississippi criminal practice. He had not moved to strike out the confessions after the deputies admitted the torture. Because of this omission the highest state court held that the defendants must die. Here is what the record showed, as summarized by two dissenting judges in the state supreme court:

> The crime with which these defendants, all ignorant negroes, are charged, was discovered about 1 o'clock p.m. on Friday, March 30, 1934. On that night one Dial, a deputy sheriff, accompanied by others, came to the home of Ellington, one of the defendants, and requested him to accompany them to the house of the deceased, and there a number of white men were gathered, who began to accuse the defendant of the crime. Upon his denial they seized him, and with the participation of the deputy they hanged him by a rope to the limb of a tree, and, having let him down, they hung him again, and when he was let down the second time, and he still protested his innocence, he was tied to a tree and whipped, and still declining to accede to the demands that he confess, he was finally released, and he returned with some difficulty to his home, suffering intense pain and agony. The record of the testimony shows that the signs of the rope on his neck were plainly visible during the so-called trial. A day or two thereafter the said deputy, accompanied by another, returned to the home of the said defendant and arrested him, and departed with the prisoner towards the jail in an adjoining county, but went by a route which led into the state of Alabama; and while on the way, in that state, the deputy stopped and again severely whipped the defendant, declaring that he would continue the whipping until he confessed, and the defendant then agreed to confess to such a statement as the deputy would dictate, and he did so, after which he was delivered to jail.
>
> The other two defendants, Ed Brown and Henry Shields, were also arrested and taken to the same jail. On Sunday night, April 1, 1934, the same deputy, accompanied by a number of white men, one of whom was also an officer, and by the jailer, came to the jail, and the two last named defendants were made to strip and they were laid over chairs and their backs were cut to pieces with a leather strap with buckles on it, and they were likewise made by the said deputy definitely to understand that the whipping would be continued unless and until they confessed, and not only confessed, but confessed in every

matter of detail as demanded by those present; and in this manner the defendants confessed the crime, and, as the whippings progressed and were repeated, they changed or adjusted their confession in all particulars of detail so as to conform to the demands of their torturers. When the confessions had been obtained in the exact form and contents as desired by the mob, they left with the parting admonition and warning that, if the defendants changed their story at any time in any respect from that last stated, the perpetrators of the outrage would administer the same or equally effective treatment.

. . . .

All this having been accomplished, on the next day, that is, on Monday, April 2, when the defendants had been given time to recuperate somewhat from the tortures to which they had been subjected, the two sheriffs, one of the county where the crime was committed, and the other of the county of the jail in which the prisoners were confined, came to the jail, accompanied by eight other persons, some of them deputies, there to hear the free and voluntary confession of these miserable and abject defendants. The sheriff of the county of the crime admitted that he had heard of the whipping, but averred that he had no personal knowledge of it. He admitted that one of the defendants, when brought before him to confess, was limping and did not sit down, and that this particular defendant then and there stated that he had been strapped so severely that he could not sit down, and, as already stated, the signs of the rope on the neck of another of the defendants was [*sic*] plainly visible to all. Nevertheless the solemn farce of hearing the free and voluntary confessions was gone through with, and these two sheriffs and one other person then present were the three witnesses used in court to establish the so-called confessions, which were received by the court and admitted in evidence over the objections of the defendants duly entered of record as each of the said three witnesses delivered their alleged testimony. . . .

The spurious confessions having been obtained — and the farce last mentioned having been gone through with on Monday, April 2d — the court, then in session, on the following day, Tuesday, April 3, 1934, ordered the grand jury to reassemble on the succeeding day, April 4, 1934, at 9 o'clock, and on the morning of the day last mentioned the grand jury returned an indictment against the defendants for murder. Late that afternoon the defendants were brought from the jail in the adjoining county and arraigned, when one or more of them offered to plead guilty, which the court declined to accept, and, upon inquiry whether they had or desired counsel, they stated that they had none, and did not suppose that counsel could be of any assistance to them. The court thereupon appointed counsel, and set the case for trial for the following morning at 9 o'clock, and the defendants were returned to the jail in the adjoining county about thirty miles away.

The defendants were brought to the courthouse of the county on the following morning, April 5th, and the so-called trial was opened, and was concluded on the next day, April 6, 1934, and resulted in a pretended conviction with death sentences. The evidence upon which the conviction was obtained was the so-called confessions. Without this evidence, a peremptory instruction to find for the defendants would have been inescapable. The defendants were put on the stand, and by their testimony the facts and the details thereof as to the manner by which the confessions were extorted from them was [sic] fully developed, and it is further disclosed by the record that the same deputy, Dial, under whose guiding hand and active participation the tortures to coerce the confessions were administered, was actively in the performance of the supposed duties of a court deputy in the courthouse and in the presence of the prisoners during what is denominated, in complimentary terms, the trial of these defendants. This deputy was put on the stand by the state in rebuttal, and admitted the whippings. It is interesting to note that in his testimony with reference to the whipping of the defendant Ellington, and in response to the inquiry as to how severely he was whipped, the deputy stated, "Not too much for a negro; not as much as I would have done if it were left to me." Two others who had participated in these whippings were introduced and admitted it — not a single witness was introduced who denied it. The facts are not only undisputed, they are admitted, and admitted to have been done by officers of the state, in conjunction with other participants, and all this was definitely well known to everybody connected with the trial, and during the trial, including the state's prosecuting attorney and the trial judge presiding.[15]

In deciding the *Moore, Powell, Mooney,* and *Brown* cases, the Court spoke of injustice to the particular defendants, saying nothing of what the convictions implied for the relationship between the rulers and the ruled. In *Chambers v. Florida* (1940),[16] unanimously reversing four murder convictions (of Negro tenant farmers) because they rested on involuntary confessions, a broader concern made its appearance. Justice Black said:

> ... in view of its historical setting and the wrongs which called it into being, the due process provision of the Fourteenth Amendment — just as that in the Fifth — has led few to doubt that it was intended to guarantee procedural standards adequate and appropriate, then and thereafter, to protect, at all times, people charged with or suspected of crime by those holding positions of power and authority. Tyrannical governments had immemorially utilized dictatorial criminal procedure and punishment to make scapegoats of the weak, or of helpless political, religious, or racial minorities and those who differed, who would not conform and who resisted tyranny.
> 
> . . . .
> 
> ... Today, as in ages past, we are not without tragic proof that the exalted power of some governments to punish manufactured crime dictatorially is the handmaid of tyranny. Under our constitutional system, courts stand against any winds that blow as havens of refuge for those who might otherwise suffer because they are helpless, weak, outnumbered, or because they are non-conforming victims of prejudice and public excitement. Due process of law, preserved for all by our Constitution, commands that no such practice as that disclosed by this record shall send any accused to his death. No higher duty, no higher responsibility, rests upon this Court, than that of translating into living law and maintaining this constitutional shield deliberately planned and inscribed for the benefit of every human being subject to our Constitution — of whatever race, creed or persuasion.[17]

Consistently with Justice Black's assignment of high priority to the task of dealing with "manufactured crime," he expressed interest in a doctrinal basis for automatically broadened Federal control over state and local police, prosecutors, and courts. He took note of a "current of opinion" that the Fourteenth Amendment *incorporates* the Bill of Rights and thus makes its provisions operate as restrictions upon the states.[18] This position had been consistently rejected by the Court — most recently in *Palko v. Connecticut*, three years before.[19] (It was to be rejected yet again;[20] but, as we shall see, the Court eventually adopted it in somewhat qualified form.)

Of more immediate consequence was the Court's manifestation of concern with tyranny. Justice Black made it clear that he used the term to mean domination over an entire population or over disfavored minority groups, not merely over the particular defendants. His characterization of involuntary confession as "dictatorial criminal procedure" suggested awareness that it is an apt device for imposing thralldom, and promised judicial opposition to any such use of the criminal law.

This was a commitment of large but uncertain extent. At a minimum, it meant that procedures substantially likely to result in conviction of the innocent would not be tolerated. That in itself would be a restraint on tyranny; it would mitigate the fear that innocent victims would be punished in order to discourage the expression of discontent. But it might also mean that "dictatorial criminal procedure" would be held unconstitutional even if the defendant's guilt was plain. Defendants and defense counsel were, in effect, invited to present new claims testing the extent of the Court's willingness to superintend all aspects of criminal law enforcement.

In response to the invitation, a growing stream of cases sought and received the Court's consideration; and as they did, some knotty problems came into view. For appreciation of the probing, step-by-step manner in which the Court evolved new constitutional rules during those early years, it will be helpful to canvass the perplexities it encountered in developing rules on *confessions*, the first aspect of the state criminal process to receive its intensive consideration.

We begin by recalling some simple facts about involuntary confessions. In the first place, voluntariness is not the same as spontaneity. Granted, there may be occasional instances of confession simply because conscience demands a clean breast. Less rarely, a neurotic urge for notoriety or a desire to protect the actual offender leads to spontaneous *false* confessions. In almost all cases, however, confessions result from pressure of some sort — anything from hope of leniency to fear of pain. In one sense, of course, that is not inconsistent with "voluntariness"; it takes an act of *will* to speak or write or affix a signature. In the legal sense, however, the voluntariness of a confession, and hence its admissibility, depends on whether the pressure that has induced it is deemed *excessive*.

Another fact worth remembering is that a confession may be true even though it has been induced by the most extreme pressure. Words uttered under torture are of course unreliable as an initial proposition, since they may have been spoken solely in order to stop the torture; but sometimes they verify themselves.[21] A statement extracted by use of a thumbscrew proves nothing in itself; but if it is a confession of murder telling where the victim's body and the murder pistol are to be found, and if the questioner has had no way of knowing their whereabouts beforehand so that he can lead the informant, and if the body and weapon are found at the places designated, the confession does acquire probative force. Guilt is not yet a certainty — the confessor *may* merely have witnessed the killing, or been told about it, or happened to stumble across the body and the pistol; but the confession (reinforced by the discoveries it has led to) is enough to satisfy the reasonable doubt standard. The prosecutor need not prove that innocence is downright inconceivable.[22] In such a case, exclusion of the confession must be based on some ground other than its unreliability; it must be based on a policy judgment that some methods of learning the truth are more dangerous than failure to convict the guilty.

One set of problems the Court faced with respect to confessions arose from its limited aptitude for factfinding. *Brown v. Mississippi* and *Chambers v. Florida* presented no difficulty on this score. On the undisputed facts, the defendants had confessed under savage mistreatment. But the 1936 *Brown* decision had taught law enforcement officials that unselfconscious admission of violence is impolitic, and subsequent cases almost invariably presented a testimonial conflict as to whether violence had been employed — the interrogating officers denying all violence or, at most, testifying that it was trivial. The jury traditionally has final authority to decide the credibility of witnesses; and the question soon arose whether, provided the jury has been properly instructed

PROTECTION OF THE SUSPECT AND THE ACCUSED        153

to disregard the confession if found involuntary, the Supreme Court should not accept its verdict of guilty. In *Lisenba v. California* (1941),[23] Justice Roberts for the Court held that the verdict should stand unless a finding of voluntariness would have been so lacking in evidentiary support as to be "fundamentally unfair" (which he said was not so in Lisenba's case). This was a stiff test, and if adhered to it would have severely limited intervention by the Court.

The test is subtly flawed. The Court adhered to it in *Lyons v. Oklahoma* (1944),[24] but ultimately detected the flaw. Voluntariness is not a pure question of fact; like "negligence" it is a mixed question of law and fact. Any *evidentiary* conflict relates not to the legal but to the factual component: Did the sheriff whip the defendant or didn't he? But the jurors may have more to do than answer the fact question. If they believe the whipping occurred, they must still decide whether such an assault constitutes *excessive* pressure; and that is an "ought question," a question of legal standards, to which their traditional prerogative of assessing credibility is irrelevant. To be sure, it is by no means unheard of for jurors to act as "judges of the law *and* facts";[25] indeed, they assume that role whenever they render a verdict on a negligence issue, which involves an evaluation of conduct as well as a determination of what actually happened. But the justification for such a role is not that jurors are the best judges of credibility, but that the law wants the "ought question" decided according to community standards — for which a cross-section jury is an apt instrument.

Thus, ascription of finality to a jury verdict of voluntariness is sensible if, but only if, community standards are to be decisive. The question is whether, if the jurors believe the defendant was in fact whipped but feel that (in the words of Deputy Dial in the *Brown* case) the whipping was "not too much for a negro," that should settle the matter. There is no reason why the Court must or should yield to community standards here. Justice Frankfurter pointed this out in *Watts v. Indiana* (1949),[26] saying that only the facts leading to the confession are for final state determination and that Federal law determines how much pressure is too much.

A practical problem remained, however. How can the Federal question be dissected out if the jurors render a *general* verdict of guilty? For all the Court can know, they may have disbelieved the defendant's testimony that he was whipped, and therefore may never have asked themselves whether whipping is a permissible kind of pressure. For a time the Court endeavored to meet this problem by holding that it would accept the defense testimony not only if *admitted* but also if *uncontradicted*; four concurring Justices proposed such a rule in *Gallegos v. Nebraska* (1951),[27] and it won majority approval in *Stein v. New York* (1953)[28] and *Thomas v. Arizona* (1958).[29] But the rule was not fully satisfactory because the jury's power to assess credibility ordinarily permits rejection of even uncontradicted testimony if the witness is deemed unworthy of belief. Ultimately the Court moved to firmer logical ground, by making prophylactic rules bypassing or minimizing credibility questions [30] and by requiring the *trial judge* to pass on the question of voluntariness.[31]

Even such solutions, however, do not reckon with another uncertainty about the jury. What if the jury has in fact disregarded the confession but found the defendant guilty on the basis of other evidence? If the record contains other evidence adequate to support a guilty verdict, and particularly if that other evidence seems to the Justices to be overwhelmingly convincing, it is not harmless error to put an involuntary confession before the jurors? Not necessarily. They themselves may not be sure whether it had any effect on their verdict, and judges certainly cannot know. The other evidence, overwhelming as it might seem to an outsider who had not heard the witnesses and observed their demeanor, could well have left the jurors in reasonable doubt if reinforcement by the confession had not been forthcoming. That is what the Court decided in *Malinski v. New York* (1945).[32] In 1967, to be sure, after long doubt, a Federal rule as to harmless constitutional error (that is, that a conviction should be affirmed despite a constitutional violation if the violation was plainly harmless to the defendant) was held applicable to other types of constitutional violation;[33] but it has never been applied to use of involuntary confessions — presumably because of the impressive weight a confession almost inevitably carries with jurors.

Until now we have been outlining problems arising from the Court's limited aptitude as a *fact-finder*. A different set of problems, even more productive of litigation, arose from its initial uncertainty as to how much it wanted to accomplish by intervening against involuntary confessions.

If the purpose were only to protect confessing defendants whose innocence seems sufficiently probable to render punishment unjustifiable, the Court would center its attention on the *reliability* of the confession. Use of a confession which verified itself, or which had been invested with strong probative value by other evidence supplementing it, would not necessitate reversal even if quite heavy pressure had been exerted to induce it. That approach would not result in exclusion of self-verifying confessions even if obtained by *barbarous* pressure such as thumbscrew, rack, or wheel. Moreover, it would place heavy demands on the Court's time, because it would often be necessary to search the whole record for evidence bearing upon the confession's reliability. At an early date the approach was rejected. *Lisenba v. California* (1941)[34] disclaimed interest in the truth or falsity of the confession; thus, the Court can limit its scrutiny to evidence as to the pressure that induced the confession.

Although Justice Jackson did attack this position in 1949,[35] his viewpoint has not prevailed. In opposing Jackson's viewpoint, Justice Frankfurter introduced a concept possessing great rhetorical force, which the Court has since found useful in justifying new constitutional rules not only for confessions but also for illegal search and seizure; for failure to provide counsel; for nonconfrontation by adverse witnesses; for jury trial; and for various other facets of the criminal process.[36] This concept, old in Anglo-American law but not previously thought to possess *constitutional* significance, is that the Constitution presupposes and requires adherence to an "underlying principle in our enforcement of the criminal law. Ours is the accusatorial rather than the inquisitorial system."[37] The *inquisitorial* system (used throughout continental Europe) places responsibility for spontaneous protection of the accused's rights upon the trial judge. In the *accusatorial* system, however, he is a neutral arbiter between two contending adversaries, and justice will suffer if one of the adversaries is put at too great a disadvantage.

The idea that the Constitution enshrines the accusatorial system was a new departure. Justice Cardozo's opinion in *Palko v. Connecticut* shows that he would have denied its essentiality to "ordered liberty." Explaining why he thought the privilege against self-incrimination to be unprotected by the Fourteenth Amendment, he acknowledged "the need to give protection against torture, physical or mental" (citing *Brown v. Mississippi*), but went on:

> Justice, however, would not perish if the accused were subject to a duty to respond to orderly inquiry.[38]

Justice Black considered it parochial to assume the superiority of *Anglo-American* notions of justice; that was one reason why, dissenting in *Rochin v. California* (1952),[39] he scoffed at Justice Frankfurter's assertion that due process of law embodies "those canons of decency and fairness which express the notions of justice of English-speaking peoples." As has been said, however, the accusatorial system is now firmly embedded in our constitutional doctrine.

The accusatorial system, the Court says, implies that the accused has more than a right not to be convicted if innocent; he has the broader right not to be convicted unless the prosecutor, *without any affirmative help from him,* can prove the charge. However guilty the accused may know himself to be, he is constitutionally entitled to remain silent and leave upon the prosecutor the entire burden of proving guilt. On this theory a confession induced by even the slightest official pressure would have to be excluded, and at one time it seemed likely that the Court would eventually so decide. In *Miranda v. Arizona* (1966)[40] it made a close approach to this position, but that was much later. For three decades after *Brown v. Mississippi*, the use of pressure was disapproved only if judged excessive.

Thus there was a problem of establishing a standard of excessiveness, both in the interest of consistency in adjudication and in the cognate interest of providing guidance to criminal investigators, lawyers, and lower courts. The choice of a standard depended on whether or not the court wished to concern itself with more than the need for justice to the confessing defendant. If so, his own particular degree of susceptibility to official pressure was immaterial; if not, it was highly material. Most of the early confession decisions imply satisfaction with the more limited objective, close attention being paid to the defendant's ignorance, his youth, his race, and other factors thought pertinent to his capacity to resist pressure.[41] Justice Black's 1940 opinion in the *Chambers* case, however, had laid the foundation for a further and broader objective: resistance to tyranny.[42] From this standpoint attention should be confined to the investigative method used, and it should be evaluated in the light of its probable impact upon the community at large. If the Court believes it to be intolerably intimidatory, it should be held unconstitutional regardless of the particular defendant's strength or weakness. The later cases appear to take that view.

Employing at first the same probing, case-by-case approach that it had used for problems of involuntary confessions, and later the more sweeping technique of "selective incorporation" (described below),[43] the Court went on to develop new safeguards for the accused in many other criminal process areas. They include illegal search and seizure; compulsory self-incrimination *not* involving confessions;[44] unavailability of defense counsel;[45] use of perjured testimony;[46] withholding of exculpatory evidence;[47] prejudicial publicity;[48] nonconfrontation by adverse witnesses;[49] lack of comprehensible definition of forbidden conduct;[50] failure to give adequate notice of the nature and cause of accusation;[51] refusal of speedy trial;[52] conviction without evidence of guilt;[53] and denial of trial by jury.[54] In criminal law administration, as in the field of freedom of expression, 1937 did not bring judicial abdication; rather it inaugurated a period of rapid growth toward the full assumption of responsibility that came in 1961 and thereafter.

The impact on the state criminal process was more drastic than on the Federal, because the wider leeway previously accorded to the state governments had led to greater abuses by them. The Court eventually raised state standards virtually to the level prescribed for the Federal Government by the Bill of Rights and the Court's glosses upon it. But Federal standards were themselves tightened in significant respects*For example, the jurisdiction of courts martial was curtailed in favor of resort to civilian courts, in which a defendant enjoys protections (such as trial by jury) that are unavailable in military tribunals.[55] All this did not happen overnight, however; the beginnings were relatively modest in scope.

The effect of World War II upon the Court's thinking was perceptible. In 1942, *Skinner v. Oklahoma*[56] displayed a sensitivity not evident in *Buck v. Bell* (1927)[57] and devised a new, strict, equal protection test to invalidate a state statute authorizing sterilization of certain habitual criminals. Justice Douglas, for the Court, declared:

> We are here dealing with legislation which involves one of the basic civil rights of man. Marriage and procreation are fundamental to the very existence and survival of the race. The power to sterilize, if exercised, may have subtle, far-reaching and devastating effects. In evil or reckless hands it can cause races or types which are inimical to the dominant group to wither and disappear.[58]

---

* Also, a few of the stricter Federal standards have been relaxed. In Warden v. Hayden, 387 U.S. 294 (1967), the Court abandoned the rule that searches could only be made to seize instrumentalities or fruits of crime, not to seize mere evidence of crime. In Terry v. Ohio, 392 U.S. 1 (1968), limited search of the person (stop and frisk) was held permissible on the basis of reasonable suspicion not amounting to "probable cause" which had theretofore been a condition of valid search. In Williams v. Florida, 399 U.S. 78 (1970), six-man criminal juries were held permissible. In Apodaca v. Oregon, 406 U.S. 404 (1972), nonunanimous juries were held permissible in state but not Federal prosecutions.

In *Adamson v. California* (1947) [59] four members of the Court were ready to hold that the Fourteenth Amendment incorporates, and thereby makes applicable to the states, the whole panoply of severe Bill of Rights restrictions that were devised to prevent tyranny on the part of the Federal Government. And in *Wolf v. Colorado* (1949) [60] the Court declared, through Justice Frankfurter, that

> security of one's privacy against arbitrary intrusion by the police — which is at the core of the Fourth Amendment — is basic to a free society. It is therefore implicit in "the concept of ordered liberty" and as such enforceable against the States through the Due Process Clause [of the Fourteenth Amendment].[61]

But the *Skinner* case involved only a peripheral innovation upon the criminal process; the *Adamson* majority rejected the incorporation proposal; and the *Wolf* case held that the Fourteenth Amendment does not require exclusion of evidence obtained in an illegal search, which is the only remedy the Court can easily apply. It was not yet ready for broad intervention.

The precise time when broad intervention in the criminal process did begin is hard to pinpoint because it came piecemeal, without announcement of a general change in approach such as would have resulted from across-the-board incorporation of the Bill of Rights into the Fourteenth Amendment. Doubtless some of the Justices became convinced sooner than others that criminal law administration was basically defective and in need of overhaul. In retrospect, however, *Mapp v. Ohio* (1961) [62] — even though it dealt only with illegal search and seizure, and built on *Wolf v. Colorado* — is seen as the likely turning point.

Between 1937 and 1961 the Court's constitutional rulings in criminal cases had rarely touched law enforcement and trial practices that were generally permitted by state law and were in widespread use. Except for reversals on account of involuntary confessions or racial discrimination in jury selection, and a series of decisions limiting the jurisdiction of courts martial, the Court refrained from attempting far-ranging reform. When it did set aside a conviction on constitutional grounds, it was typically because of some off-type practice or specialized rule, or because of circumstances peculiar to the case. In several instances denial of appointed counsel was held to be prejudicial because a *capital* offense was charged [63] or because the defendant was young, mentally retarded, or otherwise in unusual need of legal representation.[64] A statutory presumption was held irrational and therefore unconstitutional in *Tot v. United States* (1943).[65] New trials were granted in two cases because prosecutors had knowingly introduced or tolerated perjured testimony.[66] *Cole v. Arkansas* (1948) [67] held that it is a denial of due process for an appellate court to affirm a conviction on a charge different from the one passed upon by the trial court. *In re Oliver* (1948) [68] upset a contempt conviction pronounced in a closed hearing by a state judge sitting as a one-man grand jury. *Rochin v. California* (1952) [69] held that morphine capsules pumped from a defendant's stomach could not be used in evidence against him, the barbarity of the procedure being deemed a violation of due process. *In re Murchison* (1955) [70] reversed contempt convictions by a judge acting as one-man grand jury even though the hearing was public, because the tribunal was held not to be impartial. *Lambert v. California* (1957) [71] held invalid, for lack of adequate notice to defendants, a city ordinance requiring anyone who had been convicted of a felony to register with the police chief. *Irvin v. Dowd* (1959) [72] had somewhat greater potential for affecting a widespread practice, namely, "trial by newspaper"; in that case the Court held for the first time that undue publicity (the defendant's confession to six murders had been widely reported in the press) violates due process if it is likely to be prejudicial. *Thompson v. Louisville* (1960) [73] held that a conviction cannot stand if there is absolutely no evidence of criminal conduct.* And, early in 1961, *Ferguson v. Georgia* [74] held invalid the unique Georgia rule forbidding a defendant to give *sworn* testimony in his own behalf.

---

* The second Justice Harlan, concurring in Garner v. Louisiana, 368 U.S. 157, 190 (1961), said the *Thompson* case involved a situation which was "unique in the annals of the Court." But the case stands for a broad, basic principle and has frequently been cited for that principle in cases quite dissimilar on the facts. *See, e.g.,* Garner v. Louisiana, 368 U.S. 157 (1961); Gregory v. Chicago, 394 U.S. 111 (1969).

It was in *Mapp v. Ohio,* however, that the Court first struck down a common practice which, unlike involuntary confessions and racially discriminatory jury selection, had been deemed entirely legal in a great majority of the states. Twelve years earlier the Court had held in *Wolf v. Colorado* that illegally seized evidence (which typically has very high probative value) can constitutionally be introduced in state prosecutions. Now the Court repudiated that precedent. Moreover, it reached out for the opportunity to do so, departing from its usual practice of considering only contentions made by the parties; the argument that the *Wolf* case should be overruled was made only by the American Civil Liberties Union, as *amicus curiae,* not by Mrs. Mapp.[75]

Justice Clark wrote for the Court. He said that the states must adopt the exclusionary rule because it is the only practicable way to discourage the illegal police practices that the *Wolf* case had condemned.[76] In other words, the Court was asserting power to control the police, not merely to prevent conviction of the innocent. It was overriding the state's determination that conviction of the guilty is more important than discouraging illegal searches. And, as has already been noted, the new constitutional rule was of its own making.[77]

The new eagerness to speak out, and the new boldness to halt widely accepted practices, led to the forging of a series of further protections for the suspected and the accused. The cumulative effect has been a revolutionary change in the criminal process. We do not recount the well-known story in full detail, but a few milestones should be mentioned.

*Gideon v. Wainwright* (1963)[78] is noteworthy in two respects. First, it held that an indigent has a constitutional right to appointed counsel not only in Federal prosecutions, as required by the Sixth Amendment, but also in any state prosecution for serious crime — whether or not the offense is capital and whether or not the defendant shows unusual lack of capacity to defend himself. Second, it inaugurated the process of *selective* "incorporation"; Justice Black declared that those Bill of Rights provisions which are "fundamental and essential to a fair trial" [79] apply to the states just as if they had been written *verbatim* into the Fourteenth Amendment. Inasmuch as selective incorporation has been a primary vehicle for enlarging the Court's control over state prosecutions, and because it is a paradigm case of constitutional rulemaking by the Court, it deserves a word of comment.

When Justice Black had urged *full* incorporation upon the Court in the 1947 *Adamson* case,[80] his contention was that the makers of the Fourteenth Amendment intended it to subject the states to the whole Bill of Rights. In support of that thesis he adduced quotations from the Congressional debates. The weight of scholarly opinion is that, as a matter of probable historical fact, Justice Black was mistaken.[81] But unless the Justice himself *knew* he was mistaken, his proposal of full incorporation must be regarded as an effort to effectuate the original intention and not to make new law. The Court has never accepted his view, however — probably because of the difficulty of believing that the makers of the Fourteenth Amendment intended to saddle the states with the requirement of a grand jury for prosecution of infamous crime (Fifth Amendment) * and a civil trial jury for common law actions involving more than twenty dollars (Seventh Amendment).** Instead, it has embraced Justice Black's alternative contention that *some* Bill of Rights provisions, selected because they are "fundamental and essential to a fair trial," are incorporated.[82]

Incidentally, the idea *was* first approved by Justice Black,***

---

* The Fifth Amendment provides in part:

No person shall be held to answer for a capital, or otherwise infamous crime, unless on a presentment or indictment of a Grand Jury, except in cases arising in the land or naval forces, or in the Militia, when in actual service in time of War or public danger....

** The Seventh Amendment provides in part:

In Suits at common law, where the value in controversy shall exceed twenty dollars, the right of trial by jury shall be preserved....

*** As noted *supra*, pp. 105-06, Justice Cardozo used language in his 1937 *Palko* opinion which superficially seems to suggest that he regarded the First Amendment, but not the Fifth, to be incorporated in the Fourteenth. Other portions

although — using a carefully trimmed quotation from Justice Roberts' opinion for the Court in *Betts v. Brady* (1942) [83] — he modestly attributed the idea to that source and professed to add nothing but the proposition that the Sixth Amendment right to counsel *is* "fundamental and essential." The *Betts* opinion in fact had expressly rejected the notion that the Bill of Rights had any bearing at all on the right to counsel in state prosecutions and had insisted that the only question was whether the Fourteenth Amendment due process prohibition against fundamental injustice had been satisfied in the particular case.

On its face, selective incorporation involves constitutional rulemaking by the Court. There is no conceivable historical basis for believing that the Fourteenth Amendment was intended to incorporate *part* of the Bill of Rights. When the Court declares that one or another of the Bill of Rights provisions is "fundamental" and therefore incorporated, it draws only upon its own sense of what the Fourteenth Amendment *ought* to say. Justice Black, who (as already noted [84]) deplored such exercise of discretionary judicial power, had a personal defense against the charge that he himself approved it in the *Gideon* case and its successors. He persisted in maintaining that full incorporation is the only correct position and that he accepted selective incorporation solely as the closest approach to it that the intransigence of his colleagues permitted.[85] But the intransigent colleagues had no such defense, and indeed offered none. For them, the practical utility of selective incorporation was evidently a sufficient reason to approve it.

The practical utility is undeniable. On the one hand, the states can be left untouched by the grand jury and civil jury provisions. On the other, there is great economy of judicial effort. Case-by-case inquiry as to whether the particular record reveals fundamental injustice in punishing the particular defendant is an exhausting business. The Fourth, Fifth, Sixth, and Eighth Amendments focus the issues more narrowly by their more specific language. Furthermore, each of their clauses has been sharpened by interpretation in numberless Federal prosecutions, and the gloss

---

of the opinion show, however, that he would not have accepted incorporation in the literal sense approved by *Gideon v. Wainwright* and later incorporation cases.

thus accumulated is made immediately applicable to state prosecutions by the single pronouncement that the provision is "fundamental."

This availability of accumulated case law also results in a corresponding economy of effort on the part of defense counsel and thus facilitates constitutional defenses in the general run of criminal cases. Indigent defendants in such cases (which is to say, most persons accused of serious crime) are represented by lawyers serving pursuant to judicial appointment or as employees of a legal service organization. Incorporation enables these hard-pressed lawyers to cite controlling precedents; they need not start from scratch, approaching the elusive issue of fundamental injustice as an original proposition in each case.*

One by one, virtually all of the criminal safeguards contained in the Bill of Rights, save only the grand jury provision, have been "selectively" incorporated. *Ker v. California* (1963) [86] completed the job for illegal search and seizure. *Malloy v. Hogan* (1964) [87] did it for the privilege against self-incrimination, which has proved to be the most sweeping single incursion upon existing state practice. *Pointer v. Texas* (1965) [88] incorporated the right to confrontation by adverse witnesses. That same year the prospectivity doctrine made its appearance in *Linkletter v. Walker* (1965),[89] and (as already noted [90]) it liberated the Court to remold the criminal process still more freely. Then came *Klopfer v. North Carolina* (1967) (speedy trial) [91] and *Washington v. Texas* (1967) (compulsory process for witnesses).[92] *Duncan v. Louisiana* (1968) [93] incorporated the right to jury trial in criminal cases and declared *(nunc pro tunc,* actually) that the right to a public trial had already

---

*For example, in Thompson v. Louisville, 362 U.S. 199 (1960), my associate Marvin H. Morse and I spent more than 850 hours of professional time on the task of establishing that our client had been denied fundamental justice by being fined in the Louisville, Kentucky, Police Court without any evidence of wrongdoing on his part. Additional time was spent by our associate counsel in Washington, D.C., Harold Leventhal and Eugene Gressman. Had we been able to rest our contentions on precedent, rather than on painstaking analysis of the record, the case could have been handled in a small fraction of the time actually spent — if, indeed, appellate proceedings would have been needed at all.

PROTECTION OF THE SUSPECT AND THE ACCUSED   165

been incorporated by *In re Oliver* (1948).[94] *Benton v. Maryland* (1969)[95] brought in double jeopardy, overruling *Palko v. Connecticut* (1937). Cruel and unusual punishment was first explicitly declared incorporated in *Furman v. Georgia* (1972),[96] but earlier cases had evidently assumed such incorporation to have taken place.[97]

The effect of incorporation has thus been to bring the states up to Federal standards. But the Court went much further; it imposed new requirements raising state and Federal standards alike, through expansive interpretation of the Bill of Rights provisions. Again, only the main developments need be mentioned. *Massiah v. United States* (1964)[98] extended the right to counsel to all post-indictment interrogation, whether or not coercive. *Miranda v. Arizona* (1966)[99] strengthened the privilege against self-incrimination by prescribing extreme restrictions on *custodial* interrogation. *In re Gault* (1967)[100] declared a number of the Bill of Rights safeguards to be applicable in juvenile delinquency proceedings. *United States v. Wade* (1967)[101] and *Gilbert v. California* (1967)[102] held that the right to counsel applies to identification line-ups, a most drastic departure from existing practice; and *Katz v. United States* (1967)[103] — though it softened the still stricter view taken a few months before in *Berger v. New York* (1967)[104] — held that electronic eavesdropping is a "search" within the meaning of the Fourth Amendment. *Alderman v. United States* (1969)[105] put more iron into the restrictions on electronic surveillance by holding that records of eavesdropped conversations must be shown to defense counsel on request, it being insufficient for the trial judge to review them to see whether they might have affected the trial. *O'Callahan v. Parker* (1969)[106] ended court martial jurisdiction over non-service-connected crimes (in that case housebreaking, assault and attempted rape) not committed on a military base or in a combat zone. *Chimel v. California* (1969)[107] greatly narrowed the permissible scope of warrantless search incident to arrest. *Argersinger v. Hamlin* (1972)[108] held that the right to counsel exists with respect to *all* prosecutions that may lead to a jail sentence. *Peters v. Kiff* (1972)[109] stiffened the rule against discrimination in jury selection by holding that a white defendant has standing to complain of the exclusion of Negroes. And *Furman v. Georgia* (1972) [110] held that the death penalty, as imposed under then existing laws, was a cruel and unusual punishment.

This brief summary should be sufficient to show how fully the Court has brought the criminal process within its control. We now turn to a third major field of post-1937 expansion of judicial power, separation of church and state.

CHAPTER XI
## Church-State Separation

A funny thing happened to the First Amendment at the hands of the Supreme Forum. The Court rewrote the first two clauses of the Amendment, which deal with religion:

> Congress shall make no law respecting an establishment of religion, or prohibiting the free exercise thereof....

Nowadays the Court reads these two clauses, which are called the Establishment Clause and the Free Exercise Clause, as if they were designed to cover two sides of the same problem. The function of the Establishment Clause, it says, is to prevent government from *cooperating* with religion too much (and *vice versa*); the function of the Free Exercise Clause, the Court says, is to prevent government from *interfering* with religion too much. Taken together, they are held to require secularization of government on the one hand and, on the other hand, autonomy of individuals and churches on religious matters. In our society, where government provides many essential services to persons and property as such and where religious groups take great interest in the ethical quality of official behavior, there is continuing tension between the two Clauses. Sometimes, indeed, it has almost seemed that anything not forbidden by one is required by the other, and that — but for the Court's benign mediation — the same act or omission might be forbidden by one *and* required by the other. One of many possible examples is the employment of chaplains to minister to the spiritual needs of soldiers and prisoners: Employment of chaplains is governmental cooperation with religion; failure to employ them interferes with religious activity of individuals because the Government prevents them from seeking out ministers of their own choice. The Court has come to conceive of its task as the working out of a fair accommodation between the two opposing principles.

Such a conception of the Court's role cannot be faulted on pragmatic policy grounds. It reflects the deep-seated national commitments to secular government and religious toleration, and assigns to the Court a job which elected legislatures are less competent to perform because of the refractory nature of religious controversy: Theological positions, being grounded in intuitive faith rather than demonstrable social need, are not susceptible of adjustment through the process of compromise which is the hallmark of enlightened legislation. No legislature can work out a position halfway between transubstantiation and consubstantiation (the controversy about which has spilled oceans of blood), or between Sabbatarianism and Sunday observance. The Court, however, drawing on the common reverence for the Constitution whose keeper it is, can evolve lines of accommodation which command general (if sometimes grumbling) acquiescence. That is what the Court has been doing, particularly since 1947.[1]

What is not generally recognized is that this conception of the two Clauses is largely an invention of the Justices and departs radically from the Constitutors' original intent. The Constitutors intended the Free Exercise Clause as a prohibition against official persecution of religious dissenters (which had brought many of their forebears to the New World in and after 1620). At the Court's hands it has become an instrument not only for preventing discrimination motivated by religious prejudice, but also for occasionally requiring discrimination *in favor of* religious dissenters who, by reason of tenets of their faith (such as Saturday observance), are affected with particular harshness by nondiscriminatory, neutrally motivated, legislation.[2]

As for the Establishment Clause, the Constitutors of 1791 (when the First Amendment became effective) were by no means revolted by the thought of an established state church. In 1791 ten of the thirteen states (all except Connecticut, Georgia, and Rhode Island) recognized established religions [3] and the question of establishment *vel non* was considered to be for the respective state legislatures to decide. The last of the state churches (in Massachusetts) was not disestablished until 1833.[4]

Nor is there any reason to believe that the Constitutors of the Fourteenth Amendment, which became effective in 1868, intended to affect state power with respect to religion. There is room for controversy as to whether they meant to go beyond removal of the detritus of slavery and on to the protection of free business enterprise, but there is not the least indication that they were bent on preventing the reappearance of established churches — which had not existed for a generation and showed no signs of resurgence. It will be noted that even the view favoring complete and literal incorporation of the Bill of Rights into the Fourteenth Amendment would not lead to such a result, since the First Amendment literally goes no further than to forbid *Congressional* action.

The Establishment Clause, as its wording suggests, was originally intended merely to preserve state autonomy on the question of establishing churches and to keep Congress from acting on that subject in any way — either in favor of church establishment or against it — just as the Twenty-first Amendment now preserves state autonomy on liquor regulation.[5] On its face, the Clause seems to refer only to *establishment,* a term having a specific and understood meaning: financial support of an officially favored church — often, but not always, accompanied by a requirement of membership in the established church as a condition of voting, officeholding, and other official functions. The Court now reads it as a prohibition against many other types of official assistance to religious institutions.

Justice Brennan, concurring in *Abington School District v. Schempp* (1963),[6] said he was taking note of this situation but actually ignored it:

> It has been suggested, with some support in history, that absorption of the First Amendment's ban against congressional legislation "respecting an establishment of religion" is conceptually impossible because the Framers meant the Establishment Clause also to foreclose any attempt by Congress to disestablish the existing official state churches.... [But] it is clear on the record of history that the last of the formal state establishments was dissolved more than three decades before the Fourteenth Amendment was ratified, and thus the problem of protecting official churches from federal encroachments could hardly have been any concern of those who framed the post-Civil War Amendments.[7]

The kindest comment that can be made on the last sentence is that it is a lame and unconvincing rejoinder.

The present official "interpretation" of the Establishment Clause had its genesis in *Everson v. Board of Education* (1947).[8] The Justices divided five to four on the question whether New Jersey could constitutionally authorize school districts to reimburse parents for the cost of transporting their children to and from Roman Catholic parochial schools. Justice Black, for the majority, upheld the state law on the basis of a newly devised "child benefit theory." The Court made a distinction between use of public money to support religious institutions such as schools, and use of such money for at least certain kinds of financial aid to all students (including students attending such schools). Recently the Court has found itself embarrassed by the child benefit theory, as developed in *Board of Education v. Allen* (1968),[9] and has unceremoniously qualified it insofar as it permits state aid to students in *racially discriminatory* private schools.[10] In 1947, however, the distinction was rejected only by the four dissenting Justices, led by Justices Jackson and Rutledge; and the Court still clings to it in its recently modified form.[11]

Divided though the Justices were on the question of affirming or reversing, all nine of them accepted Justice Black's reinterpretation of the Establishment Clause:

> The "establishment of religion" clause of the First Amendment means at least this: Neither a state nor the Federal Government can set up a church. Neither can pass laws which aid one religion, aid all religions, or prefer one religion over another. Neither can force nor influence a person to go to or to remain away from church against his will or force him to profess a belief or disbelief in any religion. No person can be punished for entertaining or professing religious beliefs or disbeliefs, for church attendance or non-attendance. No tax in any amount, large or small, can be levied to support any religious activities or institutions, whatever they may be called, or whatever form they may adopt to teach or practice religion. Neither a state nor the Federal Government can, openly or secretly, participate in the affairs of any religious organizations or groups or *vice versa*. In the words of Jefferson, the clause against establishment of religion by law

was intended to erect "a wall of separation between church and state." [12]

The application of the Establishment Clause to the states, coupled with the expansive reading of the Clause as applied to the Federal Government, was an exercise in judicial constitution-making — and by the very Justice who in his later years objected to that process more vociferously than any other member of the Court, past or present. Interestingly enough, it was not the first time that he had announced a new constitutional principle by way of dictum in a case where the principle was held to have no application. Only three years before, in *Korematsu v. United States* (1944),[13] he had declared that "all legal restrictions which curtail the civil rights of a single racial group are immediately suspect [and] courts must subject them to the most rigid scrutiny" — *i.e.*, they are presumptively unconstitutional; nevertheless he had gone on to uphold a 1942 military order excluding all persons of Japanese descent (American citizens as well as aliens) from specified areas on the West coast.

The *Everson* dictum was not long in bearing fruit. The next year *McCollum v. Board of Education* (1948) [14] invalidated a so-called released time program in which public school classrooms in Champaign, Illinois, were made available to religious teachers for instruction of those students who wanted such instruction. The program, though nonsectarian, was condemned as a discrimination against the nonreligious, on complaint of an atheist parent. The logic of the opinion indicated that it might have quite broad application, because the released time program offered Roman Catholics an attractive means of satisfying the requirements of their church, at least in substantial measure, without undergoing the expense of sending their children to separate parochial schools. The effect of the case was sharply (and illogically) curtailed, however, four years later. *Zorach v. Clauson* (1952) [15] upheld a released time program which was similar in all respects to the Champaign program except that the religious instruction was provided off the public school premises (though during regular school hours).

As late as 1961, the Court declined to employ the Establishment Clause to strike down a widespread practice which had admittedly originated as an official effort to encourage church attendance — enforcement of the Sunday observance laws, also called blue laws. *McGowan v. Maryland*[16] and *Two Guys from Harrison-Allentown, Inc. v. McGinley*,[17] decided together in 1961, upheld blue laws on the ground that they had come to serve the purely secular purpose of requiring a universal day of rest, a purpose the Court held could not be as well served by laws requiring business establishments to close one day in every week but leaving optional the choice of the day.

Beginning in 1962, however, the Court began to hand down Establishment Clause rulings which did require abandonment of very widespread practices. (It will be recalled that this was the time when the Court also began its attacks on widespread usages in the fields of freedom of expression and criminal process.) *Engel v. Vitale* (1962)[18] invalidated a school district regulation requiring recitation at the beginning of each school day of a one-sentence nonsectarian prayer by those students who were willing to recite it. Though decided by an almost unanimous seven-man Court (Justice Stewart alone dissented, on the ground that recitation of the prayer was voluntary), the case produced a shock of seismic proportions; the movement for nullification of the decision has still not subsided.[19]

The next year, an eight-man majority struck down a practice that had been at least as widespread as prayer recitation — devotional Bible reading in the public schools. *Abington School District v. Schempp* (1963)[20] held unconstitutional a Pennsylvania statute which provided:

> At least ten verses from the Holy Bible shall be read, without comment, at the opening of each public school on each school day. Any child shall be excused from such Bible reading, or attending such Bible reading, upon the written request of his parent or guardian.

By these cases the Court made good its primary authority to decide how much governmental aid to religion is permissible and demonstrated its fearlessness in making decisions which many people, if not most, thought unwise. From that time on, its Establishment Clause rulings have not been tempered by fear of popular disapproval, so far as one can discern. What does seem to have tempered them, however, is a growing realization that Roman Catholics (and others whose churches require or encourage education of the young in a religious setting) suffer a grievous financial burden by reason of their faith. They are required, in effect, to pay twice for the education of their children — once through school taxes that support the public schools and again through tuition payments to the schools their children attend. Equally persuasive, perhaps, has been the fact that they very naturally tend to minimize this hardship by voting to minimize school taxes; and, in districts where they have significant voting power, this practice tends to result in undernourishment of the public school systems.

It has probably been for one or both of these reasons that the Court has backed off from the stern "wall of separation" doctrine of the *Everson* dictum. In *Board of Education v. Allen* (1968),[21] over the dissent of Justice Black and others, it invoked the Black distinction between subsidies to religious school and subsidies to their students, to uphold a New York statute requiring textbooks to be lent without charge to all students in grades seven through twelve, including students in private schools. Since then, a number of cases have pricked out the boundaries of permissible governmental aid to religious schools or their students, most of them being decided by narrow majorities and over bitter dissent — and some of them being reconcilable with each other only on very tenuous grounds.[22]

Not all the Establishment Clause cases have involved the schools. In addition to the blue law cases, there are decisions forbidding the courts to adjudicate questions of church dogma[23] and upholding property tax exemptions for eleemosynary institutions including churches.[24] The bulk of the litigation, however, has dealt with the schools.

Over the quarter-century or so since *Everson v. Board of Education,* the Court has gradually evolved a body of doctrine that accounts for its Establishment Clause decisions (at least, for *nearly* all of them). In *Walz v. Tax Commission* (1970) [25] it repudiated the strict "wall of separation" formulation, Chief Justice Burger saying for the Court:

> In attempting to articulate the scope of the two Religion Clauses, the Court's opinions reflect the limitations inherent in formulating general principles on a case-by-case basis. The considerable internal inconsistency in the opinions of the Court derives from what, in retrospect, may have been too sweeping utterances on aspects of these clauses that seemed clear in relation to the particular cases but have limited meaning as general principles.
>
> The Court has struggled to find a neutral course between the two Religion Clauses, both of which are cast in absolute terms, and either of which, if expanded to a logical extreme, would tend to clash with the other.... The course of constitutional neutrality in this area cannot be an absolutely straight line; rigidity could well defeat the basic purpose of these provisions, which is to insure that no religion be sponsored or favored, none commanded, and none inhibited.... No perfect or absolute separation is really possible.[26]

The Chief Justice went on to spell out a set of constitutionality tests,[27] which he refined somewhat the following year in *Lemon v. Kurtzman* (1971): [28]

> Three such tests may be gleaned from our cases. First, the statute must have a secular legislative purpose; second, its principal or primary effect must be one that neither advances nor inhibits religion, [citing cases]; finally the statute must not foster "an excessive government entanglement with religion." [29]

At this writing, this three-part test reflects the substance of the Establishment Clause as remade by the Court.

We should pause for a moment to consider the third of the three tests, which has not been suggested in the earlier discussion. The entanglement test was first articulated in its present form by Chief Justice Burger, writing for the Court in *Walz v. Tax Commission*

(1970).³⁰ Justice Harlan's concurring opinion in that case expanded upon the policy basis underlying the test and traced its antecedents:

> As Professor [Paul A.] Freund has only recently pointed out, Freund, Public Aid to Parochial Schools, 82 Harv. L. Rev. 1680 (1969), governmental involvement, while neutral, may be so direct or in such degree as to engender a risk of politicizing religion. Thus, as the opinion of THE CHIEF JUSTICE notes, religious groups inevitably represent certain points of view and not infrequently assert them in the political arena, as evidenced by the continuing debate respecting birth control and abortion laws. Yet history cautions that *political fragmentation on sectarian lines must be guarded against.* Although the very fact of neutrality may limit the intensity of involvement, government participation in certain programs, whose very nature is apt to entangle the state in details of administration and planning, may escalate to the point of inviting undue fragmentation. See my concurring opinion in *Board of Education* v. *Allen,* 392 U.S. 236, 249 (1968) and the concurring opinion of Mr. Justice Goldberg in *Abington School Dist.* v. *Schempp, supra,* 374 U.S. at 307.³¹ (Emphasis added)

The second of Justice Harlan's two case citations refers to Justice Goldberg's concurring opinion in the 1963 *Schempp* case, which Harlan joined:

> The practices here involved [devotional Bible reading in the public schools] ... involve the state so significantly and directly in the realm of the sectarian as to give rise to those *very divisive influences* and inhibitions of freedom which both religion clauses of the First Amendment preclude.³² (Emphasis added)

The other case citation refers to Justice Harlan's own concurrence in the 1968 *Allen* case, which quotes the above Goldberg statement.³³

The reason it is worth our while to trace the lineage of the entanglement test is that this test is the only indication to be gleaned from the Court's opinions as to *why it deemed itself authorized* to expand the Establishment Clause far beyond what the Constitutors could have expected. For the reason already noted,³⁴ the desirability of forestalling "political fragmentation on sectarian lines" provides a solid basis for implication of judicial constitution-making power; and such implication is essential if the Court's decisions are to be justified, since (as has been shown) the literal meaning of the Clause does not do it. Moreover, it is somewhat ironic that the Court elected to take its stand on the word "entanglement," rather than the more precisely descriptive word "divisive" that Justices Goldberg and Harlan had used. Use of the fuzzier metaphoric term "entanglement" enhances the danger of descent into mechanical jurisprudence in future cases.

Before leaving the Establishment Clause, we should note the great intensity of the Court's interest in it. The traditional rules of standing made it hard to frame a justiciable "case or controversy" even in cases involving state action,[35] and made it quite impossible to mount a judicial attack on most violations of the Clause by the Federal Government; for, after *Frothingham v. Mellon* (1923),[36] the Court had adhered steadfastly to the view that Federal taxpayers, as such, had too remote an interest in Federal expenditures to afford them standing to challenge their legality. In *Flast v. Cohen* (1968),[37] however, the Court receded from the *Frothingham* rule and held that Federal taxpayers do have standing to litigate an *Establishment Clause* claim. Thus far, the Court has extended this special privilege to no other class of litigants. Let us take a look at this significant decision.

The *Frothingham* case had precluded taxpayer attacks on Federal expenditures except in the rare case [38] where such expenditures comprised an integral part of a regulatory scheme. But the Court found a way to adjudicate the constitutionality of the Primary and Secondary Education Act of 1965, which Flast and other taxpayers had attacked as violating the Establishment Clause because it provided for grants to religious schools. Chief Justice Warren, in his majority opinion, held the *Frothingham* rule inapplicable where Congress has "breached a specific limitation upon its taxing and spending power"; [39] and he characterized the Establishment Clause as such a "specific limitation." [40] That the Clause was intended to prevent Federal religious subsidies is not open to doubt, and it may be a quibble to point out that it contains no "specific" reference to money. The mystifying question is how the *Flast* rule can logically be confined to *specific* limitations. The whole Constitution is rooted in the premise that the Federal Government possesses only the powers delegated to it, and that premise is made explicit in the Tenth Amendment.* Except for the special case of the foreign relations power (which has been held to antedate the Constitution and to result from membership in the family of sovereign nations[41]), a power not granted is officially regarded as a power denied. That was Mrs. Frothingham's contention.

The impelling reason for the *Flast* decision is probably revealed in a footnote to the Warren opinion:

> The logic of the Government's argument would compel it to concede that a taxpayer would lack standing even if Congress engaged in such palpably unconstitutional conduct as providing funds for the construction of churches for particular sects.[42]

The Chief Justice thought it was self-evidently absurd to contend that, if Congress flouted *the Establishment Clause,* the Court should stand by and leave the remedy to the electorate.

We have not yet discussed the decisions under the Free Exercise Clause. If that Clause were properly regarded as a complement to the Establishment Clause, as the Court appears to believe,[43] it would be unpardonable to discuss the one without the other. But such a complementary relationship between the two Clauses comports neither with the intent of the Constitutors nor with what the Court has *done,* as distinguished from what it has *said.* The basic thrust of the Establishment Clause, as now applied, is to forestall conditions likely to breed religious political parties; the primary thrust of the Free Exercise Clause is to require a high degree of official toleration of, and accommodation to, minority religious views. In actual practice the latter has served as a sort

---

\* The Tenth Amendment provides:

The powers not delegated to the United States by the Constitution, nor prohibited by it to the States, are reserved to the States respectively, or to the people.

of super-equal protection clause, mandating discrimination *in favor of* religious minorities under some circumstances. Review of how the Court has used that Clause is therefore better deferred,[44] to be undertaken after we have examined the Court's use of the Equal Protection Clause of the Fourteenth Amendment — our next agenda item.

CHAPTER XII

# Equality: Race — The Post-Reconstruction Heritage

The tightening of constitutional rules against racial discrimination was a bit slower in gathering headway than were the innovations we have described in the fields of speech and press freedom, criminal process, and church-state separation. For about a decade after 1937 the Court did give scattered indications of a new sensitivity to the plight of racial minorities — almost always the black minority — but the decisions involved only limited deviation from precedent.

*Missouri ex rel. Gaines v. Canada* (1938)[1] was the first of several cases to put teeth into the *equality* requirement of the "separate but equal" doctrine. By a seven to two vote, that requirement was held not to be satisfied where Negroes were excluded from the only state law school in Missouri, although the state stood ready to pay their tuition at a law school of any adjacent state (together with transportation expenses). Today this seems a minuscule step, but it contrasted strikingly with the callousness displayed in previous cases.[2]

In a related 1941 development based on the Interstate Commerce Act rather than the Constitution, racial segregation in interstate rail travel was held illegal.[3] In 1944 the Railway Labor Act was interpreted as requiring railroad unions to represent all employees in the bargaining unit, Negro and white, without discrimination.[4] Also in 1944, *Smith v. Allwright,*[5] extending the logic of *United States v. Classic* (1941)[6] which was not a discrimination case, overruled *Grovey v. Townsend* (1935)[7] and held that the Fifteenth Amendment forbids exclusion of nonwhites from party primary elections.

Then came a more sweeping innovation. *Shelley v. Kraemer* (1948)[8] held that the Equal Protection Clause prevents a state court from enforcing, through injunction against a Negro purchaser, a racially restrictive covenant forbidding the use of a house and lot by non-Caucasians. The plaintiffs contended that the Clause, which does not purport to restrict anything but *state* action, was inapplicable because the only discriminatory action had been taken by the *private* property owners who made the covenant — the state court having done no more than enforce the racially neutral state law concerning "covenants running with the land." Chief Justice Vinson, for a unanimous six-man Court, declared that state court effectuation of discriminatory private objectives was as much a denial of equal protection as if the state court itself had initiated the discrimination.

The soundness of the *decision* is not to be gainsaid. Racially restrictive covenants were being used very widely to perpetuate neighborhood segregation, religious as well as racial.[9] Under long-established common law rules, such a covenant can be abrogated only by unanimous consent of the owners of all properties bound by it (thirty in the *Shelley* case), and it endures even after all the original parties have died or transferred their properties.[10] Thus the original discrimination is perpetuated, impervious to changes in racial attitudes. In 1948 no governmental organ except the Court seemed capable of wiping it out; at that time Congress was generally believed powerless to do so.[11] The Chief Justice's opinion, however, referred to none of these considerations. Its rationale was breathtakingly simple: no official aid to private discrimination.

Unless this rule were limited in some way — and the opinion gave not the least hint of any limitation — the logical implications were startling.[12] For example, wills would be unenforceable if, because of racial hostility on a white testator's part, Negroes (or children of the testator who had married Negroes) were given no legacies. Moreover, any court or public official called upon to enforce rights of contract or property would be compelled to entertain the defense that the plaintiff's desire for enforcement was tainted with race prejudice. Of course the *Shelley* rationale was never followed to the full extent of its logic, and *Evans v. Abney* (1970) [13] (discussed in the next chapter) shows that it will not be. But the mere destruction of the racially restrictive covenant (completed five years later in *Barrows v. Jackson* (1953) [14]) cut a not insignificant swath.

In order to explain the Court's difficulty in evolving a satisfactory rationale in the *Shelley* case, it is necessary to recount the sorry tale of the Court's mutilation of the Civil War Amendments during the period 1873-1896. In 1873 the Court virtually nullified one part of the Fourteenth Amendment which could have served as a broad source of Congressional power to prohibit private as well as official discrimination. This was the "Privileges or Immunities Clause" which protects the privileges and immunities of citizens of the United States. Had Congress been held authorized to define personal privileges and immunities which the states had an affirmative duty to protect, it could have erected direct safeguards against various forms of private as well as official discrimination. It might have declared, for example, that it is a privilege of a citizen of the United States to be protected by state law against private discrimination in access to schools, jobs, housing, restaurants, and theaters; and it might have made the privilege meaningful by providing a Federal remedy for any citizen whose privilege was abridged *by the state's failure to provide one.*

It might be thought that the expansive interpretation later given to the Due Process and Equal Protection Clauses has filled the gap left by emasculation of the Privileges or Immunities Clause. This is not true, however, so far as Congressional power to prevent private discrimination is concerned. Though all three of the Clauses run against the states, only the Privileges or Immunities Clause speaks in terms of the rights of individuals rather than the disabilities of states. The Due Process Clause limits state power to deprive persons of life, liberty, or property; but life and liberty are self-defining terms, and property is traditionally defined by state rather than Federal law. The Equal Protection Clause prohibits states from denying the equal protection of the laws; but until 1966 it was thought that equal protection as defined by the courts could not be redefined by Congress, and even the decision that year in *Katzenbach v. Morgan* [15] held only that Congress can expand its definition to cover state action which the Court thought it did not include. Thus, neither Clause provided an obvious basis for a Federal statute requiring affirmative state action against private discrimination.

The Privileges or Immunities Clause, on the other hand, prohibits state abridgment of "privileges" and "immunities" belonging to United States citizens as such, and Congressional power to define those terms comports with their accepted meaning. "Immunity" is easily read to mean *protection from* affirmative action of some kind, and "privilege" is easily read to mean *the right to* affirmative action of some kind (though in legal parlance it is also used to mean protection — for example, the privilege against self-incrimination; privileged communication; executive privilege — in which sense it is a synonym for "immunity"). Congress, whose naturalization power (Article I, Section 8, Clause 4) enables it to specify the terms on which United States citizenship is to be granted, seems the natural repository of power to expand the perquisites of such citizenship.[16]

But, it will be said, the Privileges or Immunities Clause cannot be interpreted to authorize Congressional prohibition of state *inaction* (through creation of a Federal privilege requiring affirmative state action) because the Clause forbids the states only to "make or enforce any law" abridging Federal privileges or immunities. Do not the verbs "make" and "enforce" connote affirmative state action? Or do they? Let us see.

The objection would be formidable indeed if the only verb were "make." That would limit the Clause to prohibition of law newly declared. "Enforce," however, is broader. It extends the prohibition to "any law" already in existence. Whether it is broad enough to authorize Congress to require affirmative state action depends partly on the answers to two preliminary questions: (1) Does the term "law" refer only to particular statutes * or does it refer more generally to the whole network of legal rules

---

* The Contract Clause (Art. I, Sec. 10, Cl. 1) provides: "No State shall ... pass any ... Law impairing the Obligation of Contracts." It is settled that the Clause applies only to state legislative action. Hale, *The Supreme Court and the Contract Clause: III*, 57 HARV. L. REV. 852, 864-66 (1944). It was of course adopted for a purpose wholly different from that which underlay the Fourteenth Amendment.

comprising the state's *corpus juris*? (2) Does the term "abridge" imply that the "law" is forbidden only if it carries out *a purpose of the state* to effectuate private decisions calculated to hamper enjoyment of such a privilege or immunity?

The answers to both questions depend on a further basic inquiry: Did the Constitutors see slavery as a legal institution only, or did they see it as a social institution which, though buttressed by law, rested more broadly on a system of relationships between private persons which was maintained not only by law but also by private practices assigning inferior personal status to the slave? In the former event it would be reasonable — perhaps even necessary — to assume that the Constitutors intended to do no more than invalidate statutes such as the so-called Black Codes, designed to perpetuate the inferior status of blacks,* and not to provide for

---

\* The majority opinion in the Slaughter-House Cases, 83 U.S. (16 Wall.) 36, 70-71 (1873), contained this historical recital (with which the dissenters did not disagree) of the events leading to adoption of the Fourteenth Amendment:

> The process of restoring to their proper relations with the Federal government and with the other States those which had sided with the rebellion, undertaken under the proclamation of President Johnson in 1865, and before the assembling of Congress, developed the fact that, notwithstanding the formal recognition by those States of the abolition of slavery, the condition of the slave race would, without further protection of the Federal government, be almost as bad as it was before. Among the first acts of legislation adopted by several of the States in the legislative bodies which claimed to be in their normal relations with the Federal government, were laws which imposed upon the colored race onerous disabilities and burdens, and curtailed their rights in the pursuit of life, liberty, and property to such an extent that their freedom was of little value, while they had lost the protection which they had received from their former owners from motives both of interest and humanity.
> 
> They were in some States forbidden to appear in the towns in any other character than menial servants. They were required to reside on and cultivate the soil without the right to purchase or own it. They were excluded from many occupations of gain, and were not permitted to give testimony in the courts in any case where a white man was a party. It was said that their lives were at the mercy of bad men, either because the laws for their protection were insufficient or were not enforced. [Note the last four words.]
> 
> These circumstances, whatever of falsehood or misconception may have been mingled with their presentation, forced upon the statesmen who had conducted the Federal government in safety through the crisis of the rebellion, and who supposed that by the thirteenth article of amendment they had secured the result of their labors, the conviction that something more was necessary in the way of constitutional protection to the unfortunate race who had suffered so much. They accordingly passed through Congress the proposition for the fourteenth amendment, and they declined to treat as restored to their full participation in the government of the Union the States which had been in insurrection, until they ratified that article by a formal vote of their legislative bodies.

restraint upon private action. There is reason to doubt, however, that the Constitutors entertained the narrower conception of slavery.

The Court itself has consistently attributed the broader conception to the Constitutors of the *Thirteenth* Amendment, by interpreting it to authorize Congressional prohibition of purely private action subjecting anyone to slavery or peonage.[17] Contemporary Federal legislation such as the Civil Rights Acts of 1866, 1870, and 1871 [18] used the terms "custom" and "usage" as cognate with "constitution," "statute," "regulation," and "ordinance" to describe the types of local action that were not to be allowed to contravene Federal privileges or immunities.* If, as seems likely, the broader conception of slavery was current in 1868 when the Fourteenth Amendment was adopted, and if (as the Court has explicitly declared [19] and never denied) the primary purpose of the Fourteenth Amendment was to shore up the abolition of slavery, it seems to follow that the Amendment was intended (1) to apply to state common law rules as well as statutes, and (2) to provide a basis for Federal attack not only on rules of law that were themselves designed to subjugate blacks, but also on the use of racially neutral laws to effectuate private efforts to that end. In other words, the Fourteenth Amendment was designed to create Federal power commensurate with the national objective that was being declared — the rooting out of slavery in all its aspects.

This line of thought makes it clear enough that the Fourteenth Amendment was intended to authorize Federal remedies against state implementation of private racial discrimination (such as the restrictive covenant involved in *Shelley v. Kraemer*). But what if the state simply adopted a hands-off policy, doing nothing to implement private racial discrimination but also doing nothing to prevent it? More concretely: What if the state adopted a hands-off policy with respect to exclusion of nonwhites from privately owned

---

* Justice Harlan, dissenting in Jones v. Alfred H. Mayer Co., 392 U.S. 409, 454 (1968), argued that the word "custom," as used in the 1866 Civil Rights Act, meant only customary *law, i.e.,* common law. Justice Stewart, speaking for the majority, disagreed. *Id.* at 423-24.

restaurants? A proprietor could post a notice warning nonwhites not to enter his premises. Although he could not call upon the police or the courts to help him remove or exclude them if they did enter or attempt to enter, he could — with the aid of private guards — set up a cordon at his door to screen them out, and have them picked up and deposited outside if they did somehow find their way in. Was the Fourteenth Amendment intended to empower Congress to prohibit such action as abridgment of a Federal privilege?

My opinion is that an affirmative answer must be given if we adhere to the view that the Constitutors saw slavery as an institution ramifying beyond and beneath its attendant legal superstructure. We can never know whether, if the Fourteenth Amendment had not given a clear answer, the Court would have held that the Thirteenth committed the nation to anything more than abolition of the master-slave relationship itself (though the Court did give an affirmative answer, quite unnecessarily, in 1968 [20]). The very fear that the Thirteenth Amendment might be thus limited led to adoption of the Fourteenth two years later, before the question could be settled. What is clear is that the *Fourteenth* was intended to guard against any such limitation on Federal power; it was intended to empower the Federal Government to do away with servile status from whatever source derived. If the terms "make or enforce any law" and "privileges or immunities" are interpreted in the light of that central purpose, the Privileges or Immunities Clause (coupled with the Section 5 Enforcement Clause) can be read — in my opinion, can *only* be reasonably read — as an authorization of Federal legislation to prohibit private racial discrimination if the states did not. The only remaining question would be whether a particular Federal statute was legislation "appropriate" for that purpose, as required by the Enforcement Clause.

The words of the Enforcement Clause demand an interpretation at least as generous as that which *McCulloch v. Maryland* (1819) [21] accorded to the Necessary and Proper Clause of Article I, Section

8. Both clauses require appropriateness but the latter also requires, or seems to require, necessity.* In the *McCulloch* case Chief Justice Marshall had to labor mightily to demonstrate that "necessary" is a synonym for "appropriate" [22] in order to justify his classic pronouncement that the Necessary and Proper Clause gives Congress great latitude in the choice of means to be employed in exercising its delegated powers:

> Let the end be legitimate, let it be within the scope of the constitution, and all means which are appropriate, which are plainly adapted to that end, which are not prohibited, but consist with the letter and spirit of the constitution, are constitutional.[23]

He went on to focus upon the precise problem here being examined:

> No trace is to be found in the constitution of an intention to create a dependence of the government of the Union on those of the States, for the execution of the great powers assigned to it. Its means are adequate to its ends; and on those means alone was it expected to rely for the accomplishment of its ends. *To impose on it the necessity of resorting to means which it cannot control, which another government may furnish or withhold, would render its course precarious, the result of its measures uncertain, and create a dependence on other governments, which might disappoint its most important designs, and is incompatible with the language of the constitution.*[24] (Emphasis added)

Against this background, let us consider further the case of the discriminatory restaurateur and the inactive state. If Congress finds that private racial discrimination interferes with the national objective of rooting out slavery (conceived of as more than a mere *legal* institution), what do the Privileges or Immunities and Enforcement Clauses empower it to do? One conceivable alternative, of course, would be for it to command the states to

---

* The Necessary and Proper Clause provides:

   Section 8. The Congress shall have Power ... [t]o make all Laws which shall be necessary and proper for carrying into Execution the foregoing Powers, and all other Powers vested by this Constitution in the Government of the United States, or in any Department or Officer thereof.

The Fourteenth Amendment Enforcement Clause provides:

   Section 5. The Congress shall have power to enforce, by appropriate legislation, the provisions of this article.

prevent private discrimination, and provide for coercive remedies against any state *government* that failed to comply. But it has long been settled that this dangerous and painful expedient is not the only alternative. Congress can also deal with individuals, avoiding confrontation with state governments by bypassing them. One of the earliest examples of that approach was the provision in the 1789 Judiciary Act for removal of certain cases from the state courts to the Federal — notably cases between citizens of different states.[25] The reason for this so-called "diversity of citizenship" jurisdiction of Federal courts was the fear that state courts would not honor the prohibition contained in Article IV, Section 2, which forbids discrimination by a state against citizens of other states.[26] Rather than address a command to the states, Congress (on the basis of the mere fear that discrimination might occur) simply lifted the case out of the state courts and provided for Federal adjudication of the parties' rights. This is by no means the only precedent for direct Congressional action on individuals as a safeguard against state indifference to Federal rights.[27]

But, it will be said, the removal statute does not go far enough to serve as precedent for a Federal statute reaching purely private racial discrimination. The discrimination feared by the First Congress in 1789 was official discrimination by an arm of state government. Now we reach the nub of the matter and perceive the significance of interpreting the term "any law" in the Privileges or Immunities Clause to mean the whole *corpus juris* of the state. A restaurant does not operate in a social vacuum. It is unthinkable that a state would decline to intervene against private physical violence within its territory. Perhaps the states are constitutionally privileged to do so (though even that is doubtful [28]), but no state ever has and no state is likely to. Even in the field of labor relations, where contests of economic strength are allowed to proceed unchecked, the states retain power to control physical violence.[29] And the use of private guards and bouncers to keep blacks out of restaurants would involve simple battery at a minimum, with race riots a distinct possibility. Therefore, so long as the state law provides for intervention against battery and riots, a hands-off policy with respect to racial discrimination in private restaurants would inevitably lead to state intervention. The need to keep the peace has long since overridden the *code duello* and the once familiar blood feud. And when the state intervenes to keep the peace between a determined restaurateur and equally determined would-be customers, it *acts*; by enforcing laws against violence, it throws its weight on the side of whichever adversary occupies the defensive position (here, the restaurateur). If Congress has created a Federal privilege against private racial discrimination in restaurants, the state has — in the words of the Privileges or Immunities Clause — violated its obligation not to "enforce any law which shall abridge the privileges or immunities of citizens of the United States." Unless Congress must blind itself to the probability if not inevitability of this consequence of state indifference to restaurant discrimination, and ignore the certainty of later state action against violence, the logic of the removal statute (which, it will be recalled, was also based on *fear* of discrimination) justifies a statute directly prohibiting private racial discrimination in restaurants — at least if the state does not effectively prevent it.

In the *Slaughter-House Cases* (1873),[30] however, the Court held that Federal (as distinct from state) citizenship is attended by a narrow set of relatively unimportant privileges and immunities that Congress lacks power to expand by statute. It is clear from Justice Miller's majority opinion that the decision resulted from the Court's fear of that very power, which it thought Congress might use to destroy the federal character of our system:

> Was it the purpose of the fourteenth amendment, by the simple declaration that no State should make or enforce any law which shall abridge the privileges and immunities of *citizens of the United States*, to transfer the security and protection of all the civil rights which we have mentioned ["protection by the government, with the right to acquire and possess property of every kind, and to pursue and obtain happiness and safety, subject, nevertheless, to such restraints as the government may provide for the general good of the whole"], from the States to the Federal government? And where it is declared that Congress shall have the power to enforce that article, was it intended to bring within the power

of Congress the entire domain of civil rights heretofore belonging exclusively to the States?

. . . .

The adoption of the first eleven amendments to the Constitution so soon after the original instrument was accepted, shows a prevailing sense of danger at that time from the Federal power. And it cannot be denied that such a jealousy continued to exist with many patriotic men until the breaking out of the late civil war. It was then discovered that the true danger to the perpetuity of the Union was in the capacity of the State organizations to combine and concentrate all the powers of the State, and of contiguous States, for a determined resistance to the General Government.

Unquestionably this has given great force to the argument, and added largely to the number of those who believe in the necessity of a strong National government.

But, however pervading this sentiment, and however it may have contributed to the adoption of the amendments we have been considering, we do not see in those amendments any purpose to destroy the main features of the general system.[31] (Miller's emphasis)

Because the *Slaughter-House* decision has dominated all subsequent adjudication in the field of racial discrimination, and because there is still a faint possibility that the Court may be induced to reconsider it, close examination of that case and its immediate progeny is justified. For it was the crippling interpretation placed on the Privileges or Immunities Clause which led ineluctably to the better-known decision in the *Civil Rights Cases* (1883).[32] There the Court held that, because the Fourteenth Amendment restricts only state action, it gives Congress no power to forbid private discrimination. The *Slaughter-House* interpretation was thus responsible for denying Congress plenary power to legislate against private practices founded in racial stereotypes [33] that had survived from the time of slavery. That disability lay at the root of the trouble the Court had in explaining the *Shelley* decision in 1948. It is troublesome today, although the Court has mitigated it somewhat since 1966.[34] And so it will remain, as long as the *Slaughter-House* interpretation stands unrepudiated.* A careful look at this watershed case is indispensable to full comprehension of the Federal Government's slowness to intervene against private discrimination.**

In 1869 the Louisiana legislature had enacted a statute giving to a certain corporation a monopoly on the operation of slaughter houses in three parishes, including New Orleans. A number of butchers, being thus forbidden to continue their businesses as independent enterprises, attacked the statute as violating the Thirteenth and Fourteenth Amendments. The Supreme Court rejected these contentions, affirming the judgment of the Supreme Court of Louisiana which upheld the statute.

What concerns us here is not the decision itself but the rationale of Justice Miller's opinion, insofar as it interprets the Privileges or Immunities Clause of the Fourteenth Amendment, which, after providing that all persons born or naturalized in the United States and subject to its jurisdiction are its citizens, goes on to provide: "No State shall make or enforce any law which shall abridge the privileges or immunities of citizens of the United States." [35] The complaining butchers claimed that the right to pursue a lawful common calling is a privilege inherent in citizenship and that, being citizens of the United States, they enjoyed immunity from abridgment of that privilege. Their case was the first that required

---

* The decision in Jones v. Alfred H. Mayer Co., 392 U.S. 409 (1968), interpreting the 1866 Civil Rights Act as prohibiting private discrimination in the sale of realty and upholding the statute under the Thirteenth Amendment on the theory that anti-Negro discrimination in housing is a "badge of slavery," was thought by some to presage general use of that Amendment — which is not limited by the state action doctrine — to sustain Federal statutes prohibiting private racial discrimination. The later decision in Griffin v. Breckenridge, 403 U.S. 88 (1971), interpreting the 1871 Civil Rights Act (the Ku Klux Act) as prohibiting private conspiracies to detain and beat Negroes for the purpose of deterring them from claiming their Federal rights, and upholding it under the Thirteenth Amendment, is a further development in that direction. It is not at all clear, however, that the Court is yet ready to denominate every form of racial discrimination as a badge of slavery prohibitable by Congress. When and if it does, the Congressional power denied by the *Slaughter-House Cases* will have been restored, so far as Negro rights are concerned.

** The analysis of the *Slaughter-House Cases* is adapted from Lusky, *Congressional Amnesty for War Resisters: Policy Considerations and Constitutional Problems,* 25 VAND. L. REV. 525, 545-51 (1972), copyright © by Vanderbilt University School of Law. The passage appears by its permission.

the Supreme Court to interpret and apply the Fourteenth Amendment, and, as one commentator aptly wrote 40 years afterward: "Thus the Supreme Court of the United States began its series of adjudications under the Fourteenth Amendment by substantially repudiating it." [36]

Justice Miller's reasoning rejecting the plaintiffs' claim under the Privileges or Immunities Clause of the Fourteenth Amendment was founded on seven propositions, the second, third, sixth and seventh of which, I submit, do violence to the Constitutors' intent:

(1) Federal citizenship is a status distinct from state citizenship, as the very wording of the first sentence of the Fourteenth Amendment shows.

(2) Each type of citizenship, Federal and state, carries with it a distinct set of privileges and immunities *and the two sets do not overlap*; thus whatever is a privilege or immunity of state citizenship cannot be a privilege or immunity of Federal citizenship.

(3) It is state and not Federal citizenship that carries with it "those privileges and immunities which are *fundamental*; which belong of right to the citizens of all free governments, and which have at all times been enjoyed by citizens of the several States which compose this Union, from the time of their becoming free, independent, and sovereign." *

(4) The privilege of pursuing a common calling is a privilege of *state* citizenship because it is a fundamental right that had existed, subject to the regulatory power of the several states, since before the ratification of the Constitution in 1789 — *i.e.,* from the time when the colonies became free states.

---

* 83 U.S. (16 Wall.) at 76, quoting with approval from Justice Washington's opinion in Corfield v. Coryell, 6 F. Cas. 546, 551 (C.C.E.D. Pa. 1823) (emphasis as in original). The *Corfield* case, interpreting the Privileges and Immunities Clause of Article IV, Section 2, held that the privilege of digging for oysters in New Jersey waters was not a privilege or immunity of citizenship which had to be extended to Pennsylvania citizens, because enjoyment of the state's public domain was not so "fundamental" a right as to be a privilege inherent in citizenship.

(5) The second sentence of the Amendment protects only the privileges and immunities of Federal citizenship.

(6) Therefore, the right to pursue a common calling is not a privilege of Federal citizenship and so is not protected by the Privileges or Immunities Clause of the Fourteenth Amendment.

(7) It follows that the Privileges or Immunities Clause of the Fourteenth Amendment is very restricted in its scope: it protects only those privileges and immunities that "owe their existence to the Federal government, its National character, its Constitution, or its laws," [37] such as the right to go to the seat of government, the right of access to seaports, the right to petition the Federal Government for redress of grievances, the right to freedom of the high seas and protection while in foreign lands, and the right to use navigable streams. The great residue of rights — including nearly all of those that really matter to the common man — are privileges and immunities of state citizenship only, the Fourteenth Amendment not having been intended to alter the basic character of our Federal system by "bring[ing] within the power of Congress the entire domain of civil rights heretofore belonging exclusively to the States." [38]

The notion that there could be no overlap between the perquisites of state and of Federal citizenship was made from the whole cloth, a sheer invention by Justice Miller. Certainly the idea was not implicit in Justice Washington's *Corfield v. Coryell* [39] opinion, which interpreted the Privileges and Immunities Clause of Article IV, Section 2, because that 1823 case was decided long before the Fourteenth Amendment imported into the Constitution, for the first time, the protection of the privileges and immunities of Federal citizenship. To be sure, the duality of citizenship had been expounded by Chief Justice Taney in the *Dred Scott* case [40] but *not* for the purpose of showing that the perquisites appurtenant to the respective citizenships were mutually exclusive; his point, rather, was that one might be a "citizen" within the meaning of the Missouri constitution and laws, and yet not be a "citizen" as that term is used in Article III, Section 2,* and Article IV, Section 2,** of the *Federal* Constitution. Furthermore, as Justice Miller himself recognized, it was universally agreed that the purpose of the first sentence of the Fourteenth Amendment was to repudiate the *Dred Scott* ruling that Negroes, whether slave or free, were not and could not become members of the "political community created by the Constitution of the United States" — *i.e.,* "citizens of the United States." [41]

The Miller interpretation limited almost to zero the power of Congress, under the three Civil War Amendments, to intervene in the relations of a state with its citizens in order to prevent a national interest from being subverted as a result of hostility or indifference on the part of state and local officials. It also denied Congress the power to prohibit private discrimination. It is true that, as Justice Miller pointed out, a drastic shift of power from the states to the Federal Government would have resulted from a decision that the privileges and immunities of Federal citizenship include the "fundamental" rights; he seems to have assumed — quite understandably, and indeed correctly — that the *legislature* (unless forbidden) has power to define and redefine the perquisites of citizenship. As he said, this power would have enabled Congress to assume centralized control of the whole country, if — and it is an important "if" — the voters had been willing to stand for it.[42] Granting *arguendo* that the possibility of such centralization at the date of the *Slaughter-House* decision was as dangerous as Justice Miller believed, there would have been compensating advantages. Had the Court confirmed the Privileges or Immunities Clause as a source of plenary Congressional power to root out the vestiges

---

* "The judicial Power shall extend to all Cases, in Law and Equity, arising under this Constitution, the Laws of the United States, and Treaties made, or which shall be made, under their Authority... to Controversies... between a State and Citizens of another State; — between Citizens of different States, — between Citizens of the same State claiming Lands under Grants of different States, and between a State, or the Citizens thereof, and foreign States, Citizens or Subjects." U.S. CONST. art. III, § 2.

** "The Citizens of each State shall be entitled to all Privileges and Immunities of Citizens in the several States." U.S. CONST. art. IV, § 2.

of slavery, we might now, a century later, be much farther on the road to a nonracial society.*

Therefore, let us examine the soundness of Justice Miller's interpretation. Although it is supported neither by precedent nor by the words of the Constitution, this might not be a ground for criticism if, in the judgment of history, it had served the public welfare. Other such innovations, perhaps including *Marbury v. Madison*[43] itself, have survived that test. For reasons already stated, however, I think it has seriously *disserved* the public welfare by allocating to the Court rather than to Congress the primary responsibility and authority for rooting out the vestiges of slavery. Other unhappy consequences could be cited as well. But let us assume that the Court was justified, in the short view at least, in recoiling from an interpretation that would have aggrandized the power of a Congress which, for corruption and faction, has been unexcelled by any of its forebears or successors. There is still the matter of intellectual honesty.

Incredible as it may seem, Justice Miller's opinion (1) deliberately misquotes the Constitution in a material respect; (2) trims a quotation from *Corfield v. Coryell* in a manner which obscures the fact that, from his viewpoint, it was harmful rather than helpful authority; and (3) denies, erroneously, that Congress had ever undertaken to define the privileges and immunities of Federal citizenship. Let us examine these points in order.

(1) At page 75 of 16 Wallace, Justice Miller declared: "In the Constitution of the United States, which superseded the Articles

---

* Of course, the Court in the *Slaughter-House Cases* conceded that Congress possessed the power, provided by the final section of each of the Amendments, to enforce the three Civil War Amendments by appropriate legislation. But the Court initially construed these Enforcement Clauses with almost unbelievable strictness. Not until a few years ago did the Court begin to permit Congressional use of the Enforcement Clauses to broaden the self-executing coverage of the Amendments. *See* United States v. Guest, 383 U.S. 745 (1966); United States v. Price, 383 U.S. 787 (1966); Katzenbach v. Morgan, 384 U.S. 641 (1966); Cardona v. Power, 384 U.S. 672 (1966); Jones v. Alfred H. Mayer Co., 392 U.S. 409 (1968); Adickes v. S.H. Kress & Co., 398 U.S. 144 (1970); Griffin v. Breckenridge, 403 U.S. 88 (1971). Even now, the Court has by no means made them into a general charter to preempt state jurisdiction of personal status whenever Congress believes the national interest so demands.

of Confederation, the corresponding provision [defining "privileges and immunities" of state citizenship] is found in section two of the fourth article, in the following words: 'The citizens of each State shall be entitled to all the privileges and immunities of citizens *of* the several States.' " [44] This purported quotation, which substitutes the word "of" for "in," is set forth as part of the argument for dual citizenship and against the dissenting view that the makers of the Fourteenth Amendment, who had regarded certain fundamental privileges and immunities as implicit in the status of free citizen *simpliciter*, intended to add Federal protection to those same fundamental privileges and immunities already accorded protection by the several states. It would be reasonable to assume that Justice Miller's pen had merely slipped in this purported quotation from Article IV, Section 2, until one discovered that the error remained uncorrected despite the following observation in Justice Bradley's dissent: "It is pertinent to observe that both the clause of the Constitution referred to, and Justice Washington in his comment on it, speak of the privileges and immunities of citizens *in* a State; not of citizens *of* a State. It is the privileges and immunities of citizens, that is, of citizens as such, that are to be accorded to citizens of other States when they are found in any State; or, as Justice Washington says, 'privileges and immunities which are, in their nature, fundamental; which belong, of right, to the citizens of all free governments.' " [45]

(2) At page 76 of 16 Wallace, Justice Miller quotes from Justice Washington's opinion in *Corfield v. Coryell*:

> "The inquiry is," he [Justice Washington] says, "what are the privileges and immunities of citizens of the several States? We feel no hesitation in confining these expressions to those privileges and immunities which are *fundamental*: which belong of right to the citizens of all free governments, and which have at all times been enjoyed by citizens of the several States which compose this Union, from the time of their becoming free, independent, and sovereign. What these fundamental principles are, it would be more tedious than difficult to enumerate. They may all, however, be comprehended under the following general heads: protection by the government, with the right to acquire and possess

property of every kind, and to pursue and obtain happiness and safety, subject, nevertheless, to such restraints as the government may prescribe for the general good of the whole." [46] (Miller's emphasis)

This quotation appears to be consistent with Justice Miller's conception that state rather than Federal citizenship carries with it the fundamental rights that antedated the Constitution. In his dissent, however, Justice Bradley blasts this notion by the simple process of continuing the enumeration of fundamental privileges and immunities from the *Corfield* opinion at the point where Justice Miller stopped: "*the right of a citizen of one State to pass through, or to reside in, any other State* for purposes of trade, agriculture, professional pursuits, or otherwise . . . ." [47] This right certainly owed its existence to the Federal Constitution rather than to state citizenship; the Court had so held only five years before in *Crandall v. Nevada*.[48] Indeed, Justice Miller brazenly cited and quoted from that very case in another connection.[49]

(3) At page 72 of 16 Wallace, Justice Miller asserted: "The first section of the fourteenth article, to which our attention is more specially invited, opens with a definition of citizenship — not only citizenship of the United States, but citizenship of the States. No such definition was previously found in the Constitution, nor had any attempt been made to define it by act of Congress." [50] This is a remarkable assertion, because the 1866 Civil Rights Act was on its face an attempt by Congress to declare the recently freed slaves to be United States citizens, and to guarantee them certain privileges of United States citizenship.*

---

* The 1866 Civil Rights Act provided in pertinent part: "That all persons born in the United States and not subject to any foreign power, excluding Indians not taxed, are hereby declared to be citizens of the United States; and such citizens, of every race and color, without regard to any previous condition of slavery or involuntary servitude, except as a punishment for crime whereof the party shall have been duly convicted, shall have the same right, in every State and Territory in the United States, to make and enforce contracts, to sue, be parties, and give evidence, to inherit, purchase, lease, sell, hold, and convey real and personal property, and to full and equal benefit of all laws and proceedings for the security of person and property, as is enjoyed by white citizens, and shall be subject to like punishments, pains, and penalties, and to none other, any law, statute, ordinance, regulation, or custom, to the contrary notwithstanding." Act of April 9, 1866, ch. 31, § 1, 14 Stat. 27 (codified in scattered sections of 42 U.S.C.).

Disputes have arisen over the exact purposes that the Fourteenth Amendment was intended to serve. At least one great Justice of the Supreme Court has entertained doubts about whether the framers intended to create substantive due process.[51] Others have doubted whether corporations are "persons" within the meaning of the Amendment's Due Process and Equal Protection Clauses.[52] Moreover, the Court has divided almost evenly on the question whether the Fourteenth Amendment "incorporates" the Bill of Rights.[53] In addition, despite the explicit request of the Court in its order for reargument of *Brown v. Board of Education* (1954),[54] counsel were unable to find conclusive evidence one way or the other on the question whether the 1868 Constitutors regarded racial segregation as a form of racial discrimination. On one point, however, there has been no disagreement at all. The Fourteenth Amendment had its genesis in Congressional doubts whether the Thirteenth Amendment provided a sufficient constitutional basis for the 1866 Civil Rights Act — doubts that had led President Andrew Johnson to veto the bill, which was thereupon enacted over his veto.\* Thus the desire of Congress to legitimate the 1866 Act may be regarded as the "first cause" of the Fourteenth Amendment, which was designed to eliminate any question as to the power of Congress to enact it. Yet only seven years later we see Justice Miller denying that such a statute was ever enacted.

The purpose of revealing the shabbiness of the Court's reasoning in the *Slaughter-House Cases* is not to blacken the memory of Justice Miller and his four assenting brothers. We may assume that their decapitation of the Fourteenth Amendment — by stripping it of nearly all its efficacy as a source of Congressional power — was motivated by the highest patriotism. By 1873 the abolitionist crusade had almost petered out, and the abuses committed in the states of the *quondam* Confederacy by Federal troops and carpetbaggers were a festering national scandal.[55] Full and fair effectuation of the Fourteenth Amendment, initiated by

---

\* The history of the legislation is traced in Charles Fairman's *History of the Supreme Court of the United States: Reconstruction and Reunion, 1864-1888*, Part One (1971), at ch. XX.

radical Republican abolitionists and ratified only under duress,[56] would have meant legitimation of any legal advantages with which a corrupt Congress and a weak President might elect to embellish Federal citizenship — e.g., immunity from state and local taxes or immunity from arrest by state and local peace officers. This was doubtless the reason why the *Slaughter-House Cases*, unlike the three other "self-inflicted wounds" listed by Charles Evans Hughes,[57] provoked no storm of public protest. Yet the enormity of what the Court did in 1873 was publicly acknowledged even by a Richmond, Virginia, lawyer, one William L. Royall, whose struggle to reconcile his satisfaction at the result with his knowledge as a lawyer that violence had been wreaked on the Constitution was expressed in an 1878 article appearing in the *Southern Law Review*.\*

Having been so ill-mannered as to call the *Slaughter-House* ruling an enormity, I must explain why it cannot be supported as a wise exercise of implied judicial power. The short of it is that Justice Miller's "interpretation," by virtually eliminating the

---

\* "The truth is, when this amendment first came before the Supreme Court for construction, the minds of patriotic men were filled with alarm at the centralizing tendency of the government. The president of the United States was holding a half-dozen states under the armed heel of military despotism; the Congress of the United States was indicating its disposition, strongly and more strongly at each successive session, to encroach upon the reserved rights of the states; and those who wished well to their country looked with sorrowing eyes upon the prospect that the ancient landmarks of the states were to yield before the advancing strides of an imperial despotism. No one can deny that the disposition of the majority of the court to put some construction upon this amendment which would curb the progress of Federal power was a most patriotic one. But was it wise? Can it ever be wise for the court to force a meaning upon the language of the Constitution, to avert a fancied or threatened danger? It is the glory and pride of the institutions of this government that they have successfully withstood every strain to which they have been subjected; and the belief that they are equal to whatever strain may be imposed upon them in the future is the hope and comfort of those who cherish them. Would it not, therefore, have been the part of wisdom, whatever fancied danger might have flowed from giving this amendment a literal construction, to give it that construction, and leave it to the institutions themselves to cure the evils which flowed from it at the ballot-box?" Royall, *The Fourteenth Amendment: The Slaughter-House Cases*, 4 SOUTHERN L. REV. (n.s.) 558, 576-77 (1878). *See also* Borchard, *The Supreme Court and Private Rights*, 47 YALE L.J. 1051, 1063 (1938).

Charles Fairman has attacked the foregoing quotation, but mainly on *ad hominem* grounds. *See* FAIRMAN, *supra* footnote on p. 197, at 1371-73.

power of Congress to define the perquisites of national citizenship, all but foreclosed the possibility of Congressional action and *tentative* judicial review in the field of private racial discrimination. Miller and his four assenting Brothers saw only two alternatives: to restrict the Privileges or Immunities Clause to nearly nothing, or to interpret it as the self-executing source of a full panoply of legal rights (including business freedoms) to be enforced by the Court. The Court split five to four on this choice. No one spoke for a third view, probably for the understandable (if inadequate) reason that neither of the opposing sets of litigants would have been aided by it — namely, that the Clause is only partly self-executing, as a prohibition against affirmative state efforts to frustrate enjoyment of benefits already conferred by the Constitution or Federal statute, *or* predicated on "interpretation of the silence of Congress"; that, in addition, it was intended to *nationalize the regulation of personal status by giving Congress full power to define it and provide for its further protection.* Incidentally, though none of the Justices may have realized it then, this was the *only* interpretation that would give the Federal Government plenary power to regulate *private* conduct; as will be shown presently, that became clear in the *Civil Rights Cases* [58] ten years later.

The *Slaughter-House* decision protected state autonomy to a degree that the 1868 Constitutors could hardly have intended. It rested on the unspoken premise that slavery — institutionalized, complete personal bondage — was the only obstacle to a sound Federal-state relationship, and that once slavery was disestablished, that relationship ought to continue as before 1861. Had this been so, the Thirteenth Amendment would have been enough; but, as we have seen, the Fourteenth was adopted for the very purpose of remedying its possible shortcomings. The Fourteenth Amendment was adopted in the belief (1) that Federal control of personal status would be necessary for a long time if the abolition of slavery was to result in any real benefit to the Negro or in assuaging the Abolitionist sentiment that had made civil war inevitable; (2) that such control would have to be modulated from time to time, to meet current need and forestall legalistic evasions; and (3) that such control would have to cover private as well as state action.* Inasmuch as the two latter considerations both involve the need for broad-ranging Congressional action, the Miller interpretation must be recognized as being plainly contrary to the Constitutors' intention.

We may note parenthetically, however, that the Miller interpretation cannot justly be criticized on a second ground which might seem plausible in light of the subsequent development and proliferation of substantive due process — namely, the criticism that the Court deviated from the usual judicial-legislative relationship by giving *itself* broader powers than Congress over the regulation of personal status. It seems clear that the *Slaughter-House* Court was bent on limiting *Federal* power, Presidential and judicial as well as Congressional, not on limiting only the power of Congress and magnifying its own. The Court's position of self-abnegation, so far as derivation of judicial power from the Fourteenth Amendment is concerned, is revealed by *Munn v. Illinois* (1876),[59] which went very far toward denying the existence of substantive due process. Eight of the nine Justices who sat in the *Slaughter-House Cases* also sat in *Munn v. Illinois*, the only change in the Court's membership being the replacement of Chief Justice Chase (who dissented in the earlier case) by Chief Justice Waite. Five more changes in membership occurred before *Santa Clara County v. Southern Pacific Railroad Co.* (1886)[60] held that

---

* Proof of these three propositions to the satisfaction of legal historians — who have already published a roomful of books and articles on the thinking that underlay the Civil War Amendments (particularly the Fourteenth) — is a subject for a long monograph in itself. Rather than undertake it here, I simply assert that my own study of the available primary and secondary materials convinces me that the propositions are provable. Alfred Avins has collected all or nearly all of the primary materials in *The Reconstruction Amendments Debates: The Legislative History and Contemporary Debates in Congress on the 13th, 14th, and 15th Amendments*, published in 1967 by the Virginia Commission on Constitutional Government at Richmond. Perhaps the major secondary source on the Thirteenth and Fourteenth Amendments (which are the principal objects of attention here) is Part One of Charles Fairman's monumental and painstaking "Reconstruction and Reunion, 1864-1888," published in 1971 (pursuant to the Oliver Wendell Holmes Devise) as Volume VI of the *History of the Supreme Court of the United States*.

corporations are "persons" within the meaning of the Fourteenth Amendment, and *Mugler v. Kansas* (1887)[61] voiced, by way of approving dictum, the first sure indication that the Court was prepared to examine the substantive reasonableness of state legislation under the Amendment's Due Process Clause.

Even though the *Slaughter-House* Court is thus innocent of self-aggrandizement, it cannot be acquitted of defying the plain intention of the Constitutors — expressed only five years before, when the Amendment was adopted; nor can an acquittal be predicated on the doctrine of implied judicial power, since there was little reason to believe that the Court was better qualified than elected officials to deal with the problem of recovery from slavery and civil war. In this regard, the most that can be said is that Congress was perhaps a sorrier mess in 1873 than in 1868; but that is a slim basis for the making of a constitutional rule designed to endure for generations, as this one has in fact done.

The apparent solidity of the *Slaughter-House* interpretation of the Privileges or Immunities Clause, even in the present era of constitutional flux when the life expectancy of a newborn constitutional precedent is shorter than it has ever been, is quite remarkable. It probably results from the fact that during Franklin D. Roosevelt's administration, when the controversy over "government by judiciary" was boiling, Justice Stone led the ultimately victorious "liberal wing" of the Court in opposition to a more expansive interpretation of the Clause.[62] The actual dominant reason for opposition was doubtless Stone's disinclination to activate a new constitutional fountainhead of judicial power, at a time when he and his supporters were doing their best to *de*activate the Due Process Clause as a protection of *laissez faire*.[63] Stone's principal *stated* reason, however, was that invigoration of the Privileges or Immunities Clause, which protects "citizens" rather than "persons," involved uncalled-for discrimination against aliens.[64]

Whatever validity the latter point may have had in 1935 or 1940, it had little significance in 1868 and has even less today. In 1868, when the Fourteenth Amendment was adopted, aliens were not an important minority. A great many aliens had come here, but in a generation or two the melting pot had brought them within the bond of community kinship. The word "citizens" was probably used in the Clause not because of a purpose to exclude aliens from its protection but because the purpose of the Clause and the sentence which precedes it was to overrule the *Dred Scott* decision, a decision about Federal citizenship, and extirpate the untouchability which that decision undertook to legitimate. Today the distinction between official treatment of citizens and aliens has been minimized by a series of recent cases holding that discrimination against aliens is a presumptive violation of the Equal Protection Clause.[65]

By stretching that Clause and the Due Process Clause, the Court has now retrieved a part, but only a part, of the ground lost in 1873. Later on we shall take note of what the Court has itself done in recent years to devise new protections of personal status and how it has encouraged and permitted Congress to do likewise.[66] But the effects of the 1873 tragedy are still felt, and the cost of smothering the first purpose of the Fourteenth Amendment has been heavy.

Suppression of the fact that Congress was intended to have power to say what the privileges and immunities of Federal citizenship consist of — a power which it had undertaken to exercise in the 1866 Civil Rights Act and which the Amendment was designed to confirm beyond any possible doubt — left the healing of the cancer of slavery almost entirely in the hands of the Court. The Privileges or Immunities Clause having been denuded of nearly all significance by the decision that Federal privileges and immunities are a closed category incapable of expansion (and a uselessly narrow one at that), the Due Process and Equal Protection Clauses were left as the effective provisions of the Amendment; and, as already noted, those Clauses provided no obvious basis for prohibiting or limiting private discrimination. For that purpose Federal legislation was needed, and it was the Privileges or Immunities Clause that could and should have served as the source of Congressional power.

EQUALITY: RACE—THE POST-RECONSTRUCTION HERITAGE 203

The decade following the Civil War, when the horror of racial subjugation and its capacity for tearing the nation in two were fresh in memory, and when Congress was therefore politically capable of enacting one civil rights act after another,[67] was a precious moment. But the *Slaughter-House Cases* minimized Congressional action under the Fourteenth Amendment against racial discrimination, both public and private. In 1883 the *Civil Rights Cases*[68] formalized the "state action" doctrine, and thereby excluded Congress entirely from the prevention of racial discrimination by private persons, except insofar as it utilized powers such as the war and commerce powers which had been granted by constitutional provisions other than the Fourteenth Amendment Enforcement Clause (Section 5).

The state action requirement was implicit in the *Slaughter-House* interpretation, and the *Civil Rights Cases* did no more than spell it out in plain words. Granted that the Fourteenth Amendment by its very terms controls the states, not their people, the question remained: What does it prevent the states from doing? Except for the *Slaughter-House* interpretation, it would have prevented them from abridging the privileges or immunities of Federal citizenship as prescribed by the Constitution *or established by Congress*. Congress would have been able to declare that in certain types of transactions (such as property purchases) and relationships (such as employment), Federal citizens possess a privilege against racial discrimination at the hands of private persons as well as public officials and that a state abridges the Federal privilege not only if it enforces its law of contract or property to effectuate private discrimination, but also if it fails to provide effective legal remedies against discrimination accomplished by strictly private means. The Fourteenth Amendment Enforcement Clause would then have enabled Congress to intervene against private discrimination if the states did not; as already shown, this would clearly be "appropriate legislation" to prevent abridgment of the Federal privilege, once Congress had defined it.

Congressional power to define privileges and immunities was thus the fulcrum of its enforcement power; and when the *Slaughter-House* interpretation had shattered that fulcrum, the words of the Amendment did the rest. Private persons are simply incapable of granting or withholding due process of law or of denying the equal protection of the laws. They can break the law, but only government can make, change, and administer it. And so it was a simple matter to hold in the *Civil Rights Cases* that the Fourteenth Amendment gives Congress no power to forbid racial discrimination in "inns, public conveyances on land or water, theatres, and other places of public amusement," as it had undertaken to do in the 1875 Civil Rights Act.[69] The Enforcement Clause does not help. As Justice Bradley observed for the Court, that Clause empowers Congress to enforce the substantive prohibitions found elsewhere in the Amendment,[70] but *not* to take over the state's job of regulating private conduct. For, as Justice Bradley quite correctly added: "The wrongful act of an individual, unsupported by ... [state] authority, is simply a private wrong, or a crime of that individual"[71] for which the Fourteenth Amendment may require the state to provide a remedy. It is for the state, however, to decide what private acts *are* wrongful. When the state's law of trespass forbids Negroes to enter a restaurant whose proprietor says they are not wanted or invited, or when its law of restrictive covenants forbids Negroes to purchase and occupy real property because property owners have agreed to exclude them, all the state has done is to decide that the discriminatory private conduct is not wrongful.[72]

As I have said, the *Slaughter-House* interpretation automatically gave state action the central significance which the *Civil Rights Cases* accorded to it. It was a matter of mere textual exegesis to hold that the Amendment gives Congress no power to forbid racial discrimination in privately owned places of public amusement and accommodation.

Justice Bradley, for the Court, began the exegesis by quoting the crucial second sentence of the Amendment:

No State shall make or enforce any law which shall abridge the privileges or immunities of citizens of the United States;

nor shall any State deprive any person of life, liberty, or property without due process of law; nor deny to any person within its jurisdiction the equal protection of the laws.[73]

He went on to explore the meaning of the words:

It is state action of a particular character that is prohibited. Individual invasion of individual rights is not the subject-matter of the amendment. It has a deeper and broader scope. It nullifies and makes void all State legislation, and State action of every kind, which impairs the privileges and immunities of citizens of the United States, or which injures them in life, liberty or property without due process of law, or which denies to any of them the equal protection of the laws. It not only does this, but, in order that the national will, thus declared, may not be a mere *brutum fulmen,* the last section of the amendment invests Congress with power to enforce it by appropriate legislation. To enforce what? To enforce the prohibition. To adopt appropriate legislation for correcting the effects of such prohibited State laws and State acts, and thus to render them effectually null, void, and innocuous.[74]

The exegesis proceeded:

[C]ivil rights, such as are guaranteed by the Constitution against State aggression, cannot be impaired by the wrongful acts of individuals, unsupported by State authority in the shape of laws, customs, or judicial or executive proceedings. The wrongful act of an individual, unsupported by any such authority, is simply a private wrong, or a crime of that individual; an invasion of the rights of the injured party, it is true, whether they affect his person, his property, or his reputation; but if not sanctioned in some way by the State, or not done under State authority, his rights remain in full force, and may presumably be vindicated by resort to the laws of the State for redress. An individual cannot deprive a man of his right to vote, to hold property, to buy and sell, to sue in the courts, or to be a witness or a juror; he may, by force or fraud, interfere with the enjoyment of the right in a particular case; he may commit an assault against the person, or commit murder, or use ruffian violence at the polls, or slander the good name of a fellow citizen; but, unless protected in these wrongful acts by some shield of State law or State authority, he cannot destroy or injure the right; he will only render himself amenable to satisfaction or punishment; and amenable therefor to the laws of the State where the wrongful acts are committed.[75]

Not only did the Court, in the *Civil Rights Cases,* minimize the power of Congress under the Enforcement Clause of the Fourteenth Amendment; in later cases it also interpreted the self-executing Due Process and Equal Protection Clauses quite narrowly so far as their effect on racial discrimination was concerned. It did hold that a state statute which expressly discriminates against nonwhites, such as a statute making them ineligible for service on juries, is a denial of equal protection.[76] It also held that equal protection is denied by discriminatory administration of a law that speaks in impartial terms: the Court set aside the conviction of a Chinese for violating a San Francisco ordinance forbidding operation of a laundry in a wooden building without permission of a city official, because the ordinance had been enforced against hundreds of Chinese laundry operators and virtually no one else.[77] Thus, state action that was plainly predicated on the assumption that a disfavored racial minority was unworthy of equal treatment was condemned. But the Court found no constitutional defect in racial segregation laws, if equal though separate facilities were provided to blacks and whites. In *Plessy v. Ferguson* (1896)[78] it upheld a Louisiana statute requiring "equal but separate accommodations" for white and Negro railway passengers, saying:

> The object of the [Fourteenth] amendment was undoubtedly to enforce the absolute equality of the two races before the law, but in the nature of things it could not have been intended to abolish distinctions based upon color, or to enforce social, as distinguished from political equality, or a commingling of the two races upon terms unsatisfactory to either. Laws permitting, and even requiring, their separation in places where they are liable to be brought into contact do not necessarily imply the inferiority of either race to the other, and have been generally, if not universally, recognized as within the competency of the state legislatures in the exercise of their police power. The most common instance of this is connected with the establishment of separate schools for white and colored children....[79]

The single dissenter, the first Justice Harlan, was more sensitive to the realities. He saw that racial segregation laws are designed to perpetuate a caste system inherited from slavery days. Unlike

EQUALITY: RACE—THE POST-RECONSTRUCTION HERITAGE 207

the Court, he thought that equality of the separate facilities was not enough. In his view, the Constitution not only forbade inequality of treatment but authorized Congress to eradicate the social cleavages which provide a continuing impetus for unequal treatment by government and private persons alike. He declared:

> There is no caste here. Our Constitution is color-blind, and neither knows nor tolerates classes among citizens. . . . Sixty millions of whites are in no danger from the presence here of eight millions of blacks. The destinies of the two races, in this country, are indissolubly linked together, and the interests of both require that the common government of all shall not permit the seeds of race hate to be planted under the sanction of law. What can more certainly arouse race hate, what more certainly create and perpetuate a feeling of distrust between these races, than state enactments, which, in fact, proceed on the ground that colored citizens are so inferior and degraded that they cannot be allowed to sit in public coaches occupied by white citizens? That, as all will admit, is the real meaning of such legislation as was enacted in Louisiana.[80]

It was many years before the Court conceded the soundness of his perception and overruled the *Plessy* case.[81] Meanwhile, racial segregation laws became prevalent throughout the southern and middle states where slavery had persisted until the Civil War, and such laws were not unknown in other states as well. Not only were common carriers and public schools segregated, but also private schools; recreation facilities such as parks, beaches, and golf courses; and places of public accommodation such as hotels and restaurants.[82]

During this period the Court's efforts on behalf of equality were limited to the condemnation of provable official discrimination. It seems to have been oblivious to the fact that official discrimination reflects underlying social attitudes toward estranged minority groups [83] and that if nothing modifies these attitudes, the condemnation of particular official acts resulting from them is no more than a palliative. At the same time, moreover, the Court maintained its own jurisdictional monopoly over equality problems. Thus, on the one hand, it permitted the use of segregation laws to solidify the status of nonwhites as an untouchable caste. On the other hand — under the state action doctrine — it denied the power of Congress to weaken caste barriers by prohibiting private discrimination in education, housing, employment, and public accommodations.

There was one remaining avenue to relief from inequality — political action at the state level. The Fifteenth Amendment prohibited denial of the vote because of race or color; and if Negroes had been able to exercise voting power in proportion to their numbers they might, over a period of time, have been able to cause the state governments to discontinue racial segregation and forbid the more oppressive forms of private discrimination. In several different ways, however, this road to relief was blocked — particularly though not exclusively in the southern states, where the official and private barriers to interracial contact were strongest and where potential Negro voting power was most formidable because Negroes were so numerous. The Supreme Court did invalidate one method that was used to disfranchise the Negro — the establishment of very stiff requirements for voting registration, with so-called "grandfather" clauses exempting from those requirements persons who had been entitled to vote before 1867, *and their descendants*.[84] But other restrictive devices were held constitutional.

One such device was the literacy test. It took many forms, but a typical statute made voting registration conditional upon ability to read and write a section of the state constitution and interpret it to the satisfaction of the local registrar. The tests lent themselves to discriminatory administration by petty voting officials; and though such discrimination was theoretically unconstitutional, the would-be registrant could obtain relief only through a lawsuit that involved too much difficulty, expense, and delay to be a practical remedy. Beyond this, the segregated education system — in which the separate Negro schools were rarely if ever equal in quality to the white schools, despite the nominal equality requirement of *Plessy v. Ferguson* — tended to hold Negro literacy to a low level, so that even a fairly administered literacy test would eliminate much of the voting power that might otherwise have been exerted to end segregation. Nevertheless the Court held literacy tests not to violate the Fifteenth Amendment.[85]

Another device was to make payment of a head tax, commonly known as a "poll tax," a prerequisite to voting. The tax was small, often only a dollar or two, but even that was a deterrent to the very poor; and a disproportionate number of Negroes were in that category. Moreover, the tax was often made cumulative so that the right to vote depended on payment for previous years as well as the current year. The Court held it constitutional.[86]

A third device was the so-called white primary. For more than half a century after Reconstruction the Republican party (the antislavery party of Abraham Lincoln) was virtually powerless in the deep South, and nomination as candidate of the Democratic party was tantamount to election; Republican Herbert Hoover broke into the Democratic "solid South" in the 1928 presidential election, but it remained a reality until the election of Dwight D. Eisenhower in 1952.* In those southern states where candidates were nominated by party primary elections, the only important election was the Democratic primary. In 1927 a Texas statute excluding Negroes from the Democratic primary was held to violate the Equal Protection Clause.[87] A successor statute empowering the party's state executive committee to fix the qualifications of primary voters, and the Democratic committee's subsequent order for a white primary, suffered a like fate five years later.[88] In both cases the "state action" requirement (which had been declared applicable to the Fifteenth as well as the Fourteenth Amendment) was held to be satisfied. At that point the Texas legislature abandoned all control, and still the Democratic party adhered to the white primary. In *Grovey v. Townsend* (1935)[89] the Supreme Court held that there was no constitutional violation because no state action was involved. Thus, the white primary remained an obstacle to Negro political power.

---

* The ebb and flow of party strength is summarized by V. O. Key, Jr., in Chapter 7 ("The Party Battle, 1896-1960") of his *Politics, Parties, and Pressure Groups* (5th ed. 1964). The 1928 and 1952 elections are described at pages 185-86 and 193-95, respectively.

Backstopping the literacy test, the poll tax, and the white primary, was private terrorism. The Ku Klux Klan, which became powerful shortly after the Civil War, sought to maintain white supremacy through lawless (but usually unpunished) violence against Negroes who were politically active or otherwise asserted their equality with whites. Congress responded with an 1870 statute making it a felony for two or more persons to band together to intimidate a citizen with intent to hinder his exercise of a constitutional right,[90] and an 1871 statute penalizing private conspiracies to deprive a person of the equal protection of the laws.[91] The latter provision was carried forward into the broader Civil Rights Act of 1875.[92] The Court, construing the statutes restrictively and invoking the state action requirement, repeatedly set aside convictions under these statutes and virtually denied the power of Congress to interfere with Klan violence.[93]

This brief précis reveals the extent to which inequality remained beyond the reach of the law prior to World War II, even for the black minority which was by far the most deeply submerged of all the many minority groups in the United States. The Supreme Court not only failed to fulfill the promise of the Civil War Amendments, but invoked the Constitution to prevent Congress from doing so. And so long as Negro inequality remained pervasive, legal recourse against the milder discriminations suffered by other disadvantaged groups was not to be expected. Against this background, the more recent developments stand out in high relief.

CHAPTER XIII*

# Equality: Race — the Post-World War II Development

The consequences of governmental indifference to the plight of minority groups became painfully evident during World War II. After the attack on Pearl Harbor had crippled the Pacific fleet and exposed the west coast to the danger of Japanese invasion, the possibility of sabotage by American residents of Japanese ancestry aroused military concern. Although many of them were American citizens, they had long been subjected to extensive discrimination; and at least some disaffection very probably did exist. Indeed, about five thousand of them "refused to swear unqualified allegiance to the United States and to renounce allegiance to the Japanese Emperor, and several thousand evacuees requested repatriation to Japan";[1] at least some of these, however, were doubtless motivated by the hostile treatment they had received in 1942. In that year the military authorities declared that individual loyalty determinations could not be quickly made, and therefore ordered an entire group of 112,000 to be excluded from specified areas in California where they lived and worked.[2] The hardship visited alike upon citizen and alien, upon the loyal and the disloyal, was very great.

In 1944 the Supreme Court held the military orders to be constitutional.[3] There were vigorous dissenting opinions deploring racial discrimination, but six Justices were persuaded that military necessity justified the order. Yet the Court revealed deep concern at the anomaly involved in discrimination against a racial minority at the very time that the nation was waging a great war in the name of liberty and equality. While insisting that military need was paramount, the Court declared that racial classification is subject

---

* Most of this chapter, and portions of Chapter XIV, are adapted from Lusky & Botein, *The Law of Equality in the United States,* in THE CONSTITUTIONAL PROTECTION OF EQUALITY (1975), a comparative law symposium edited by T. Koopmans and published by A. W. Sijthoff, Leiden, copyright © 1975. They appear by permission of the copyright holder.

to "the most rigid scrutiny." [4] There could no longer be any doubt that the continued existence of disaffected minorities was a grave *national* problem and that the dissolution of barriers that held such minorities separate from the rest of society was a legitimate Federal objective. This called for relaxation of the restrictions the Court had placed upon Congressional power, and greater sensitivity to social realities by the Court itself in enforcing constitutional equality requirements.

The first large step in that direction was taken in *Smith v. Allwright* (1944),[5] holding that the white primary is unconstitutional. The first indication of a new determination to overthrow *private* racial barriers came in *Shelley v. Kraemer* (1948),[6] the restrictive covenant case previously discussed.[7] The racially restrictive covenant was a prime candidate for prohibition as a major evil, for reasons already noted. And it is at least arguable that Congress did prohibit it, in a provision of the 1866 Civil Rights Act [8] which has been carried forward into present law as 42 U.S.C. § 1982:

> All citizens of the United States shall have the same right, in every State and Territory, as is enjoyed by white citizens thereof to inherit, purchase, lease, sell, hold, and convey real and personal property.

Whatever one may think of the interpretation given to this statute in *Jones v. Alfred H. Mayer Co.* (1968),[9] where it was held to require an *unwilling* property owner to sell to a Negro, it could reasonably be held to mean not only that ex-slaves were endowed with legal capacity to own property, but that they were granted a substantive right to buy it from a *willing* seller. Indeed, the Court in the *Shelley* case quoted it but, as we have seen, did not decide the issue by saying that it covered the case and that it was "appropriate legislation" within the meaning of the Enforcement Clause of the Fourteenth Amendment.[10] Given the fact that the initial impetus for adoption of the Amendment had come from a desire to ensure the validity of this very statute, it is hard to imagine a statute that would more clearly qualify as "appropriate legislation."

The state action doctrine, however, stood in the way. That is what (1) diverted the Court to the impossibly broad position that state action to implement *any* private racial discrimination in the exercise of property rights violates the Equal Protection Clause; (2) gave rise to similar difficulty in the later sit-in cases,[11] and delayed the enactment of Federal legislation [12] against private discrimination in employment, housing, and public accommodations; and (3) makes it so hard to prevent the present exodus of white children to racially discriminatory private schools.[13] Attention is focused on the extent of affirmative state participation rather than on citizen rights, and there is disingenuous resort to the commerce power which the state action doctrine does not confine.

But we are ahead of our story. The 1948 *Shelley* decision left no doubt that racial discrimination had become one of the Court's prime concerns, justifying heroic measures. There was no longer any room for confident optimism on the Court's part that the melting pot, which had served and was serving so well to bring immigrant groups and religious minorities within the common bond of American kinship, could ever melt the refractory barriers that set apart the large and congenitally visible black minority. Such optimism may have comforted the eight Justices who approved the majority opinion in the *Civil Rights Cases* (1883).[14] There Justice Bradley declared in effect that it was time for Negroes, having been relieved of the unique degradation of slave status, to take their place alongside the many other minority groups:

> When a man has emerged from slavery, and by the aid of beneficent legislation has shaken off the inseparable concomitants of that state, there must be some stage in the progress of his elevation when he takes the rank of a mere citizen, and ceases to be the special favorite of the laws.... [15]

In 1883 the Court may well have hoped and expected that the separateness of Negroes would gradually give way to the universal solvent of common humanity, without further governmental help. By 1948 any such hope and expectation had faded, and the Court showed its readiness to intervene on a broad front. If it was prepared to intervene against private discrimination, so difficult to handle because of the state action requirement, it was *a fortiori* prepared to intervene against official discrimination. Racial equality had won a place, alongside freedom of expression, protection of the accused, and church-state separation, as a major object of its solicitude.

It was in 1954 that the Court launched a full-scale offensive against isolation of the Negro minority, repudiating the "separate but equal" doctrine of *Plessy v. Ferguson* in the field of public education. In *Brown v. Board of Education* and three companion cases, legally required racial segregation in the public schools was held to violate the Equal Protection Clause.[16] Also, on the same day, such segregation in the District of Columbia was held to violate the Fifth Amendment Due Process Clause; the Court declared that the concepts of equal protection and due process stem from "our American ideal of fairness" and that both of them therefore prohibit discrimination which is "not reasonably related to any governmental objective."[17] Both cases rest on the central proposition that inequality can result from segregation even though the separate educational facilities are equal.

This proposition involved a broadening of the previous conception of discrimination. Decisions in 1948 and 1950 had enforced the equality requirement of the "separate but equal" doctrine with a new strictness, but had not held that segregation is itself a form of discrimination.[18] Now the Court found that the separate education of Negro children "generates a feeling of inferiority as to their status in the community that may affect their hearts and minds in a way unlikely ever to be undone."[19] On this basis, the Court concluded: "Separate educational facilities are inherently unequal."[20] Plainly the Court was using the term "unequal" in a new sense. The "inequality" prohibited by the Constitution was no longer thought limited to unequal distribution of governmental burdens and benefits, but was held to include measures perpetuating the social isolation of minority groups. Suddenly the Court was concerned not only with what the state did, but with the "hearts and minds" of black children—which are affected by private as well as official discrimination, though perhaps not as much.

This new conception called for extensive reconsideration of existing constitutional doctrine, including the "state action" restriction on Federal power. The Court did not at once acknowledge the magnitude of the innovation, however. It elected to establish the new dimension of equality gradually, dealing with specific situations case by case. The resulting doubt and confusion, which has not yet fully abated, has led to severe aggravation of racial tensions. Negroes and other racial minorities have been exasperated by the slowness in recognition of their claim to full acceptance into the general community, and recalcitrant whites have been angered by what has appeared to them as endless judicial pursuit of an insatiable egalitarian ideal. Hindsight suggests that it might have been wiser for the Court (a) to acknowledge explicitly that the Civil War Amendments were intended as a mandate for extirpation of racial caste by the Federal Government, not simply as a requirement of official even-handedness; (b) to admit the full extent of its own past responsibility for frustrating that mandate; but (c) to recognize that the social barriers which it had helped to solidify could only be dissolved over a period of time.[21] In that way, racial integration might have been more generally understood as a defined (though not instantly attainable) objective, prescribed by the people through constitutional amendments, rather than as a product of judicial policy still being developed and therefore debatable at every step. But the Court chose a step-by-step development which it doubtless believed would encounter less public resistance. The broad position implicit in the *Brown* opinion has eventually been approximated fairly closely, but it has taken a long time.

The breadth of that opinion was itself something of a departure from the third of Justice Brandeis's seven *Ashwander* principles,[22] because, as already said,[23] the cases could probably have been decided the same way on a narrower ground. But Chief Justice Warren's preference for the broader rationale was not startling. The Court had long been recognized to have legitimate leeway in its choice of grounds, and there was a practical reason to choose the broader one. If, as suggested above, the Court had become convinced that the melting pot was not working for Negroes and could never be expected to work in a community having segregated public schools, and if the Court therefore found it inconceivable that any of the thousands of segregated school districts could pass constitutional muster, then delay in letting the school boards know would result in a great deal of wholly pointless litigation over the equality of this school and that.

Criticism of the *Brown* ruling is less justly directed against the breadth of the Court's opinion than against the Court's failure to follow the opinion with a normally firm mandate. Its boldness on the substantive side was qualified by seeming uncertainty with respect to remedy. The Court, aware that a very extensive reorganization of public education would be required in twenty-two of the fifty states, did not order immediate desegregation. Instead, after a year's wait for presentation and consideration of arguments in favor of delay, the district courts were directed to pass upon desegregation plans submitted by local school boards and to approve plans which provided for desegregation "with all deliberate speed." [24]

This was a radical innovation in judicial method. In adopting the "deliberate speed" formulation, the Court was attempting to bring about the quick disappearance of legally required racial segregation from *all* public school systems. Citing the discretionary power of equity courts to shape remedies so as to reconcile public and private needs, the Court applied that power in an unprecedented way. *It left open the possibility that the particular plaintiffs would be denied any relief whatever* from the legal wrong they were found to have suffered, in order to hasten relief for Negro children generally. (Ten years later, at least one of the school districts involved in the 1954 decision had not desegregated.[25]) Adjudication was subordinated to constitution-making.

Even if the Court's mandate had issued in normal form (reversal and remand to the trial courts for further proceedings consistent with the Warren opinion), there would doubtless have been some weeks of delay in the five school districts while attendance areas and bus routes were revised. There might also have been somewhat longer delay — for months, or possibly a year or two — for supplementary rulings needed to determine how far the local statutes and regulations had been displaced by the Court's decision. After that, legally required segregation would have ended in those five districts.[26] The plaintiffs would have received their legal due, as required by the *Marbury v. Madison* conception of judicial review.

But there were 2,283 school districts in the eleven states of the old Confederacy, all of them segregated by law. There were also many districts segregated by law in other states. It could be assumed that all these would eventually conform to the new rule — some spontaneously, but many or most after protracted additional litigation. The Court evidently believed that the process would be faster in these thousands of districts if it acknowledged the permissibility of some delay in the working out of local administrative and legal problems. The school boards, instead of being branded as lawbreakers by a sudden requirement of immediate desegregation, would be told that they still had time to comply with the law. In that way, it was hoped, their willing cooperation might be obtained and school segregation might disappear more quickly and easily.

The Court did not disguise its interest in framing a mandate that the thousands of districts could live with. In its 1955 opinion on implementation, it said:

> Because these cases arose under different local conditions and their disposition will involve a variety of local problems, we requested further argument on the question of relief. In view of the nationwide importance of the decision, we invited the Attorney General of the United States and the Attorneys General of all states requiring or permitting racial discrimination in public education to present their views on that question.[27]

Outside the deep South, public school desegregation proceeded with some rapidity; but in the eleven states whose attempt at secession had precipitated the Civil War, the program was a failure. The elective school boards were paralyzed by adverse local opinion, and even the Federal district courts were often influenced by it. Only 0.4% of the black students in these eleven states had been brought into schools attended also by white children by the end of 1962, and 2,013 biracial school districts out of 2,283 were still fully segregated.[28] In extreme cases, state officials openly defied the Court's interpretation of the Constitution and opposed it with the whole weight of the state's resources, including use of the militia and harassment of desegregation advocates with groundless but burdensome criminal prosecutions.[29] In one Virginia county, the public schools were closed until the Supreme Court ordered them reopened.[30] More commonly, resistance took the form of stubborn refusal to develop meaningful desegregation plans, and protracted appeals from plans eventually formulated by the Federal district courts. In 1963 the Court warned that the time for "deliberate speed" was running out,[31] and in 1968 it eventually held that delay was "no longer tolerable." [32]

What proved to be the decisive factor in public school desegregation, however, was Congressional action. The 1964 Civil Rights Act prohibited discrimination on the ground of race, color, or national origin in any "program or activity receiving Federal financial assistance," and directed Federal agencies to issue supporting regulations.[33] Pursuant to this statute, the Department of Health, Education and Welfare issued regulations cutting off Federal monetary grants to segregated school systems until they adopted acceptable desegregation plans. Under this pressure general compliance with the decision in *Brown v. Board of Education* is at last being obtained. By 1973, 79% of black children in the South were attending schools also attended by whites as compared with 23% in 1968.[34]

The reason why deliberate speed *retarded* effectuation of the *Brown* ruling, contrary to the hope and expectation of the Court, was that its temporization on the form of relief was widely believed to signify ambivalence as to the merits, and thus very probably served to stimulate the organization of prosegregation White Citizens Councils (which began to spring up right after the postponement of the mandate) and much obstructive state legislation. The 1954 opinion had placed heavy emphasis on the importance of education, the unique role of the public schools as instruments of acculturation, and the fact that school attendance (unlike recreation and travel, for example) is compelled by law; this emphasis likewise encouraged segregationists by suggesting that "separate but equal" treatment might still be permissible in other public facilities.

The deliberate speed experiment was eventually abandoned even for public schools, and the Court has not again resorted to that tactic. Thus, in dealing with officially required racial segregation outside the public schools, it has declared a flat prohibition with no grace period. It has summarily invalidated laws and regulations requiring segregation of other facilities which the government provides or helps to finance, such as graduate schools, beaches, golf courses, parks, municipal buses, courtrooms, and prisons.[35] (The Court never took the trouble to explain why the *Brown* case required these results, but the breadth of its position is clear; "it is no longer open to question," the Court declared in 1963, "that a State may not constitutionally require segregation of public facilities."[36]) The bitter obstructionism that had been encouraged by the deliberate speed doctrine required and received the Court's repeated attention, and brought forth far-reaching new protections for *freedom of expression.*

Primary responsibility for prescribing the pace of public school desegregation had been left with local school boards which are completely exposed to the pressure of local opinion. Judicial enforcement had been left primarily to the discretion of Federal district courts, which, though much less susceptible to local influences than the school boards, are much more susceptible than the Federal appellate courts.[37] The question whether desegregation was to be accomplished in weeks or years or decades or generations was therefore made to depend, to a considerable degree, upon the mobilization of supporting public opinion and the prosecution of necessary litigation. These functions were undertaken by a number of private organizations, of which the NAACP and its offshoot, the NAACP Legal Defense and Education Fund, Inc. (sometimes called the Defense Fund) were the most prominent — particularly insofar as litigation was concerned. These organizations, and the protests they sponsored, were natural targets for diehard segregationist effort. Since, in a sense, the Court relied on them to provide an essential push toward realization of its objective, and since indignant Negro protest against further delay in enjoyment of established constitutional rights had been stimulated by the Court's own startling tolerance for continued violation of the Fourteenth Amendment, it is not astonishing that the Court resisted segregationist counterattack against the organizations and their protests. What is interesting is the *form* its resistance took, which typically characterizes the failure to justify new constitutional rules on the basis of implied judicial power and which reflects a general weakness in judicial lawmaking and constitution-making — difficulty in limiting a new rule to the problem it is primarily designed to deal with. In each of the situations about to be reviewed, the Court was very probably moved by the uniquely desperate plight of the Negro (partly attributable to the Court's previous crippling of Congressional power under the Fourteenth Amendment). It may also have recoiled from the transparent hypocrisy of announcing a new constitutional right against racial segregation but countenancing its frustration through suffocation of effective demand for its enjoyment. But each case was treated as a problem in freedom of expression rather than race relations, and rules were accordingly announced for *all* protest or for *every* organization, whether or not it was concerned with racial discrimination.

*NAACP v. Button* (1963) [38] held invalid a 1956 Virginia statute designed to curb the NAACP and the Defense Fund. It was (and is) the practice of those organizations to encourage the bringing of desegregation suits, provide lawyers, and pay all litigation expense. The 1956 statute prohibited solicitation of legal business by an organization, for litigation to which it was not a party and in which it had no pecuniary interest. On its face, the statute simply prescribed an ethical standard for the conduct of lawyers, a subject matter that has long been recognized to be within state regulatory power. But *this* statute was enacted, along with several others, as part of Virginia's well-advertised program of "massive resistance" to desegregation, and (as the NAACP argued) could have been struck down as an obstacle to enforcement of the Equal Protection Clause. Instead, the Court held it invalid as an abridgment of political expression in violation of the First Amendment.

Justice Brennan's opinion stretched the concept of political expression beyond recognition. Speech, press, and association had long been recognized as part of the political process of assembling majority support — for (or against) candidates, for (or against) change in the law, and for improvement of public administration. The courtroom, however, was a place not for the propagation of political ideas but for enforcement of rights established through the political process. Now Justice Brennan says:

> In the context of NAACP objectives, litigation is not a technique for resolving private differences; it is a means for achieving the lawful objectives of equality of treatment by all government, federal, state and local, for the members of the Negro community in this country. It is thus a form of political expression. Groups which find themselves unable to achieve their objectives through the ballot frequently turn to the courts.... And under the conditions of modern government, litigation may well be the sole practicable avenue open to a minority to petition for redress of grievances....
>
> The NAACP is not a conventional political party; but the litigation it assists, while serving to vindicate the legal rights of members of the American Negro community, at the same time and perhaps more importantly, makes possible the distinctive contribution of a minority group to the ideas and beliefs of our society. For such a group, association for litigation may be the most effective form of political association.[39]

Having thus bestowed the Court's blessing upon use of the courtroom as a political forum — a practice that has since been pressed to remarkably destructive extremes* — Justice Brennan

---

* A number of lawyers have considered themselves authorized, and perhaps obligated, to defend their clients by means of obstructive courtroom histrionics and other newsworthy tactics of a type normally leading to disciplinary action and punishment for criminal contempt. Justice Brennan's rationale in the *Button* case provides at least a colorable justification for this approach — which one well-known lawyer referred to as an effort to work within the judicial system in order to destroy it. The Court, somewhat belatedly (and with some of the Justices filing concurrences that suggested a more tolerant position for what they called "political trials"),

went on to emphasize the racial neutrality of the First Amendment rationale. If one did not know from his other opinions [40] that he did not mean it, one might believe he was (with fine impartiality) inviting resort to politically motivated litigation by the NAACP's adversaries, to "arouse the society" against desegregation:

> Because our disposition is rested on the First Amendment as absorbed in the Fourteenth, we do not reach the considerations of race or racial discrimination which are the predicate of petitioner's challenge to the statute under the Equal Protection Clause. That the petitioner happens to be engaged in activities of expression and association on behalf of the rights of Negro children to equal opportunity is constitutionally irrelevant to the ground of our decision. The course of our decisions in the First Amendment area makes plain that its protections would apply as fully to those who would arouse our society against the objectives of the petitioner.[41]

This reliance on First Amendment associational freedom has caused the *Button* case to be used as a precedent in later cases having nothing to do with racial discrimination or public advocacy. For example, the Court now strictly limits state interference with labor unions' exertion of influence in their members' personal injury cases, declaring that freedom of association is at stake.[42]

*Edwards v. South Carolina* (1963)[43] was another case where the Court preferred to expand freedom of expression for everyone rather than recognize the special plight of Negroes. Negro student demonstrators gathered on the South Carolina State House grounds to protest against racial discrimination. They sang, chanted, stamped feet, clapped hands, and carried placards with such messages as "Down with Segregation." After a large crowd of onlookers gathered, the demonstrators were ordered to disperse within fifteen minutes. When they did not, 187 of them were arrested and convicted of breach of the peace. The Supreme Court

---

rejected this view. *See* Illinois v. Allen, 397 U.S. 337 (1970). This case involved courtroom disruption by a defendant who was representing himself, as did Mayberry v. Pennsylvania, 400 U.S. 455 (1971). For cases involving lawyers, *see* Taylor v. Hayes and Codispoti v. Pennsylvania, 418 U.S. 488, 506 (1974); United States v. Seale and *In re* Dellinger, 461 F.2d 345, 389 (7th Cir. 1972), and the sequel to the latter case on remand, 370 F. Supp. 1304 (N.D. Ill. 1973).

reversed the convictions, Justice Stewart speaking for an eight-man majority. Justice Clark dissented.

Twelve years before, the Court had held in *Feiner v. New York* (1951)[44] that a street speaker can be stopped by a policeman who senses imminent disorder because of the hostility of the audience, and can be punished for disorderly conduct if he persists. Justice Stewart attempted to distinguish the *Feiner* decision, saying the *Edwards* facts were "a far cry from the situation" in the *Feiner* case.[45] He offered several grounds of distinction, none of them convincing. Justice Clark was plainly justified in concluding that the *Feiner* situation was "no more dangerous than that found here,"[46] adding:

> It is my belief that anyone conversant with the almost spontaneous combustion in some Southern communities in such a situation will agree that the City Manager's action may well have averted a major catastrophe.[47]

What the Court actually did, in holding that the Fourteenth Amendment "does not permit a State to make criminal the peaceful expression of unpopular views,"[48] was to extend the constitutional protection of provocative expression generally.

The Court came somewhat closer to resting decision on the special plight of Negroes and the special need for Negro organizations, in blocking state efforts to weaken the NAACP by publicly identifying its members and thus exposing them to private reprisals; but still it spoke of freedom of association rather than equal protection. In 1958, *NAACP v. Alabama ex rel. Patterson*[49] first established the right of "associational privacy," setting aside a $100,000 fine for contempt of court that had been imposed because the NAACP refused to produce its membership lists as evidence in a case brought by Alabama to exclude it from the state. The next year a contrary result was reached in a nonracial case: *Uphaus v. Wyman* (1959)[50] held that a pacifist group that was suspected of pro-Communist activity could be required to reveal, in an investigation conducted by the New Hampshire Attorney General at the direction of the state legislature, the list of guests who had attended a summer camp operated under its auspices. In 1960, however, *Bates v. City of Little Rock*[51] held that the NAACP could not be required to disclose its membership lists in an Arkansas city license tax proceeding, on the ground that such disclosure "would work a significant interference with the freedom of association."[52] Later that year, in *Shelton v. Tucker* (1960),[53] the Court struck down on the same ground an Arkansas statute compelling every teacher in a state-supported school or college, as a condition of employment, to file annually an affidavit listing every organization to which he had belonged or contributed during the five preceding years. The class suit was brought by a teacher who was not a member of any left-wing organization but was a member of the NAACP.

At this point the rule seemed to be that, though the Court had not acknowledged it, associational privacy was the constitutional right of black but not red organizations. In 1963 a case arose that could not be decided on that simplistic ground. *Gibson v. Florida Legislative Investigation Committee*[54] involved a legislative investigation to find out whether the Communist Party had infiltrated the Miami branch of the NAACP. The president of the branch refused to produce its membership list, which could have been compared with lists of known or suspected Communist Party members, and was sentenced for contempt. Clearly, here was an investigation of both the red Communist Party *and* the black NAACP. Justice Goldberg, for the Court, purported to solve the problem by simply declaring that the NAACP, unlike the Communist Party, is a "legitimate" organization and that its members cannot be "exposed" unless and until the state has first proved a "nexus" between the NAACP and subversive activities.[55] It is hard to follow the logic; the very question under investigation was whether the Miami branch had fallen under Communist Party domination and was engaged in subversive activities. The decision can be accounted for only on the ground that the need to protect the NAACP overrode the rule of *Uphaus v. Wyman* — which the Court failed to distinguish on any other comprehensible ground. The NAACP, unlike pacifist organizations, was not considered expendable.

A fourth example of the impact of racial discrimination on the law of free expression was *New York Times Co. v. Sullivan* (1964).[56] In 1960 the *Times* carried a paid advertisement appealing for funds to support the cause of Negro students and Negro voting rights and to defend Dr. Martin Luther King, Jr., against a pending perjury indictment. The advertisement included ten paragraphs stating factual particulars of hardships said to have been suffered by Negroes at the hands of "Southern violators." Two of the paragraphs included partly inaccurate statements about actions of the Montgomery, Alabama, police. L. B. Sullivan, who as Montgomery Commissioner of Public Affairs was in charge of the police force, sued the *Times* for libel claiming that the advertisement cast a slur on his performance of official duty. The Alabama state court jury was instructed in accordance with settled Alabama libel law — which followed the accepted common law rules that (1) the defendant has the burden of proving truth, (2) written words tending to bring an individual into public contempt are libelous *per se,* (3) it is for the jury to say whether the words referred to the plaintiff, and (4) the jury can award substantial damages without proof of pecuniary injury. The jury awarded $500,000 in damages. The Supreme Court reversed, laying down a new constitutional rule that statements about the official conduct of public officials are not actionable, even if false and defamatory, unless the defendant knew they were false or was recklessly indifferent to their truth or falsity.

The *Sullivan* rule has been applied to nonracial situations [57] and has been expanded to cover defamatory statements about the *private* lives of public officials [58] and defamation of prominent *private* persons.[59] Indeed, the Court indicated it would apply the rule to defamation of *nonentities* by statements on matters of general interest to the public,[60] though it eventually declined to do so.[61] Today there is little disposition to question the Court's subordination of the interest in reputation to the interest in unhampered political expression.[62] But this significant incursion into state tort law might never have taken place had not the *Sullivan* case confronted the Court with the danger that huge libel judgments would deter the news media from airing the facts of *racial discrimination* and thus stifle the drive for remedial legislation.

There is no intention here to suggest that the bolder protection of free speech was an unwholesome development. Possibly it would have come even without the stimulus of the drive for Negro equality. The point is, rather, that the Court's determination to help Negroes extricate themselves from the status of untouchables did in fact impel it — particularly in the *Button* and *Sullivan* cases — to invade traditional areas of state autonomy on a broader front than it had been willing to do in response to repression of religious evangelism or the crusade against suspected subversion.

Freedom of expression was not the only field where the plight of the Negro very probably helped stimulate the Court to drastic intervention. Another such field was criminal process (already reviewed in Chapter X). A great many of the criminal cases that were coming to the Court's attention involved black defendants. The disproportionate frequency of Negro arrests and prosecutions meant one or both of two things: (1) that a great many Negroes lacked the sense of political obligation, the inner compulsion to obey the law simply because obedience to the law is right,[63] and therefore had to be coerced into compliance by fear of punishment; (2) that the criminal law enforcement apparatus was being arbitrarily used against Negroes, as it had once been used against wage workers, to keep them to their lowly place in the social and economic structure. That is to say, the frequent involvement of Negroes in the criminal process was either a *result* of deep disaffection on the part of the large Negro minority (some 11% of the total population, and a much higher percentage in the larger cities), or it was a persistent *source* of the disaffection, or it was both. The existence of such disaffection being a matter of national concern, there was reason for closer Federal supervision of the treatment of suspected and accused persons; the methods used for controlling crime could no longer be regarded as a matter of local consequence only.* And the Court is the Federal organ best situated to supervise closely the performance of policemen, prosecutors, and courts.

Of course, Negro disaffection was not the only reason why the Court took increased interest in the criminal process. Revulsion against practices routinely employed by totalitarian governments in the so-called police states must also have been a factor. But the fact that intensification of the Court's interest came at about the same time as its heavier intervention against overt racial discrimination, rather than during or immediately after the 1941-1945 war against Germany, indicates that racial considerations were the triggering cause here as in the field of political expression.

\* \* \* \* \*

In the last chapter we traced the source of the Court's predicament in *Shelley v. Kraemer.* The *Slaughter-House* interpretation, as unfolded in the *Civil Rights Cases,* had denied the power of Congress to identify and prohibit particular types of private discrimination as especially harmful to the national interest in clearing away the residues of slavery — and to do it without outlawing private discrimination across the board, which would have cut deeply into the freedom of the individual to make most of his choices without being called upon to justify them to any government.[64] It is easier for a legislature than for a court to single out the worst evils and, at least temporarily, ignore others similar in quality but less destructive in effect. There is no sense of shock if a legislature, being the traditional agency for balancing and compromising competing interests, deals only with the most urgent part of a problem. A court, on the other hand, hears charges of logical inconsistency if it does so. An issue of *legitimacy* arises.

Initially the Court evaded the delicate question whether miscegenation (racial intermarriage) can be forbidden by law, an issue which stirred feelings even deeper than those aroused by school desegregation. In 1956 it refused to decide the question,

---

\* This is *not* to say that different criminal conduct standards should be applied to whites and blacks.

giving no comprehensible explanation for the refusal.[65] In 1964 it invalidated a statute penalizing illicit cohabitation more severely if the parties were of different races, but chose not to pass on the validity of the antimiscegenation statute which it implemented.[66] In 1967, however, without explanation of the delay, antimiscegenation laws (which then existed in sixteen states) were declared to violate the Equal Protection and Due Process Clauses.[67]

Although the distinction between official and private discrimination has not been obliterated,[68] the concern that the Court has shown for dissolution of caste barriers has led to incompletely rationalized inroads upon the state action doctrine. For one thing, the government is forbidden to encourage or facilitate private discrimination. One device employed by prosegregation state governments to dampen pressure for racial equality was to provide targets for private reprisals by publicizing membership in organizations dedicated to promoting Negro rights. The Court's resistance to that tactic has been discussed earlier in this chapter.[69]

Similar sensitivity to official encouragement of private discrimination was displayed in cases involving trespass prosecutions of Negroes for "sit-ins" at restaurants that served whites only. Prior to the 1964 Civil Rights Act, the Court never went so far as to deny the right of a restaurant proprietor to exclude Negroes on his own initiative; nor did it hold that Negroes have a constitutional privilege to protest against such discrimination by "sitting in," *i.e.,* requesting service at a table or counter and refusing to leave upon demand.[70] Sit-in demonstrations took place in a number of Southern cities, as a form of civil disobedience, and criminal convictions resulted. In some such cases the Court temporized;[71] but in *Lombard v. Louisiana* (1963)[72] it reversed such a conviction on the ground that, within the week before the alleged offense, the local mayor and police chief had made public statements condemning sit-ins. There was no proof that the proprietor was in fact influenced by the statements, which in any event did not expressly advocate refusal to serve whites and blacks together. Evidently the Court believed that the statements necessarily encouraged discrimination by promising use of the criminal law to enforce a decision by the proprietor to exclude Negroes, so that his decision resulted at least partly from state action.

The Court has also held that discrimination by the private lessee of state-owned property is state action. In *Burton v. Wilmington Parking Authority* (1961)[73] a private company conducted a restaurant business in a state-owned parking garage building under a 20-year lease which contained no provision either requiring or permitting exclusion of Negroes from the restaurant. Such exclusion by the private lessee was held to be a denial of equal protection, the Court finding that the state was involved in the restaurant operation because (a) it owned the building, (b) its adjacent garage benefited from the restaurant's proximity, and (c) the private lessee claimed that exclusion of Negroes had a favorable effect on the restaurant's profits, from which rents were paid to the state.

An even thinner governmental involvement was held to constitute state action in *Reitman v. Mulkey* (1967).[74] A 1963 California statute forbidding discrimination in the sale or rental of any dwelling containing more than four apartment units, aroused great criticism. By popular referendum, the state constitution was amended the next year to provide:

> Neither the State nor any subdivision or agency thereof shall deny, limit or abridge, directly or indirectly, the right of any person, who is willing or desires to sell, lease or rent any part or all of his real property, to decline to sell, lease or rent such property to such person or persons as he, in his absolute discretion, chooses.[75]

The effect was to nullify the 1963 statute.

It had previously been thought that the people of a state could limit the power of their legislative representatives at will; but the Court held, in effect, that state and local lawmakers must be left free to deal with racial discrimination, at least in the field of housing. The state constitutional amendment *forbidding* legislative action was held to be discriminatory state action itself. The California Supreme Court had held — evidently on the basis of judicial notice, since no evidence was introduced to support the conclusion — that the amendment in fact encouraged private discrimination; and in *Reitman v. Mulkey* the Court could find "no sound reason for rejecting this judgment." [76] It ignored the complaint of the four dissenters that there was no evidence to support the state court's factual conclusion.[77]

The decision in *Reitman v. Mulkey* brought the Court fairly close to the position that would have resulted from repudiation of the rationale of the *Slaughter-House Cases* and the *Civil Rights Cases* (discussed in the last chapter) — but not quite. The *Reitman* ruling rests heavily on a factual finding by a state court sensitive to the realities of private racial discrimination, and thus may not be followed in a similar case arising in the deep South. Again, it does not recognize *Congressional* power to define the privileges and immunities of Federal citizenship. Moreover, the shakiness of its doctrinal foundation — revealed by Justice Harlan's powerful dissent — leaves it vulnerable to reconsideration and overruling after a change in the Court's membership. The cases now to be considered show that the mutilation of the Fourteenth Amendment at the hands of the post-Reconstruction Court has not yet been fully repaired.

The Court has vacillated on the question whether the mere application of racially neutral laws to enforce discriminatory private decisions is state action and therefore subject to the Equal Protection and Due Process Clauses. As already noted, *Shelley v. Kraemer* (the 1948 restrictive covenant case) seemed to give a broad affirmative answer, but was not applied to the full extent of its logic in different factual settings.[78] In 1957 the Court held that a testamentary trust establishing a school for "poor white male orphans" could not be administered *by the city of Philadelphia as trustee*,[79] but the next year it refused to interfere after the state court had allowed the city to resign and had appointed successor trustees who continued the racial discrimination.* [80] In 1966 the

---

* Eventually the school was opened to nonwhites. In 1966, after the Court had begun to manifest still greater sensitivity to racial discrimination, a new injunction action was brought. It succeeded, on the ground that the school was "municipal in nature" so that its operation was state action and, as such, was governed by the Equal Protection Clause of the Fourteenth Amendment. Pennsylvania v. Brown, 392 F.2d 120 (3d Cir. 1968), *cert. denied*, 391 U.S. 921 (1968).

Court rejected an effort to preserve a similar testamentary trust establishing a park in Macon, Georgia, for whites only, although the state court had replaced the city with private trustees; but the decision was rested partly on the Court's assertion that the service rendered by a park is inherently "municipal in nature," and partly on its doubt that a change of trustees would alter the public nature of a park which had been operated by the city for many years.[81] Thereafter the state court terminated the trust on the ground that its purpose had been frustrated and decided that the park property should revert to the donor's estate. The result was that Negroes (as well as whites) were denied use of the park, but in *Evans v. Abney* (1970) [82] the state decision was upheld. The Court said the result might be different if "the State and not a private party [were] ... injecting the racially discriminatory motivation" [83] — a distinction that would be immaterial under the logic of *Shelley v. Kraemer*. The next year, however, the Court held that the city of Jackson, Mississippi, had not acted unconstitutionally in closing its public swimming pools *as soon as they had been ordered desegregated.*[84]

Mention should be made of recent cases approving drastic remedies devised by the district courts to dissipate the effects of school segregation previously accomplished by law. The most controversial feature of these plans arises from the fact that neighborhoods in many cities have become exclusively or very preponderantly white or nonwhite, and from the further fact that it is considered desirable for children — particularly the younger ones — to attend schools near their homes. In response to the Court's directive to replace dual school systems with "unitary" ones,[85] a number of district courts have ordered that children be assigned to distant schools and transported back and forth by school buses, so that the racial mix in each school will approximate that in the community at large. Great resentment has been generated against "busing" for this purpose, but the Court has held it to be a justifiable means of disestablishing officially segregated school systems.[86] The Court came close to deciding that children are to be exchanged between separate school districts when racial concentrations within the districts otherwise preclude effective integration. In 1973 it divided four to four on that question in a case from Richmond, Virginia, one Justice abstaining;[87] but the next year the full Court gave a negative answer, by a vote of five to four, in a similar case that arose in Detroit, Michigan.[88]

The Court has not passed upon the constitutionality of so-called *"de facto* segregation." This is the term that has been coined to describe a condition of racial concentration in particular schools which is not attributable to governmental efforts to separate the races, but results from local population patterns not themselves brought about by official action. It is a rather odd expression, since "segregation" ordinarily connotes a *process* resulting in separateness, rather than separateness as such. The term *"de facto* segregation" has entered current usage, however, being distinguished from *"de jure* segregation" which is brought about by public authority. In *Keyes v. School District* (1973),[89] where the Court found *de jure* segregation to exist in Denver, Colorado, two of the Justices declared themselves ready to provide judicial remedies against *de facto* as well as *de jure* segregation. Should the Court take that step, little if anything would remain of the state action doctrine; it would have given way to the view that the Court is omnicompetent to utilize the public schools as a means of maximizing interracial association.

As desegregation of public schools has become more and more complete, there has been a perceptible movement of white students into all-white private schools. Until now the Court has not questioned the legality of such schools, but it has forbidden governmental assistance to them or their students. They have been declared ineligible for federal tax benefits extended to other nonprofit educational institutions,[90] and a state law providing free textbooks to their students (and also to public school students) has been held unconstitutional.[91]

The foregoing review of the Court's attack on caste barriers does not touch every aspect of its effort. Enough has been shown, however, to reveal the reality and magnitude (as well as the logical asymmetry) of the effort and to suggest that it has been impelled by (a) awareness of the wretched condition of socially isolated minorities in the United States and (b) belief that full relief is unlikely to be obtained through the political process alone. The great bulk of the cases deal with the black minority, which is much the largest and which is uniquely disadvantaged by the cultural residue of slavery; but equality requirements developed initially for the protection of Negroes apply to other socially isolated minorities as well. For example, in *Hernandez v. Texas* (1954)[92] the Court held that discrimination against persons of Mexican descent in the selection of juries violates the Equal Protection Clause, saying: "The Fourteenth Amendment is not directed solely against discrimination due to a 'two-class theory' — that is, based upon differences between 'white' and Negro." [93]

Thus the Court, considering itself blocked off from tentative judicial review by the logic of the *Slaughter-House Cases* and the *Civil Rights Cases,* has undertaken to build *its own* protections of personal status, not only for Negroes but for all persons. Each new individual constitutional right it establishes becomes, in effect, a Federal "privilege or immunity" that must be shielded (a) from attack by the state, and (b) from private attack encouraged or facilitated by the state.

However, this is a difficult assignment for a *court* acting without the cooperation of a legislature. Courts cannot easily collect facts needed for intelligent lawmaking; they find it hard to correct their mistakes for the future without impugning the justice of established case-law long thought settled; they cannot easily generate cases in which to announce needed improvements in the law — unlike legislatures, which are self-starting. But after World War II, when the Court awoke to the enormity of the national peril arising from emasculation of the Civil War Amendments and faced the urgent need to repair the deficiency, it found itself blocked off from Congressional assistance by its own nineteenth-century rulings.

At that point the Court began to signal Congress for help. Possibly such a signal was intended, for example, in *Collins v. Hardyman* (1951),[94] where the Court held that the 1871 Civil Rights Act (the Ku Klux Act) did not provide a right to damages against private individuals for breaking up the plaintiffs' political meeting. Justice Jackson, for the Court, referred to "constitutional problems" [95] but avoided resolving them. He rested decision on a point of statutory construction (later repudiated by the Court [96]), not taking issue with the assertion of the three dissenters that the statute, if interpreted to cover the case, would be valid despite the state action doctrine.[97]

*Bell v. Maryland* (1964) [98] provided an unequivocal signal. The question was whether trespass convictions of Negro "sit-in" demonstrators, for refusal to leave a restaurant at the proprietor's request, violated the Equal Protection and Due Process Clauses of the Fourteenth Amendment. Three of the Justices gave an affirmative answer; three others gave a negative answer but said they would uphold a Federal statute outlawing such convictions; and the remaining three did not reach the merits. Ten days later Congress responded to the invitation by enacting the long-delayed Civil Rights Act of 1964.[99]

Even then, however, the Court could not bring itself to send out the one signal that would have been immediately understood — retraction of the *Slaughter-House* interpretation of the Privileges or Immunities Clause. Instead, it began to exhume the old Civil Rights Acts, many of whose provisions had been allowed to remain on the books in a state of innocuous desuetude long after they had lost their teeth. For example, in *Jones v. Alfred H. Mayer Co.* (1968)[100] the Court not only upheld the validity of a long dormant provision of the 1866 Civil Rights Act, but, as already noted,[101] gave it an interpretation so broad as to set its authors spinning in their graves. (We have seen[102] that a far narrower interpretation would have sufficed to justify the decision in *Shelley v. Kraemer* twenty years earlier, without resort to the impossible Vinson rationale in that case, which has unsettled the law ever since.) The

Court has also signaled that Congress has power to *expand* — but, contrary to principles of tentative judicial review, *not to contract* — the meaning of "equal protection of the laws," as interpreted by the Court.[103]

Despite the confusion engendered by such bizarre and seemingly arbitrary signals, Congress — after the fashion of a psychiatrist searching out the rationale of seeming irrationality — has responded with several highly effective Civil Rights Acts. And, warily keeping one foot always on the Commerce Clause, Congress (or one might say the thoroughly alarmed electorate, acting through Congress) has, by these statutes, regulated private discrimination in important ways and has even undertaken to *narrow* some of the individual immunities bestowed by the Court. The Court has not yet shifted over to tentative judicial review by upholding the power of Congress to take away what the Court has given. Yet it has not yet *refused* to take that step; and the validity of such legislation as the Omnibus Safe Streets and Crime Control Act of 1968,[104] which purports to modify the *Miranda* safeguards, remains unadjudicated.

It is quite clear, however, for the first time since 1868, that the Court is ready to concede to Congress some sort of partnership status in the implementation of the Civil War Amendments. No longer does it treat Congress as the mere servant of its own will. Therefore this discussion would be incomplete without a review of recent Federal legislation.

In that field, the past decade has witnessed two parallel developments. First, the broad equality provisions contained in the Civil Rights Acts of 1866,[105] 1870,[106] 1871,[107] and 1875,[108] enacted in the wake of the Civil War and then quickly emasculated (by hostile interpretation and the state action doctrine) have been revivified by new interpretations giving them greater effect. Second, Congress has enacted a series of new antidiscrimination statutes.

The 1866 Civil Rights Act [109] contained a provision (which, slightly reworded, is now 18 U.S.C. § 242) for criminal prosecution of anyone who, "under color of any law, . . . wilfully subjects any inhabitant of any State ... to the deprivation of any rights, privileges, or immunities secured or protected by the Constitution or laws of the United States." The 1870 Civil Rights Act [110] contained a provision (which, slightly reworded, is now 18 U.S.C. § 241) for criminal prosecution of conspiracy "to injure, oppress, threaten or intimidate any citizen in the free exercise or enjoyment of any right or privilege secured to him by the Constitution or laws of the United States." These were the statutes involved in *United States v. Price* (1966).[111] Three Mississippi law enforcement officers and fifteen private individuals were prosecuted under both statutes. The charges were based on allegations that the defendants had killed three civil rights (Negro rights) workers, but the Federal prosecution was not for murder (which is a *state* crime). Rather, it was for "punishing" the victims without due process of law in violation of their rights under the Fourteenth Amendment. The district court dismissed most of the charges, adopting restrictive interpretations of the Federal statutes, which it quite reasonably thought to be required by earlier Supreme Court decisions.[112] On appeal, the Court reinstated the charges. It held that a private individual acts "under color of law" when he is "a wilful participant in joint activity with the State or its agents," so that § 242 applies to him. It also held — which it had refused to do fifteen years earlier [113] — that § 241 covers rights protected by the Fourteenth Amendment Due Process Clause.

On the same day, the Court decided *United States v. Guest,* [114] involving a prosecution of six private individuals under § 241. They were charged with conspiracy to engage in violence and other illegal acts to deter Negroes from equal use of (1) theaters, restaurants, and other places of public accommodation, (2) state and city facilities, and (3) streets and highways. The district court dismissed. For technical reasons the Supreme Court held it lacked jurisdiction of the first charge,[115] but it reinstated the other two. It held that § 241 covers frustration of the Equal Protection Clause, which guarantees equal enjoyment of public facilities, and also covers interference with the Federal right of interstate road travel.

The Court has also broadened its interpretation of the civil provisions of the old Civil Rights Acts. The 1871 Act contained a provision which, as formally revised by 42 U.S.C. § 1985(3), created a right to damages against those who conspire "for the purpose of depriving ... any person ... of the equal protection of the laws, or of equal privileges and immunities under the laws." [116] In 1951 the Court construed the statute as reaching only conspiracies under color of state law, or by private groups so large and powerful as to dominate the state government.[117] Twenty years later, in *Griffin v. Breckenridge* (1971),[118] it discarded that interpretation. It upheld a damage suit by Mississippi Negroes who were allegedly beaten by two private individuals for the purpose of preventing them and other Negroes "from seeking the equal protection of the laws and from enjoying the equal rights, privileges and immunities of citizens." As so construed, the Court held the statute constitutional under the Enforcement Clause of the *Thirteenth* Amendment and did not pass on the applicability of the Fourteenth — which would have required reconsideration of the state action doctrine. That doctrine does not apply to the Thirteenth Amendment, which abolished slavery and has been held to empower Congress to eliminate "badges and incidents of slavery" resulting from private as well as state action.[119]

It will be observed that expansive interpretation of the Thirteenth Amendment provides a basis for tighter restriction of private discrimination against Negroes than other minorities. The Court proceeded down this road in *Jones v. Alfred H. Mayer Co.* (1968),[120] applying a provision of the 1866 Civil Rights Act (now 42 U.S.C. § 1982) which (as stated above [121]) provides:

> All citizens of the United States shall have the same right, in every State and Territory, as is enjoyed by white citizens thereof to inherit, purchase, lease, sell, hold, and convey real and personal property.

In 1948 the Court had interpreted the statute as being directed against governmental action only.[122] In the 1968 *Jones* case, however, it was held to entitle a Negro couple to civil relief against a private company which, because of their race, had refused to sell them a home. The Court said the statute was designed "to prohibit all racial discrimination, whether or not under color of law, with respect to the rights enumerated therein — including the right to purchase or lease property." [123] The earlier case was overruled. As so construed, the statute was upheld under the Thirteenth Amendment.

These are not the only decisions broadening Federal remedies under the old Civil Rights Acts.[124] They suffice, however, to indicate the extent to which they have been revived by repudiation of earlier restrictive interpretation. They have now been strongly supplemented by new Federal legislation, a brief overview of which will be helpful.

The 1964 Civil Rights Act [125] is the most comprehensive ever enacted by Congress. It created new Federal rights of equal access to privately owned places of public accommodation and to private employment. It also provided for Federal assumption of the enforcement burden in major areas, notably through suits by the Attorney General for relief against many forms of official discrimination and through cessation of Federal financial assistance to discriminatory programs and activities of state and local governments. Other provisions strengthened voting rights, established administrative aids to desegregation, and created the Community Relations Service to conciliate racial disputes.

Title II, dealing with public accommodations, was the most controversial. It covers hotels, motels, and other transient lodgings which have more than five rooms for rent; restaurants and other eating places; gasoline stations; and places of exhibition and entertainment such as theaters and sports arenas. It forbids "discrimination or segregation on the ground of race, color, religion or national origin." Because the 1883 *Civil Rights Cases* [126] had applied the state action doctrine to invalidate a similar statute, Congress laid a basis for reliance on the Commerce Clause (Article I, Section 8, Clause 3) which empowers it to regulate interstate and foreign commerce without regard to state action.[127] The coverage of the statute was therefore limited to establishments having some connection with interstate or foreign "travel, trade, commerce, transportation or communication," except that transient lodging facilities were considered to satisfy this requirement *per se.*

Within less than a year, the Court held Title II valid. A restaurant in Birmingham, Alabama, that refused to serve Negroes was held to have the requisite connection with interstate commerce because it bought meat from a local supplier which procured it from outside Alabama.[128] The Court also pointed to evidence that Negro travel had been impeded by racial discrimination in restaurants and held that the Commerce Clause authorizes Congress to remove the impediment. Later, it held even a much more tenuous connection with interstate or foreign commerce to be sufficient;[129] and except for private clubs, which the statute exempts, the coverage of the restaurant provisions is now recognized to be universal for all practical purposes.

On the same day, the statute was upheld as to an all-white motel in Atlanta, Georgia, 75% of whose customers were from outside the state.[130] Here too the Court based its decision on the power of Congress to eliminate hindrances to interstate Negro travel. It pointedly left open the question whether the statute could also have been sustained under the Fourteenth Amendment Enforcement Clause.[131] Therefore one cannot now say whether the rule of the *Civil Rights Cases* is still good law.

The employment provisions of the 1964 Act (Title VII) cover employers of 15 or more employees in businesses affecting interstate or foreign commerce — which, in practice, means virtually all sizeable companies. Labor unions and employment agencies are also regulated. Discrimination on the ground of sex, as well as race, color, religion, and national origin, is forbidden. The statute established the Equal Employment Opportunity Commission to receive complaints and refer them to state agencies having power to act on them. If resolution of a complaint is not effected by a state agency, the Commission may investigate the charge and attempt conciliation itself. All else failing, Title VII authorizes suit by the aggrieved individual in Federal court. Its lack of direct enforcement power and the necessity of delay for possible conciliation somewhat impaired the effectiveness of Title

VII, but a 1972 amendment has eliminated the former weakness. There has also been considerable controversy about the scope of statutory exemptions for "bona fide occupational qualification" [132] and for job screening by "professionally developed ability tests," [133] and even more controversy about the availability of preferential hiring quotas ("reverse discrimination") as a remedy.[134]

The Voting Rights Act of 1965 [135] provided the first effective remedy against racial discrimination in voting, though such discrimination has been illegal since adoption of the Fifteenth Amendment in 1870. The problem arose because the Constitution leaves the states in charge of administering all elections, subject to the power of Congress to alter state regulations as they affect Congressional elections.[136] Hostility to Negro political activity, prevalent throughout the South, led to widespread abuses.[137] Judicial relief was slow and expensive and had been limited by the repeal or invalidation of most of the Federal statutes on voting rights which Congress enacted shortly after the Civil War.[138] The Civil Rights Acts of 1957,[139] 1960,[140] and 1964 [141] strengthened Federal remedies somewhat, but none of them took the essential step of displacing state control of the voting registration machinery. That step was finally taken in the 1965 Act.[142]

The central provisions of the Act dealt with literacy tests, which had become a preferred vehicle for discrimination. The use of such tests was suspended for five years in any state or other governmental unit where less than half of the otherwise qualified voters were registered as of November 1, 1964. To prevent the substitution of other discriminatory devices, adoption of new voting regulations was forbidden unless the Attorney General or the Federal district court in the District of Columbia found that their use would not result in discrimination. Most importantly, the Act provided for appointment of Federal examiners empowered to receive applications and register applicants if found qualified. These provisions were held constitutional under the Enforcement Clause of the Fifteenth Amendment.[143]

The main thrust of the Act was against anti-Negro discrimination in the South; but there was one provision for the benefit of Puerto Ricans, several hundred thousand of whom had migrated to New York City and, though literate in Spanish, were prevented from voting by an English literacy test. The 1965 Act prohibited enforcement of the English literacy requirement against persons who had completed the sixth grade of school in Puerto Rico (a United States dependency where the language of instruction is Spanish). The Fifteenth Amendment did not apply, since the discrimination was on the basis of language rather than race, but the provision was upheld under the Enforcement Clause of the Fourteenth.[144]

The 1965 Act was continued and broadened by the Voting Rights Act Amendments of 1970,[145] where literacy tests were abolished for all elections. That statute also lowered the voting age to 18, in recognition of a claim that voting equality should be extended to young adults who were old enough to be drafted into military service. Late in 1970 the Court sustained the prohibition of literacy tests, and held the 18-year provision valid as to Federal but not state elections.[146] Three months later Congress proposed the Twenty-sixth Amendment, lowering the voting age to 18 for *all* elections. It took only another three months for three fourths of the states to ratify it and render it effective.*

Meanwhile, Title VIII of the Civil Rights Act of 1968 [147] had significantly extended the Federal law against discrimination in the sale or rental of housing. Subject to exemptions for most single-family houses and for apartment buildings containing four units or less (one unit of which is occupied by the owner), it covers all housing aided by Federal financing since 1962. It goes beyond the 1866 Act, upheld in *Jones v. Alfred H. Mayer Co.,*[148] by prohibiting discrimination on account of religion and national origin as well as race and color; by covering discrimination in the provision of financing, brokerage, and other services and facilities in connection

---

* Oregon v. Mitchell (1970), *supra* note 146, was decided December 21, 1970. The Twenty-sixth Amendment was proposed by Congress on March 23, 1971, and the ratification process was completed on June 30, 1971.

with the sale or rental of dwellings; by outlawing advertisements or other representations that indicate discriminatory preferences; and by empowering a Federal administrative agency to assist aggrieved parties. On the other hand, the 1866 Act is broader in some respects since it is not limited as to type of dwellings and is not subject to the exemptions mentioned above.

* * * * *

Since World War II the ideal of a caste-free society has become a dominant objective in the law of the United States. Not only has the Supreme Court ceased its obstruction to Congressional implementation of the Civil War Amendments. It has also taken the lead in publicizing and condemning the discrimination against racial minorities that has so long pervaded American society. Moreover, as the recent Federal statutes show, its efforts have stimulated a broad political movement which in the long run may prove to be the most solid basis of further progress toward unification of the national community.

Beyond all this, the Court has generalized the concept of legally required equality beyond protection of minority groups from hostile discrimination and insists on the greatest possible equality in enjoyment of rights which it considers to be "fundamental." This has been the basis of a tremendous expansion in constitution-making, particularly since 1969; and in order to give some sense of the diversity of the new *corpus juris* and its sheer bulk, it will be necessary to summarize decisions in a good many different fields, any one of which could fill a chapter of its own. With an expression of regret for the sketchiness of the treatment, which is unavoidable if we are not to be distracted from our primary inquiry as to whether the Court's performance can be squared with neutral principle, I now turn to that development.

CHAPTER XIV
## Equality: Beyond Race

The discerning reader may have noticed an unusual omission in the two preceding chapters. There was no resort to the doctrine of implied judicial power to justify the very extensive protection the Court has given to racial minorities. That was because the Constitutors of the Civil War Amendments *intended* to accord Negroes more protection than the Federal Government has given them even yet. Whatever the worth of Justice Miller's *interpretation* of the Fourteenth Amendment in the *Slaughter-House Cases* (1873),[1] it is impossible to disagree with his recital of the *main purpose* that underlay the Thirteenth, Fourteenth, and Fifteenth Amendments:*

> Twelve articles of amendment were added to the Federal Constitution soon after the original organization of the government under it in 1789. Of these all but the last were adopted so soon afterwards as to justify the statement that they were practically contemporaneous with the adoption of the original; and the twelfth, adopted in eighteen hundred and three, was so nearly so as to have become, like all the others, historical and of another age. But within the last eight years three other articles of amendment of vast importance have been added by the voice of the people to that now venerable instrument.
>
> The most cursory glance at these articles discloses a unity of purpose, when taken in connection with the history of the times, which cannot fail to have an important bearing on any question of doubt concerning their true meaning. Nor can such doubts, when any reasonably exist, be safely and rationally solved without a reference to that history; for in it is found the occasion and the necessity for recurring again to the great source of power in this country, the people of the States, for additional guarantees of human rights; additional powers to the Federal government; additional restraints upon those of the States. Fortunately that history is fresh within the memory of us all, and its leading features, as they bear upon the matter before us, free from doubt.

---

* *See* footnote on p. 200 *supra*; and *see* TEN BROEK, EQUAL UNDER LAW (1965) (originally published in 1951, in somewhat less comprehensive form, as "The Antislavery Origins of the Fourteenth Amendment") *passim.*

The institution of African slavery, as it existed in about half the States of the Union, and the contests pervading the public mind for many years, between those who desired its curtailment and ultimate extinction and those who desired additional safeguards for its security and perpetuation, culminated in the effort, on the part of most of the States in which slavery existed, to separate from the Federal government, and to resist its authority. This constituted the war of the rebellion, and whatever auxiliary causes may have contributed to bring about this war, undoubtedly the overshadowing and efficient cause was African slavery.

In that struggle slavery, as a legalized social relation, perished. It perished as a necessity of the bitterness and force of the conflict.... The proclamation of President Lincoln expressed an accomplished fact as to a large portion of the insurrectionary districts, when he declared slavery abolished in them all. But the war being over, those who had succeeded in reestablishing the authority of the Federal government were not content to permit this great act of emancipation to rest on the actual results of the contest or the proclamation of the Executive, both of which might have been questioned in after times, and they determined to place this main and most valuable result in the Constitution of the restored Union as one of its fundamental articles. Hence the thirteenth article of amendment of that instrument....

The process of restoring to their proper relations with the Federal government and with the other States those which had sided with the rebellion, undertaken under the proclamation of President Johnson in 1865, and before the assembling of Congress, developed the fact that, notwithstanding the formal recognition by those States of the abolition of slavery, the condition of the slave race would, without further protection of the Federal government, be almost as bad as it was before. [The opinion continued with the description of the Black Codes which is quoted in the footnote on page 183 *supra.*]

These circumstances,... forced upon the statesmen who had conducted the Federal government in safety through the crisis of the rebellion, and who supposed that by the thirteenth article of amendment they had secured the result of their labors, the conviction that something more was necessary in the way of constitutional protection to the unfortunate race who had suffered so much. They accordingly passed through Congress the proposition for the fourteenth amendment, and they declined to treat as restored to their full participation in the government of the Union the States which had been in insurrection, until they ratified that article by a formal vote of their legislative bodies.

Before we proceed to examine more critically the provisions of this amendment, on which the plaintiffs in error rely, let us complete and dismiss the history of the recent amendments, as that history relates to the general purpose which pervades them all. A few years' experience satisfied the thoughtful men who had been the authors of the other two amendments that, notwithstanding the restraints of those articles on the States, and the laws passed under the additional powers granted to Congress, these were inadequate for the protection of life, liberty, and property, without which freedom to the slave was no boon. They were in all those States denied the right of suffrage. The laws were administered by the white man alone. It was urged that a race of men distinctively marked as was the negro, living in the midst of another and dominant race, could never be fully secured in their person and their property without the right of suffrage.

Hence the fifteenth amendment, which declares that "the right of a citizen of the United States to vote shall not be denied or abridged by any State on account of race, color, or previous condition of servitude." The negro having, by the fourteenth amendment, been declared to be a citizen of the United States, is thus made a voter in every State of the Union. . . .[2]

The Justices' problem has been not to deal with contingencies unforeseen by the Constitutors, but to squirm loose from the straitjacket that their own revered predecessors wrapped around the Civil War Amendments. Such strained rationales as those in *Shelley v. Kraemer* (1948),[3] *Evans v. Newton* (1966),[4] *Reitman v. Mulkey* (1967),[5] and *Jones v. Alfred H. Mayer Co.* (1968)[6] reflect not an effort to push beyond the Constitutors' intention, but an effort to approximate it as closely as possible without overtly repudiating the rules of the *Slaughter-House Cases* and the *Civil Rights Cases.* And decisions such as *Evans v. Abney* (1970),[7] *Palmer v. Thompson* (1971),[8] and *Moose Lodge v. Irvis* (1972)[9] are — in my opinion — more accurately perceived as failures to effect such an approximation, than as rearguard defenses of neutral principle.

More than once in recent years, Justices have declared in general terms that race is the core of the Fourteenth Amendment, and that racial discrimination is therefore more "suspect" than other inequalities. (One is reminded of George Orwell's animals, all of whom were equal but some of whom were more equal than others.) Notwithstanding these affirmations, if the Court's recent administration of the Fourteenth Amendment is justly subject to any broad criticism whatever, it is on the ground that it has paid no more than lip service to the historically solid proposition that the Amendment's central purpose was to clear away the vestiges of slavery — of *slavery,* the only issue that has ever been so divisive as to precipitate an American civil war. Too often the Court has treated discrimination against blacks as if it differed only quantitatively, not qualitatively, from discrimination against other minorities that do not suffer under the heritage of remembered enslavement.

I am compelled to recognize, of course, that the Constitutors did not intend the protection of the Civil War Amendments to be limited to Negroes or ex-slaves. The Thirteenth Amendment prohibits "involuntary servitude," which is broader than slavery; [10] the Fifteenth forbids denial of the vote on the ground of race or color as well as "previous condition of servitude," so that Orientals and Chicanos (for example) are literally covered; and the Fourteenth is the most expansive of all, speaking of "persons." My position is not that the Amendments should be held effective only for protection of Negroes,* but that anti-Negro discrimination should occasion particularly determined judicial condemnation because the central purpose of the Constitutors was to cure an affliction which, like sickle-cell anemia, has afflicted that race virtually alone — at least in this country.

I recognize further that the Constitutors themselves very probably viewed the Amendments as protecting against racial discrimination generally, not only against anti-Negro discrimination. Their words make that clear, and the Court has doubtless been justified in applying the Amendments as strictly in favor of Orientals and Chicanos, for example, as it has applied them in favor of Negroes.[11] The point remains, however, that the Amendments reflect a national allergy to *racial* discrimination that

---

* *Compare* footnote on p. 227 *supra.*

is more intense than the national allergy to discrimination against nonracial minorities.

A number of the free expression cases reviewed in the preceding chapter exemplify the Court's curious reluctance to admit the obvious. The new constitutional rule announced in *NAACP v. Button* (1963),[12] born out of the need for eliminating untouchability, has been partly discredited by the Court's persistent de-emphasis of the race factor, which has led to mechanical extension of the rule to other situations not involving racial discrimination or any other issue reasonably considered as having constitutional dimension. The same is true of the doubtfully legitimate progeny of (a) the clearly legitimate ruling in *New York Times Co. v. Sullivan* (1964);[13] (b) *Edwards v. South Carolina* (1963)[14] and other cases opening wider the "forum of the streets";[15] and (c) cases such as *Shelton v. Tucker* (1960),[16] protecting Negro organizational activity. These decisions have been noted in the preceding chapter.[17]

Also noted in the preceding chapter is the probable racial element in the broad offensive the Court has mounted against archaic and callous aspects of the criminal process.[18] Of the thousands of criminal cases brought to the Court in the past quarter-century, many if not most involved black defendants complaining of coerced confessions, unlawful searches, denial of counsel, double jeopardy, and other such abuses. Perhaps the disproportionate number of black defendants resulted from racial discrimination, perhaps from the higher incidence of crime in this socially handicapped group, perhaps from both. Whatever the reason, it was clear that the criminal process was a particularly important element in the relationship between blacks and society at large, and that abuses had dangerous potential for increased racial tension. Awareness of this fact may well have helped induce the Court to institute the sweeping reforms of recent years, during which most of the safeguards contained in the Fourth, Fifth, Sixth, and Eighth Amendments — originally adopted as restrictions on the Federal Government alone [19] — have been extended to state prosecutions,[20] and new safeguards of fairness and privacy have been ordered for

Federal and state prosecutions alike.²¹ In most cases the Court has made no reference to the significance of race; but it seems to have been decisive in *Furman v. Georgia* (1972),²² which held that the death penalty as then administered violated the constitutional prohibition against "cruel and unusual punishments." The vote was five to four. Of the five Justices in the majority, only two declared the death penalty unconstitutional *per se.* Its discriminatory aspect was decisive for Justice Douglas, one of the other three. Pointing to the disproportionate number of Negroes who had been executed, he declared it " 'cruel and unusual' to apply the death penalty — or any other penalty — selectively to minorities whose numbers are few, who are outcasts of society, and who are unpopular." ²³

\* \* \* \* \*

The Court's awareness of racial inequality has not only made its mark on the law of freedom of expression and on the criminal process. Reluctance to assign special legal status to racial minorities has also led to generalization of the law of equality itself. Equality doctrine now extends well beyond caste problems and narrowly restricts governmental classification in a number of other fields.

### The doctrinal framework

The Constitution has long been understood to require some degree of consistency in governmental action. A typical formulation is that "cities, states and the Federal Government must exercise their powers so as not to discriminate between their inhabitants except upon some reasonable differentiation fairly related to the object of regulation." ²⁴ This is called the "rational relationship" test because it requires a rational connection between the discrimination and the governmental objective. In practice it has been a highly permissive one. Except where the discrimination has plainly been motivated by hostility to a socially isolated minority and not by a purpose to serve the needs of the public at large, judicial doubts have been resolved in favor of validity. In a 1935 case the Court said:

> It is a salutary principle of judicial decision, long emphasized and followed by this Court, that the burden of establishing the unconstitutionality of a statute rests on him who assails it, and that courts may not declare a legislative discrimination invalid unless, viewed in the light of facts made known or generally assumed, it is of such a character as to preclude the assumption that the classification rests upon some rational basis within the knowledge and experience of the legislators. A statutory discrimination will not be set aside as the denial of equal protection of the laws if any state of facts reasonably may be conceived to justify it.[25]

In that case a state statute allowing a longer time for suits on claims against out-of-state insurance companies than against local ones was upheld, the Court saying that the legislature *might* have thought there was a difference in the time claimants needed to prepare for litigation — though the legislature had not so declared, and the legislative history reflected no such idea.

This permissive judicial approach reflected recognition that nearly all legislation involves classification of one kind or another, that classifications often result from expedient compromise rather than logical principle, that articulation of a coherent legislative purpose is frequently impossible because different legislators have had different reasons for approving the result reached, and that the difficult business of assembling legislative majorities would be paralyzed by a requirement of rigid consistency. Moreover, the electorate has ultimate power to bring about the repeal or improvement of statutes which deviate too far from the ideal of equality, and the availability of a political remedy lessens the Court's responsibility.

In some cases, however, the Court has applied a stricter standard; it has invalidated discriminations even though they might be rationally related to a permissible objective, unless a "compelling governmental interest" could be demonstrated. Occasionally, as in the *Korematsu* case involving relocation of Japanese-Americans for military reasons, the compelling governmental interest test has been satisfied and the discrimination upheld.[26] The test is a severe one, however, and its application usually results in a declaration of unconstitutionality.

Initially the stricter test was applied rather sporadically and on a particularistic basis. For example, *Skinner v. Oklahoma ex rel. Williamson* (1942)[27] invalidated a state statute providing for sterilization of habitual criminals (persons convicted of three "felonies involving moral turpitude") because embezzlement, tax violations, and other so-called white-collar crimes were excepted from its operation. The rational relationship test would probably have led to a contrary result, since the legislature *might* have had a basis for believing that criminal tendencies are more inheritable for some crimes than for others. The Court, however, held that "strict scrutiny" was required because procreation is "one of the basic civil rights of man."[28] That would have been more understandable as a reason for denying all legislative power to sterilize criminals, than for an abnormally strict *equality* requirement. In any event, there was no indication that the category of "basic civil rights" might be a broad one; the Court emphasized the special dangers of sterilization, and referred obliquely to Hitler's genocide efforts as showing the potential enormity of the deprivation.

For more than twenty years the Court maintained its deferential attitude toward the legislative judgment with respect to classification,[29] except for racial classification, which it treated as inherently "suspect." As it said in the 1964 interracial cohabitation case:

> Normally, the widest discretion is allowed the legislative judgment in determining whether to attack some, rather than all, of the manifestations of the evil aimed at; and normally that judgment is given the benefit of every conceivable circumstance which might suffice to characterize the classification as reasonable rather than arbitrary and invidious. . . . But we deal here with a classification based upon the race of the participants, which must be viewed in light of the historical fact that the central purpose of the Fourteenth Amendment was to eliminate racial discrimination emanating from official sources in the States. This strong policy renders racial classifications "constitutionally suspect," . . . subject to the "most rigid scrutiny," . . . and "in most circumstances

irrelevant" to any constitutionally acceptable legislative purpose. . . .

...That a general evil will be partially corrected may at times, and without more, serve to justify the limited application of a criminal law; but legislative discretion to employ the piecemeal approach stops short of permitting a State to narrow statutory coverage to focus on a racial group. Such classifications bear a far heavier burden of justification.[30]

Then, in a series of nonracial cases involving the right to vote, the stricter standard was applied because of the basic importance of the elective franchise.[31] And in 1968 the Court invalidated a state statute allowing legitimate but not illegitimate children to recover damages for their mother's wrongful death, describing "the intimate, familial relationship between a child and his own mother" as a basic civil right.[32] The Court was taking a more expansive view of its authority to strike down classifications which it considered inhumane or unwise.

*Shapiro v. Thompson* (1969) [33] crystallized a broad rationalizing principle. The case involved welfare (poor-relief) laws in Connecticut, Pennsylvania, and the District of Columbia. Each state has its own welfare law and fixes its own scale of payments and eligibility requirements, but must conform to Federal standards in order to receive large Federal grants which cover most of the cost. In the District of Columbia, welfare payments are dispensed by the Federal Government directly. The question was whether the two states and the District could require newly arrived residents to wait a year before receiving payments for dependent children and for disability. The Court held that the Equal Protection Clause forbade the two states, and the Fifth Amendment Due Process Clause forbade the District, to discriminate between old and new residents in this way.

First, the Court declared that the waiting period could not be justified as a means of discouraging the entry of poor people, even if they had moved in order to obtain higher welfare payments than they had received in the states they had left. Citing earlier cases holding that there is a constitutional right of unimpeded movement across state lines, the Court said that the withholding of benefits was a deterrent to the exercise of that right and was not a permissible objective. Then it dealt with four other claimed justifications: that the waiting period facilitated the planning of the welfare budget; provided an objective and easily administered test of residency; minimized the opportunity for recipients fraudulently to obtain double welfare payments by continuing on the relief rolls in the states they had left; and encouraged the new arrivals to take jobs. In rejecting these arguments on the ground that the state had other ways to accomplish these purposes which did not discourage interstate movement, the Court formulated a broad principle:

> At the outset, we reject appellants' argument that a mere showing of a rational relationship between the waiting period and these four admittedly permissible state objectives will suffice to justify the classification.... The waiting-period provision denies welfare benefits to otherwise eligible applicants solely because they have recently moved into the jurisdiction. But in moving from State to State or to the District of Columbia appellees were exercising a constitutional right, and any classification which serves to penalize the exercise of that right, unless shown to be necessary to promote a *compelling* governmental interest, is unconstitutional....
>
> ... the traditional criteria do not apply in these cases. Since the classification here touches on the fundamental right of interstate movement, its constitutionality must be judged by the stricter standard of whether it promotes a *compelling* state interest.[34] (Emphasis in original)

It should be noted that the Court, in justifying application of the stricter standard, first characterized interstate movement as a "constitutional right" and later referred to it as a "fundamental right." The two terms may not be coextensive; but the difference between them, if any, is unimportant because the Court exercises the power (1) to coin new constitutional rights, and (2) to characterize as fundamental any "right" (more precisely, any *interest*) which it thinks should enjoy extraordinary judicial protection. The Court, in later cases, has usually resorted to the "fundamental right" terminology to rationalize its use of the compelling governmental interest test where *the especially important nature of the right affected* has been the basis for insistence on rigid equality; and that terminology will be used here.

This strict test has also been applied on a separate ground involving not the nature of the right affected but *the nature of the classification*. Certain classifications of persons are held to be "suspect" and are held unconstitutional unless essential to the furtherance of a compelling (and permissible) governmental objective. As noted above, racial classifications were the first to be called suspect. As the equality concept has broadened beyond concern with caste, the category of suspect classifications has been extended.

For comprehension of the doctrinal basis of the decisions about to be reviewed, it should be understood that many of them have depended both on the nature of the right affected *and* on the nature of the classification. One commentator has written:

> The interaction of these two factors can be visualized by imagining two gradients. Along the first of these gradients is a hierarchy of classifications, with those which are most invidious — suspect classifications based on traits such as race — at the top. Along the second, arranged in ascending order of importance, are interests such as employment, education, and voting. When the classification drawn lies at the top of the first gradient, it will be subject to strict review even when the interest it affects ranks low on the second gradient — for example, the denial of a driver's license on the basis of race. As the nature of the classification becomes less invidious (descending on the first gradient) the measure will continue to elicit strict review only as it affects interests progressively more important (ascending on the second gradient). Thus, restrained review might be applied when a state disqualifies indigents by requiring a fee from all persons desiring a driver's license or a university education, whereas strict review is applied when indigents are disqualified from voting through a fee imposed for the exercise of that right.[35]

There also appears to be an interrelationship between the nature of the right affected and the kind of governmental interest that will be held sufficiently compelling to justify its curtailment. Justice White has declared:

> ... as the Court's assessment of the weight and value of the individual interest escalates, the less likely it is that mere administrative convenience and avoidance of hearings or investigations will be sufficient to justify what otherwise would appear to be irrational discriminations.[36]

## Poverty

Inequality of wealth has been a prolific source of litigation. The Court has never gone quite so far as to hold that the withholding of governmental services because of inability to pay for them is in itself enough to warrant strict review. In other words, it has not declared wealth to be an inherently suspect basis of classification. Yet it has done much to mitigate legal disadvantage resulting from poverty.

This is particularly evident in the criminal process area. The right to appointment of a defense lawyer without cost, for accused persons who are unable to pay a fee, was first declared to be necessary for ignorant and friendless defendants in capital cases;[37] later, in all cases where a substantial prison sentence was possible;[38] and, recently, in all cases involving the possibility of any imprisonment whatever.[39] Although there is no constitutional right of appeal, appellate review — if provided, as it is in all but the most trivial cases — must be equally available to rich and poor. Thus, if the appellant is too poor to pay for a typed transcript of the trial proceedings (for review by a higher court),[40] or if he cannot afford to pay a lawyer to present his appeal,[41] they must be provided without cost; and if he cannot pay a filing fee, it must be waived.[42] Many states have statutes requiring criminal defendants to reimburse the state for legal fees paid on their behalf. The Court has refused to hold that this is an unconstitutional burden on the right to counsel, but has invalidated one such statute because the defendants were not allowed the same exemptions as other debtors.[43]

The Court has also limited the practice of imprisoning convicted persons because of their failure to pay fines, under statutes providing that unpaid fines must be "worked off" in jail at a specified rate (typically $5 per day of confinement). Indigent defendants cannot be jailed for nonpayment of fines if the result will be to increase their term of incarceration beyond the maximum imprisonment otherwise authorized by the penal statute.[44] Thus, if a sentence up to five years and $10,000 is authorized, it is pointless to add a fine to a five-year prison sentence where the defendant is indigent. Applying this principle, the Court has held that inability to pay fines for traffic offenses punishable *only* by fine results in freedom from any punishment whatever [45] — an indication of the extent to which equality is exalted above other social values in criminal cases.

Less has been done to mitigate the disadvantage of poverty in private litigation. The Court did hold that due process requires the waiver of court fees for indigent plaintiffs in divorce cases, such cases being deemed to involve a unique need for access to judicial relief because marriages cannot be dissolved by agreement of the spouses;[46] but such relief has been held unavailable for other civil proceedings such as petitions in bankruptcy and appeals from administrative rulings on welfare benefits.[47] Legal assistance to the poor is available to some extent through legal services programs financed partly or wholly by public funds, but the demand outruns the supply and the quality of the service is uneven.[48]

The 1969 opinion in *Shapiro v. Thompson,* already referred to, contained a hint that the Court might be about to intervene freely against all inequalities in welfare programs, on the theory that the right to poor-relief is fundamental; in disapproving the one-year waiting period there involved, it remarked that such benefits are "the very means to subsist — food, shelter, and other necessities of life." [49] The later cases, however — all decided over the dissent of three or four Justices — have rejected unlimited judicial intervention in this area. A state law prescribing maximum benefits of $250 per month for families with dependent children was held not to violate the Equal Protection Clause, although the effect was to reduce the payment per child in larger families.[50] A state statute scaling down benefits for dependent children to 75% of estimated need, while paying 100% of estimated need to the aged and 95% to the disabled and the blind, was also upheld; the Court held it immaterial that 87% of recipients of dependent child benefits were Negroes and Mexican-Americans, whereas the other three categories contained a smaller proportion of those minority groups, because it said the "naked statistics" did not prove "racial motivation."[51] A Federal statute reducing disability benefits to reflect receipts from workmen's compensation (compensation for injury in the course of employment, under compulsory insurance carried by employers) was held valid although persons receiving other kinds of disability compensation (*e.g.*, tort damages, and insurance benefits under their own disability policies) do not have their Federal benefits reduced.[52]

The one case that clearly looks in the other direction invalidated a provision of the Federal food stamp program. Under the statute, only households comprised of related persons — *i.e.*, families — could obtain the stamps, which permit food purchases at very low prices. The decision that this was unconstitutional was influenced by the belief that Congress intended to discriminate against "hippie communes"; Justice Brennan, for the Court, said that "a bare congressional desire to harm a politically unpopular group cannot constitute a *legitimate* governmental interest."[53] Thus it seems that, in the field of welfare benefits, the Court is sensitive to discriminatory purpose but not to fiscal provisions which simply happen to result in inequality.

In the related field of subsidized housing, the Court has also been relatively unresponsive to complaints of discrimination. Federal loans and grants are made to state agencies for slum clearance and low-rent housing projects. In 1971 the Court upheld a California requirement that such a project be undertaken only after approval at an election conducted in the community where it was to be located. The requirement was attacked as discriminating against the poor, the three dissenting Justices calling it "an explicit classification on the basis of poverty — a suspect classification which demands exacting judicial scrutiny." The Court, however, did not agree that poverty was a suspect basis of classification. It held that the will of the local majority should be respected because part of the fiscal burden would rest on the local community.[54]

The next year the Court addressed itself explicitly to the question whether housing is so fundamental as to justify a rigid equality requirement for laws affecting the rights of tenants against their landlords. It gave a negative answer to that broad question, and yet invalidated a procedural provision erecting a special financial obstacle against appeals from court orders of eviction for nonpayment of rent — which it called a "discrimination against the poor." [55]

The five to four decision in *San Antonio Independent School District v. Rodriguez*,[56] though it rejected an equal protection claim, reflects the seriousness with which wealth differentials are evaluated even in matters of general tax policy — where, traditionally, legislatures rather than courts have been considered supreme. In every state but Hawaii, public schools are financed mainly by local property taxes raised in the respective school districts. Since the districts vary greatly in taxable property and in school-age population, there are substantial inequalities in the property tax revenues per pupil — and, consequently, in expenditures per pupil. These inequalities are mitigated to some extent by state and Federal grants (and perhaps, in some places, are fully balanced — or even overbalanced — by such grants), but it is not unusual for one district to spend twice as much per pupil as another.

In several states, the state constitutions have been held to forbid such inequality.[57] The Court declined to accept that position for the whole country, however. It pointed out that no correlation had been established between the wealth of a district and the wealth of its residents: a district inhabited mainly by poor people may contain valuable factories and commercial buildings which give it a high tax base, and may have few school-age children. Inhabitants of the tax-poor districts, the Court said, comprise "a large, diverse, and amorphous class ... [having] none of the traditional indicia of suspectness." [58] Nor, as the Court said, is public education a "fundamental right." And with a humility that seems somehow quaint and old-fashioned, it acknowledged that

> the Justices of this Court lack both the expertise and the familiarity with local problems so necessary to the making of wise decisions with respect to the raising and disposition of public revenues.... No scheme of taxation ... has yet been devised which is free of all discriminatory impact. In such a complex arena in which no perfect alternatives exist, the Court does well not to impose too rigorous a standard of scrutiny lest

all local fiscal schemes become subjects of criticism under the Equal Protection Clause.... We are unwilling to assume for ourselves a level of wisdom superior to that of legislators, scholars, and educational authorities in 50 States, especially where the alternatives proposed are only recently conceived and nowhere yet tested.[59]

As noted, four of the nine Justices dissented.

### Illegitimate birth and alienage

In other fields the Court has been more confident of its superior wisdom. For example, it has held that various legal disabilities resulting from illegitimate birth violate the Equal Protection Clause: disability to recover damages for a mother's wrongful death;[60] disability of a mother to recover damages for the wrongful death of her illegitimate child;[61] subordination of an illegitimate child's workmen's compensation claim to that of a legitimate child, in case of the death of their father;[62] disability of an illegitimate child to claim financial support by his father;[63] and exclusion of some dependent illegitimate children from consideration in computing their fathers' Social Security benefits for disability.[64] However, a statute withholding inheritance rights from illegitimate children whose father had not formally acknowledged paternity was upheld by a vote of five to four.[65]

The same policy of favoring licit sexual relations that underlay state discriminations against illegitimate children, also motivated a state statute forbidding distribution of contraceptives to unmarried persons for the prevention of pregnancy (as distinguished from the prevention of disease). The statute was held unconstitutional as a discrimination against unmarried persons.[66]

Several recent cases have invalidated laws discriminating on the basis of citizenship, which has now been denominated a suspect basis of classification. Declaring that "classifications based on alienage, like those based on nationality or race ... are inherently suspect and are therefore subject to strict judicial scrutiny whether or not a fundamental right is involved," the Court struck down (1) a Pennsylvania law providing state-funded welfare benefits only for American citizens, and (2) an Arizona law providing Federally financed welfare benefits only for American citizens and for aliens who had resided in the United States for fifteen years or more.[67] Later decisions invalidated laws making citizenship necessary for admission to law practice [68] and to the state competitive civil service.[69] But the Court held that the refusal of a private company to employ aliens does not violate a Federal statutory prohibition against employment discrimination on the basis of national origin, which was held to be quite different from citizenship as a basis of classification.[70] It noted, without evident disapproval, that the Federal Government employs citizens only — not explaining why aliens can be excluded from the Federal but not the State competitive civil service. More recently, however, the Court has heard argument on whether to extend its condemnation to the Federal discrimination also.[71]

## Sex discrimination

The grosser forms of sex discrimination, such as denial of the franchise to women and the disability of married women to control their own property, have long since disappeared; but a heavy cultural residue persists. It is reflected partly in laws premised on the assumption that women are less capable than men in work involving physical strength or business acumen, and partly in laws attributing significance to women's status as nurturing parents and homemakers — such as alimony provisions for divorcees, special limitations on working hours, and exemptions from compulsory jury duty. A vigorous new feminist movement is pressing for ratification of a proposed Twenty-seventh Amendment, providing:

> Equality of rights under the law shall not be denied or abridged by the United States or by any State on account of sex.

The Amendment was approved by Congress in 1972 and at this writing has received thirty-four* of the thirty-eight state

---

* The thirty-four include two states, Nebraska and Tennessee, which first ratified the proposed Amendment and then rescinded, or attempted to rescind, their ratifications. It is an open question whether the attempted rescissions are effective. In favor of recognizing them, it can be argued that the Article V requirement of

ratifications necessary for adoption. If and when it is adopted, every law and administrative practice which treats women more or less favorably than men, or in any way differently, will be at least presumptively unconstitutional. In order to allow time for the extensive statutory changes that it will require, the Amendment is not to become effective until two years after its ratification.

Meanwhile, a great many attacks on sex discrimination have been launched on the basis of present law, and they are beginning to reach the Court. In *Reed v. Reed* (1971) [72] an Idaho law giving males preference over females as administrators of decedent estates was held to violate the Equal Protection Clause. (The father and mother of a deceased child were competing for the right to administer his estate.) In *Frontiero v. Richardson* (1973) [73] the Court invalidated a Federal statute enabling a male soldier to obtain increased pay by reason of marriage, without proving that his wife was in fact financially dependent on him, but granting such increase to a female soldier only upon proof that she supported her husband. Four of the Justices believed that sex should be declared a suspect basis of classification. Three others, without flatly rejecting that step, thought it should be deferred while the Twenty-seventh Amendment was under consideration by the states:

... democratic institutions are weakened, and confidence in

---

approval by three fourths of the states means that there should be some single point of time when three quarters of the states do approve. On the other side stands the stark fact that, if this argument were accepted, the Fourteenth Amendment was promulgated without proper ratification. *See* THE CONSTITUTION OF THE UNITED STATES OF AMERICA, SEN. DOC. NO. 82, 92d Cong., 2d Sess. 31 n.6. Another question is whether a state's rejection of an Amendment prevents later approval. Note, *Ratification of Child Labor Amendment by a State Legislature After Previous Rejection,* 47 YALE L.J. 148 (1937). Complicating the whole problem is uncertainty as to whether the question is entirely "political" and therefore nonjusticiable, so that the answer will have to be given by elected officials, or whether the Court has a part to play. *Compare* the majority opinion of Chief Justice Hughes *with* the concurring opinion of Justice Black (for four members of the Court) in Coleman v. Miller, 307 U.S. 433 (1939). Useful analyses include: ORFIELD, THE AMENDING OF THE FEDERAL CONSTITUTION (1942); Heckman, *Ratification of a Constitutional Amendment: Can a State Change Its Mind?,* 6 CONN. L. REV. 28 (1973); Note, *Reversals in the Federal Constitutional Amendment Process: Efficacy of State Ratifications of the Equal Rights Amendment,* 49 IND. L.J. 147 (1973); Note, *The Equal Rights Amendment: Will States Be Allowed to Change Their Minds?,* 49 NOTRE DAME LAW. 657 (1974).

the restraint of the Court is impaired, when we appear unnecessarily to decide sensitive issues of broad social and political importance at the very time they are under consideration within the prescribed constitutional processes.[74]

This seems to hold open the possibility that, if the Amendment does fail of ratification, the Court will then proceed to effectuate it nevertheless — by declaring sex classifications suspect and applying the compelling governmental interest test.

Although the Court has not yet taken that step, which would create a sweeping presumption of unconstitutionality, it has made clear the depth of its concern by giving sex equality priority over freedom of the press (which it usually defends as a constitutional value second to none*) in one important respect. In *Pittsburgh Press Co. v. Pittsburgh Commission on Human Relations* (1973) [75] it upheld a local order prohibiting a newspaper from listing advertisements for jobs in sex-designated help-wanted columns. (The four dissenters protested the decision as a dangerous encroachment on press freedom, believing that no government "can tell a newspaper in advance what it can print and what it cannot.") Very recently the Court held, however (by a vote of six to three), that a state does not unconstitutionally discriminate against women by establishing a program of disability benefits for

---

\* *See, e.g.,* the Court's unanimous decision in Miami Herald Pub. Co. v. Tornillo, 418 U.S. 241 (1974), holding invalid as an infringement of press freedom a Florida "right of reply" statute requiring the press media to publish responses of political candidates to attacks upon them. The Florida Supreme Court had upheld the statute on the ground, among others, that the defendant newspaper had a local monopoly which left candidates with no effective means of responding to unwarranted attacks upon them unless the statutory right of reply were recognized.

Incidentally, it is hard to see how the United States Supreme Court had jurisdiction of the appeal; there had been no "final" judgment in the state court within the meaning of 28 U.S.C. § 1257 (the statute delimiting the Court's appellate jurisdiction) as the Court had interpreted it prior to abandonment of the "passive posture." *See* p. 113 *supra.*) The Florida Supreme Court had reversed a lower court decision that the statute was unconstitutional and remanded the case for further proceedings. The United States Supreme Court, without significant analysis, found the judgment final on the basis of North Dakota State Bd. of Pharmacy v. Snyder's Drug Stores, Inc., 414 U.S. 156 (1973), one of the recent cases in which the Court has stretched the concept of finality in order to decide important questions that might not reach it otherwise. *See* discussion of *Mills v. Alabama* and *Organization for a Better Austin v. O'Keefe, infra,* ch. XV, p. 306.

sick and injured workers without including maternity benefits.[76] A number of other sex equality issues are raised by cases now pending in the Court.

### Electoral rights

In Chapter IX we have reviewed the Court's work in the field of electoral rights. We have seen that, at the same time that it has been endeavoring to equalize voting power (or at least to achieve equality in the number of eligible voters per legislator, which is one of the determining factors), the Court has steadily broadened the franchise by striking down restrictions on voting eligibility as violations of the Equal Protection Clause. It has characterized the right to vote as fundamental and has unsparingly applied the compelling governmental interest test. As noted above,[77] the right to vote in a local school board election cannot be limited to persons who own or rent taxable property in the district, or whose children attend public school there; this was held to be an unconstitutional discrimination against a bachelor who resided with his parents at their home in the district.[78] For like reason, military personnel cannot be denied the capacity to acquire local residence for voting purposes in the place where they are stationed,[79] and residents of Federal enclaves within a state are entitled to vote in state elections there.[80] In elections to pass upon proposed municipal bond issues, we have seen [81] that the franchise cannot be limited to property taxpayers but must be extended to all residents.[82] The Court held in 1969 that prisoners awaiting trial need not be provided with absentee ballots,[83] but in 1973 it held that they may nevertheless have a right to vote — which, unless absentee ballots are provided, would seem to require establishment of voting facilities in jails.* [84]

The most sweeping decision on voting eligibility was *Dunn v. Blumstein* (1972).[85] It dealt with durational residence requirements (denying the franchise to those who had resided in the state and

---

* O'Brien v. Skinner, 414 U.S. 524 (1974), held that New York's denial of absentee ballots to pre-trial detainees and convicted misdemeanants if, but only if, they were confined in the county of their residence (and thus were not eligible for absentee ballots) violated the Equal Protection Clause. This leaves open the question whether the franchise can be denied to all such prisoners. Richardson v. Ramirez, 418 U.S. 24 (1974), held that convicted felons can be disfranchised.

county for less than specified periods), which were found in nearly all states. The Court invalidated the typical statute of Tennessee, which made voting eligibility dependent on residence in the state for one year and in the county for three months. It said no governmental interest was sufficiently compelling to warrant such curtailment of the fundamental rights of voting and interstate movement. The Court said it would not object to a requirement of registration thirty days before the election, and later cases have in fact upheld fifty-day periods.[86]

The Twenty-fourth Amendment, adopted in 1964, forbade use of the poll tax to prevent voting in Federal elections. Two years later, the Court held that the Equal Protection Clause leads to the same result for state elections.[87] A contrary 1937 decision[88] was overruled.

The compelling governmental interest test has been applied to prevent not only discrimination in voting eligibility, but also discrimination in the eligibility of political parties and candidates for a place on the ballot. An Ohio election law was held unconstitutional on two grounds: first, because it permitted established parties to retain their position on the ballot simply by obtaining 10% of the vote at the last election for state governor, while requiring other parties to obtain signatures totaling 15% of the votes cast at that election; and second, because it required submission of the signatures too long (nine months) before election day.[89] In another case, heavy filing fees for candidates, ranging up to $8,900, were held to discriminate unlawfully against poor candidates and their probably poor supporters.[90]

\* \* \* \* \*

At the same time that the Court was holding the franchise to be supremely valuable — so valuable that the weight of votes cannot be allowed to vary from 1/9717 to 1/10313 of the total that can be cast for a legislative representative,[91] so valuable that the vote cannot be withheld from recently arrived residents[92] or diverted from splinter parties[93] — it was busily engaged in stripping the vote of much of its significance. In the years since 1962, one large subject matter after another has been put beyond majority rule in a dazzling display of seemingly freehand constitution-making without apparent concern for the intention of the Constitutors. Having converted the requirements of justiciability and standing into mere guidelines to be followed or disregarded almost at will,[94] the Court has plunged into the full-scale remodeling of the people-government relationship.

The bolder the Court's incursions upon majority rule, the less convincing were the justifications it offered. As we have seen,[95] it held in *Shapiro v. Thompson* (1969)[96] that a state cannot constitutionally make eligibility for welfare payments depend upon residence in the state for a year or more. Justice Brennan, for the Court, condemned the discrimination against recent arrivals as a denial of equal protection because the waiting period requirement failed to pass the "compelling governmental interest" test. In the years since 1969, that test has become a favorite formula for justification of constitution-making. Its beauty, from the viewpoint of a Court bent upon expanding its power, is that it sidesteps the need to explain why the judgment of the Court should be preferred to that of the legislature. That is treated as self-evident where a "fundamental" right or interest is involved. Therefore everything turns on whether a particular right or interest is denominated as "fundamental," and *that* depends upon a value judgment so broad that the Court's solemn affirmation of "fundamentality" cannot be verified by reference to any known standard. For all that one can tell, the only value judgment the Court makes is that it ought to take control of the particular subject matter; but one cannot be sure. Conveniently lost in the shuffle is the question why fundamental rights or interests, *whatever* they are, should be wards of the Court.

Justice Harlan was outraged at what he regarded as a verbal trick, and his dissent in *Shapiro v. Thompson* was caustic:

> ... I know of nothing which entitles this Court to pick out particular human activities, characterize them as "fundamental," and give them added protection under an unusually stringent equal protection test....
>
> ... Today's decision, it seems to me, reflects to an unusual degree the current notion that this Court possesses a peculiar wisdom all its own whose capacity to lead this Nation out of its present troubles is contained only by the limits of judicial ingenuity in contriving new constitutional principles to meet each problem as it arises.[97]

EQUALITY: BEYOND RACE 265

But the Court's drive toward omnicompetence was not to be halted, and the "compelling governmental interest" was too useful to be abandoned.

The test has also been found serviceable outside the equality field. For example, in *Roe v. Wade* (1973) [98] it was used to delimit the extent to which a state can enter a zone marked out by the Court as predominantly private (in the *Griswold v. Connecticut* sense); the Texas abortion laws were held to violate due process. Wherever it is used, the test reverses the presumption of constitutionality; the challenged official action is held invalid unless it can be shown that the statute is the only possible way to attain an important public objective, a burden that can rarely be sustained. It counts for nothing that the voters, through their elected representatives, have approved or acquiesced. And the Court, at its own discretion, decides when the stringent test is to be applied.

The freedom with which the Court now promulgates new constitutional rules is indicated by the number of unaccustomed fields it has entered in recent years. It has swept away some (but not all) state laws subjecting illegitimate children or their parents to legal disadvantage; [99] it has struck down long-established procedures for wage garnishment and repossession of goods; [100] it has invalidated ancient rules of evidence;[101] it has relieved indigent divorce plaintiffs (though not other civil litigants) of court costs;[102] it has significantly limited imprisonment for financial inability to pay fines;[103] it has extended its protection of verbal expression to the use of shock-words in public;[104] it has denied a state legislative house the power to punish summarily the calculated disruption of its proceedings by demonstrators (taking the astonishing position that summary punishment could only have been imposed by *immediate* adoption of a contempt resolution, which the disruption itself had rendered impossible).[105] The catalogue could be extended. The point is not that the uprooted laws and practices were enlightened, humane, and fair; by and large, they were not. The point is that issues long left for legislative resolution have become grist for the judicial mill.

As several of the Justices have noted in dissent,[106] there is only a verbal difference between the "fundamental rights" branch of the compelling governmental interest test and the now discredited substantive due process doctrine of such cases as *Lochner v. New York* (1905).[107] Both of them leave the Court entirely at large, with full freedom to enact its own natural law conceptions. The only difference is in the type of interests that are protected, and even that difference is beginning to disappear.[108]

Any statute can be attacked as "unequal" if (a) it applies to persons differently situated, as all or nearly all statutes do, and (b) "equality" is a matter of equality of effect rather than the legislators' state of mind — their *good-faith effort* to effect fair compromise between the competing interests of all segments of the population. This is because, if all persons are treated the same, the several burdens of hardship will be unequal by reason of the difference in individual circumstance, and if the statutory requirement is waived or softened for some persons in order to equalize the individual burdens, then the statute itself is "unequal" in that it treats different people differently.[109] In a moment we shall examine the most striking illustration of this dilemma, the cases applying the Free Exercise Clause of the First Amendment to religious minorities.

While the "fundamental rights" branch of the compelling governmental interest test is wholly subjective, there being no way to appraise objectively the decision of the Court to apply the label "fundamental," such total subjectivity does not infect the "suspect basis of classification" branch of the test — *if* applied in the manner contemplated by the third paragraph of the *Carolene Products* footnote. So applied, it simply leads the Court to be more skeptical of denials that there was a discriminatory legislative *purpose*. The reasonableness of the Court's suspicion that the legislators have not attempted to serve the whole people can be assessed by consideration of (a) the social isolation of the complaining minority group,* and (b) whether the legislature has

---

* Indicia of social isolation were enumerated by the Court in San Antonio Independent School Dist. v. Rodriguez, 411 U.S. 1, 28 (1973). *See* the quotation from

been callous to claims of great hardship that could so easily have been accommodated that failure to do so justifies an inference of unconcern for the complaining minority.

At the end of Chapter XI [110] we observed that the First Amendment Free Exercise Clause has served as a sort of super-equal protection clause. The Court has not been called upon, at least in recent years, to adjudicate the validity of purposeful discrimination *against* religious minorities. The tradition of religious toleration has sufficed to prevent enactment of statutes of that type. In the typical free-exercise case, the question has been whether a statute fair on its face is unconstitutional as applied to a religious minority, because it *fails to make accommodation for special hardship* suffered by members of such a group by reason of their religious tenets.

The pre-1937 Court brushed off such a contention in *Hamilton v. Regents* (1934),[111] where pacifist students at the University of California claimed a constitutional right to exemption from a requirement that all male students take military science courses. A similar contention was rejected in *Minersville School District v. Gobitis* (1940),[112] where children who were members of the Jehovah's Witnesses claimed a constitutional right to exemption from a requirement that public school students salute the flag at the beginning of each school day; they asserted that such a salute would violate the Second Commandment's precept against bowing down to a graven image. This time, however, there was a vigorous though solitary dissent by Justice Stone, who invoked the principle articulated in the third paragraph of his 1938 *Carolene Products* footnote: "more searching judicial scrutiny" of statutes directed against (or, more precisely, in this case, failing to accommodate the needs of) "discrete and insular minorities." In 1943, after the tide of military fortune in World War II had begun to run in favor of the Allies, and after some changes in the Court's membership, the *Gobitis* decision was overruled in *West Virginia State Board of Education v. Barnette* (1943); [113] but Justice Robert M. Jackson's

---

Justice Powell's opinion at p. 312 *infra* where the point is discussed further. *See also* Hernandez v. Texas, 347 U.S. 475, 478-80 (1954).

majority opinion did not rely on the Free Exercise Clause. It relied instead on a broader First Amendment freedom of (non)expression.

That same year, however, in *Murdock v. Pennsylvania* [114] and several companion cases,[115] the Free Exercise Clause was found to entitle Jehovah's Witnesses to exemption from nondiscriminatory local taxes imposed on the business of selling books or other literature. The weight accorded to Free Exercise considerations in those cases is not clear, because the element of press freedom was also involved. In *Braunfeld v. Brown* (1961) [116] a free-exercise claim to exemption from Pennsylvania blue laws, asserted by orthodox Jewish merchants, won the votes of only two Justices (Brennan and Stewart). But in *Sherbert v. Verner* (1963) [117] a religious claim was upheld under the Free Exercise Clause.

In that case a Seventh-Day Adventist was discharged by her South Carolina employer because she would not work on Saturday, the Sabbath Day of her faith. When she was unable to obtain other employment because conscientious scruples led her to decline Saturday work, she filed a claim for unemployment compensation under the South Carolina Unemployment Compensation Act. The Act provided that, to be eligible for benefits, a claimant must be able to work and available for work; and, further, that a claimant is ineligible for benefits "[i]f . . . he has failed, without good cause . . . to accept available suitable work when offered him by the employment office or the employer." [118] The claim for compensation was rejected, and the highest South Carolina court held that the rejection violated no constitutional rights. The United States Supreme Court reversed, only two Justices (Harlan and White) dissenting.

Justice Brennan's majority opinion did not deny that the state statutory eligibility requirement satisfied the "rational relationship" test, being a rational means of safeguarding the state's permissible interest in protecting its treasury from claims by loafers. However, in one of the earliest applications of the compelling governmental interest test, it was held that this was insufficient justification because the state could have achieved its legitimate objective in some other way. Justice Harlan, in dissent, pointed out that the Court was in effect requiring discrimination *in favor of* a religious minority:

> The State ... must *single out* for financial assistance those whose behavior is religiously motivated, even though it denies such assistance to others whose identical behavior (in this case, inability to work on Saturdays) is not religiously motivated.[119] (Emphasis in original)

For example, compensation could and would have been denied to a woman who could not work Saturdays because of inability to find or afford day care for her school-age children.

The Court ignored Harlan's protest, however, obviously because of extreme solicitude for the claim of *religious* hardship, and it has maintained that solicitude ever since. In *Welsh v. United States* (1970)[120] it extended the Selective Service Act exemption for religious conscientious objectors to include nonreligious objectors (obviously influenced by the rule of *McCollum v. Board of Education* (1948),[121] that nonbelievers are entitled to the protection of the religious clauses of the First Amendment). Four of the Justices predicated their votes on an impossibly strained "interpretation" of the Act; a fifth (Justice Harlan) could not swallow that interpretation, but concurred on the ground that the exclusion of nonbelievers from the benefits of the exemption violated the Establishment Clause.

The holding in *Gillette v. United States* (1971)[122] that the exemption need not be extended to objectors to particular wars rather than all wars, cannot be regarded as a backward step. A contrary ruling would have amounted to invalidation of military conscription and would have presented in aggravated form a general difficulty with the conscientious objector exemption — namely, that it discriminates in favor of college-trained objectors who are able to articulate clearly their moral standards, and against the equally unwilling but less articulate young men who know they oppose a particular war but cannot say exactly why.

The Court's continuing sensitivity to religious hardship was demonstrated in its amazing decision, rendered without substantial dissent, in *Wisconsin v. Yoder* (1972),[123] already referred to.[124] There the Court held that Amish children are entitled, under the Free Exercise Clause, to exemption from the Wisconsin compulsory school attendance statute insofar as it requires them to attend high school — which they and their parents believe involves exposure to the values of the outside world and therefore, in the long run, would destroy their close-knit religious communities.

\* \* \* \* \*

In the eight chapters comprising this Part Two we have reviewed the Court's constitutional rulings in controversial areas since 1937. The purpose is to lay a basis for ascertaining whether the principle of implied judicial power, as a measure of the legitimacy of constitution-making, can rightly be considered a neutral principle or whether it is so vague as to be illusory. As stated in Chapter I,[125] that is the question on which the validity of the thesis set forth in this book must stand or fall.

Our method of approach to that question is to see whether the principle can in fact be used for evaluation of the Court's work. In Part Three, I shall attempt to do it.\* It will be for the reader to judge whether I am right in believing that the attempt is successful.

---

\* Note that my objective is to show that the principle of implied judicial power *can* be used to evaluate the Court's work and can therefore serve to defend the Court from the accusation that it has cast off all restraint and set itself above the law. There is no need for me to say whether I believe that the need to justify the Court's decisions on the basis of implied judicial power is cause for rejoicing, *i.e.,* that the public interest has been better served by the Court's actual performance than it would have been served by its adherence to the Constitutional text. (Copernicus might have *regretted* that the Ptolemaic conception of the solar system was so hard to reconcile with Tycho Brahe's astronomical observations; but would this have justified him in remaining silent?) William F. Young's observation, quoted in the footnote on page 34 *supra,* is pertinent here.

There is of course a further question. Suppose that the evaluation shows (as I think it does) that some small part of the Court's recent constitution-making cannot be justified on the basis of implied judicial power. Is that small part so valuable that (unless someone else can devise another neutral principle or set of principles by which *all* the Court's actions can be justified, which I have found myself unable to do) it should be preserved even at the cost of acquiescing in the proposition that the Court ought to be above the law? This is the "stark choice between misgovernment by law and enlightened government by decree" to which I referred in Chapter VII.[126] Part Three will enable the reader to make his own judgment as to which alternative should be chosen.* My vote is for law.

We now proceed to examine the Court's present conception of its role, and then to apply the yardstick of implied judicial power to its constitutional decisions and pronouncements.

---

* My friend Milton Handler, who has served both as my law teacher and as my colleague, has written to me his own practical views on this question:

> I have always been very sympathetic to the position taken by Adolph Berle in his Carpentier lectures. Since the courts seem destined to be policy makers and to operate as a constitutional convention in continuous session, shouldn't the focus of attention be on how the Court can be helped to make policy wisely? I think that after a while one gets a bit fed up with all of the debates on methodology. Let me hasten to say that I think it is wrong for this to come about, but I am really describing what I think is the fact. We get tired of Viet Nam and we recoil from hearing anything more about it. I have an idea that most people today, even well trained lawyers, are likely to say, "If the results of the Court's cases are wise, isn't that all that should matter?" You would answer that question emphatically in the negative. You would say that the way in which the result is achieved is of signal importance. I believe you are right. It is a position that I have always taken in the past. But I veer towards the other point of view, namely, shouldn't we concentrate on whether the end results are good or bad for our country and shouldn't our energies be directed towards improving the way the Court operates so as to assure that it approaches policy making with the very best of the available tools.

# Part Three
# A Modest Proposal

CHAPTER XV
## The Court's New Role

The changes the Court has wrought in the substantive law of the Constitution since World War II, dramatic as they have been, are insignificant in comparison with the change it has wrought in its own role. Beginning in 1961 (the year John F. Kennedy reawakened the optimistic New Deal faith in rational government achieved through bold experiment) or 1962 (the year Justice Goldberg took the seat of Justice Frankfurter and added a fifth vote to the Court's "liberal wing" which had previously included Chief Justice Warren and Justices Black, Douglas, and Brennan), the orthodox *Marbury v. Madison* conception of judicial review has gradually given way to a broader one.\* Hesitantly at first, then ever more confidently, the Court emerged from the cocoon it had spun for itself since 1803, and unfolded its wings.

In Chapter VII [1] we have observed that the shift in constitutional doctrine that took place in the first years after 1937 was accomplished without abandoning the passive posture that was contemplated by Hamilton in his reference to "the least dangerous branch," was assumed by Chief Justice Marshall in *Marbury v. Madison,* and was glorified by Justice Brandeis in his *Ashwander* concurrence. Prior to 1937 there had been no need to abandon that passive posture. The pre-1937 Court had formulated its constitutional rules against a backdrop of private law derived from other sources — statutes, state common-law rules, treaties, customary international law. The rich structure of property and contract law already provided a full array of legal rights and

---
\* As early as 1960 Justice Brennan, speaking for the Court in United States v. Raines, 362 U.S. 17, 22, noted a number of deviations from strict orthodoxy. He called them "rules of practice."

remedies for protection of bargains and vested rights, so that the Court could defend free business enterprise simply by curbing legislative innovations. That is why so staunch a champion of *laissez faire* as Justice Sutherland, with all his uninhibited zeal to control unorthodox economic expedients undertaken by Congress and state legislatures, could be content with adjudication of *preexisting legal rights.* Speaking for the whole Court in *Frothingham v. Mellon* (1923),[2] he put judicial review in a narrow framework:

> We have no power *per se* to review and annul acts of Congress on the ground that they are unconstitutional. That question may be considered only when the justification for some direct injury suffered or threatened, presenting a justiciable issue, is made to rest upon such an act. Then the power exercised is that of ascertaining and declaring the law applicable to the controversy. It amounts to little more than the negative power to disregard an unconstitutional enactment, which otherwise would stand in the way of the enforcement of a legal right.... If a case for preventive relief be presented, the court enjoins, in effect, not the execution of the statute, but the acts of the official, the statute notwithstanding.[3]

Mrs. Frothingham claimed as a taxpayer that Congress lacked constitutional authority to pay over Federal funds to the states under the Maternity Act of 1921, thus increasing her Federal taxes in some degree. Her claim was rejected not on the ground that Congress possessed the questioned authority but on the ground that the lady had no *legal right* which the tax collector was infringing. The Court was indifferent to the fact that the constitutionality of the Maternity Act could be adjudicated in no other way. It felt no compulsion to purge the statute books of invalid legislation, so long as the *legal rights* of litigants were not infringed.

We have also observed that the Court maintained its traditional passive posture down to 1961 or 1962 and then, in one field after another, demanding more and more sweeping reforms, it moved to a more active attack on five major flaws it perceived in American society. In retrospect, it is not difficult to see what led the Justices to the drastically enlarged conception of their role. They had felt the effect of the thousands of entreaties for help, heard in steadily swelling volume in the years after 1937, from dissenters, accused persons, and members of minority groups. Those entreaties, which it had stimulated by its own interventions on behalf of the oppressed, in turn triggered further interventions on a far grander scale. The petitions for certiorari could be denied, the appeals summarily dismissed, but the papers were read and pondered; and case after case provided, in specific and often shocking detail, a glimpse of life on the underside.

As the glimpses multiplied, it must have become ever harder for the Justices to believe that the people-government relationship was fundamentally healthy; that deviations from the professed ideals of liberty, rationality, and equality of opportunity were exceptional; and that the Court's traditional passive posture was suited to the needs of the times. In 1940 its opinions had breathed optimism. They seemed to say that realization of the great ideals was in sight and that the Court only needed to step in for correction of occasional aberrations. A quarter-century later most of the Justices had abandoned the passive posture. They chafed at rigid jurisdictional and procedural requirements that interfered with adjudication of constitutional issues, and found ways around them. They were not content to decide the case before them and declare the constitutional rules that applied; they concerned themselves also with the universal and speedy enforcement of those rules. And they no longer hesitated to call for sweeping changes in the existing order.

The first tentative struggles to excape the confining cocoon were *Barrows v. Jackson* (1953), fleshing out *Shelley v. Kraemer,* the 1948 restrictive covenant decision,[4] and the 1955 implementation decision in *Brown v. Board of Education,* the public school segregation case.[5] Apart from these experimental efforts at rehabilitation of the Fourteenth Amendment as an instrument for extirpation of the remnants of slavery, the Court was content with its old jurisdiction-limiting rules, content to accord the immediate parties their legal rights without caring how soon or completely its decisions were accepted throughout the land (*e.g.*, by Congress and the state governments).*

It was able to assume that, because it had related its decisions to the written Constitution, the rest of government would comply with the Constitution as interpreted by the Court. It could assume that other organs of government would respect the Constitution because the Court had enabled them to *understand* it. Its meaning was thought to depend ultimately on the words of the Constitutors, and the Court said its job was to decide how the Constitutors would have dealt with current problems. When constitutional decisions were overruled, the Court said it was to get closer to the Constitution as the Constitutors made it. And the Court rarely called for change in any *widespread practice;* it dealt mainly with the rare and exceptional cases (so far as the Constitution was concerned — statutory construction was another matter).

Beginning about 1962, the Court began to take an ever more intense interest in the *effectuation* of its rulings. It began to think in terms of constitutional *rights* rather than constitutional *powers* — *i.e.*, to look at the law through the eyes of the people affected by it rather than the government officials who declared and enforced it; to be worried about cynicism of the people if their constitutional rights were not valuable in fact. From this viewpoint it was important for the Court to see to it that its rulings were backed by accessible remedies and were generally complied with. This soon led to a much more active role in which the Court was relatively less concerned with justice to the immediate parties, and more concerned with the need to change social conditions. The

---

* For example, the Court held in Tumey v. Ohio, 273 U.S. 510 (1927), that the then familiar system under which magistrates received as their fees a percentage of the fines they imposed, was a violation of due process because it made the magistrate a judge in his own case. For twenty-nine years the decision was a dead letter in Kentucky, and very probably in other states as well, because there was no way to mount a collateral attack on a magistrate's fine; collateral attack was held unavailable because a trial *de novo* could be had on appeal to a higher court. (It was nearly always cheaper to pay the fine, however, than to take the appeal.) Finally, the Kentucky Court of Appeals took notice of the lawlessness of the existing fee system and ordered it abolished — after expiration of the then current terms of office of incumbent magistrates (justices of the peace). Roberts v. Noel, 296 S.W.2d 745 (Ky. 1956).

change of role was not announced, but is plain from a study of the Court's performance in various fields. It makes the *Marbury* conception of judicial review obsolete, and a number of the practice rules that are its corollaries have been heavily modified. But even today the Court clings to the *form* of the *Marbury* approach and reverts to its substance when expedient.

The Court used to apply judicial review only in a negative way. Adjudications of unconstitutionality operated as a veto on some initiative taken by another organ of government, endeavoring to change the status quo. The underlying assumption was that the status quo was pretty good and that, in case of doubt, the prohibition of a change was less likely to be socially harmful than the change would be, if permitted. The present use of judicial review includes a large element of innovation, the Court acting as a prime mover rather than a modulator of efforts at change initiated elsewhere. As a mere modulator, the Court could not accelerate change farther than was desired by electoral majorities. As a prime mover, it is not subject to that limitation; and it has demanded a number of social changes which do not command majoritarian support. That may be why the Court has thought it necessary to concern itself with *effectuating* its judgments. The Court is now often declaring a rule of law that is unpopular and is likely to win no enthusiastic support from elected officials; its task is not simply to allow or prevent enforcement of a law which, by hypothesis, the electoral majority presumably wants. This involves great technical difficulties with the passive posture. In order to understand them, one must keep in mind some obvious propositions about the mechanics of enforcement.

Governmental action consists partly of regulation (including taxation) and partly of services, such as on-the-scene police and fire protection, welfare payments, delivery of the mails, and education. By regulation, government controls an individual's own conduct and protects him from the interfering conduct of others. It is easy for the Court, without departing from the passive posture, to limit regulatory controls if they are judicially enforced, as they usually are in our society. It is hard for the Court to limit them if they are enforced extra-judicially, or to compel effective extra-judicial enforcement, or to substitute its own control for extra-judicial enforcement. Any controls of individual conduct, in our "free" society, work poorly unless backed by public opinion; and, in this connection, it is not to be overlooked that the Court's every encouragement of the assertion of individual constitutional immunities has initially weakened the sense of political obligation — the compulsion to obey the law simply because constituted authority declares it to be the law — and has made it harder (not only for elected officials, but for the Court) to induce voluntary compliance.

When the Court limits the government's *regulatory controls,* large social change* — what we have called sweeping reform — results if (but only if) the controls are necessary to suppress conduct that disrupts Everyman's life (*e.g.,* prosecution of burglary) or to compel conduct essential to Everyman's life (*e.g.,* coercion of child support). Any social change that does result will come rather gradually, since many persons will continue to conform to the previously enforced standard even though compulsion to do so has ceased (*e.g.,* continue to respect racially restrictive covenants by "gentleman's agreement" long after they have become legally unenforceable).

As for *governmental services,* different considerations come into play. The Court can easily modify the manner in which they are rendered [6] and can prevent elected officials from withholding, from some disfavored class,[7] benefits made available to the rest of the population. What is hard, without the support of elected officials — *i.e.,* of public opinion — is for the Court (a) to prevent discrimination in services rendered by private individuals, or (b) to

---

* Perhaps the term "large social change" needs no definition, but it is appropriate to state my own conception of its meaning. I believe that the essence of large social change is a shift in many people's perception of their relationship with others. The particular kind of change which the Court has usually wrought is an alteration — for better or worse — of security felt by people because of their confidence, or lack of it, that the government will protect them from harm or interference by others. Some of my colleagues believe that this definition is too narrow to be useful, and that it merely identifies one of the *consequences* of large social change. My own view is that the core of the change is in the hearts and minds of men, and not in the technological or legal or environmental or other changes that have *affected* their hearts and minds.

compel either elected officials or private individuals to render, or continue to render, services *on the Court's terms.*[8] Large social change frequently results from initiating, modifying, or discontinuing governmental or private services.

We have seen in Chapter V that it was in *Linkletter v. Walker* (1965),[9] the first explicit prospectivity ruling, that the Court candidly revealed that it was departing from the *Marbury* conception of judicial review.[10] To be sure, there were earlier cases in which dissenting Justices accused the majority of making new constitutional rules; but the majority routinely ignored or denied the accusations, claiming to be controlled by the words and intent of the Constitutors. When a prior constitutional interpretation was discarded in favor of a new one, which happened with some frequency, the assigned reason was that the earlier interpretation had erroneously disregarded the Constitutors' intention and therefore could not be allowed to stand. *Stare decisis* was declared to be inapplicable in such situations for the very reason that the Court lacked power to amend the Constitution; the prior erroneous interpretation, it was said, would have the same effect as an amendment unless repudiated as soon as it was perceived to be wrong.[11] Cases since 1965 explain the Court's readiness to revise constitutional rules on the quite different ground that the amendment procedure prescribed by Article V is so difficult that the Court can rightly bypass it.[12]

These are the principal considerations that bear upon one of the major practical limits on the Court's power to institute large social change. The other major limit is imposed by the Court's inability to carry more of a caseload than is consistent with its tiny size, the need for time to deliberate and exchange views, and the ideal of technical excellence in opinion-writing.

Since 1962 the Court has discovered a number of ways in which it can develop leverage — increase the impact of its decisions by giving them, in effect, the quality of wholesale rather than tailor-made adjudication. They fall under two main headings: (1) Adoption of new doctrines that extend the Court's effective reach and bring the lower Federal courts into situations formerly reserved for the state courts (with Federal review available only in the Supreme Court). (2) Adoption of opinion-writing techniques which, in effect, anticipate and prejudge a large number of cases that would otherwise arise in the same general field as the particular case *sub judice.*

Before examining the particulars, it will be helpful to review in detail one great exploit in constitution-making, where the Court not only showed how thoroughly it has emancipated itself from the *Marbury v. Madison* conception of judicial review, but also illustrated the injustice that can result from achieving such emancipation as a matter of *substance* while adhering to the *formal practices* that grew up around the now superseded conception. The case is *Miranda v. Arizona* (1966).[13]

For a long time the Court had been troubled by the virtual impossibility of finding out, with any degree of certainty, what pressure (if any) the police have used to obtain a confession from a suspect in their custody. Typically the suspect would testify that he had been subjected to physical or mental torture and the police would deny it. On both sides credibility was weakened by interest. In the *Miranda* case the Court devised a set of prophylactic rules which it hoped would largely bypass the credibility question. It held that no statement given by the suspect after custodial interrogation is admissible in evidence unless he has been advised of his right to remain silent; has been warned that his words may be used against him; has been told he is entitled to have his lawyer present during the interrogation; and has been offered appointed counsel for that purpose if he lacks the means of getting a lawyer on his own.[14] The Court also held that no waiver of these rights is effective unless it is convincingly proved to be voluntary.[15]

The new rules were designed to change existing interrogation practice greatly, and they very probably did. The most drastic departure from existing practice was the requirement that the prisoner be offered appointed counsel to assist him at the interrogation. It is doubtful that the lawyer's presence was thought valuable because of the professional advice he might give. Except in the unusual case, his advice to his client is simply to remain silent; and the other warnings convey that message. The lawyer's main function is as an outside observer whose very presence will either deter coercive practices or make him an available witness to any coercion that does take place. The Court, by resorting to judicial control over the legal profession, thus devised an ingenious means of making the voluntariness requirement more effective.

In his majority opinion, Chief Justice Warren said that "our holding is not an innovation in our jurisprudence, but is an application of principles long recognized and applied in other settings." [16] It is hard to accept his words at face value. Unless the Court was consciously making new constitutional rules, it was chargeable with the most egregious injustice; for at the same time that it decided the *Miranda* case and its three companion cases, it denied certiorari in some 75 other cases presenting the same issue.[17] Only if new rules were being laid down could those other convictions rightly be left untouched. And even on that assumption (which the Court confirmed a week later in *Johnson v. New Jersey,* [18] holding that the *Miranda* decision applied only to cases tried after announcement of the new rules), the four *Miranda* reversals constitute a serious departure from the ideal of equal justice. Quite clearly, these four cases — which Justice Douglas, a member of the five-man *Miranda* majority, later said had been selected at random [19] — were employed as a vehicle for making the new rules, and the four lucky defendants were mere incidental beneficiaries. As in *Powell v. McCormack* (1969),[20] the *Marbury v. Madison* conception of judicial review was completely inverted. Instead of deciding a constitutional question in order to adjudicate the legal rights of litigants, the Court was using the litigation as an occasion for expressing its constitutional views. Adjudication was subordinated to constitution-making.

The *Miranda* ruling is interesting also as demonstrating how far the Court has surmounted its handicap in devising remedies. It lacks the power of the purse which enables Congress to create new offices and agencies — even raise armies — to carry out its objectives. Yet, by relying on the zeal of lawyers in defense of their clients' rights, and simplifying the task of those lawyers as well as itself by adopting blunt prophylactic rules, it can accomplish great change.

Other cases show how the Court has even surmounted to a considerable extent the handicap resulting from its inability to legislate administrative structures into existence. The 1955 implementation ruling in *Brown v. Board of Education*[21] inaugurated extensive use of the device of compelling other organs of government (there, the local school boards) to formulate "plans" establishing needed administrative structures, and to submit the plans for judicial approval or disapproval. The same device has done yeoman service in the legislative malapportionment cases.[22] And, of course, the familiar device of appointing a master in chancery — long used in litigation between states where the Court has original jurisdiction — is also available to the lower Federal courts in cases deemed important enough to justify its use.[23]

## NEW DOCTRINES

### Broadened collateral attack

The first of the new jurisdiction-broadening doctrines was announced in *Fay v. Noia* (1963).[24] In 1942, Noia was convicted of murder in a New York state court and was sentenced to life imprisonment. He considered appealing to a higher court on the ground that the conviction was based on his involuntary confession, but decided against that course because he feared that if he won reversal and new trial he might receive the death sentence — the fate that had overtaken Palko five years before.[25] In 1942 the Federal constitutional safeguards against use of involuntary confessions were still in a rudimentary stage [26] and Noia had reason to doubt that he would be granted a reversal *without* retrial.

Noia's two co-defendants did appeal. They were unsuccessful; but they were able to sustain their own involuntary confession claims in collateral challenges to their convictions, in 1955 and 1956, after the Court's involuntary confession doctrine had matured. Noia initiated a similar collateral attack by a petition for habeas corpus in the Federal district court, but lost because the highest state court held that, under a (valid) New York rule of procedure, failure to appeal precluded collateral attack. The United States Supreme Court granted certiorari and reversed by a vote of six to three, Justice Brennan writing the Court's opinion.

Under the Court's previous decisions Noia would have been denied relief because, whether or not it had been unconstitutional to receive his confession in evidence against him, his conviction was sustainable on the adequate non-Federal ground mentioned above — so that, even if the Court had held his confession involuntary, Noia's conviction and imprisonment would have stood (by reason of his failure to appeal in 1942). But by 1963 it had become apparent to the Court that many aspects of the state criminal process needed improvement, and that often — under existing law — the only way to bring about such improvement was for a Federal court to take the time to reconsider the record and decide whether a miscarriage of justice had occurred. That might well have imposed a crushing caseload burden on the Court, one that could be lightened if the lower Federal courts were empowered to take the laboring oar. And that is what the Court decided to do. It held that the adequate non-Federal ground rule did not apply if the state ground was based on a procedural rather than a substantive rule, unless the defendant had deliberately abused the state procedure to gain a tactical advantage.

Justice Brennan's opinion for the Court did not relate the decision to these considerations. Instead, he adopted a novel "interpretation" of the 1867 Habeas Corpus Act, which he said empowered the lower Federal courts to liberate a prisoner if his *detention* was unlawful, even if he was detained pursuant to a judgment of conviction whose validity could not be challenged. Justice Harlan, joined by Justices Clark and Stewart, demolished this reasoning by showing that the Court had always treated the validity of the detention as being inseparable from the validity of the judgment, and had held that any detention pursuant to a valid judgment is lawful. But they dissented in vain. Not only did the

Court uphold Noia's habeas corpus petition; it also held, in the companion case of *Townsend v. Sain* (1963),[27] where Justice White joined the three *Fay v. Noia* dissenters, that the Federal district courts must grant evidentiary hearings in habeas corpus proceedings in any of a large number of situations which the Court described in detail. Chief Justice Warren, for the Court, remarked that a main purpose of the 1867 Habeas Corpus Act was to permit the trial, in a Federal tribunal, of facts on which a Federal claim depends.[28] Shortly afterward, in *Sanders v. United States* (1963),[29] the Court applied the same rules to collateral attacks brought by *Federal* prisoners under 28 U.S.C. § 2255, the Federal analog of the habeas corpus procedure provided for *state* prisoners.

We pause to reflect upon Justice Brennan's ingenious rationale in *Fay v. Noia*. He declared that, although noncompliance with the New York limitation on the time in which criminal appeals must be taken would preclude direct review of the *conviction* since its affirmance by the highest state court was based on an adequate state ground, the *prison sentence* was open to collateral attack on habeas corpus:

> ... while our appellate function is concerned only with the judgments or decrees of state courts, the habeas corpus jurisdiction of the lower federal courts is not so confined. The jurisdictional prerequisite is not the judgment of a state court but detention *simpliciter*.[30]

This deft and novel distinction between the blood and the pound of flesh enabled the Federal district courts to frustrate unreversible convictions by liberating prisoners incarcerated pursuant to them. The state court judgment was "valid" but useless. A prisoner could of course be retried (if prosecution witnesses were still available) but his original conviction was nullified as completely as if it had been reversed.

The effect of this trilogy of cases was seismic. On the one hand, the Court was enabled to make a single constitutional ruling do the work of many, since it provided numberless prisoners with access to the Federal district courts which, on the whole, apply the Supreme Court's decisions much more sympathetically than do the state courts; and the effect was multiplied as the Court extended its control over the criminal process in the years after 1963. The grant of relief by a lower Federal court relieved the Supreme Court of the need to do more than deny certiorari — even if the respondent prison officials were so bold as to file a certiorari petition (which rarely happened).

On the other hand, the lightening of the Supreme Court's caseload was matched by a corresponding increase in the caseload of the lower Federal courts. Chief Judge Henry J. Friendly, in his 1972 Carpentier Lectures at Columbia Law School,[31] has noted that

> [b]etween 1961 and 1970, . . . state prisoner petitions, including both those seeking release and those complaining of maltreatment, increased from 1,020 to 11,812, or 1158%.[32] (Footnote omitted)

Justice Clark, who had predicted this in his *Fay v. Noia* dissent, thus proved to be a prophet. Between 1961 and 1972 the total number of filings in the Federal district courts increased from 86,753 to 143,216, and the corresponding figures for the eleven Federal courts of appeals were 4,204 and 14,535.[33]

Another consequence has been a considerable increase of the wait between the time a judgment of conviction is entered and the time it becomes final beyond possibility of further review on appeal or collateral attack. Criminal law practitioners, including the many lawyers who service the poor under the auspices of the Legal Aid Society and other legal service organizations, were not slow to discern the possibility of such delay — rendered more attractive by the new constitutional rules affording free appellate service to indigent convicts [34] and by the recent liberalization of rules for enlargement of such appellants on bail. It requires no great professional skill for a lawyer to keep his client's state court conviction from becoming "final" in the sense described above — and in some cases, if he can afford a bail bond, keeping him out of jail — for a period of months or years (regardless of the merit of his objection to the conviction), while appeals are taken through the state court hierarchy, followed by a habeas corpus petition* in

---

*The defendant may or may not remain free on bail during the period of delay, but he often does. In any event, delay can benefit the defendant by allowing the passions aroused by the crime to cool; and it is reasonable to assume that the defendant *expects* to benefit from any delay resulting from his own initiative.

the Federal district court, an appeal to the Federal court of appeals if the trial court denies relief, and a certiorari petition to the Supreme Court. The prospect of such delay is a substantial consideration in plea bargaining, and often helps a defendant to effect a compromise settlement based on a guilty plea to a much-reduced charge.\* Alternatively, such delay impairs the deterrent

---

\* One such situation is very clear in my memory. On September 19, 1972, as I was getting down to work on this book, I had lunch with my colleague Wolfgang Friedmann who had agreed to give me his reactions to the précis I had just published in the *New York Law Journal* entitled, "The Unwritten U.S. Constitution." See pp. 11-13 *supra*. A distinguished scholar of jurisprudence (see, *e.g.*, his *Law in a Changing Society* (2d ed. 1972) which was then just off the press), he was generous with his ideas and his ideas deserved the respect that I have accorded them in what I have written here. I still have the handwritten notes I made at that lunch (with some of his own notes scrawled in the margin).

Thirty hours later he was dead. Though as a judge he had successfully defied Hitler's brownshirts, ousting them from his courtroom when they attempted disruption, and fleeing Germany (though he was not a Jew) when the National Socialists assumed power, he was done in by a miserable mugger — in broad daylight, two blocks north of the campus, while dozens of onlookers ignored his calls for help. He had given his money to the mugger and his two companions but had refused to surrender a watch that had sentimental value to him. A knife in the heart was the result.

The police succeeded in arresting the three young males, one of whom was aged 16, one was 17, and the third was an adult. The adult had been under treatment at a rehabilitation center for several months, after hospitalization for methadone detoxification. In August, however, two bench warrants had been issued for him, one for failure to appear for sentencing in a grand larceny conviction resulting from a plea bargain to settle a robbery charge, and the other for failure to appear for a hearing on three drug-related charges.

The three were tried for robbing and murdering Wolfgang Friedmann. There was eyewitness testimony that the adult defendant wielded the knife. He testified, however, that the younger of his two co-defendants did the actual knifing and that he himself had tried to prevent it. It would seem that this was not in itself a legal defense to the murder charge. Section 125.25 (3) of the New York Penal Law, sometimes called the "felony murder" provision, imposes liability for murder on all participants in felonies such as robbery if a nonparticipant is killed, unless the defendant proves each of four extenuating circumstances. The statute provides, in pertinent part:

    A person is guilty of murder when:
    . . . .
    3. Acting alone or with one or more other persons, he commits or attempts to commit robbery . . . and, in the course of and in furtherance of such crime . . . he, or another participant, if any there be, causes the death of a person

effect of the conviction, which most criminologists believe to depend more importantly on the swiftness of punishment than on its severity.

> other than one of the participants; except that in any prosecution under this subdivision, in which the defendant was not the only participant in the underlying crime, it is an affirmative defense that the defendant:
> (a) Did not commit the homicidal act or in any way solicit, request, command, importune, cause or aid the commission thereof; *and*
> (b) Was not armed with a deadly weapon, or any instrument, article or substance readily capable of causing death or serious physical injury and of a sort not ordinarily carried in public places by law-abiding persons; *and*
> (c) Had no reasonable ground to believe that any other participant was armed with such a weapon, instrument, article or substance; *and*
> (d) Had no reasonable ground to believe that any other participant intended to engage in conduct likely to result in death or serious physical injury. (Emphasis added)

However, the cross-section jury reported twice to the court that it was unable to reach agreement on the felony murder charge; and at that point the prosecutor agreed to dismiss the murder charge if the adult defendant would plead guilty to robbery.

The plea bargain was carried out, and the defendant was sentenced to prison. He immediately commenced an attack on the sentence as based on a coerced agreement, contending that he had not committed the robbery (which very possibly was true). So far as I know, that proceeding has not run its course.

I must confess shame for my failure to speak up at one point. After the arrests, an article in the *Columbia Law School News* said (October 16, 1972, p. 1, col. 3) (reprinted by permission of Columbia Law School News, Inc.):

> "They've been accused of murdering one of the system's darlings," William Kunstler said last week, explaining why he had accepted a court appointment to defend one of the three neighborhood youths accused of the murder of Professor Wolfgang G. Friedmann on September 20.
> 
> "I don't think his death is any more to be mourned than that of a derelict in the slums," Kunstler said in an interview with the Law School News.
> 
> "These boys have been accused of murdering a middle-class person highly placed in the system. He is given more value than they in the eyes of society. This reflects both the classism and the racism of society," he added.
> 
> "If it had been a derelict and not Dr. Friedmann," Kunstler said, "I never would have heard of the case. You would never have heard of the case. I think that's wrong. I resent that.
> 
> "When the middle class reacts to the death of one of their own, they react with ferocity," he said. "Kent State was an example — and I think a good one — of that.
> 
> "But unless these defendants get the most vigorous and imaginative of defenses, I think their right to a fair trial is going to be jeopardized. Not only jeopardized, but destroyed.
> 
> "In any event," Kunstler said, "I will try to equalize the odds against these three young men."

Mr. Kunstler was not heard to demand a retraction, so I assume that the

It should be noted that the continuance of this state of affairs appears to depend on the acquiescence of Congress, since the *Fay v. Noia* trilogy rests on interpretations of the 1867 Habeas Corpus Act and 28 U.S.C. § 2255 rather than on constitutional grounds. If this is so, it has the quality of tentative judicial review. But Justice Douglas has asserted that although Congress can curtail the habeas corpus jurisdiction of Federal *courts,* it cannot curtail such jurisdiction of Federal *judges*;[35] and, so far as I can ascertain, no other Justice has expressed disagreement.

The expanded availability of collateral attack on criminal detention was probably the largest single factor in broadening the Court's power to institute reforms in the criminal process. There were other doctrinal changes, however, whose effect has been far from insignificant. A number of them can be grouped under the rubric

*Devices for changing the criminal process without emptying the prisons.*

We have already quoted Justice Black's objection to the new prospectivity principle of *Linkletter v. Walker* (1965):[36] that, by eliminating the concern that wholesale liberation of hardened criminals might result, prospectivity set the Court entirely free to remodel the criminal process conformably to the Justices' personal perceptions of public policy.[37] We have also pointed out that the very point and purpose of the prospectivity doctrine was to attain flexibility.[38] Prospectivity, however, was not the only doctrine the Court developed to attain flexibility (both in the criminal process field and elsewhere). Other devices enabling the Court to announce new constitutional rules without reopening final judgments and settled transactions were: (1) the doctrine of harmless constitutional error; (2) the doctrine of abstention; and (3) the practice of declaring a new constitutional right but not enforcing it in the instant case.

---

quotation was accurate. *Not one member of the Columbia Law Faculty, or any alumnus, uttered a word of public protest.* Perhaps some of them thought that Professor Friedmann deserved what he got; he was a leader in the struggle for freedom of the press and prisoner rights. That was not my excuse; I have none.

Before the era of "selective incorporation," when the Court still adhered to the older view that the Fourteenth Amendment afforded protection in criminal cases only against serious miscarriage of justice — the teaching of *Palko v. Connecticut* [39] — the idea of harmless constitutional error, in the state criminal process field at least, was a logical impossibility, the legal equivalent of Maurits C. Escher's weirder drawings. Any error in a state court prosecution which was held to be of constitutional dimension was necessarily "harmful" in the sense that it gave rise to an unacceptable risk that the innocent might be convicted. The 1952 ruling in *Rochin v. California*,[40] reversing the narcotics conviction of a plainly guilty defendant, does not fit this formulation, but at the time it seemed explainable as a rare exception resulting from an odor suggestive of the medieval torture chamber: a narcotics suspect, about to be seized in his bed, swallowed two morphine capsules which, having been retrieved with a stomach pump, were used as evidence against him. It was only when most provisions of the Fourth, Fifth, and Sixth Amendments, with their accompanying exclusionary rules, were declared to be incorporated bodily into the Fourteenth, that a Federal rule on harmless constitutional error in state prosecutions became an obvious possibility. Time and again, the rigors of selective incorporation led to the liberation of state prisoners who, there was every reason to believe, were a menace to society. Unfortunate as this might be in the case of Federal prisoners, it was still more dangerous in the case of many state prisoners; for state criminal law contains the primary check on crimes of violence, which most directly impair security of person and property.

After a few years the proponents of selective incorporation, perceiving that this absurdity was deterring the Court from "incorporating" as freely as it otherwise might, declared in *Chapman v. California* (1967) [41] that establishment of a Federal constitutional violation in the course of a state criminal prosecution would not automatically lead it to reverse the judgment of conviction. Instead, the Court would reverse *unless* it was clear beyond reasonable doubt that the defendant would have been convicted even if the violation had not occurred.

So long as the Court intervened in the state criminal process only to prevent conviction of the probably innocent, it would have been anomalous to say that any constitutional error should be disregarded as harmless. If the substantial rights of the accused were not prejudiced, there simply was no constitutional error. Justice Harlan quite correctly observed that a Federal harmless error rule is inconsistent with the notion that constitutional limitations apply only to the result the state court has reached and not to the procedures used to reach it. His dissent expressed disapproval:

> I regard the Court's assumption of what amounts to a general supervisory power over the trial of federal constitutional issues in state courts as a startling constitutional development that is wholly out of keeping with our federal system and completely unsupported by the Fourteenth Amendment where the source of such a power must be found.[42]

But the Court had in fact assumed the power to prescribe rules for the conduct of state prosecutions. That was the effect of selective incorporation. Having done so, the Court found it useful to say it would excuse departure from its rules if convinced that reversal was pointless because a new trial conducted in compliance with the rules would almost certainly yield another conviction. Such flexibility rendered somewhat more palatable the prescription of new Federal standards for state prosecutions.

The strange doctrine of abstention is another one that would have been logically impossible under the earlier law, which reflected the *Marbury v. Madison* conception of judicial review as elaborated in *Cohens v. Virginia* (1821).[43] In the *Cohens* case, Chief Justice Marshall declared for the Court:

> It is most true, that this court will not take jurisdiction if it should not: but it is equally true, that it must take jurisdiction, if it should.[44]

That proposition, already possibly undermined by the 1925 Judiciary Act which sanctioned the discretionary denial of certiorari, was in effect repudiated in *Railroad Commission v. Pullman Company* (1941)[45] where the Court, under Justice

Frankfurter's leadership, held that the Federal courts should abstain from the exercise of jurisdiction they admittedly possess, in order to permit state court adjudication of an unclear state law issue which, if resolved in a certain way, might make decision of a Federal constitutional claim unnecessary. Later on, the Court pressed the abstention doctrine into service in cases that Justice Frankfurter himself said were beyond its reach.[46] It has become an established, though still controversial, means of softening the impact of judicial constitution-making. And in the last year of his life Justice Black, for a plurality of the Court in *Younger v. Harris* (1971),[47] announced a curious refinement of the abstention doctrine which that apostle of constitutional literalism, with Olympian indifference to the constitutional text, called "Our Federalism." [48] The general nature of our federal system, he said, forbids the Federal courts to interfere with certain state prosecutions even though no constitutional provision or Federal statute says so.

As for the useful but infuriating practice of declaring a new constitutional right but not enforcing it in the instant case, we have already adverted to the paradigm case of *Wolf v. Colorado* (1949).[49] *Brown v. Board of Education*[50] was also such a case. There have been others.

\* \* \* \* \*

We now turn to the examination of four other methods whereby the Court has enabled itself to enhance the practical effect of its judgments and multiply its opportunities for constitution-making. They are: (1) Modifying doctrines limiting its freedom of action. (2) Instituting practices having the purpose and effect of increasing the flow of constitutional claims presented to it for adjudication. (3) Weakening the orthodox aversion to advisory opinions. (4) Interpreting restrictively jurisdiction-limiting statutes.

## Modification of doctrines limiting freedom of action

We have already seen how the Court plasticized the justiciability and standing requirements in *Baker v. Carr* (1962)[51] and then, in *Powell v. McCormack* (1969),[52] relaxed the justiciability requirement still further and trivialized the rule against adjudication of moot cases.[53] We have also seen how *Flast v. Cohen* (1968)[54] laid a doctrinal foundation for ignoring the standing requirement to whatever extent the Court thought desirable.* Those are by no means isolated cases in these respects. The doctrines of justiciability, standing, and mootness, though still honored by lip service, no longer bind the Court any more tightly than it elects to be bound.

We have also pointed out that the Court has flatly repudiated the doctrine of *stare decisis* on constitutional issues.[55] Justice Black, dissenting in *Boys Markets, Inc. v. Retail Clerks Union* (1970)[56] because the Court had refused to adhere to its own prior interpretation of a *statute,* nevertheless conceded:

---

\* The present Court may be endeavoring to restore some vitality to the standing requirement. In Sierra Club v. Morton, 405 U.S. 727 (1972), it held that a conservationist club lacked standing to attack the development of Mineral King Valley, a part of Sequoia National Forest, into a recreational area. In Laird v. Tatum, 408 U.S. 1 (1972), it held that persons who claimed to have been the object of Army surveillance lacked standing to question the legality of such surveillance. In United States v. Richardson, 418 U.S. 166 (1974), it held that taxpayers, as such, lack standing to claim violation of the Statement and Account Clause (Art. I, Sec. 9, Cl. 7) by a statute relieving the Central Intelligence Agency of the obligation to account for its expenditures except by certificate of its Director. In Schlesinger v. Reservists Committee to Stop the War, 418 U.S. 208 (1974), it held that citizen-taxpayers lack standing to claim violation of the Incompatibility Clause (Art. I, Sec. 6, Cl. 2) by membership of Congressmen in the Armed Forces Reserve.

These decisions, however, do little to weaken the impression that the Court resorts to the standing requirement on an *ad hoc* basis, to provide a reason for avoiding decision of questions it is not ready to deal with or which it believes, for other reasons, are unsuitable for judicial determination. For example, in United States v. SCRAP, 412 U.S. 669 (1973), it held that SCRAP (Students Challenging Regulatory Agency Procedures) had standing to attack railroad rate increases which allegedly discouraged the use of recyclable goods and thereby tended to degrade the forests, rivers, streams, mountains, and natural resources that SCRAP's members used, and to pollute the air they breathed. Predication of standing on such slender grounds suggests that the Court's approval of judicial intervention on environmental issues was the decisive factor.

> In the area of constitutional law, ... where the only alternative to action by this Court is the laborious process of constitutional amendment and where the ultimate responsibility rests with this Court, I believe reconsideration is always proper.[57]

The boldest innovation by which the Court extended its reach was *Bivens v. Six Unknown Named Agents* (1971).[58] The plaintiff sued six Federal narcotics agents for damages, alleging that, without a warrant and without probable cause, they had arrested him and searched his apartment. The Civil Rights Acts of the Reconstruction era provided a damage remedy for the violation of Federal rights by the state or local police, but there was no corresponding provision for Federal officials. If Federal officials *threatened* to abuse their authority, injunctive and declaratory relief was available; but that remedy was useless in the case of a completed violation. The rule excluding illegally seized evidence had no application unless a victim of illegal search was subsequently brought to trial, which Bivens was not. Thus there was no applicable Federal remedy under the pre-existing law. On the other hand, the law of every state does provide a damage remedy for assault and trespass. If Bivens had sued the six agents under the state law, their status as Federal officials would have shielded them from liability only to the extent that Federal law made their action privileged; and the Federal privilege, having been conferred by the Court,[59] could also have been withdrawn by it. If it were withdrawn, the Federal officials, lacking legal authority for the arrest and search, would have stood in the same position as private individuals who had committed the same acts. Thus the existence of Federal privilege did not in itself make the state law remedy unsatisfactory.

The Court nevertheless held that a Federal damage remedy was necessary because the state law might not cover all Fourth Amendment violations. Justice Brennan, for the majority, pointed out that state law might not give damages for nontrespassory eavesdropping, such as wiretapping, or for a search consented to after an unauthorized official demand to be admitted. In response to the argument that Congress had not provided the damage remedy, he said that Congress had not forbidden the courts to supply it. (It would seem to follow that the statutory remedies against state and local officials, provided by the nineteenth-century Civil Rights Acts, were entirely unnecessary.) As in *Flast v. Cohen* (1968),[60] the distinction between Federal action specifically prohibited by the Constitution (here, the Fourth Amendment), and Federal action simply not authorized by it, was declared to be material; a 1963 case denying damages against a staff member of the House Un-American Activities Committee for unlawful issuance of a subpoena was distinguished on that doubtful ground.

The decision opens new vistas of Federal litigation. Unlike injunction and declaratory judgment, which merely tell defendant officials what the law requires of them, the damage remedy touches them personally [61] and is therefore likely to be a more effective deterrent.[62] Moreover, it can be sought at leisure; there is no need to sue before the questioned action is taken. It remains to be seen whether the Court will limit it to cases where specific constitutional prohibitions have been violated. Even if it does, the First, Fourth, Fifth, and Sixth Amendments will provide a broad field for its application.*

## *Protecting the source of supply*

Since, unlike Congress, the Court is not self-starting, its capacity for constitution-making depends on a large and steady flow of cases from which it can select those presenting issues on which it desires to speak. Decisions protecting such organizations as the

---

\* Two of the Justices think it at least possible that Article I, Section 9, Clause 7 of the Constitution, which provides that "a regular Statement of Account of the Receipts and Expenditures of all public Money shall be published from time to time," is a source of private rights. We have noted that in United States v. Richardson, 418 U.S. 166 (1974), the Court held that a taxpayer has no standing to attack the statute regulating the Central Intelligence Agency, insofar as it permits the Agency to account for its expenditures "solely on the certificate of the Director." Justice Stewart, joined by Justice Marshall, dissented saying (*id.* at 203):

> Seeking a determination that the Government owes him a duty to supply the information he has requested, the respondent is in the position of a traditional Hohfeldian plaintiff. He contends that the Statement and Account Clause gives him a right to receive the information [C.I.A. expenditures] and burdens the Government with a correlative duty to supply it. Courts of law exist for the resolution of such right-duty disputes. (Footnote omitted)

NAACP, which have been referred to in Chapter XIII, [63] serve this purpose, as do a set of cases invalidating practices which tend to discourage resort to the appellate process. Typical examples from this latter category are *United States v. Jackson* (1968),[64] *Johnson v. Avery* (1969),[65] and *North Carolina v. Pearce* (1969).[66]

The *Jackson* decision invalidated a provision of the Federal Kidnaping Act (the so-called Lindbergh Law) which authorized capital punishment if, but only if, "the jury shall so recommend." [67] This provision tended to encourage defendants to avoid jury trial by pleading guilty; and such pleas, coupled with the soon-to-be-announced rule [68] favoring plea bargaining by insulating most bargained guilty pleas from appellate review (including collateral attack), could have easily interfered with the Court's case flow.

*Johnson v. Avery* gave qualified endorsement to "jailhouse lawyers" as a source of assistance to prisoners who would otherwise be hampered in seeking adjudication of claims to post-conviction remedies. The Court found invalid, as a restriction on access to Federal habeas corpus, a Tennessee prison regulation that barred inmates from assisting other prisoners in preparing "[w]rits or other legal matters."

*North Carolina v. Pearce* dealt with the problem that had plagued Noia and had deterred him from appealing his life sentence for murder,[69] namely, the possibility of a heavier sentence after reversal and retrial. The *Pearce* case held that in such a situation the second sentence cannot be heavier than the first unless the trial court shows that the increase was based on facts unknown when the first sentence was imposed, and was not a reprisal for the appeal.

An unusually precise reading on the Court's sensitivity to the importance of its case flow is permitted by decisions imposing an apparently illogical limitation on the prospectivity doctrine. The Court has consistently held that, even if the benefits of a new constitutional rule are not to be extended to some or all past convictions, those benefits *will* be extended to the defendant who has first induced the Court to declare the new rule.

Thus the Court never applies what is sometimes called "pure" prospectivity, under which the old rule would apply to all past convictions *including the one under review.* Pure prospectivity is an entirely feasible doctrine, and indeed is applied in many if not most of the state prospectivity cases.[70] The Court, however, rejects it. Strange reasons have occasionally been assigned for the rejection, such as the assertion that unless the instant defendant is granted the benefit of the new rule there will be no justiciable "case or controversy" [71] (clearly not so, since the Court disposes of a real case whether it affirms or sets aside the conviction), and the self-evidently groundless contention [72] that constitutional rules are never made by way of dictum.[73] The real reason for prospectivity was made plain in *Jenkins v. Delaware* (1969),[74] where Chief Justice Warren declared for the Court:

> [Petitioner's contention, that it is incongruous to deny his *Miranda* claim, presented on direct review by certiorari, solely because he was tried before June 13, 1966, when *Miranda v. Arizona* was decided, is not] more disconcerting than applying the new standards for in-custody interrogation to Ernesto Miranda while denying them to other defendants whose cases, for wholly fortuitous reasons, simply reached this Court at a later date, although the defendants in those cases may have been both interrogated and tried after Ernesto Miranda.
>
> In short, petitioner's concern for what he refers to as "visible imperfection[s] in a judicial process" merely highlights the problem inherent in prospective decision-making, *i.e.,* some defendants benefit from the new rule while others do not, solely because of the fortuities that determine the progress of their cases from initial investigation and arrest to final judgment. The resulting incongruities must be balanced against *the impetus the technique provides for the implementation of long overdue reforms, which otherwise could not be practicably effected.*[75] (Emphasis added)

The real reason for "impure" prospectivity had previously been disclosed, somewhat less explicitly, in the Court's opinion in *Stovall v. Denno* (1967),[76] written by Justice Brennan. He admitted that Wade and Gilbert, who got the benefit of the new rule on identification line-ups announced in their cases,[77] were "chance beneficiaries" of the new rule, but said that this was justified by the Court's need for "incentive of counsel to advance contentions requiring a change in the law." [78] It will hardly be contended that this reflects the conception of judicial review embodied in *Marbury v. Madison* and Justice Brandeis's *Ashwander* principles.

An index of the importance the Court attributes to the prospectivity doctrine (and the qualification upon it) is provided by considering the high price paid for it in terms of doctrinal confusion and capriciousness in the judicial process. The above quotation from Chief Justice Warren's opinion in *Jenkins v. Delaware* reveals his inability to deny that — contrary to the inscription "Equal Justice Under Law" which adorns the Court's marble palace — the prospectivity doctrine results in arbitrary discrimination that the Chief Justice cannot approve, but only explain. As for doctrinal confusion, consider Justice Harlan's dissenting opinion in *Desist v. United States* (1969),[79] where the Court held the new electronic eavesdropping rule of *Katz v. United States* (1967)[80] applicable only to cases in which the prosecution seeks to introduce in evidence the fruits of electronic surveillance conducted after the date of the *Katz* decision. Justice Harlan said:

> The unsound character of the rule reaffirmed today is perhaps best exposed by considering the following hypothetical. Imagine that the Second Circuit in the present case had anticipated the line of reasoning this Court subsequently pursued in *Katz* v. *United States, supra,* [389 U.S.] at 352-353, concluding — as this Court there did — that "the underpinnings of *Olmstead* and *Goldman* have been so eroded by our subsequent decisions that the 'trespass' doctrine there enunciated can no longer be regarded as controlling." *Id.,* at 353. Would we have *reversed* the case on the ground that the principles the Second Circuit had announced — though identical with those in *Katz* — should not control because *Katz* is not retroactive? To the contrary, I venture to say that we would have taken satisfaction that the lower court had reached the same conclusion we subsequently did in *Katz.* If a "new" constitutional doctrine is truly right, we should not reverse lower courts which have accepted it; nor should we affirm those which have rejected the very arguments we have embraced. Anything else would belie the truism that it is the task of this Court, like that of any other, to do justice to each litigant on the merits of his own case. It is only if our decisions can be justified in terms of this fundamental premise that they may properly be considered the legitimate products of a court

of law, rather than the commands of a super-legislature.[81] (Emphasis in original)

Another such absurdity (not, however, involving prospectivity) is discussed in a recent *Columbia Law Review* note.[82] The ruling in *United States v. Jackson* (1968),[83] invalidating the death penalty provision in the Federal Kidnaping Act, was held to afford no basis for post-conviction relief to one Brady who, in 1959, had been indicted under the Act and had pleaded guilty, thus avoiding a jury trial with its possibility of death penalty. He was sentenced to 50 years imprisonment, later reduced to 30. After Jackson had won his case in the trial court the defendant, Brady, sought post-conviction relief under 28 U.S.C. § 2255, claiming that his guilty plea had been made under compulsion because of his fear of the death penalty and was therefore invalid. The claim of invalidity was based on a long line of cases beginning with *Bram v. United States* (1897)[84] and carried to a remarkable climax in *Garrity v. New Jersey* (1967),[85] holding invalid the waiver of a constitutional right (including the waiver of the right to a jury trial) if made under fear of legal disadvantage — even, in the *Garrity* case, a policeman's fear of losing his job if he availed himself of the privilege against self-incrimination in an official investigation into the fixing of traffic tickets. On the precedents, the contention seemed ironclad, and neither the Court's opinion (by Justice White) nor Justice Brennan's concurrence effectively refuted it. Yet in *Brady v. United States* (1970)[86] the Court rejected it, without a dissenting vote. Evidently the need for logical consistency was thought to be outweighed by the need to preserve plea bargaining by insulating guilty pleas from attack. A similar decision was rendered in a companion case, *McMann v. Richardson* (1970),[87] where the facts favoring the prisoner were even stronger than in the *Brady* case.

By reason of the implacable candor and true humility of Justice Harlan, we have been afforded a unique glimpse of prospectivity's seamy side. A few months before he died, he wrote (dissenting in *Williams v. United States* (1971)[88] and concurring specially in two companion cases):

Today's decisions mark another milestone in the development of the Court's "retroactivity" doctrine, which came into being somewhat less than six years ago in *Linkletter v. Walker,* 381 U.S. 618 (1965). That doctrine was the product of the Court's disquietude with the impacts of its fastmoving pace of constitutional innovation in the criminal field. Some members of the Court, and I have come to regret that I was among them, initially grasped this doctrine as a way of limiting the reach of decisions that seemed to them fundamentally unsound. Others rationalized this resort to prospectivity as a "technique" that provided an "impetus . . . for the implementation of long overdue reforms, which otherwise could not be practicably effected." *Jenkins v. Delaware,* 395 U.S. 213 (1969). . . .

What emerges from today's decisions is that in the realm of constitutional adjudication in the criminal field the Court is free to act, in effect, like a legislature, making its new constitutional rules wholly or partially retroactive or only prospective as it deems wise. I completely disagree with this point of view. . . .

. . . the retroactivity analysis currently ascendant in this Court proceeds on the false and unacceptable premise that constitutional interpretation is not purely a judicial, but, rather, something akin to a legislative, process. If, in fact, that premise is true we ought not to be writing retroactivity opinions but instead relinquishing some of our powers of judicial review.

. . . the distinction between judicial and legislative power is . . . woven deeply into the fabric of our positive law. So, too, is the notion that this Court definitively interprets the Constitution only because its role as a court of law requires it to do so. . . .

In conclusion, the Court in deciding these cases seems largely to have forgotten the limitations that accompany its functions as a court of law. For the retroactivity doctrine announced today bespeaks more considerations of policy than of legal principle. . . . As a court of law we have no right on direct review to treat one case differently from another with respect to constitutional provisions applicable to both.[89]

## *The trend toward advisory opinions*

The Court's oft-repeated protestation that it is constitutionally powerless to render advisory opinions has never meant that it can express no views except on the precise case before it. It means only that the Court lacks power to expatiate upon wholly abstract questions not presented in the course of adversary litigation. Virtually every opinion it writes, however, goes beyond the instant case; it *must* do so, in order to demonstrate the consistency between the instant decision and earlier ones, and that is a primary function of judicial opinions.

Even so, if the rule against advisory opinions means anything, the Court must recognize some self-imposed limits on how far afield its opinions will roam. It is conceivable, for instance, that an opinion might reconcile the instant decision with every single case which the Court has ever decided or which it could ever be called upon to decide. We would call it a treatise or a commentary or a legal encyclopedia, however — in times past it would have been called an institute — rather than a judicial opinion; and we would correctly characterize it as a mass of advisory opinions.

It is therefore necessary for a somewhat arbitrary line to be drawn, and no one begrudges the Court the prerogative of deciding, within broad limits, how far it will cast its eye. I certainly disclaim any purpose to suggest that the Court's current practice has obliterated the distinction between advisory opinions and adjudication of cases and controversies. Nevertheless, in this review of the methods whereby the Court has enhanced the effectiveness of its actions, it is pertinent to note that the current practice has been moving closer to advisory opinion writing — that is to say, the Court has been pronouncing dicta more freely on issues not before it for decision.

Constitution-making by dictum, as in *Wolf v. Colorado* (1949),[90] has long been a common practice; it can even be plausibly argued that *Marbury v. Madison* (1803) was a prime example.* Therefore

---

\* FAIRMAN, AMERICAN CONSTITUTIONAL DECISIONS 24 (1948):

> It was not really necessary . . . for the Court to declare an act of Congress unconstitutional. Had it not been that Marshall thought it opportune to establish such a precedent, he could have reconciled Section 13 of the Judiciary Act with Article III of the Constitution without any real difficulty. He could have treated it as a simple matter of statutory construction.

Compare the seventh of the Brandeis *Ashwander* maxims, *supra* p. 52.

nothing can be made of the continued prevalence of that practice. Some of the cases since 1962, however, do reveal an unaccustomed eagerness to reach out for the opportunity to articulate a previously unannounced constitutional rule. In *Brady v. Maryland* (1963),[91] for instance, the Court went out of its way to declare its approval of the invalidation, by Maryland's highest court, of a death sentence imposed by a jury after the defendant, an admitted murderer, had been wrongly denied access to evidence that might have helped him get off with a prison sentence. Justice White concurred in the result but declined to join Justice Douglas's majority opinion on the ground that "the due process discussion by the Court is wholly advisory."[92]

Justice White himself, however, subsequently showed in a somewhat different way that he was not above reaching out for a constitutional question. In *Stanley v. Illinois* (1972)[93] an unwed father claimed that the Equal Protection Clause of the Fourteenth Amendment prevented the state from denying him custody of his two youngest illegitimate children after their mother's death, without first granting him the opportunity for a *hearing* on the question whether he was a fit custodian. The Court was persuaded that Stanley had a constitutional right to a hearing, but that his right was granted by *the Due Process Clause,* on which he had not relied in the state courts. As Chief Justice Burger, joined by Justice Blackmun, pointed out in his dissent, the Court had long interpreted 28 U.S.C. § 1257, the applicable jurisdictional statute, as denying it the *power* to adjudicate constitutional claims not previously urged upon the highest state court, or actually passed upon by that court. Justice White neatly, if unconvincingly, circumvented the objection by adding a paragraph to his majority opinion saying that the Equal Protection Clause had indeed been violated because

> all Illinois parents are constitutionally entitled to a hearing on their fitness before their children are removed from their custody. It follows [*sic*] that denying such a hearing to Stanley and those like him while granting it to other Illinois parents is inescapably contrary to the Equal Protection Clause.[94] (Footnote omitted)

He made no response to the Chief Justice's tart (and accurate) rejoinder:

> This "method of analysis" is, of course, no more or less than the use of the Equal Protection Clause as a shorthand condensation of the entire Constitution: a State may not deny *any* constitutional right to some of its citizens without violating the Equal Protection Clause through its failure to deny such rights to *all* of its citizens. The limits on this Court's jurisdiction are not properly expandable by the use of such semantic devices as that.[95] (Emphasis in original)

Much more significant from a quantitative viewpoint is the Court's apparently growing propensity to announce whole systems of rules covering not only the instant case but the entire subject matter to which they relate. Of course, the result has been merely an extension of the method of choosing a broad, in preference to a narrow, rationale — which in our discussion of *Brown v. Board of Education* (1954)[96] we agreed might well be justified. It *is* a material extension, however, and has drawn the fire of dissenting Justices as being tantamount to an advisory opinion. Thus, Justice Stewart objected on behalf of himself and the other three dissenters in *Townsend v. Sain* (1963),[97] to the Court's formulation of detailed rules governing the right to evidentiary hearing on a petition for habeas corpus in the Federal district court, saying that the Court was "attempting to erect detailed hearing standards for the myriad situations presented by federal habeas corpus applications . . . ." He continued:

> . . . the enunciation of an elaborate set of standards governing habeas corpus hearings is in no sense required, or even invited, in order to decide the case before us, and the many pages of the Court's opinion which set these standards forth cannot, therefore, be justified even in terms of the normal function of dictum. The reasons for the rule against advisory opinions which purport to decide questions not actually in issue are too well established to need repeating at this late date. [Citations anyway][98]

Such rule formulation, however, is a valuable means of extending the effective power of the Court. It amounts to the decision of cases at wholesale rather than retail, and the stated rules enable the lower Federal courts to dispose of many cases that would otherwise encumber the Supreme Court docket. That is probably why the practice has been continued, both by Chief Justice Warren in *Miranda v. Arizona* (1966) [99] and by Chief Justice Burger in *Miller v. California* (1973), [100] the recent obscenity case that will be discussed in the next chapter.

The very most effective power-enhancing device, however, is the well-known "exclusionary rule" under which the Court reverses convictions based on unconstitutional evidence regardless of guilt, and thereby puts teeth into the Fourth, Fifth, and Sixth Amendments. It would be inaccurate to equate the exclusionary rule with advisory opinions, since the Court does render a judgment having real consequences to adversary litigants. Yet, it has much the same potentiality for extending the Court's effective power. The actual controversy between the state and the defendant is whether he has committed an alleged crime and thus made himself eligible for punishment which would presumably serve as a deterrent to would-be offenders. Because this question is entirely separate from the question whether the state broke the law in gathering the evidence, many states [101] accepted the Cardozo maxim that the criminal should not "go free because the constable has blundered." [102] One might put it differently by saying that two wrongs do not make a right.

The Court, after initially agreeing that the states had power to embrace the Cardozo maxim if they so elected,[103] ultimately decided in *Mapp v. Ohio* (1961) [104] and a host of later cases that the value of the maxim was outweighed by the danger that open acquiescence in official lawlessness would engender cynicism destructive of the open society. The value judgment was that of Justice Brandeis, dissenting in *Olmstead v. United States* (1928),[105] where the Court held that the Fourth Amendment does not forbid wiretapping:

> Our Government is the potent, the omnipresent teacher. For good or ill, it teaches the whole people by its example. Crime is contagious. If the government becomes a lawbreaker, it breeds contempt for law; it invites every man to become a law unto himself; it invites anarchy. To declare that in the administration of the criminal law the end justifies the means — to declare that the Government may commit crimes in order

to secure the conviction of a private criminal — would bring terrible retribution.[106]

This, I suggest, is the reason why the Court thought it necessary, by means of a lawyer's maneuver — simply broadening the issues of the initial controversy by declaring material the constitutionality of the state's investigative methods — to embrace the exclusionary rule. From the beginning the Court has known that the rule is not a perfect tool.[107] But it is the most powerful one presently available, and a very powerful one at that.

Although, as has been said, it is doubtful whether the exclusionary rule should be grouped with practices that somewhat resemble the advisory opinion, rather than put in a class by itself, there is one other device that *does* resemble the advisory opinion quite closely: The artificial splitting out of issues.\* The Court does not use this practice often, but seems to reserve it for a few particularly difficult and controversial cases.

The conception underlying the "case or controversy" requirement is that judicial business properly consists of settling disputes between litigants. Of course that does not mean that the Court is precluded from deciding different issues at different stages of the litigation in the interest of efficient judicial administration. But it does mean that the Court should ordinarily decide the whole issue presented to it — not, without good reason, decide half of it and leave the other half for another appeal on another day.

As we have observed, the issue in *Baker v. Carr* (1962) [108] was whether the complaint stated a claim upon which relief would be granted if the facts alleged were proved.[109] To meet that issue fairly, it was necessary for the Court to decide not only whether the requirements of jurisdiction, justiciability, and standing were satisfied, but also whether it was possible to grant at least some effective relief. Justice Brennan's opinion brushed aside this latter problem with the offhand remark that remedies for equal protection violations are "well developed and familiar" — surely

---

\* The legal mind has been defined as "a mind that can think of one of two things that are inescapably related without thinking about the other." See p. 316 *infra.*

the overstatement of the year, since effective judicial remedies for legislative malapportionment were not worked out until long afterward. The obscurity of the majority opinion even misled Justice Stewart into the belief that the Court had not decided the merits of the case — a belief that impelled him to join with four other Justices to make a five-man majority.

The year before, the Court had resorted to a similar device in *Communist Party of the United States v. Subversive Activities Control Board* (1961).[110] The issue was whether the registration order which the Board had issued against the Party was constitutional. To meet that issue fairly, it was necessary for the Court to decide not only whether the issuance of the order violated the First Amendment and other constitutional provisions, but also whether it was possible to grant at least some effective relief. Justice Frankfurter, for the five-man majority, declared that the latter question was premature — even though counsel for the Party had informed the Court that every Party member qualified to sign a registration statement could and would refuse to do so on the ground that he might thereby incriminate himself. The Court proceeded to uphold the registration order in the abstract. Thereafter the Party members did refuse to sign, and in *Albertson v. Subversive Activities Control Board* (1965)[111] the Court unanimously upheld the refusal, under the Fifth Amendment.

In both *Baker v. Carr* and the first *SACB* case, the decision was incomplete. It did not settle the concrete controversy that the parties had tendered to the Court. Like an advisory opinion, it enabled the Court to exert the power of its prestige on one side of a hot political controversy without committing the Court one way or the other with respect to the ultimate decision. And there was no discernible reason for such a course, in terms of orderly judicial administration.

### Restrictive interpretation of jurisdiction-limiting statutes

There is one further device that the Court employs to maximize its power, namely, astonishingly narrow "interpretation" of statutes designed to limit its jurisdiction.

The statute that grants the Court appellate jurisdiction over state court judgments (28 U.S.C. § 1257) permits review of *"[f]inal judgments or decrees rendered by the highest court of a State in which a decision could be had."* (Emphasis added) In *Mills v. Alabama* (1966)[112] and *Organization for a Better Austin v. Keefe* (1971)[113] the Court winked at the nonfinality of a judgment in order to render a decision on an issue — press freedom in the *Mills* case, privacy in the *Keefe* case — which the Court evidently thought it important to adjudicate without delay.

Another example: Section 10 (b) (3) of the Universal Military Training and Selective Service Act was amended in 1967 to provide that there shall be

> [n]o judicial review ... of the classification or processing of any registrant by local boards, appeal boards, or the President, except as a defense to a criminal prosecution instituted under section 12 of this title, after the registrant has responded either affirmatively or negatively to an order to report for induction, or for civilian work in the case of a registrant determined to be opposed to participation in war in any form: *Provided,* That such review shall go to the question of the jurisdiction herein reserved to local boards, appeal boards, and the President only when there is no basis in fact for the classification assigned to such registrant.[114]

In *Oestereich v. Selective Service System Local Board No. 11* (1968)[115] the Court nevertheless upheld district court jurisdiction of a civil injunction suit brought by a registrant who claimed a statutory exemption as a student in a theological school; and, in an opinion by Justice Douglas, the Court decided the student's claim would be upheld if he proved his allegation that he was such a student. The vote was six to three.

Fairly included under this heading is *Mitchum v. Foster* (1972).[116] There the Court interpreted 28 U.S.C. § 2283, which provides that a Federal court "may not grant an injunction to stay proceedings in a State court except as expressly authorized by Act of Congress, or where necessary in aid of its jurisdiction, or to protect or effectuate its judgments." In numberless cases, over a period of years and years, the Court had declined to say whether 42 U.S.C. § 1983, the basic provision granting civil relief against state deprivations of civil rights, which was first enacted as a part of the 1871 Civil Rights Act, is an express authorization by Act of Congress within the meaning of § 2283. The Court maintained its silence even after a conflict on the question developed among the Federal courts of appeals.[117] Ultimately, in the *Mitchum* case, which involved an issue of press freedom, the Court gave an affirmative answer in an opinion by Justice Stewart from which there was no dissent.

## OPINION-WRITING TECHNIQUES

Finally, we must take note of a number of methods whereby the Court has avoided public responsibility for decisions such as those just reviewed.

One method has been to interpret the text of the Constitution and its Amendments in ways not explainable in terms of the intent of the Constitutors. In Chapter VI we have seen how, at an early date, a broad Federal foreign affairs power was declared to exist, in the teeth of the Tenth Amendment.[118] This is not the only instance in which the constitutional text has been overridden. The Second Amendment, for example, which provides that "the right of the people to keep and bear Arms, shall not be infringed," has long been treated as a dead letter which does not preclude strict gun control legislation. This "interpretation" technique cannot be regarded as a recent phenomenon.

Nor is it a recent phenomenon for the Court to pretend it still adheres to the conception of judicial review embodied in *Marbury v. Madison* — that the Court voices not its own will but that of the Constitutors — which, as noted above, is a protection against popular outcry.[119] We have quoted Justice Roberts's classic resort to this protective coloration technique in *United States v. Butler* (1936).[120]

In recent years, however, the Court has refined the technique to a new level of sophistication. The selective incorporation doctrine described in Chapter X [121] is one example. The compelling governmental interest test, described in Chapter XIV,[122] is another; and, among the Justices still sitting, only Justice Rehnquist has questioned its validity.[123]

The most exquisitely ingenious method the Court has devised for masking the basis for its constitution-making, however, is (a) the imputation to Congress or a state legislature of an intention to make a person's rights dependent on a particular fact when it has actually provided that the fact shall be immaterial, coupled with (b) invocation of the long-established rule that irrational factual presumptions (whereby one fact is declared to imply another which in actuality it does not tend to prove) are inconsistent with due process. For example, in 1971 Congress provided that food stamps (for the purchase of groceries at low prices) should not be issued to any household that included a member over 18 years old who had been claimed as a dependent by an income taxpayer who was not himself eligible to receive the stamps. In *United States Department of Agriculture v. Murry* (1973) [124] the Court imputed to Congress an intention to make eligibility for stamps depend on the fact of dependency rather than the taxpayer's *claim* of dependency, and held the statute invalid on due process grounds because it established a "conclusive presumption" that anyone claimed as a dependent is in fact a dependent — which of course he is not, if the taxpayer has made a false claim. The Court thus avoided discussing the real question in the case, which was whether the statutory classification on the basis of dependency claims rather than dependency in fact was an impermissible departure from equality. Instead, it spoke in terms of the due process requirement of procedural fairness.

Until quite recently, the Court had examined into the rationality of statutory presumptions only where a statute *said* it was establishing a presumption. For example, in *United States v. Romano* (1965) [125] the defendant was convicted of violating a statute penalizing *possession* of an illegal still. The statute declared that a person's presence at an illegal still created a presumption that he was in possession of it. The Court held the presumption irrational and reversed the conviction because one can easily be present at a still without being in possession of it; that would be true, for example, of a helper or customer of the moonshiner. Justice White, for the Court, held that the case was governed by the rule of *Tot v. United States* (1943) [126] where Justice Roberts declared:

> Under our decisions, a statutory presumption cannot be sustained if there be no rational connection between the fact proved and the ultimate fact presumed, if the inference of the one from proof of the other is arbitrary because of lack of connection between the two in common experience.[127]

In the *Romano* case the Government contended that the presumption should be upheld because Congress could have made it a crime to be *present* at an illegal still. Justice White for the Court responded, in effect, that the statute's validity depended on what it said rather than on what it constitutionally could have said:

> It may be, of course, that Congress has the power to make presence at an illegal still a punishable crime, but we find no clear indication that it intended to so exercise this power. The crime remains possession, not presence, and, with all due deference to the judgment of Congress, the former may not constitutionally be inferred from the latter.[128] (Footnote omitted)

Under the approach of the *Murry* food stamp case, however, the power to prohibit presence could easily be denied to Congress. The Court could say that Congress really meant criminality to depend on possession, and established a "conclusive presumption" that anyone present at a still was in possession of it — an even more irrational presumption than the *rebuttable* presumption held invalid in the *Romano* case.

On a moment's reflection it will be seen that this technique can be used to convert any equal protection objection, if based on assertedly impermissible classification, into a due process case. All the Court needs do is look behind the words of the statute, find a legislative intent to make a person's rights depend on a particular fact, show that the classification is not exactly congruent with the presence or absence of that fact, and condemn the classification as an irrational "conclusive presumption." The beauty of the technique, from the viewpoint of a Court bent on masking the basis of decision, is that its authority to decide questions of procedural fairness is much more widely accepted than its authority to override the legislative judgment as to permissible classification. Nearly every statute includes classifications of some sort, and few if any of them produce in every single application the result the legislature would have wanted. Some variation from the ideally desired effect is the inevitable consequence of what is generally called "the rule of law" — government through general rules enacted in advance rather than through wholly discretionary disposition of each individual case. The technique therefore gives the Court great freedom to invalidate statutes it considers unwise, so long as it refrains from articulating a principle prescribing when the Court will look behind the words of the statute and when it will not. It does not do so in every case where it could,[129] but it does not tell us why.

Ever since the technique was first employed, in *Stanley v. Illinois* (1972),[130] it has provoked exasperated dissent by some of the Justices [131] as well as acid scholarly criticism.[132] Professor Gerald Gunther of Stanford Law School reports that his colleague William Cohen calls it "New Old Equally Protective Substantively Procedural Due Process." [133] The Court, however, shows no sign of abandoning it.

\* \* \* \* \*

Having canvassed the new role in which the Court has cast itself, we now proceed to evaluate its performance.

CHAPTER XVI
# What Difference It All Makes

We have already noted [1] the important difference between the first paragraph of the *Carolene Products* footnote and the second and third; and I have said [2] that the "fundamental rights" branch of the compelling governmental interest test is derived from the first paragraph of the footnote and is wholly subjective, but not the "suspect basis of classification" branch which traces back to the third paragraph of the footnote.[3] As a preliminary to evaluating the new role assumed by the Court, I should make it clear why I regard the "fundamental rights" branch as wholly subjective, leaving the Court entirely free to attach the talismanic label or not, at the whim of the Justices.

The word "fundamental" does have a dictionary meaning. According to Webster, it means: "Of or pertaining to the foundation or basis; serving for the foundation. Hence: Essential, as an element, principle, or law; important; original; elementary; primary; basal; as, a *fundamental* truth, or axiom." [4] But if it means essential or important — the senses that most closely approximate the Court's usage — the question immediately arises: Essential or important to whom or by what standard? That is the question on which the Court has wholly neglected to commit itself. "Fundamental" *might* mean essential or important to preserving self-government and the open society, which are entitled to be regarded as basic constitutional objectives. That, indeed, is the sense in which the Court appears to have used the term when the compelling governmental interest test made its public debut in full-fledged form.[5] At least four of the Justices, however, and probably more, have used the term in a quite different sense. They have used it to mean essential or important from the viewpoint of the general populace; they have asserted — often with great passion — that a "right" (more accurately, an *interest*) is fundamental if Everyman would so describe it.

Quite clearly, the Court has not consistently adhered to this latter definition. Had it done so, the decisions holding fundamental the "right" of recent residents to vote, without restriction by a one-year durational residency requirement,[6] and decisions holding *not* fundamental the "rights" to housing, education, and a subsistence income [7] would reflect such an obvious inversion of values as to betoken psychotic departure from reality. In point of fact, the Court has never addressed itself to the question of what standard of fundamentality it does or should apply; and the division between Justices who vaguely feel the first standard to be appropriate and those who strongly espouse the second has caused decisions to turn on small points that have swung a single vote, so that the decisions handed down in the "new equal protection" field form a crazy quilt every bit as bizarre as the Tennessee legislative apportionment condemned in *Baker v. Carr* as a denial of equal protection.[8] Moreover, *not one* of the Justices has said anything that precludes him from attaching or withholding the label "fundamental" in future cases.

Such subjectivity does not infect the "suspect basis of classification" test, at least to the same degree. There, it is possible for the Court to articulate meaningful criteria of "suspectness," and it has occasionally done so. For example, in rejecting a proposed "suspect" basis of classification in *San Antonio Independent School District v. Rodriguez* (1973),[9] Justice Powell observed in his majority opinion:

> The system of alleged discrimination and the class it defines have none of the traditional indicia of suspectness: the class is not saddled with such disabilities, or subjected to such a history of purposeful unequal treatment, or relegated to such a position of political powerlessness as to command extraordinary protection from the majoritarian political process.[10]

Thus, though the *Carolene Products* footnote has left its mark on constitutional doctrine, the difference in approach between its first paragraph and its second and third — which the Court has failed to articulate — has blurred that mark. While he lived, Justice Stone might have brought the difference to his colleagues' attention; but even he seems to have underestimated its importance, since it was he who first applied the term "preferred position" to freedom of the press [11] and thereby fostered the impression that the footnote mainly stood for judicial defense of rights that are in some sense important — the teaching of the first paragraph. There is little doubt that Justice Frankfurter's repudiation of the footnote in his *Kovacs v. Cooper* (1949) [12] concurrence resulted from his disapproval of the first paragraph with its "preferred position" corollary, since he said:

> My brother Reed speaks of "the preferred position of freedom of speech".... This is a phrase that has uncritically crept into some recent opinions of this Court. I deem it a mischievous phrase, if it carries the thought, which it may subtly imply, that any law touching communication is infected with presumptive invalidity.... I say the phrase is mischievous because it radiates a constitutional doctrine without avowing it. Clarity and candor in these matters, so as to avoid gliding unwittingly into error, make it appropriate to trace the history of the phrase "preferred position."[13]

After tracing that history, with a comment that "[a] footnote hardly seems to be an appropriate way of announcing a new constitutional doctrine, and the *Carolene* footnote did not purport to announce any new doctrine," Frankfurter continued:

> The objection to summarizing this line of thought by the phrase "the preferred position of freedom of speech" is that it expresses a complicated process of constitutional adjudication by a deceptive formula. And it was Mr. Justice Holmes who admonished us that "To rest upon a formula is a slumber that, prolonged, means death." Collected Legal Papers, 306. Such a formula makes for mechanical jurisprudence.[14]

This criticism was well justified, if limited to the first paragraph, which implies that the Court should take primary responsibility for protecting interests it deems "preferred" because they are in some undefined sense *important* — the idea being that some interests are too important to be exposed to majoritarian regulation, just as Clemenceau is reputed to have said that war is too important a matter to be left to the generals. But the criticism is inappropriate if directed against the second and third paragraphs, which call for determining the Court's relative competence to deal with particular types of problems. Justice Frankfurter would probably have conceded as much.

Turning more directly now to an evaluation of the new role that the Court has fashioned for itself, we observe that a great many of its actual *decisions* can be justified more successfully as being based on implied judicial power than on the reasons actually given by the Court. Take *Powell v. McCormack* (1969) [15] for example. As pointed out in Chapter IX,[16] no decision has departed more radically from the *Marbury v. Madison* conception of judicial review. Yet the decision may well be justifiable on the ground that in 1969 the Court reasonably thought it very important to show Negroes that the political process is for them as well as for whites, coupled with the fact that the Court may well have been better fitted to make the showing than other organs of government.

If, as Adam Clayton Powell claimed, the House of Representatives judged his delicts with unwonted harshness because of his race, there was no effective remedy at the polls: Most voters in the *other* 434 Congressional districts, who controlled the House majority, very probably did not feel threatened by Powell's exclusion from his seat, since he was black and they were preponderantly white; consequently, the House majority probably did not feel threatened either. Lacking an effective political remedy, his Harlem constituents may well have thought that, even though Powell *was* seated after his reelection in 1968, it took blacks an extra two years to put their chosen representative into Congress — and meanwhile, during his two-year wait, they may have thought that he couldn't get into Congress at all unless he behaved like an "Uncle Tom" or else satisfied higher ethical standards than were applied to whites. It was therefore important for reassurance to be given, and the Court — being the only organ of government that *could* give it quickly — stretched the mootness and justiciability rules in order to do so (without waiting years for maturation of a new lawsuit in the Court of Claims for salary wrongfully withheld, as suggested by Justice Stewart in dissent).

So far as mootness is concerned, the decision contrasts strangely with *DeFunis v. Odegaard* (1974).[17] DeFunis, a rejected white applicant for admission to the University of Washington Law School, sued to compel his admission on the ground that he had been the victim of discrimination in favor of nonwhite applicants. Having been allowed to matriculate and attend law school while the case was working its way through the state courts, he was about a month short of graduation when the Court reached his case for decision. By a vote of five to four, the Court dismissed the appeal as moot. The case had aroused tremendous public interest, because it involved one of the most difficult and fiercely disputed of current racial issues (of which the controversies relating to "busing" and benign racial quotas are examples): To what extent is it permissible to load the burden of righting the racial injustices of the past century upon unluckily situated individuals or small groups, rather than upon the national community as a whole? Moreover, as the four dissenters pointed out, there was still a possibility — even if a slight one — that DeFunis might not graduate on schedule.[18] The only way to account for the dismissal is that the Court was not ready to express itself on the vexed issue and, lacking the privilege of Congress to table such an issue, it resorted to the mootness rationale as the best available excuse.

Adoption of the approach I have posed for *Powell v. McCormack* would have enabled the Court to acquit itself more creditably in the great case of *United States v. Nixon* (1974).[19] The case involved the question whether President Nixon was legally obligated to produce tape recordings and memoranda of his office and telephone conversations, for possible use as evidence in a criminal trial. The Court, in an opinion by Chief Justice Burger joined by seven other Justices (Justice Rehnquist abstaining), held that he was. The opinion dealt meticulously with various legal issues, such as justiciability and the scope of executive privilege, but one first-magnitude question — perhaps the basic one — was left untouched.

Counsel for President Nixon had contended that the subpoenas for the tapes were mainly significant as an aid to impeachment proceedings, and that impeachment was simply outside the sphere of legitimate judicial action. His reply brief, after referring to "the utter impropriety of this Court becoming involved in the constitutional process of impeachment," went on:

> Surely this Court can judicially notice the fact that proceedings are under way in the House Judiciary Committee looking to possible impeachment of the President.
>
> The late Thomas Reed Powell is said to have defined the legal mind as a mind that can think of one of two things that are inescapably interrelated without thinking about the other. Only those who would attempt this cynical view of the legal process would suppose that this case and the investigation in the Judiciary Committee are wholly unrelated, or that this Court can render a decision in this case without that decision having a heavy impact, one way or the other, in the impeachment process that is so clearly committed exclusively to the House and the Senate.[20]

The issue thus tendered was surely of the first magnitude, and was possibly the main one in the minds of the public. The President's fundamental position was that the question whether his private conversations should be disclosed was for him alone to decide, and that the sole remedy for a wrongful decision on his part was a political one. If the people disapproved, he said, they could register their disapproval by their votes at the next presidential election or, through their elected representatives, by impeachment and removal. It is unfortunate that the Court elected to dispose of the case without adverting to this great separation of powers problem.

The problem could have been squarely faced and convincingly handled — without changing the result in the case, which in my opinion is sound — on the following rationale:

  1. Prosecutions for official malfeasance serve a broader purpose than prosecutions for ordinary crimes. The latter are undertaken primarily to deter other potential offenders; the former serve also, and perhaps more importantly, to publicize the facts in an authoritative way and thereby facilitate the corrective political processes by informing the electorate.\*

---

\* This is the rationale that justified the Court in deciding *NAACP v. Button*, discussed *supra* at pages 220-22, on First Amendment grounds. Though I cannot concur in Justice Brennan's actual rationale, which encourages lawyers and parties to abuse courtroom procedures by using criminal trials as opportunities for political

2. The particular corrective political process which the Constitutors established for removal of an unfit president is impeachment by the House of Representatives and removal by the Senate.

3. For various reasons, not the least of which is the unhappy fate that history tells us has befallen many regicides, the House of Representatives is even more reluctant to impeach a president than to enact controversial legislation. However persuasive the argument for impeachment may be, the House is unlikely to impeach unless pushed by unmistakable electoral demand.

4. Prosecutions for political malfeasance are the most effective way to generate electoral demand for the ousting of scoundrels; and prosecutions of lower ranking officials are the most effective way of loosening their tongues and inducing them — in order to exculpate themselves or mitigate their punishment — to reveal the misdeeds of their superiors. Such prosecutions are therefore a useful and perhaps essential preliminary to the impeachment of an unfit president.

5. Prosecutions are judicial business, and the Special Prosecutor acts in the judicial mainstream when he seeks to uncover evidence for use in prosecutions for political malfeasance. The prosecutions and the subpoenas are an integral part of the corrective political process that the Constitutors have prescribed, which includes Congressional action but is not limited to it. As stated in Point 4, judicial action is an essential preliminary to activation of the Congressional process, which would be useless unless judicial action were available for generation of the indispensable public understanding and outcry.

---

dialectic within a sanctuary protected against liability for defamation, I do agree that freedom of political expression is importantly aided by *authoritative determination of the facts.* Many who disapproved the Nuremberg trials as a means of establishing legal rules against international aggression (as did Chief Justice Stone) might have agreed that they served the useful purpose of establishing — in an impartial and orderly proceeding — the facts that led up to World War II and the way in which it was fought. For the Stone position, *see* MASON, HARLAN FISKE STONE: PILLAR OF THE LAW 715-16 (1956).

Such a rationale would have involved candid resort to the principle of implied judicial power, and the Court may have avoided it for that reason. But it would have provided better justification for the decision, at a time when a troubled and divided nation desperately needed the clearest justification possible.

Analysis of this type would provide justification for the overwhelming majority of the Court's decisions from 1937 down to about 1969. That was the premise on which my original five-theorem approach, set out in Chapter I, was based. Even before 1969, however, the Court's failure to develop an implied power doctrine led to a few aberrations; and after 1969, when four changes in Court membership occurred very quickly, the aberrations began to appear at an accelerating rate. That is why my five-theorem approach had to be abandoned as an oversimplification.[21]

At the end of Part One, after postulating the principle of implied judicial constitution-making power, I acknowledged that it can serve to defend the Justices against the accusation that they have set themselves above the law only if it is not so vague as to be illusory — that is to say, only if it is sufficiently knowable to permit detection of judicial usurpation. Proposing to test that question by reviewing the Court's work in controversial areas and attempting to evaluate it on the basis of the postulated principle, I undertook such a review in Part Two. In Chapter XV, I have canvassed an observed change in the Court's methodology which facilitates constitution-making and is most easily explainable as reflecting its assumption of broader constitution-making power than it previously claimed. Now it is time to see what happens when the principle of implied judicial constitution-making power, with its corollary preference for tentative rather than definitive judicial review, is used to evaluate the new constitutional rules. To avoid undue repetition I shall — except where the skimpiness of the previous discussion forbids — avoid extended explanations by making use of back references, and shall state rather summarily my reasons for considering particular decisions or opinions to be aberrational.

I believe it will be seen (a) that the principle is not so vague as to be illusory — *i.e.,* that it can be used, with its corollary, as a yardstick; (b) that although a few of the Court's constitutional decisions (mainly quite recent ones) appear to transcend the limits of implied judicial power, the great majority of them are consonant with it; but (c) that the Court can rightly be criticized for failure to explain, in a good many cases, the justification for its exercise of constitution-making power. The reader will have to make his own judgment as to whether the result is to disapprove any part of the Court's work that is worth preserving; in my opinion, the answer is no.

The standard against which I propose to measure the Court's performance is *demonstrable necessity;* in Chapter II, I said that the Court must look down a dark road whenever it utilizes judicial review beyond the boundaries of demonstrable necessity. This calls for examination of the decisions to see (a) whether implied judicial power has been utilized in cases where it was not needed for attainment of some national objective, some "great purpose" of the Constitutors — not needed because elected officials were as well qualified as the Court to attain it; and (b) whether definitive judicial review has been utilized in cases where tentative judicial review would have been adequate to the need.

\* \* \* \* \*

In the field of freedom of expression (Chapter IX) the major aberration is in the law of obscenity. It cannot be seriously contended that the Constitutors of the *First* Amendment thought they were establishing a general constitutional right to publish or receive pornographic literature. Possibly they intended to keep *Congress* from regulating that subject matter; the unqualified ban upon Congressional abridgment of "freedom of speech, or of the press" does seem to say so, though a respectable argument can be made that the quoted phrase carried in 1791 the specific technical meaning that Blackstone attributed to it, namely, freedom from *preventive administrative censorship.*[22] But even if that argument must yield to the supposed "plain meaning" of the constitutional text, no restriction on regulation by the *states* was then intended.[23]

Nor is it plausible to suppose that the Constitutors of the *Fourteenth* Amendment, if asked, would have said it had anything to do with protecting pornography. It must be remembered that the original Federal postal censorship statute was passed in 1865,[24] and the more ferocious Comstock Law was enacted in 1873 [25] — both of them by many of the same Senators and Representatives who had proposed the Fourteenth Amendment on June 13, 1867. Moreover, for more than three quarters of a century thereafter, the Court gave no indication that traffic in pornographic literature deserves any greater constitutional protection than traffic in beef or buttons. Indeed, in *Mutual Film Corp. v. Industrial Commission* (1915),[26] the Court went so far as to declare that moving pictures, being predominantly entertainment rather than politically significant expression, were excluded from constitutional protection — a position that was questioned in *Winters v. New York* (1948) [27] with the remark, "What is one man's amusement, teaches another's doctrine"; [28] was repudiated by way of dictum in *United States v. Paramount Pictures, Inc.* (later in 1948); [29] and was abandoned in *Joseph Burstyn, Inc. v. Wilson* (1952).[30]

In 1957 the Court once again initiated new constitutional doctrine by way of dictum, as it had done in *Korematsu v. United States* (1944) [31] and *Wolf v. Colorado* (1949),[32] in an opinion of Justice Brennan disposing of two companion cases: *Roth v. United States,* involving a Federal prosecution for mailing pornographic material, and *Alberts v. California,* involving a state prosecution for keeping pornographic books for sale and advertising them.[33] In both cases convictions were affirmed, Justice Brennan quoting a 1942 opinion of the Court saying that pornography has no constitutional protection because "such utterances are no essential part of any exposition of ideas, and are of such slight social value as a step to truth that any benefit that may be derived from them is clearly outweighed by the social interest in order and morality." Justice Brennan went on: "We hold that obscenity is not within the area of constitutionally protected speech or press."

Despite the seeming universality and finality of this pronouncement, there was a difficulty with it that made Justice Brennan and the Court uneasy. Not a few books have been attacked as pornographic when the real objection to them was that they propagated unpopular political ideas. Such books as *The Grapes of Wrath* and *1984* have suffered censorship under obscenity laws.[34] Thus, while it seemed clear that no pornographic book or movie should be granted constitutional protection against state action simply because it is published by the "press," there might well be a basis for an exercise of implied judicial power to protect a book or movie despite its salacious qualities. Therefore, by way of dictum, Justice Brennan rejected the strict English rule of *The Queen v. Hicklin* (1869)[35] which allowed material to be judged by the effect of an isolated excerpt upon particularly susceptible persons, and instead approved this test:

> whether to the average person, applying contemporary community standards, the dominant theme of the material taken as a whole appeals to prurient interest.[36]

And as a *reason* for believing that this test consists with the need to protect dissenting expression, he said:

> All ideas having even the slightest redeeming social importance — unorthodox ideas, controversial ideas, even ideas hateful to the prevailing climate of opinion — have the full protection of the [constitutional] guaranties, unless excludable because they encroach upon the limited area of more important interests. But implicit in the history of the First Amendment is the rejection of obscenity as *utterly without redeeming social importance.*[37] (Emphasis added; footnote omitted)

Chief Justice Warren, concurring in the result, voiced an idea that was to be embraced by the Court nine years later in *Ginzburg v. United States* (1966),[38] under the name of the "pandering" rule. For the Chief Justice, the dominant fact was that the defendants "were plainly engaged in the *commercial exploitation* of the morbid and shameful craving for materials with prurient effect."[39] (Emphasis added)

On the same day that it decided the *Ginzburg* case, the Court — swayed by the consummate advocacy of my justly admired law school friend Charles Rembar, who represented the publisher of the first white-market edition of *Fanny Hill* in the two centuries of that classic's harried existence — took its first step up the Tower of Babel. In the case known as *Memoirs v. Massachusetts* (1966),[40] the Massachusetts judgment condemning the book as "obscene" was reversed by a vote of six to three.

There was no opinion of the Court. Justices Black and Douglas voted for reversal because, in their view, the First and Fourteenth Amendments forbid the punishment of expression of whatever sort; as they put it, the First imposes an unqualified ban on abridgment of press freedom and should be applied in accordance with its plain language. They pretermitted the uncomfortable fact that *literally,* and without support by implication of judicial power, the Amendment restricts only Congress. (One is reminded of the justice of the peace who decided every bill collection case in favor of the plaintiff on the ground that, if a man owes money, he ought to pay it.) Justice Black adhered to this position until his death, and Justice Douglas still does.

Justice Stewart voted for reversal in the *Memoirs* case on the ground that *Fanny Hill* is not "hard-core pornography," a term he admitted in *Jacobellis v. Ohio* (1964)[41] that he could not define:

> I shall not today attempt further to define the kinds of material I understand to be embraced within that shorthand description; and perhaps I could never succeed in intelligibly doing so. But I know it when I see it....[42]

In what is sometimes politely called the prevailing or plurality *Memoirs* opinion (which actually means the opinion representing a lowest common denominator on which at least a majority of the Justices could agree), Justice Brennan was joined only by Chief Justice Warren and Justice Fortas. He purported to follow the test previously laid down in *Roth,* but actually prescribed a much more severe one:

> ... three elements must coalesce: it must be established that (a) the dominant theme of the material taken as a whole appeals to a prurient interest in sex; (b) the material is patently offensive because it affronts contemporary community

standards relating to the description or representation of sexual matters; and (c) *the material is utterly without redeeming social value.*[43] (Emphasis added)

"Redeeming social value" is thus promoted from the status of an explanation of the other two elements of the test, to the status of an independent element in its own right. Bewildered, Justice White in dissent protested this transmutation; but his protest fell on deaf ears. As a practical matter, the third Brennan test became the decisive rule, since (a) the three Justices who approved it could count on the concurrence of Justices Black and Douglas in any case where the three deemed the test not to have been satisfied and (b) the third test was so very restrictive that it was nearly always impossible to satisfy it, so that the other two were unimportant. For the whole seven years that it remained in effect, the only case in which the Court held it to be satisfied was *Mishkin v. New York* (1966),[44] decided the same day the test was announced.

From the viewpoint of judicial administration the test was a monstrosity. Defenders of pornography consistently trained their fire on the "redeeming social value" question — whether or not they also relied upon the other two tests — and, unlike prurient appeal and offense to community standards, utter lack of "redeeming social value" is *wholly subjective.* No lower court can know what will be held to be "utterly without redeeming social value" until the Supreme Court has spoken. From 1966 on, appeals to the Court were therefore taken as a matter of course, and seven of the Justices (all except Black and Douglas) had to take the time to read or view every questioned book or movie brought before them.

The Court did lay down three rules that eased its burden slightly: (1) The "pandering" rule of *Ginzburg v. United States* (1966),[45] which held that distribution of material not obscene under the three-part *Memoirs* test can be made punishable if it is *marketed* with flamboyant appeal to prurient interest; (2) the rule of *Ginsberg v. New York* (1968),[46] which held that even material which is constitutionally protected with respect to distribution to adults can nevertheless be made punishable if it is distributed to *juveniles* and is reasonably believed to be too raw for their tender minds; and (3) the rule of *Rowan v. United States Post Office Department* (1970),[47] which held that distribution of sexually oriented material to *nonconsenting* persons can constitutionally be prevented even if not obscene under the *Memoirs* test. These three rules, however, are easily enough avoided to render them of little use in lightening the Justices' burden of cinema-going and nonlegal reading.

Obscenity cases also presented a number of fringe issues. From time to time the Court announced especially stringent procedural requirements for attacks on pornography, such as the rule that movie censorship is constitutional only if a very quick judicial decision is made available [48] and the rule (recently modified [49]) that a warrant authorizing seizure of allegedly pornographic material is valid only if issued after an adversary hearing — which, as a practical matter (given the time needed for appeals and the pervading uncertainty as to the meaning of "redeeming social value" until the Court has spoken or refused to speak) means that any lawyer can keep a client's book or movie on the market for a long time, regardless of its noncompliance with the obscenity statute, and the validity of the statute.

Beyond all this, there was the very real problem that originally led Justice Brennan to utter his protective dictum in the *Roth* case — the danger that obscenity laws can be used (or, rather, abused) to suppress material not because it is thought salacious but because it expresses obnoxious ideas. The difficulty of formulating a precise definition of obscenity, which Justice Stewart so candidly admitted, has given rise to a chronic vagueness; and even statutes which declare quite specifically what is forbidden, such as depiction of sexual intercourse, might easily be so broad as to condemn much of the world's great art and literature. (Justice Douglas is fond of citing chapters 7 and 8 of the Song of Solomon.[50])

Moreover, it is hard to discern a material distinction between a movie film depicting a sexual act and a live show in which the same act is performed in the flesh. To be sure, the one is a form of *publication* which literally comes within the ambit of *press* freedom, whereas the other is not. But such a difference is unlikely to impress Justices accustomed to look through form to substance in adjudicating constitutional questions. Indeed, the Justices encountered great difficulty in finding a plausible ground for allowing revocation of the liquor licenses of night clubs whose mode of entertainment was delicately described by Justice Rehnquist, speaking for the Court in *California v. LaRue* (1972),[51] in these terms:

> Customers were found engaging in oral copulation with women entertainers; customers engaged in public masturbation; and customers placed rolled currency either directly into the vagina of a female entertainer, or on the bar in order that she might pick it up herself.[52]

The Court happened to find a basis for reversing the judgment of a three-judge district court forbidding the license revocations, in the peculiarly extensive regulatory control over liquor which the Twenty-first Amendment has been held to allow to the states. It avoided saying, however, whether the entertainers' and customers' conduct itself could constitutionally be made punishable.

In 1973 the Court decided it had had enough of this. In *Miller v. California* (1973)[53] Chief Justice Burger succeeded in assembling a majority of five — the first time since the 1957 *Roth* case that a majority of the Justices agreed on a single obscenity test — to modify the *Roth* test (and the *Memoirs* formulation which superseded it) in this way:

> The basic guidelines for the trier of fact must be: (a) whether "the average person, applying contemporary community standards" would find that the work, taken as a whole, appeals to the prurient interest [citations]; (b) whether the work depicts or describes, in a patently offensive way, sexual conduct *specifically defined* by the applicable state law; and (c) whether the work, taken as a whole, lacks *serious* literary, artistic, political, or scientific value.[54] (Emphasis added)

The Chief Justice went on to give examples of a sufficiently specific statutory definition:

(a) Patently offensive representations or descriptions of ultimate sexual acts, normal or perverted, actual or simulated.

(b) Patently offensive representations or descriptions of masturbation, excretory functions, and lewd exhibition of the genitals.[55]

The Chief Justice also said that the "community" whose "standards" are material under the first part of the test is not the national community but a local community. He did not say how local a community he had in mind — the state, the county, the city, or the judicial district.[56]

On June 24, 1974, after the foregoing words were written, the Court rendered two more obscenity rulings which Warren Weaver, Jr., writing in the *New York Times,* describes as follows:

> The Supreme Court ruled today that the motion picture "Carnal Knowledge" was not obscene but that an advertisement for an illustrated version of the report of the Presidential commission on obscenity was.
>
> Divergent decisions in the two related cases raised the possibility, despite guidelines issued by the Court a year ago, that the Justices would be called upon to decide what is obscene on a case-by-case basis in the future, a course they have tried to avoid.
>
> Both of today's rulings hinged on the Supreme Court's own independent finding that the film or publication involved was obscene because it fell within one of the broad generalities of its past decisions, as "patently offensive" or "hard-core pornography," without defining these categories further.
>
> "Our own view of the film," Justice William H. Rehnquist wrote for a unanimous Court, "satisfies us that 'Carnal Knowledge' could not be found under the [Court's 1973] standards to depict sexual conduct in a patently offensive way."
>
> But when it came to the book ad, Mr. Rehnquist said: "It is plain from the Court of Appeals' description of the brochure involved here that it is a form of hard-core pornography well within the types of permissibly proscribed depictions described in" the principal 1973 decision.
>
> These statements prompted Justice William J. Brennan Jr. to charge that the new decisions do not "extricate us from the mire of case-by-case determinations of obscenity" and to protect "the attendant uncertainty of such a process and its inevitably [*sic*] institutional stress upon the judiciary."

In the case involving the advertisement, the high court held for the first time that Federal court jurors were entitled to apply their "own knowledge of the view of the average person in the community" in deciding obscenity cases.

Under this theory, Justice Brennan declared, "The guilt or innocence of distributors of identical materials mailed from the same locale can now turn on the dicey course of transit or place of delivery of the materials," with distributors "forced to cope with the community standards of every hamlet into which their goods may wander."

Dissenting in the case involving the advertising brochure were Mr. Brennan and Justices William O. Douglas, Potter Stewart and Thurgood Marshall. While expressing reservations about the majority reasoning, they all concurred in the result of the "Carnal Knowledge" ruling.

The brochure found obscene by the lower courts was mailed to advertise an illustrated version of the report of the President's Commission on Obscenity and Pornography, issued in 1970. The report, denounced by President Nixon, urged an end to all legal bars on adults buying sexually explicit books and magazines or attending such films.

The Federal court jury convicted the distributors of the advertisement on a charge of mailing obscene material. But the jury was unable to agree on whether the book itself was obscene. According to the Court of Appeals, which affirmed the conviction, the brochure included pictures of "heterosexual and homosexual intercourse, sodomy and a variety of deviate sexual acts."

Under the Court's 1973 ruling, Justice Rehnquist said, jurors trying the mail case in the Southern District of California had properly applied the standards in deciding that the advertisement was obscene.

. . . .

Concurring in the result of the motion picture case but objecting to the reasoning, Justice Brennan repeated his 1973 objection that "one cannot say with certainty that material is obscene until at least five members of this Court, applying inevitably obscure standards have pronounced it so."

Describing "Carnal Knowledge," Justice Rehnquist said that "while there are scenes in which sexual conduct including 'ultimate sexual acts' is understood to be taking place the camera does not focus on the bodies of the actors at such times."

"There is no exhibition whatever of the actors' genitals, lewd or otherwise, during these scenes," he added.

In his dissent in the commission report case, Justice Douglas said, "If officials may constitutionally report on obscenity, I see nothing in the First Amendment that allows us to bar the use of a glossary factually to illustrate what the report discusses."[57]

That is where obscenity law stands as this book goes to press. There is no reason to believe that it has reached its final form. On the one hand, a storm of anguished protest has arisen from the intelligentsia and from certain publishers and movie makers; even if the present five-to-four rule proves durable, state legislatures may be impressed by their arguments. On the other hand, as will appear in the next chapter, it is quite difficult to justify even a rule as permissive as the present one, on the basis of implied judicial power; and, as noted above, it finds no foundation in the intent of the Constitutors.

In comparison with the obscenity quicksand in which the Court has mired itself by reason of its disregard of the principle of implied judicial power, other vagaries in the field of speech and press freedom are insignificant. They can be listed summarily:

(1) By insisting (unnecessarily) that its decisions in the field of defamation, subsequent to *New York Times Co. v. Sullivan* (1964),[58] be tied to the words of the First Amendment, the Court has extended its intrusion upon state tort law farther than the national interest demands. Not only has the state law of defamation been thrown into needless disarray,[59] and the protection of reputation been subordinated to journalistic greed much more than the public interest requires, but the state law of privacy has been wantonly thrown into confusion.[60]

(2) By the same insistence on tying its decision in *NAACP v. Button* (1963)[61] to the words of the First Amendment, coupled with its stubborn refusal to recognize that anti-Negro discrimination stands in a class by itself, the Court has been led by that eminently sound ruling to supersede state control over the legal profession far more completely than is required by any perceptible national interest.[62]

(3) By the same insistence on tying its probably sound decision in *Marsh v. Alabama* (1946)[63] to the words of the First Amendment, the Court has superseded Congressional and

administrative solution of the delicate labor relations problem of regulating picketing on private property, and has confused the lower courts and the bar by rendering decisions that are hard to reconcile with each other.[64]

(4) By its autohypnotic devotion to its own dictum that the First Amendment requires expression to be left "uninhibited, robust, and wide open," first voiced in *New York Times v. Sullivan* (1964) [65] and tracing back to a still more vigorous dictum in *Terminiello v. Chicago* (1949),[66] the Court has led itself into erecting constitutional protections for excessive street demonstrations [67] and pointless incivility in discourse, such as the wearing in a courthouse corridor of a leather jacket emblazoned "Fuck the draft"; [68] repeated use of the epithet "mother fucking" * by a speaker at a school board meeting attended by about 150 people, including women and children; [69] repeated use of the same epithet by a speaker at a meeting in a university chapel; [70] and the scolding of policemen engaged in an arrest as "God-damned fucking police." [71] ** For the same reason, the Court has repeatedly ducked the question whether flag desecration statutes are constitutional, evidently being reluctant to hold either that they are valid or that they are not.[72]

---

*Exhibiting a delicacy not manifested in Cohen v. California, 403 U.S. 15 (1971), four Justices used the term "m- - - - - f- - - - - -" in quoting the defendants in the later 1972 cases, referred to immediately below.

**A nonlegal protest on unorthodox grounds has been lodged by my friend Louis B. Salomon, in *The Atlantic,* October, 1967, at page 125, under the title "Stop the Dirty-Word Drain" (copyright © 1967 by the Atlantic Monthly Company, Boston, Mass.; reprinted with permission):

> At Free Speech and Filthy Speech, I neither gag nor groan,
> For every little Movement has a meaning all its own.
> There's not a word I've ever heard that makes me ill or queasy,
> But look, you guys, four-letter-wise it pays to take it easy.
> When billingsgate you escalate, you know not what you do:
> It takes a heap of abstinence to make a term taboo,
> And every dirty word that gets infected with propriety
> Is one more natural resource lost to the Great Society.
> Are we so rich in phrases which it takes some guts to utter?
> At Parent-Teacher teas can we afford both buns and gutter?
>
> CHORUS
>
> With tea-table talk gone all hairy and tough,
> What can you use when the going gets rough?
> What'll you shout when a two-ton truck

(5) By its wooden application of overbroad dicta concerning freedom of association, the Court has swept into the field of *definitive* judicial review a problem more suitably handled by tentative judicial review: the extent to which student organizations must be permitted to destroy academic values in pursuit of political objectives.[73] On the basis of personal experience I believe that such thick-fingered handling of a most difficult conflict of important interests may spell the doom of the modern university.[74]

(6) By its almost hysterical distaste for restraints on expression, the Court has been led to the precipitate disposition, without ample time for deliberate consideration, of one of the most important and difficult issues that has ever come before it — the question whether the Federal executive can obtain an injunction against the publication of purloined official documents, concealment of which may help prolong a war but disclosure of which may harm the national interest.[75] Justices Black, Douglas, and Brennan went so far as to condemn the grant of temporary injunctions (to prevent the case from becoming moot before the Court could decide it) as violating the First Amendment.[76]

In the related field of electoral rights, the valuable if masochistic decision in *Baker v. Carr* (1962)[77] has led to condemnation of

> Splatters your coat with water and muck —
> *Oh, mercy me?*
> What can you scrawl
> On the men's-room wall —
> *Fiddle-de-dee?*
> *Gee?*
> When doing slow burns
> Over tax returns,
>     Will you cry *What a dilly?*
> When your car won't budge,
> Will you holler *Oh, fudge?*
>     Don't be silly!

ENVOI

> Our dirtiest words
> Don't come in herds.
>   Please keep 'em dirty.
> We haven't got more
> Than three or four.
>   We sure could use thirty!

inequalities far too small to be significant, because of the Court's desperate need for a rule simple enough for it to manage without unacceptable demands on its time.[78] For the same reason, the Court has unjustifiably imposed doctrinaire limitations on efforts of state and local governments to grant the franchise to persons most interested in the election results and deny it to a few others.[79] Very recently, the Court has begun to back off from these extreme positions — by way of *ipse dixit,* however, rather than reasoned recognition of the limits of implied judicial power.[80]

* * * * *

In its regulation of the criminal process (Chapter X), the aberrational decisions made by the Court stem almost entirely from the underemphasis on protecting the basic security of person, property, locomotion, and reputation which results from across-the-board application of the Bill of Rights guarantees as limitations on state and local law enforcement. The Bill of Rights was devised for the very purpose of making it quite difficult for the *Federal* Government to obtain criminal convictions. What made it tolerable to erect such high barriers against Federal prosecution was the fact that the basic securities just mentioned are primarily protected by state and local rather than Federal law. We have acknowledged the practical utility of the selective incorporation doctrine,[81] but — utilized as the Court does utilize it, *i.e.,* by way of *definitive* judicial review — it has a drawback. The problem in each case is to balance (a) the collective need for security from attack, against (b) the equally important individual need for protection from unwarranted police intrusion, groundless prosecution, and erroneous conviction. Except for the fact noted above [82] that political remedies for denial of the latter protection tend to be ineffectual, such balancing could be done far better by legislators than by courts. Legislators are exposed to the anguished complaints of the victims of crime, as well as the admonitions of the criminal courts bar and of civil liberties organizations; appellate courts get a close look only at the often pitiful defendant, whereas victims and potential victims are dim and faceless abstractions. That being so, it is perhaps understandable that some of the Justices, and in the years 1967-1969 most of them, wrote as if it were a cause for unalloyed rejoicing — a demonstration that justice is alive and well in America — that a plainly guilty defendant had won his liberty by invoking the Bill of Rights.

In this connection it is pertinent that although, as we have seen, the Court has surmounted its intrinsic handicap in the matter of remedies in several quite astoundingly successful ways, it is powerless to do the job of a police force in protecting the citizenry from the depredations of criminals. All its sheriffs and marshals and bailiffs and masters and receivers, backed by every conceivable injunction and writ and mandate, cannot intervene between the determined murderer or rapist and his intended victim. Therefore no one can blame the Court for failing to perform the function of a constabulary, as it has occasionally undertaken to perform the function of a legislature. By the same token, however, the Court ought not to deprecate the importance of the constabulary in defending the people against marauders, or — as it has sometimes seemed to do — imply that its own important task of assuring justice to the suspect and the accused is nobler than the task of the policeman on the beat and the prosecutor who seeks judicial approval of the fruits of the policeman's labors.

It would extend this chapter beyond reasonable limits to list the particulars in which the Court has underemphasized the importance of the basic function of government — a function that the judiciary itself is incapable of performing unaided — namely, preserving the public peace. Instead, I offer two illustrations of the remarkable extremes to which the Court has gone in applying one of the most precious but most costly of the Bill of Rights safeguards, the privilege against self-incrimination.

The first such case is *Garrity v. New Jersey* (1967),[83] which has been briefly noted.[84] A policeman was called as a witness in an investigation of the fixing of traffic tickets. He was given his choice of testifying or losing his job. He elected to testify and incriminated himself. On his own admissions, he was convicted. The Court reversed. This, I submit, is absurd.

The other illustrative case is *California v. Byers* (1971) [85] which, from the defendant's point of view, arose about two years too late. A California "hit and run" statute required a driver involved in an auto accident to stop at the scene and give his name and address. Byers was indicted for failing to do so. The extremely able California Supreme Court, which in recent years has been second to none in its energetic implementation of the directions of the United States Supreme Court, held that the statute required the defendant to subject himself to "substantial hazards of self-incrimination," and that in order to save the statute from invalidity under the Fifth Amendment privilege (incorporated into the Fourteenth), it was necessary to forbid the state to use information supplied pursuant to the statute, in a subsequent prosecution of the informant. Since Byers could not have known, at the time of the accident, that this "use immunity" would be created by the court, the California Supreme Court held that it would be "unfair" to punish him and therefore threw out the indictment. The United States Supreme Court reversed, by the narrowest of margins. The vote was five to four, and none of the four opinions was accepted by more than four of the Justices.

Only the opinion of Justice Harlan, who wrote for himself alone, commends itself to the seeker after rational government. He acknowledged that the driver who is required to stop and identify himself after an accident does expose himself to greater risk of prosecution — perhaps for reckless or drunken driving — than if he were allowed to hightail it down the road and disappear from view (particularly if he is lucky enough to be the only surviving witness to the accident). He also conceded that the privilege against self-incrimination is the keystone of the accusatorial system. He declared, however, that preservation of the accusatorial system is not the only value worthy of protection; that the state is also entitled to concern itself with enabling accident victims to identify persons who may be liable to them (and whose liability insurance may be available to them). Weighing such considerations as these, Justice Harlan arrived at the only conclusion that is consistent with humanity and common sense. He voted to reverse the judgment of the California Supreme Court.

Four others — Chief Justice Burger and Justices Stewart, White, and Blackmun — arrived at the same result by a route worthy of the Lord Chancellor in Gilbert and Sullivan's *Iolanthe*. They simply denied that compliance with the hit-and-run statute would have exposed Byers to substantial risk of self-incrimination. It is hard to accept such a view without abandoning the long-settled proposition that any compelled statement which provides a link in a chain of incriminatory evidence — even though not itself a confession of crime — is protected by the Fifth Amendment privilege.[86]

The other four Justices dissented in scornful terms, claiming that the Court was sterilizing the self-incrimination privilege. Justice Black wrote one dissent, in which Justices Douglas and Brennan joined. Justice Brennan wrote another, in which Justices Douglas and Marshall joined. It seems likely that, had the case reached the Court two years earlier, before Chief Justice Warren was replaced by Chief Justice Burger and Justice Fortas resigned (eventually to be succeeded by Justice Blackmun), the vote would have been five to three for affirmance. And the California Supreme Court cannot be faulted for deciding the case in the way it believed, with good reason, would be required by a majority of the Justices.

We have endeavored to pinpoint the main trouble with the Court's recent decisions in the criminal process field. Later on, we shall inquire what can be done to correct it.

\* \* \* \* \*

In the field of church-state separation (Chapter XI) the Court was in deep trouble until 1970, when in *Walz v. Tax Commission*[87] it broke free from the "wall of separation" concept and began to focus on real problems. In the later cases it has righted itself, and no aberrational decisions appear to encumber the reports. It may be said, however, that articulation of the implied power basis for rulings in this field would increase the life expectancy of existing precedents and would lessen the danger that the three-part test announced in *Lemon v. Kurtzman* (1971)[88] — particularly the metaphoric "entanglement" element of the test — may lead future Courts astray.

\* \* \* \* \*

In the field of racial discrimination (Chapter XIII) the aberrational decisions, such as *Evans v. Abney* (1970),[89] *Palmer v. Thompson* (1971),[90] and *Moose Lodge v. Irvis* (1972)[91] are attributable — as is a fair amount of doctrinal confusion — to one basic cause: the Court's failure to reconsider and reject the rationale of the *Slaughter-House Cases* (1873)[92] and the appendant *Civil Rights Cases* (1883).[93] Unless and until the Court takes that step, Negroes will not receive what the Civil War Amendments were designed to give them, namely, full relief from the heritage of chattel slavery. Yet the Court has performed more valiantly in the cause of racial equality in the years since World War II than has any other organ of government.

Even if the two basic cases remain undisturbed, the Court can do a great deal, and very probably will, to ease the plight of the blacks. It could and would very probably do more, however, if it could bring itself to accept the notion that anti-Negro discrimination has a special history and a special constitutional status, enshrined in the Thirteenth, Fourteenth, and Fifteenth Amendments, which cries out against its being dealt with no more firmly than other inequalities.[94] As noted above, it has thus far stubbornly rejected that notion. By insisting that the black minority receive the same degree of solicitude as other out-groups, no less but no more, the Court withholds acknowledgment of a just national obligation and imposes a drag on the effort to eradicate the vestiges of slavery. Other groups — women, Jews, Roman Catholics, Jehovah's Witnesses, Chicanos, Nisei, Puerto Ricans, aliens, bastards, homosexuals — may well deserve protection from majoritarian tyranny. But their claims are minuscule compared to those of the descendants of slaves.

\* \* \* \* \*

In the field of nonracial discrimination (Chapter XIV) there have been so many aberrational decisions since 1969, when the compelling governmental interest test came to full flower in *Shapiro v. Thompson,* that there is no point in doing more than refer back to comments already made on many of the "new equal protection" decisions [95] (as the cases applying the compelling governmental interest test have come to be called) which are based on "fundamental interests." Along with the neo-privacy decisions, about to be discussed, they comprise the heart of the case for accusing the Court of setting itself above the law.

I have coined the term "neo-privacy" to characterize cases in which the Court has claimed to be protecting privacy but has invested that term with a strange and novel meaning. These cases have little if anything to do with immunity from unwarranted intrusion on person or property, or with control over the dissemination of information about oneself — the two senses in which the term privacy is ordinarily used. Rather than acquiesce in the blurring of that useful term, I call such cases as the recent abortion and contraceptive decisions neo-privacy cases.*

There is a temptation to call them *pseudo*-privacy cases, but that would involve covert denigration. If they are to be criticized, they should be fairly criticized on their merits; the scales of judgment should not be biased by calling them a bad name. Therefore I use the unloaded term neo-privacy, which carries a reminder of their newness without imputing artificiality.

What these cases relate to are certain zones of personal autonomy in which the individual's decision must be allowed to

---

*Perhaps my unwillingness to stand unprotesting while the term privacy is ruined for descriptive use is a consequence of my own struggle to sharpen the term. *See* Lusky, *Invasion of Privacy: A Clarification of Concepts,* 72 COLUM. L. REV. 693 (1972), 87 POL. SCI. Q. 192 (1972). It is probably too late to salvage the term "invidious" which the Court has long used simply as an epithet describing discrimination which is constitutionally impermissible, with no regard whatever for dictionary meaning or previously accepted usage. The comparable degradation of the term privacy, however, is a much more recent development. There may still be time.

prevail over that of the majority. This must be because the Court thinks there is no substantial collective interest to be served, since no other plausible reason exists. Such discredited substantive due process cases as *Lochner v. New York* (1905) [96] did answer this description. They held, for example, that the individual's decision as to the price and terms on which he would buy or sell goods or services was his business, and his alone. The Court wiped these cases off the books in and after 1937, and for two decades or so adhered rigorously to the self-denying principle that it is for legislatures and not courts to pronounce the existence of a collective interest, an interest occasioning rightful official concern. Substantive due process became a pejorative term, and freedom of contract — the slogan emblazoned on the banner of free business enterprise — was consigned to the limbo of obsolete constitutional doctrine.

Then in 1965 substantive due process began to reappear, this time under a different banner bearing the watchword privacy. The Court, having renounced its constitutional protection of *laissez faire* in the economic field, commenced to establish it in the field of noneconomic liberties.

This development was a momentous departure from the self-denying principle to which the Court had adhered for more than a quarter-century. The drastic contraction of judicial review which began in 1937 had two major aspects: (1) rejection of the pre-1937 Court's belief in the sanctity of states' rights which had led to erection of constitutional barriers against plenary Federal regulation of "local business" such as manufacturing, mining, and farming; and (2) repudiation of the pre-1937 Court's view that it was entitled to speak the last word on the question whether a particular issue involves a collective interest justifying majoritarian control through legislative action. Despite the explosive constitutional innovations in the period 1937-1965 that we have examined in Part Two, the Court steadfastly refused to recede from the position that it is for legislatures and not courts to decide whether a collective interest exists — that it is for legislatures and not courts to determine which issues each individual should be left free to resolve for himself.

The Court did limit legislative action in many ways during that period, but without questioning the conclusiveness of legislative judgments as to the *existence* of a collective interest. Sometimes, as in the field of speech and press freedom, it invalidated a statute on the ground that an acknowledged collective interest (such as prevention of violent rebellion) was so attenuated in the particular circumstances that it should be *overridden* by an imperative public need for personal autonomy. Sometimes, as in the criminal process cases, the Court restricted the *methods* to be employed in serving the legitimate collective interest in controlling socially harmful behavior. Sometimes, as in the equality cases, it held the legislature to a requirement of *consistency* in the measures it took to implement concededly permissible public policies. However, unless it had firm support in the text of the Constitution or in the need to preserve the people's control of their government, it refrained from bringing itself into flat confrontation with the people's elected representatives on the fundamental question whether a particular issue *is any of the government's business.*

Such a confrontation compels a choice between relatively enlightened judicial government and possibly inferior self-government.* If the people, thus confronted, were to opt for

---

*Justice Jackson, concurring in Railway Express Agency v. New York, 336 U.S. 106, 112 (1949), pointed out that equal protection and substantive due process have quite different impacts on self-government:

> The burden should rest heavily upon one who would persuade us to use the due process clause to strike down a substantive law or ordinance. Even its provident use against municipal regulations frequently disables all government — state, municipal and federal — from dealing with the conduct in question because the requirement of due process is also applicable to State and Federal Governments. Invalidation of a statute or an ordinance on due process grounds leaves ungoverned and ungovernable conduct which many people find objectionable.
> Invocation of the equal protection clause, on the other hand, does not disable any governmental body from dealing with the subject at hand. It merely means that the prohibition or regulation must have a broader impact.

At the time those words were written the Equal Protection Clause was viewed as nothing more than a prohibition against impermissible official classification, and the Clause was administered pursuant to the highly permissive "rational

self-government (as I believe they would), the Court as an institution could be badly damaged and the great values of judicial review lost. We must not forget that, through a confrontation of that sort, the Court nearly wrecked itself in the years prior to 1937. The neo-privacy cases are steps down the same path — not long steps, perhaps, but steps in the same direction.

The efflorescence of constitutional protection for newly established personal liberties got under way in *Griswold v. Connecticut* (1965).[97] A Connecticut statute made it a crime to use contraceptives or advise their use. The Court held the statute invalid as an infringement upon constitutionally protected privacy. Justice Douglas, in his majority opinion, staked a broad claim having little to do with privacy as previously understood — freedom from unwanted intrusion (as by an illegal search) and ability to control information about oneself.[98] He did ask: "Would we allow the police to search the sacred precincts of marital bedrooms for telltale signs of contraceptives?" [99] But no such search had taken place or been threatened; the defendants were the director of the Planned Parenthood League of Connecticut and one of its consulting physicians who had been convicted of advising married couples on the use of contraceptives.

The Justice therefore did not emphasize the danger of bedroom searches, but took the much broader position that constitutional

---

relationship test" (see pp. 248-49 *supra*). Later decisions now require the second quoted paragraph to be qualified: In some cases, such as those which hold that indigent defendants in criminal cases must be exempted from fee requirements, the Clause has been held to require a *narrower* rather than a *broader* impact. Moreover, the reach of the Clause is no longer limited to cases of impermissible official classification; it is held also to forbid official facilitation or encouragement of private discrimination, as by the 1964 California ban upon "fair housing" laws. In addition, some of the "new equal protection" cases impose such high standards of legislative consistency as to make it very difficult or impossible for the legislature to avoid offending them, except by abandoning the substantive legislative objective. Thus, the words "Invocation of the equal protection clause" introducing the second quoted paragraph would today be revised to read, "Invocation of the equal protection clause to invalidate official classification (or refusal to classify) without resort to the 'compelling governmental interest' test," etc.

Justice Jackson's main point, however — that the Court should be slow to confront legislatures with a "thou shalt not" so broad as to prevent *any* regulation of conduct they consider objectionable — remains valid.

provisions protecting individual liberties cover more than their words suggest. He cited *NAACP v. Alabama* (1958) [100] to show that the First Amendment has a "penumbra where privacy is protected from governmental intrusion"; [101] the Amendment does not expressly mention associational privacy, and yet was held to protect it in that case. He listed other Bill of Rights provisions protecting privacy — the Third Amendment, on quartering of soldiers; the Fourth, on searches and seizures; and the Fifth, on self-incrimination. For good measure he threw in the Ninth, which has no substantive content but makes clear that the guaranty of certain rights does not imply that the people possess no others. All this added up to a respectable argument for constitutional protection of privacy. What it did not explain was how privacy (as previously understood) was involved in the case: *NAACP v. Alabama* had to do with enforced disclosure of information — the NAACP membership lists. Compulsory self-incrimination, by definition, also involves enforced disclosure. The quartering of soldiers, and searches and seizures, constitute *physical intrusions.* All of them deal with privacy in the previously accepted sense.

Justice Douglas sought to bridge the logical gap by stressing the sacredness and intimacy of the marriage relationship. He "reaffirmed the principle" [102] of two pre-1937 cases holding that the due process clause protects personal liberties the Court deemed sacrosanct — the right to study the German language in a private school,[103] and the right to educate a child in a school of the parents' choice.[104] That principle formed the actual basis of the *Griswold* decision. The Court was simply forbidding regulation of an activity in which it thought there was no legitimate collective interest. The case held that it is none of the state's business whether married couples use contraceptives or not; but the Court *said* it was protecting privacy, and thereby gave privacy a new and indefinitely extensible dimension.*

---

*Incidentally, the majority opinion in the *Griswold* case (by Justice Douglas, at 381 U.S. 481-82) took issue with Justice Black's dissenting observation (*id.* at 514 et seq.) that substantive due process à la *Lochner v. New York* was being revived:

> Coming to the merits, we are met with a wide range of questions that implicate the Due Process Clause of the Fourteenth Amendment. Overtones

Another case in this same vein is *Stanley v. Georgia* (1969),[105] where the Court held that one has a constitutional immunity — based on a so-called right of privacy — against criminal punishment for possessing and viewing pornographic movies in his own home. *Eisenstadt v. Baird* (1972),[106] though ostensibly decided on equal protection grounds, is more properly classified as a neo-privacy case. It extended the *Griswold* decision's protection of "marital privacy" in the use of contraceptives, to cover unmarried persons as well. And in Chapter I we have already reviewed at length the cases which thus far represent the high water mark of neo-privacy, the 1973 abortion decisions.[107]

Although we now see *Griswold v. Connecticut* as the first neo-privacy case, neo-privacy became identifiable as a major constitutional doctrine only in *Roe v. Wade,* the principal 1973 abortion case. The *Griswold* decision was most plausibly interpreted as establishing no more than a unique right of "marital privacy" with little potential for extension to other fields. *Stanley v. Georgia* was easily accounted for as a manifestation of the Court's intense allergy to interference with expression. Not until *Roe v. Wade* did the Court (with only two dissents) propound a rationale so broad and conclusory as to provide convenient precedent for extension of noneconomic *laissez faire* as far as the Court chooses to enlarge it. That was when it became obvious that the Court has taken a course which, if pursued as far as its logic seems to permit, will result in a conflict of cataclysmic proportions between judicial review and self-government.

The neo-privacy cases cannot be justified on the basis of an expressed mandate from the Constitutors, and the Court has tendered no other persuasive justification. The closest I can come

---

of some arguments [*e.g.,* the Black dissent] suggest that *Lochner* v. *New York*, 198 U.S. 45 [1905], should be our guide. But we decline that invitation. . . .

Justice Black may well have been tempted to make the same rejoinder that his own majority opinion drew from Justice Robert H. Jackson in Everson v. Board of Education, 330 U.S. 1, 19 (1947):

> The case which irresistibly comes to mind as the most fitting precedent is that of Julia who, according to Byron's reports, "whispering 'I will ne'er consent,' — consented."

to explaining the decisions in terms of implied judicial power is to admit the possibility that religious taboos on the matter of sex may have clogged the corrective political processes so greatly that legislators have not dared to carry out the actual wishes of their constituents. As a factual matter, I doubt that this has been true in all of the cases.

Concerning contraceptives, for example, it is significant that the Connecticut legislature was on the point of repealing the statute involved in the *Griswold* case — proving once again the soundness of the maxim that the best way to assure quick repeal of a stupid law is to enforce it (as the Court had already goaded the reluctant Connecticut prosecutors into doing [108]) — when the Court obligingly preempted the question. The Massachusetts statute which the Court invalidated on "new equal protection" grounds in *Eisenstadt v. Baird* (1972),[109] for the stated reason that it discriminated illegally against fornicators, must be deemed simply a victim of doctrinaire analysis unless the majority Justices either (a) have forgotten that fear of pregnancy does deter illicit sexual intercourse to some extent, or (b) believe that no sexual intercourse between consenting adults can constitutionally be the object of official prohibition or discouragement. In the former event, there was simply a factual error. In the latter event, the Court must be faulted for failure to explain (if, indeed, it can explain) why there is no legitimate collective interest in discouraging extra-marital sex.

Concerning the freedom to enjoy pornography in one's home: Prohibitions against *possession* of pornographic materials exist only to implement restrictions on *distribution* of such materials. Therefore *Stanley v. Georgia* must be appraised as part of the Court's position on control of pornography generally. As a matter of fact, hindsight suggests that *all* the recent pornography cases ought to be classified under the heading neo-privacy rather than freedom of the press. I doubt that the Court's protective rules on pornography reflect the majority will of any single state or municipality — either with respect to the type of material that enjoys the Court's protection, or with respect to the status of the home as a sanctuary for display of otherwise illegal movies and literature; and I doubt that religious dogma plays a significant part in shaping community attitudes toward pornography today, at least in most communities.

Concerning abortions, the question is closer. Shortly before 1973, a few states had indeed abandoned the inhumane position so long adhered to under Roman Catholic pressure; but most of these had come only part of the way toward humanistic rationality, and the great majority of states seemed likely to persist indefinitely in their callous disregard of myriad social and physical tragedies wrought by the old rules. There was reason to believe that religious dogma was still a potent factor. That was enough to justify tentative judicial review. Query whether it was enough to justify definitive judicial review, particularly along the rigid lines that I have criticized in Chapter I.

One other defense of the neo-privacy decisions can be made, and it is not without substance. Even if it is true that Americans have emancipated themselves from the bondage of social taboos sufficiently to permit their elected officials to carry out the people's actual desires, it can be said that this is true only because the Court — in a series of decisions dating back at least to the *Lady Chatterley's Lover* case (1959) [110] — has cleansed away the foul-minded, debilitating, sexist precepts of Victorian morality. And it may well be so.

The argument provides a justification in terms of implied judicial power if, as may be the case, the Court was the only organ of government capable of doing this valuable job with respect to abortion, contraceptives, and pornography. It falls short of justifying everything the Court has done in the neo-privacy field, however, and it is still less adequate to justify what the Court's announced doctrines promise for the future. The washing away of Victorian morality, once done, is a *fait accompli*. If the cleansing job is now virtually complete (and I suspect that it is), the overruling of the neo-privacy decisions would not bring back the taboos, at least not for a long time. Their eradication is not reversible in less than a generation or two. Therefore, tentative judicial review seems adequate to the need. And even if one accepts as legitimate the decisions in neo-privacy cases (as opposed to their shoddy doctrine), it does not follow that the Court is justified in claiming for itself, as it seems to have done, the primary power to protect *every* interest that it chooses to bless with the label "private."

\* \* \* \* \*

Before leaving this canvass of decisions that do not measure up to the standards of implied judicial review, we should take note of one practice of the Court that has often been *erroneously* condemned as unprincipled: the grant or denial of certiorari without explanation, and the dismissal of appeals for want of a "substantial Federal question" without full briefs or oral argument. I have said in Chapter I that, as a law clerk, I found myself unable to demonstrate that the Court adheres undeviatingly to the Wechsler view that even the grant or denial of certiorari should be governed by neutral principles.[111] For example, I knew that certiorari had been granted (and the Ninth Circuit's decision reversed) in *United States v. O'Donnell* (1938),[112] which turned on the interpretation of an 1853 opinion by Attorney General Caleb Cushing concerning an obscure point of practice under the 1848 Treaty of Guadalupe Hidalgo. In no way could the case be regarded as presenting "an important question of federal law which has not been, but should be, settled by this court"; nor did it fit any of the other categories of cases listed by Supreme Court Rule 19 (1)(b) as deserving review, on certiorari, of a Federal court of appeals judgment. The only conceivable reason why the Court had exercised its discretionary power to grant certiorari in that case was that the Ninth Circuit's decision had undertaken to abrogate the Government's title to a sizeable part of the Mare Island Navy Yard, and it would have cost millions to regain title through eminent domain.

Not only this. The Rule 19 provision that the Court will review cases presenting "important" questions that "should be" reviewed is hardly a model of objectivity, and even in 1937 the Justices differed widely as to what kinds of questions it included. Still wider differences appear when different time periods are compared: Forty years ago, financial and commercial problems were considered more "important" than problems of civil liberties. Today the opposite is true. More striking yet was the Court's refusal to review many cases which, though they satisfied all the statutory requisites for *mandatory* review on *appeal,* as opposed to discretionary review on certiorari, were deemed to present no "substantial Federal question" because the decision of the lower court was so clearly right. In short, the Court's summary method of handling preliminary application for review leaves it quite free to act in an unprincipled manner if it is so inclined. Moreover, the so-called Rule of Four, which calls for the grant of certiorari if four of the Justices favor it (even where it seems plain as day that the other five will ultimately vote to affirm the lower court's decision on the merits), is a curious departure from usual deference to the principle of adjudication by majority vote. It seemingly injects an irrational element into the appellate process, somewhat impairing predictability.

For several reasons, these things did not trouble me in 1938 (and do not trouble me now). First, the 1925 Judiciary Act expressly gave the Court full discretion to grant or deny certiorari.[113] In nearly all cases two or more lower courts, bound by the same constitutional oath as the Supreme Court, had given the issues their full attention; it was not unjust to say that this was enough to accord to the immediate parties a fairly tolerable brand of justice, and that further appellate review could rightly be limited to cases having significance for many people *other than* the parties. So long as the Court adhered to the view that a denial of certiorari nowise committed it to any position on the merits (a view that may well have been modified now that the Court has become readier to grant certiorari simply because it thinks the decision below is wrong), liberal exercise of the power to deny certiorari without explanation called for no serious criticism. Indeed, if the Court *had* taken the trouble to explain each denial of certiorari, a principal objective of the 1925 Act — conservation of the Court's time — would have been largely frustrated.

Second, Rule 19's reference to "importance" could be defended from criticism as being too vague. It could be explained as a direction to the Court to "prick out" actual standards by "the gradual process of judicial inclusion and exclusion," a process familiar to courts in the common law system.[114] The word "important" is no vaguer on its face than "reasonable man" or "reasonable search" — standards that the courts administer with no departure from principle. The significant question was whether the rulings on certiorari petitions were in fact reconcilable with standards that the Justices *could* articulate without embarrassment if they took the trouble to do it.

A few such standards had indeed been crystallized. For example, there was tacit agreement among the Justices that certiorari would be denied in cases involving only the validity of a patent, unless courts of appeals had rendered conflicting decisions on the validity of *one particular* patent; a conflict with respect to the applicable legal rule was not a basis for certiorari in patent litigation, though it was enough in other types of cases.

With a little stretching, even the *O'Donnell* case could be made to fit a pattern. The recondite legal point on which the case hung was hardly of general interest, but the very fact that the *Government* stood to lose some millions of dollars might arguably invest the case with public significance since the burden would fall on every taxpayer. To be sure, *Frothingham v. Mellon* (1923) [115] had held that the cost imposed on each taxpayer by a wrongful Federal expenditure was too slight to give him standing to object; but it does not follow that abrogation of the Government's title to a valuable tract of realty — a deprivation which *it* had clear standing to complain of — was such an unimportant matter that it had no claim on the Court's time, even though no important question of Federal *law* was involved.

Third, as to the dismissal of appeals for want of a substantial Federal question: This seemed contrary to the literal mandate of Congress,[116] but there were countervailing considerations. If the ultimate outcome of a case on the merits was a foregone conclusion, it would be no favor to the losing party (unless he valued delay for its own sake, an interest hardly worthy of judicial respect) to put him to the trouble and expense of full briefs and oral argument. And it was at least arguable that Congress could not have *intended* for the Court to waste its time on frivolous or near-frivolous questions, and that the literally rigid terms of the jurisdictional statute should be softened by "equitable construction" [117] to permit this leeway.*

Finally, the Rule of Four does have much to recommend it unless the Court's caseload is so heavy that plenary consideration of even a few borderline cases is a matter of serious concern. Though one suspects that each Justice is able, in the great majority of cases, to make up his mind on the basis of the required preliminary papers (certiorari petition, or jurisdictional statement on appeal), there are undoubtedly a number of cases where his vote is affected by the more extensive briefs submitted on the merits or by the oral argument or by both. Were it not so, full briefing and oral argument would be empty rituals. There have even been cases where the Justices have agreed upon one decision at their initial conference immediately after oral argument, but have arrived at a contrary result after the more intensive study made by the Justice assigned to write the Court's opinion.[118] So it is not illogical for the Court to take the position that if its members divide almost evenly on the question of granting certiorari, the case is close enough to warrant plenary consideration which, as already acknowledged, *may* lead at least one of them to change his mind.

Indeed, one need not look even this far for a justification of the Rule of Four if, as the Court always professes to do, it keeps the decision on granting certiorari entirely separate from the decision

---

* Since dismissal for want of a substantial Federal question is the functional equivalent of summary affirmance, *i.e.*, affirmance on the basis of the preliminary papers alone, and since the jurisdictional statute does not forbid summary affirmance, the Court could avoid even the appearance of defying the statute by merely altering the wording of its dismissal mandates. The Court's present practice, reflected by its Rule 16, is to dismiss for want of a substantial Federal question in plainly unfounded appeals from state courts, but to affirm summarily in such appeals from lower Federal courts. If the latter practice were followed in appeals from state courts also, the statutory command would not be violated and still there would be no material difference in the effect of the decision.

on the merits (a proposition which has now become a bit doubtful). If the grant of certiorari depends solely upon the considerations listed in Rule 19, and if the decision on the merits depends solely upon the facts of the case and the applicable law, a Justice's vote to deny certiorari is no indication at all that he will vote to affirm on the merits.[119] On that assumption, there is no reason why the Court should not adhere to the Rule of Four because it effectuates a presumption of reviewability, in the same way that the requirement of jury unanimity reinforces the presumption of innocence. Just as it is thought better to acquit a guilty defendant than to convict an innocent one, so the Court *might* believe it is better to review than to risk an erroneous result, if the desirability of review is so close a question that four presumably intelligent and impartial Justices favor it.

Actually, a Rule of *One* might be justified on the same reasoning; and though outsiders can never know such things, it is not impossible that if a single Justice is seen to feel very deeply, three or more of his colleagues may sometimes go along with him for that reason alone. Moreover, though the Court has never acknowledged such a practice with respect to the *grant* of certiorari, Chief Justice Burger (like his immediate predecessors) has said that a Rule of One is followed in deciding whether a certiorari petition which he puts on his list for proposed denial without discussion at conference, should be removed from the list and exposed to debate among the assembled Justices.[120]

It is true that the Rule of Four is currently under some adverse critical pressure; but that is not because it is illogical or incompatible with the principle of adjudication by majority vote. It is because of the Court's enormous caseload — its docket has more than quadrupled since the Rule was laid down. A Court so beleaguered may be unable to afford the luxury of a presumption of reviewability.

CHAPTER XVII
## Quo Vadimus?

The reader may have observed that none of the decisions that are criticized as aberrational in the last chapter are related to the cases, summarized in Chapter XV, whereby the Court moved beyond the conception of judicial review expressed in *Marbury v. Madison* and fashioned a new role for itself. Those decisions cannot justly be criticized (except perhaps for lack of candor) without first arriving at a judgment as to whether or not the new role is itself subject to criticism. That is the purpose of the present chapter.

Approval or disapproval of the Court's abandonment of the passive posture called for by the *Marbury v. Madison* conception of judicial review depends on one's appraisal of implied judicial constitution-making power. If one believes, with Justice Black and Lord Acton, that "[p]ower tends to corrupt; absolute power corrupts absolutely," [1] then one will deplore the assertion of the implied judicial power to revise the Constitution.

It must be admitted that the aberrational decisions cited in the preceding chapter provide strong evidence in support of the proposition that, however sincerely the Justices who first exercise an implied power may intend to keep within boundaries fixed by the political philosophy of the Constitutors and however strictly they may have respected those boundaries, the boundaries tend to disappear when other Justices, not privy to the thoughts of their predecessors but seeing only their printed opinions in the *United States Reports,* take their places. Then the conflict of interest noted in Chapter I [2] may well result in the casting off of all external constraint. In my opinion, however, a countervailing consideration is decisive. It is now nearly two centuries since the original text was written at Philadelphia and over a century since the Civil War Amendments were adopted. The years since then have witnessed very great changes in the shape of our society and its economy and in our place on the world scene. Further changes, probably at an accelerating rate, are to be expected as the decades pass. Partly because of our nation's size, heterogeneity, and readiness for social change, and partly because of our propensity for keeping our constitutional ideals in the forefront of public consciousness — in rash but wholesome disregard of Justice Holmes's warning that one should never articulate his major premises [3] — adherence to the limitations on governmental power which the Constitutors would have prescribed if they had been consulted during their own lifetimes must (the formal amendment process being so difficult) lead to one of two results: (1) Increasingly serious inadequacy of government power to serve collective needs by providing political and legal remedies as substitutes for self-help. (2) Increasing resort to strained and artificial "interpretations" of the constitutional text, of the kind to which Justice Black, as we have seen, perforce resorted. Since I believe that either of these consequences — let alone both together — would be so great an evil as to outweigh the risk of judicial usurpation which acceptance of implied judicial constitution-making power ineluctably involves, I cast my vote in favor of accepting that risk.

This is not to say, however, that I think it necessary or wise for the Court to exercise such implied power in the covert manner it has in fact adopted. That involves considerations of an entirely different order. The argument against judicial candor is that, however clearly the Justices and the *cognoscenti* may understand that the Court's "interpretations" of the constitutional text are to be taken with a grain of salt, it is important for the general populace to believe that the Court really enforces the commands and prohibitions prescribed by the words of the Constitutors. Otherwise, it can be argued, the Court's power, dependent as it is upon continued popular acquiescence,[4] will fade away as the general public becomes more fully aware that the Justices do in fact remake the Constitution, and have been doing so since before the birth of any American now living. Only by use of emotion-laden slogans such as "fundamental rights" and "invidious discrimination," it may be said, can the Court put elected officials on the defensive and maintain its own primacy.

The argument on the other side can be summed up in Benjamin Franklin's aphorism that honesty is the best policy, or in Abraham Lincoln's warning that it is impossible to fool all of the people all of the time. There is simply no way, given the freedom with which ideas are communicated within our open society, to confine knowledge of the holy mysteries to a select priesthood comprised of bench and bar. Any attempt to do so will only produce festering suspicion and cynicism. Therefore, if we are to retain the open society, it is best to lay bare the real dynamics of the Court's work — hoping all the while that we Americans have attained sufficient political maturity to enable us, like the philosophers in Plato's cave, to look toward the sunlight rather than the shadows without blinding ourselves.

There are also compelling short-term reasons favoring judicial candor and calling for express publicly-avowed acceptance by the Justices of the limitations on their authority that are instinct in the principles of implied power. The most obvious of these reasons is that, unless such a course is taken, the Court's caseload will soon overwhelm it.

Addressing the American Bar Association in August, 1973, Chief Justice Burger said:

> In the past five years the increase in docketed cases has been 20 percent. Twenty years ago the Court issued 65 full signed opinions; in 1969, 88; this year, 140. The enormous increase in docketed cases from 1,463 in 1953 to 4,640 this past year, while staggering, is not the whole story. The cases presented to district and circuit judges in the past few years, and consequently those coming to the Supreme Court, contrast sharply in content and difficulty with those twenty-five or even ten or fifteen years ago.... Because of this new complexity of cases, the docketing of forty-five hundred Supreme Court cases today represents more than a four and a half multiple of one thousand cases twenty-five years ago.[5]

The Chief Justice took particular note of the increased number of *constitutional* cases. For more than half a century after *Marbury v. Madison* (1803) first held a Federal statute unconstitutional, he said, not a single act of Congress was declared invalid by the Supreme Court for variance with the Constitution, and only thirty-six state statutes were invalidated in fifty-four years from 1803 to 1857. I have not checked each of the cases coming to the Court in those fifty-four years to see how often statutes were challenged as unconstitutional, but I suggest it was a relatively infrequent event. During this past term of the Supreme Court, 57 of the 177 argued cases involved claims that a state or federal statute or a city ordinance violated the Federal Constitution — and many such claims were sustained.[6]

Since some 95% of the docketed cases are disposed of without oral argument, the total volume of constitutional cases now tendered to the Court annually on certiorari or appeal, and disposed of on the preliminary papers, must run well into the hundreds.

Chief Justice Burger thinks the quality of the Court's work is endangered:

> ... no person who looks at the facts can rationally assume that nine justices today can process four or five times as many cases as the Courts that included Taft, Holmes, Brandeis, and Hughes — to mention only a few — and do this task as it should be done.[7]

Some of the Chief Justice's colleagues disagree. Justices Douglas and Brennan have emphatically denied that the Court is overworked.[8] If the present trend continues, however, even they might become concerned; and the problem is under serious study. In 1971 Chief Justice Burger, as chairman of the Judicial Center, appointed a group of distinguished scholars and practitioners (chaired by Professor Paul A. Freund of Harvard Law School) to examine the caseload situation and make such recommendations as its findings warranted. Their report,[9] issued late the following year, concluded that the problem was acute. They recommended a series of remedial measures, the most far-reaching of which was to establish a new National Court of Appeals just below the Supreme Court to assume the main burden of preliminary screening of appeal statements and petitions for certiorari and to pass on to the Supreme Court only those cases (about 400 per year) which the National Court considers most worthy of the Supreme Court's attention. Chief Judge Henry J. Friendly, in his 1972

Carpentier Lectures at Columbia Law School, disapproved this proposal but, agreeing that the caseload had reached crushing proportions, recommended a number of less dramatic changes to bring it under control.[10] In 1974 another distinguished committee, chaired by my colleague Maurice Rosenberg, offered a modified version of the National Court of Appeals proposal, under which the Supreme Court would retain the ultimate power to bring up for review any case of a type now reviewable by it.\* [11]

None of the recommended measures will be more than a temporary expedient unless the Court acknowledges understandable limits to its power. There is literally no ceiling on the number of cases that can and will be presented for adjudication if litigants have a basis for hope that the Court will devise a new legal right or a new constitutional rule to afford relief from any official action or inaction that offends its sense of justice. Our statutes consist largely of measures that cannot be fully justified

---

\* More recently, the Commission on Revision of the Federal Court Appellate System has given added impetus to the movement for a National Court of Appeals. The Commission, established by Pub. L. No. 92-489 (1972) and directed by Pub. L. No. 93-420 (1974) to report by June 21, 1975, consisted of four Senators, four Representatives, four members appointed by the President, and four members appointed by the Chief Justice. Senator Roman L. Hruska served as chairman, Judge J. Edward Lumbard as vice-chairman, and Professor A. Leo Levin as executive director.

After issuing a preliminary report, the Commission held extensive hearings to receive comment and criticism by numerous witnesses including Professors Freund and Rosenberg. Its final report, rendered June 20, 1975, shows that it drew extensively on their views. For example, the final report moves in the direction of Professor Rosenberg's opinions with respect to the staffing of the National Court of Appeals and the desirability of vesting it with jurisdiction over categories of cases rather than cases selected individually on the basis of relatively vague criteria. Further debate and development is to be expected when the Commission's recommendations are embodied in proposed legislation and court rules, as they surely will be.

For a summary of the work done thus far, with citations to the literature, *see* pages 119-21 of the 1975 Supplement to ROSENBERG, WEINSTEIN & SMIT, ELEMENTS OF CIVIL PROCEDURE (2d ed. 1970). For a lucid and lively account, *see* Rosenberg, *Enlarging the Federal Courts' Capacity to Settle the National Law,* 10 GONZAGA L. REV. (Summer issue, 1975). Senator Hruska has explained the work of his Commission in the July, 1975, *American Bar Association Journal.* Hruska, *Commission Recommends New National Court of Appeals,* 61 A.B.A.J. 819 (1975).

on principle, for the simple reason that it is the proper job of legislatures to effect practical compromise between competing interests. Statutes speak in terms of universal rules that are almost certain to operate harshly in some situations, but that is the price of a government of laws. Few if any criminal trials are entirely free from error, though substantial justice can nevertheless be done. If the Court elects to be hypercritical of the other organs of government, it will nearly always be able to detect a flaw of some kind in their work.

During the years since 1937, the Justices must have known that their increased concern for free expression, criminal justice, church-state separation, and equality would not pass unnoticed. They must have known that each extension of the Court's protection would generate the hope of further extension, at least if the Court had announced a principle reaching beyond the particular issue it had decided; and that was very often what it did. For example, the assertion in *Schneider v. New Jersey* (1939) [12] that the Court would not defer to the legislative judgment but would weigh for itself the justification advanced for restraints on expression, reached far beyond the question whether handbill distribution can be forbidden to prevent littering. Likewise, the condemnation of involuntary confessions as "dictatorial criminal procedure" in *Chambers v. Florida* (1940) [13] suggested that the intrinsically hard-boiled business of investigating and punishing crime, in all its aspects, would receive the Court's scrutiny. The assertion in *Shelley v. Kraemer* (1948) [14] that enforcement of racially restrictive covenants is a denial of equal protection opened measureless possibilities for relief against private discrimination.

Moreover, being lawyers themselves, the Justices must have known that private legal practitioners would explore these new possibilities. In our adversary system, lawyers are not only permitted but obligated to pursue any substantial hope of furthering their clients' interests through litigation. And so it was entirely predictable that many more cases would be offered for review by the Court.

QUO VADIMUS? 355

This was no cause for immediate alarm, since the Court has ways to modulate the flow. The bulk of its cases are brought to it on certiorari, nearly all the rest on appeal. There is a quick screening on the basis of preliminary papers — a petition for certiorari or a jurisdictional statement setting forth grounds of appeal — each of which can be passed upon in a small fraction of the time needed for plenary consideration on full briefs and oral argument.

It was indeed possible that the number of offered cases could grow so large that even their *summary* disposition would strain the Court's capacity, and that has now happened. At first, however, and for a long time, the Justices seem to have regarded the increasing case flow as a wholesome development; and, as pointed out in Chapter XV, they have gone to considerable lengths to forestall its constriction.[15] That is why, if *half a dozen* intermediate stages of review are prescribed as protective barriers between the presently existing lower courts and the Supreme Court, the Supreme Court will still be increasingly overworked unless it acknowledges some understandable limits to its power.

Another short-term consideration argues for candid acknowledgment by the Court that it is and has been exercising implied judicial constitution-making power. Unless it does so, paradoxical discriminations of the type described in Chapter XV, involving callous disregard of the need for justice in the instant case,[16] will generate destructive skepticism about the genuineness of the Court's professed concern for "equal justice under law."

How can the Court go about *acknowledging* its resort to implied judicial constitution-making power, should it elect to follow that course? It might conceivably do the job all at once, of course, by issuing a grand manifesto; but that is not to be expected. A less radical approach to the problem is not outside the realm of the possible, however improbable it may be. The Court could inaugurate a practice of explaining, in each case where implied judicial constitution-making power is resorted to, (a) the national objective (commitment or goal) that is involved; (b) why it is that the national objective can be attained by the action the Court is taking; and (c) why it is that the national objective can probably be attained *only* (or much more surely) if the Court takes such action. That would quell the suspicion that the Court acts purely on a paternalistic, arrogant, opportunistic basis. It would mark off the area in which it accepts primary responsibility for the result and thus limit its caseload by making known the areas in which it is futile to petition it to override the judgment of elected officials. It would shore up confidence in the Constitution as a symbol of national unity, since the Constitution would be recognized once again as a set of objectively knowable principles setting limits on the power of all governmental organs, not excluding the Court, regardless of political pressure on particular issues. And it would take account of the fact that laws made by elected officials command general compliance more successfully than court-made law, because they are understood (a) to represent an attempt at balancing the competing needs of all segments of the population by elected representatives who are more closely in touch with them and their needs than are Justices appointed for life or good behavior, and (b) to be open to revision and repeal, if they work badly, by the same political processes that led to their enactment.

In each of its new opinions, the Court might do even more. It might go back and reinterpret in the same manner its previous opinions in the same field as the instant case. That would considerably accelerate the process of dispelling the suspicion that the Justices consider themselves to be above the law.

There is one other measure the Court might find productive. Liberated by its candor from the need to relate its every constitutional ruling to the words of the constitutional text, it could resort more freely to the process of tentative judicial review, reserving definitive judicial review for situations in which tentative judicial review is logically impossible or pragmatically pointless. From time to time throughout this book, we have taken note of cases in which the Court might profitably have utilized tentative judicial review. It is now time to take a closer look at this possibility and bring it down from the jurisprudential stratosphere to the level of practical affairs. Enlightenment needs translation into action, just as electricity did not serve mankind until a kite had captured lightning in a jar that could be held in the hand.

Let us first recall the rationale of tentative judicial review, as revealed in the familiar fields of interstate and foreign commerce and Federal tax immunity.[17] The rationale is that although the Commerce Clause, and probably the Supremacy Clause, operate primarily as grants of power to *Congress,* they also implicitly grant to the *Court* the secondary, interim power to implement the intent of the Constitutors in situations that Congress has not yet elected to deal with — to "interpret the silence of Congress," as it is said. If and when Congress does act, the Court yields. The effect is to shift the burden of legislative initiative but not to oppose the Court's will to that of the electorate as *affirmatively expressed* by elected officials.

Two familiar facts should also be recalled. First, the Court arrived at frank recognition of tentative judicial review, in the fields of commerce and tax immunity, only after a long transition period during which the Court spoke in terms of definitive rather than tentative judicial review. From the initial dictum of Chief Justice Marshall in *Gibbons v. Ogden* (1824)[18] until the ultimate clarification in *Prudential Insurance Co. v. Benjamin* (1946),[19] the Court applied the Commerce Clause at least partly as an *unyielding* limitation on that state action which, in the Court's opinion, unduly burdened interstate or foreign commerce. Then (with the aid of perceptive scholarly analysis [20]) the Court conceded that the will of Congress, if and when expressed, was supreme. In the field of Federal tax immunity, there was a similar transition period that began with *McCulloch v. Maryland* (1819)[21] and ended only in *Helvering v. Gerhardt* (1938).[22] Thus there is good precedent for substitution of tentative for definitive judicial review despite long delay.

Second, the Court has repeatedly held that more than a broad affirmation of legislative policy in abstract and general terms may be needed to convince the Court that Congress or a state legislature has actually attempted to deal with a particular subject matter. In a number of cases the Court has insisted that the legislative intent be expressed in a narrowly drawn statute directed at the specific problem, before the Court would defer. This idea appears to have been first adumbrated in *Cantwell v. Connecticut* (1940).[23] There the conviction of a Jehovah's Witness for inciting breach of the peace — a common law crime — was reversed as a violation of due process even though the Court said it might uphold a conviction for the same conduct if proscribed by a narrowly drawn statute. Speaking through Justice Roberts, it declared:

> Conviction on the fifth count was not pursuant to a statute evincing a legislative judgment that street discussion of religious affairs, because of its tendency to provoke disorder, should be regulated, or a judgment that the playing of a phonograph on the streets should in the interest of comfort or privacy be limited or prevented. Violation of an Act exhibiting such a legislative judgment and narrowly drawn to prevent the supposed evil, would pose a question differing from what we must here answer. Such a declaration of the State's policy would weigh heavily in any challenge of the law as infringing constitutional limitations. Here, however, the judgment is based on a common law concept of the most general and undefined nature.
>
> . . . .
>
> Although the contents of the [phonograph] record not unnaturally aroused animosity, we think that, in the absence of a statute narrowly drawn to define and punish specific conduct as constituting a clear and present danger to a substantial interest of the State, the petitioner's communication, considered in the light of the constitutional guarantees, raised no such clear and present menace to public peace and order as to render him liable to conviction of the common law offense in question.[24] (Footnotes omitted)

The *Cantwell* case involved a conviction of common law crime, with no action at all by the legislature; but later the Court began to apply the same principle to broadly drawn *statutes*. In *Aptheker v. Secretary of State* (1964),[25] for example, Section 6 of the Subversive Activities Control Act of 1950 [26] — banning passports for members of Communist-action organizations — was held invalid. The Court did not deny that a narrowly drawn statute might constitutionally restrict the foreign travel of Party *leaders,* but held Section 6 invalid because of its "overly broad scope." Justice Goldberg's majority opinion explained that the section "sweeps within its prohibition both knowing and unknowing members" and "renders irrelevant the member's degree of participation in the organization and his commitment to its purpose." The fact that, in the particular cases then under consideration, the Secretary of State had attempted to apply the statute to party leaders (Elizabeth Gurley Flynn, Chairman of the American Communist Party, and Herbert Aptheker, editor of the Party magazine) was held immaterial; the Court held Section 6 to be unconstitutional "on its face." Repeatedly since that decision the Court has insisted that statutes impinging upon constitutionally important interests be *narrowly drawn*.[27] Such a rule can be explained only on the ground that, even though the Court may not claim the *last* word on certain issues, it will not defer to the legislative will unless convinced that the legislature has put its collective mind squarely on the particular problem involved in the case. The principle has not yet been directly declared applicable to tentative judicial review, but there is no logical reason why it should not be.

Against this background, it is possible to formulate some fairly precise opinions as to (1) the fields in which the Court should retain definitive judicial review, (2) the fields in which the Court should move from definitive to tentative judicial review, and (3) the extent to which such tentative judicial review ought to reverse the burden of legislative initiative. For this purpose it is more important to raise the right questions than to give the right answers and — as will be seen — I remain uncertain on a few of the answers.

(1) Unless and until the vestiges of black slavery are truly extirpated from American society, the Court should adhere to definitive judicial review of official action based on purposeful anti-Negro discrimination — that is, action grounded in hostility to blacks or indifference to their race-related needs. Indeed, I have argued that the Court should go even further. I have argued [28] that it should repudiate the *Slaughter-House* interpretation of the Fourteenth Amendment Privileges or Immunities Clause — that it should acknowledge plenary Congressional power to define the

perquisites of national citizenship under the authority of that Clause, and thereby to control or prohibit *non*official discrimination — thus liberating Congressional power from artificial limitations that result from reliance on the commerce, spending, and war powers. Moreover, I have also acknowledged that a strong case can be made — on the basis of the language used by the Constitutors of the Thirteenth, Fourteenth, and Fifteenth Amendments, and their probable intent — for the proposition that these Civil War Amendments mandate the same protection of all racial minorities as they mandate for blacks.[29] It is less clear that other socially isolated ("discrete and insular") minority groups — such as aliens, bastards, and homosexuals — should be accorded the same degree of judicial protection as racial minorities, either on the basis of the Constitutors' intent or on the basis of implied judicial power. And definitive judicial review is quite clearly *in*appropriate in dealing with "discrimination" resulting not from hostility or indifference to particular minorities but from unsought differences in the hardship wrought on particular persons or groups by official action that is nondiscriminatory in form and purpose.

In the field of freedom of speech and press, definitive judicial review is *logically* necessary for protection of politically significant expression. Such judicial protection should continue not only with respect to direct restraints on political expression and organization, as through sedition laws, loyalty programs, and invasion of "associational privacy" (anonymity), but also with respect to indirect restraints, as through overstrict libel laws and unnecessarily vague prohibitory laws.

In the field of church-state separation, definitive judicial review should continue with respect to official action that involves genuine potential for stimulating political division along religious lines, as with measures importing religion into the public schools or providing public funds for religious education. Since the Court is the only governmental organ that can cope with this problem at the source, its continued intervention is justified by principles of implied judicial power.

In the field of criminal process, definitive judicial review is desirable for prevention of probable conviction of the innocent — the "fundamental justice" or "ordered liberty" standard called for by *Palko v. Connecticut* (1937).[30] The Court's special competence in evaluating lower court performance, and its consequent unique ability to decide what hardship is "so acute and shocking that our polity will not endure it," [31] justify its uncompromising refusal to permit use of the judicial process for conviction of the probably innocent. A strong case can also be made for retaining definitive judicial review in state as well as Federal cases involving conviction of the probably guilty, where the conviction has been obtained through investigative methods that involve lawless police intrusion on privacy — at least if the intrusion or the lawlessness is so blatant as to threaten a police-state relationship between the government and the people, or any part of the people. Here the justification, so far as state cases are concerned, results from the practical unavailability of political remedies to redress lawless police measures against the guilty; as for Federal cases, even broader definitive judicial review is called for by the intent of the Fourth Amendment's Constitutors.

(2) We consider now the areas where tentative should be substituted for definitive judicial review.

In the field of criminal process, Congress should be recognized to have power — under the Enforcement Clause of the Fourteenth Amendment and the Necessary and Proper Clause of Article I, Section 8 — to narrow as well as extend the protections the Court has erected for the suspected and the accused in *state* investigation and prosecution of crime. The intent of the Constitutors of the Fourth, Fifth, Sixth, and Eighth Amendments may preclude similar deference to Congressional judgment where Federal action is involved, though an arguable case can be made for the proposition that implied judicial power should extend to mitigation of the Constitutors' stern limits on Federal prosecution — imposed, as they were, at a time when effective Federal prosecution was less important to the national welfare than it has now been rendered by the greater interdependence of American society and by the communications explosion.

The main question involved in many of the cases restricting state police and prosecutorial action is: Where should the balance be struck between fairness to suspected and accused persons, and solicitude for the potential victims of crime? It is right that the Court should reverse the burden of legislative initiative in striking that balance, because public indifference to unpopular targets of the state criminal process tends to hamper political remedies. Moreover, deference to *state* legislatures is not prudent — if only because a number of such legislatures are likely to be indifferent to the grievances of nonwhites. That is not true, however, with respect to Congress; and if the national electorate is so fearful that overprotection of criminals and probable criminals is impairing personal security, as to prompt a demand upon elected officials to alter the balance in favor of law enforcement, there is no reason why their will should not prevail. Congress is actually better equipped to strike the balance than is the Court, if only it can be induced to put its collective mind on the problem.

In the field of freedom of speech and press, I have acknowledged [32] that respect for the intent of the First Amendment's Constitutors *may* forbid deference to Congressional judgment as to the desirability of any Federal statute (and perhaps Federal action of any kind) which directly or indirectly restrains expression of *any* sort, whether or not it is politically significant. No such argument can plausibly be made in favor of definitive judicial review of *state* action restraining politically nonsignificant expression — such action as the suppression of nonpolitical pornography (and probably the prohibition of public use of shock-words). Here, tentative judicial review may be justified by the fact that religious dogma based on faith rather than reason may clog the corrective political processes. If, however, the national electorate mandates Congress to ease the strict limitations with which the Court still surrounds state action in this field, there is no reason why the Court should not defer to Congress; and an argument can also be made for deference to state legislatures if

Congress remains inactive, though divergent standards in different locations may just conceivably create such distribution difficulties as to provide a respectable argument for tentative judicial review in obscenity cases under the *Commerce Clause.*

The notion that punishment of the so-called "victimless crimes" — such as participation by consenting adults in prostitution or sexual display — offends natural law and must therefore (*sic*) be held unconstitutional, is a meretricious fallacy. There is no such thing as a truly victimless crime; there are only crimes that harm society in ways that people feel but cannot prove through statistical analysis. The Constitutors never intended to condition self-government on the consent of the sociologists, and there is no *general* basis for implication of judicial power to that end. The most that can be said is that tentative judicial review is justified if the corrective political processes are clogged by social taboos.\*

In the field of freedom of religious exercise, definitive judicial review will be justified — by the intent of the First Amendment's Constitutors with respect to Federal action, and by implied judicial power with respect to state action — if and when the American tradition of religious toleration breaks down so far as to permit purposeful discrimination by elected officials against religious minorities. It may also be justified if and when the failure of elected officials to adjust to the special needs of such groups is fairly attributable to callous insensitivity rather than opposition to special privilege. No more than tentative judicial review is justified with respect to official actions that simply happen to burden particular religious groups more heavily because of their religion; and even tentative judicial review is justified only if the burden is very heavy.

---

\* Conceivably the same is true of other "victimless crimes" such as violation of laws prohibiting gambling, the use of narcotics or alcoholic beverages, and usury. In fact, the crusaders for personal liberty have made less headway on these fronts — none of which, except usury, involve taboos based on *religious dogma.* And the crusaders have not uttered a word, so far as I have been able to ascertain, against the usury laws — perhaps because even they recognize economic duress as a legitimate object of governmental control.

In the neo-privacy cases, which involve not freedom from unwanted intrusion or control of information about oneself, but only the claim of unrestrained personal autonomy in making certain "private" decisions, judicial review should be tentative. Indeed it should be *nonexistent* in the absence of reason to doubt the efficacy of the corrective political processes. These neo-privacy cases, beginning with *Griswold v. Connecticut* (1965),[33] deal with such matters as contraception, abortion, and the enjoyment of pornography in one's home. It is here that the Court has wandered farthest from any easily justifiable role. Even where judicial intervention is warranted, as it may well have been in the abortion cases, definitive judicial review ought to be avoided. The doctrinal rigidity of *Roe v. Wade* (1973),[34] which (as shown in Chapter I) appears to preclude a wholly rational approach to the problem of the viable fetus and its possible "right" to be killed, is unfortunate. Tentative judicial review could avoid it.

Finally a judgment must be made about the Court's protean application of the equal protection principle in the years since *Shapiro v. Thompson* (1969)[35] heralded — or acknowledged — the advent of the "new equal protection." It will not do to say, as Justice Jackson once maintained,[36] that insistence on equality amounts to tentative judicial review only — because, he said, the Court does not say *what* elected officials can constitutionally do, but only *how* they must (or cannot) do it. Political realities, and considerations of administrative efficiency, very often mean that prohibition of the means *via* the strict "compelling governmental interest" test amounts to prohibition of the end. A great many of the Court's recent equality decisions must be recognized as efforts at definitive judicial review.

I have already in effect agreed that this is justifiable in dealing with discrimination against racial minorities.[37] I am inclined to go further, and agree that it is justifiable in dealing with discrimination against any socially isolated minority group (though I have some doubt that the Court has correctly placed aliens in that category). I do not agree that definitive judicial review is warranted, beyond the limits fixed by the "rational relationship" test, by reason of the "fundamental" nature of the interests affected. The "fundamental rights" branch of the "compelling governmental interest" test is simply a breeding ground for judicial usurpation — *except* where some constitutionally protected value such as self-government is involved, as it is in cases on political expression and electoral rights. I am not convinced that the constitutional right of interstate travel is significantly affected by durational residency requirements for welfare aid, voting, and low-cost college education. This may be unimportant, however, because of the Fourteenth Amendment provision conferring state citizenship on United States citizens who reside in the state. That provision can reasonably be interpreted as forbidding or limiting discrimination against recently arrived residents; and, if it is, the Court might be led to the same results in durational residency cases as it has already reached under the Equal Protection Clause.

Even in the electoral rights cases, adherence to doctrinaire verbalism has carried the Court too far. The wholly sound initial decisions on legislative malapportionment, which were needed to prevent elected officials from insulating themselves against majority control by the voters, have been extended to ridiculous extremes of meaningless mathematical equality — from which the Court has now begun, with unnecessary clumsiness, to recede. And I am not persuaded that in protecting the access of splinter parties to the ballot, the Court has so completely demonstrated its superior competence to mold the party system as to justify more than tentative judicial review.

(3) Until now I have used the term "tentative judicial review" without indicating how tentative such judicial review ought to be. That is to say, I have not indicated how careful the Court should be to assure itself, before receding from a tentative invalidation of some type of action by elected officials, that Congress has made a considered judgment in favor of such recession. My opinion on this point can be expressed simply. I believe that, in any case where constitutional values are sufficiently implicated to warrant the exercise of tentative judicial review, the Court ought not yield to general, abstract propositions enacted by legislatures without

demonstrated consideration of the facts and value judgments that have moved the Court to action. Thus, for example, a modification of the *Miranda* rule [38] based on careful study of its operation in practice and evaluation of possible alternatives, should pass muster. A general joint resolution condemning the decision should not. Judicial review, even where tentative, is serious business. It ought to be undertaken seriously by the Court, and taken seriously by Congress.

\* \* \* \* \*

I close with two general thoughts.

*First.* I have often asked myself, as I have worked on this book: For whom am I writing it? Not primarily for the present Justices. They are probably too far committed by their past opinions to permit them to adopt the suggestions here made, even if they would have been inclined to embrace them had they been able to write on a clean slate. Not primarily for the bar; constitutional practitioners already know most of what I have said. Not primarily for Congress; unless and until the Court moves on a broader front from definitive to tentative judicial review, Congress cannot resist the Court.

I write mainly for people who want to understand what is really happening in areas that affect them deeply. Even if the ultimate conclusion is that self-government won't work in America as broadly as we had hoped and believed, and that we cannot do without the services of what Learned Hand called "a bevy of Platonic guardians," there is some satisfaction in *understanding* that we lack the political maturity to handle some of our important problems. Moreover, be it noted that this tough-minded group, this group of Americans who insist on facing reality, most probably includes the *next* Justices who will grace the supreme bench.

*Second.* The tower at Pisa is a delight to the spirit. Praise and thanks are due to the artists and master craftsmen who created it. We would be still more heavily indebted to them, however, if they had built on a firmer foundation. Because they paid more attention to the beauty of the visible superstructure than to the solidity of the footing, the soaring edifice will some day tumble in ruins — unless the underpinning is made firm.

A similar hidden weakness menaces the constitutional edifice reared by the Supreme Court in the past third of a century for the better protection of individual liberty, equality, justice, and rational government. The lack of a firm conceptual foundation was less troublesome in the first years after 1937, when the present structure began to take form amid the crumbling remnants of the proud citadel of free business enterprise and vested property rights. The first modest defenses against official censorship, racial discrimination, wrongful conviction, and theistic government seemed likely to endure. As ever loftier turrets have been added, however, the danger of collapse has grown.

If collapse does come, it will not be limited to the topmost pinnacles of the structure — the more extreme curbs on majority rule in the name of humanity, compassion, and natural justice. The whole edifice may topple. That is why it is worth great exertion to shore up the lovely structure that now gives Americans cause for pride in their national heritage.

# NOTES

## APOLOGIA

1. *See, e.g.,* Uphaus v. Wyman, 364 U.S. 388 (1960); May v. United States, 280 F.2d 555 (6th Cir. 1960); *cf.* Braden v. Commonwealth, 277 S.W.2d 7 (Ky. 1955), 291 S.W.2d 843 (Ky. 1956); Braden v. Lady, 276 S.W.2d 664 (Ky. 1955); Thompson v. Louisville, 362 U.S. 199 (1960); Brief for American Civil Liberties Union as Amicus Curiae, Dombrowski v. Pfister, 380 U.S. 479 (1965).
2. *E.g.,* Lusky, *Minority Rights and the Public Interest,* 52 YALE L.J. 1 (1942); Lusky, *Racial Discrimination and the Federal Law: A Problem in Nullification,* 63 COLUM. L. REV. 1163 (1963); Lusky, *The Stereotype: Hard Core of Racism,* 13 BUFF. L. REV. 450 (1964); Lusky, *Justice with a Southern Accent,* HARPER'S, March 1964, at 69; Lusky, *The King Dream: Fantasy or Prophecy?,* 68 COLUM. L. REV. 1029 (1968).
3. I have been unable to trace this quotation to its source. It was first given to me by the late E.C. Frank, M.D., of Louisville, Ky., who, however, was unable to say who wrote or said it. Numerous efforts to locate the source have thus far been unsuccessful.
4. *Cf.* Braden, *The Search for Objectivity in Constitutional Law,* 57 YALE L.J. 571, 572 n.5 (1948).
5. Board of Educ. v. Barnette, 319 U.S. 624, 646 (1943).
6. *Cf.* R. DAHL, WHO GOVERNS? (1961).
7. *Cf.* Griggs v. Duke Power Co., 401 U.S. 424 (1971).
8. 330 U.S. 552, 564 (1947).
9. *See, e.g.,* MALCOLM X, THE AUTOBIOGRAPHY OF MALCOLM X (1965); E. CLEAVER, SOUL ON ICE (1968).
10. *See, e.g.,* NEWSWEEK, Feb. 25, 1974, at 18, 21; NEWSWEEK, May 27, 1974, at 18.
11. *See* A. BURGESS, A CLOCKWORK ORANGE (1963) *passim.*
12. Reprinted as *Toward Neutral Principles of Constitutional Law* in H. WECHSLER, PRINCIPLES, POLITICS AND FUNDAMENTAL LAW: SELECTED ESSAYS, at 3, 21 (1961).
13. A. BICKEL, THE LEAST DANGEROUS BRANCH ch. 4 (1962).
14. *See The Supreme Court, 1971 Term,* 86 HARV. L. REV. 1, 303 (1972).
15. Gunther, *The Subtle Vices of the "Passive Virtues" — A Comment on Principle and Expediency in Judicial Review,* 64 COLUM. L. REV. 1 (1964).

16. CBS News Special, Dec. 3, 1968, "Justice Black and the Bill of Rights," Dec. 3, 1968 (Telecast Interview of Justice Hugo L. Black by Eric Sevareid), reprinted at 27 CONG. QUAR. WEEKLY REP. 4 (Jan. 3, 1964).

## CHAPTER I

1. *See* B. SEVERN, MR. CHIEF JUSTICE: EARL WARREN 164-65 (1968).
2. *See* the First Report by the Special Subcommittee on H.R. 920 of the House Comm. on the Judiciary, 91st Cong., 2d Sess., pursuant to H.R. 93 (1970).
3. Lusky, *The Unwritten U.S. Constitution,* N.Y.L.J., Aug. 31 and Sept. 1, 1972, at 1, col. 5 (2-part article).
4. Roe v. Wade, 410 U.S. 113 (1973); Doe v. Bolton, 410 U.S. 179 (1973).
5. *See, e.g.,* Barlow v. Collins, 397 U.S. 159 (1970); Association of Data Processing Serv. Orgs., Inc. v. Camp, 397 U.S. 150 (1970); *cf.* Sierra Club v. Morton, 405 U.S. 727 (1972).
6. *See, e.g.,* Police Dep't of City of Chicago v. Mosley, 408 U.S. 92 (1972); James v. Strange, 407 U.S. 128 (1972); Argersinger v. Hamlin, 407 U.S. 25 (1972); Brooks v. Tennessee, 406 U.S. 605 (1972); Apodaca v. Oregon, 406 U.S. 404 (1972); Wisconsin v. Yoder, 406 U.S. 205 (1972); Eisenstadt v. Baird, 405 U.S. 438 (1972); Dunn v. Blumstein, 405 U.S. 330 (1972); Bullock v. Carter, 405 U.S. 134 (1972); Groppi v. Leslie, 404 U.S. 496 (1972); Graham v. Richardson, 403 U.S. 365 (1971); Organization for a Better Austin v. Keefe, 402 U.S. 415 (1971); Rogers v. Bellei, 401 U.S. 815 (1971); Tate v. Short, 401 U.S. 395 (1971); Williams v. Illinois, 399 U.S. 235 (1970); Baldwin v. New York, 399 U.S. 66 (1970); Walz v. Tax Comm'n, 397 U.S. 664 (1970).
7. 408 U.S. 238 (1972).
8. 406 U.S. 404 (1972).
9. *See* Johnson v. Louisiana, 406 U.S. 356, 369-71 (1972).
10. 406 U.S. 205 (1972).
11. 410 U.S. 113 (1973).
12. Vern. Tex. Code Ann. P.C. §§ 1191-94, 1196 (1907), now VERN. ANN. CIV. STATS. art. 4512.1-.4, 4512.6.
13. 410 U.S. at 152-53.
14. *Id.* at 154.
15. *Id.* at 155.
16. *See* ch. XIV *infra.*
17. 410 U.S. at 163.
18. *Id.* at 163-64.
19. *See, e.g.,* United States v. Wade, 388 U.S. 218 (1967); Gilbert v. California, 388 U.S. 263 (1967).

20. Roe v. Wade, 410 U.S. 113, 164-65 (1973).
21. United States v. Vuitch, 402 U.S. 62, 71-72 (1971).
22. *See* Tribe, *Toward a Model of Rules in the Due Process of Life and Law,* 87 HARV. L. REV. 1, 22 (1973).
23. 17 U.S. (4 Wheat.) 316 (1819).
24. *See* pp. 90-91 *infra.*
25. 379 U.S. 241 (1964).
26. 379 U.S. 294 (1964).
27. Quoted in 1 C. WARREN, THE SUPREME COURT IN UNITED STATES HISTORY 501 (rev. ed. 1926). Reprinted by permission of Little, Brown & Co.
28. JOHN MARSHALL'S DEFENSE OF MCCULLOCH V. MARYLAND 173 (G. Gunther ed. 1969). Reprinted by permission of Stanford University Press.
29. *Id.*
30. *See* p. 74 and its note 27 *infra.*

# CHAPTER II

1. 1 C. WARREN, THE SUPREME COURT IN UNITED STATES HISTORY 264 n.4 (rev. ed. 1926).
2. *See* p. 80 *infra.*
3. Dred Scott v. Sandford, 60 U.S. (19 How.) 393 (1857).
4. United States v. Nixon, 418 U.S. 683 (1974).
5. 1 A. DE TOCQUEVILLE, DEMOCRACY IN AMERICA 290 (Vintage ed. 1954).
6. *Cf.* Collins v. Hardyman, 341 U.S. 651 (1951).
7. Bantam Books, Inc. v. Sullivan, 372 U.S. 58 (1963).
8. *Cf.* Barsky v. Board of Regents, 347 U.S. 442 (1954).
9. Anderson v. Dunn, 19 U.S. (6 Wheat.) 204 (1821); *see* T. TAYLOR, GRAND INQUEST: THE STORY OF CONGRESSIONAL INVESTIGATIONS 33, 309-10 n.7 (1955).
10. THE FEDERALIST No. 78, at 395, 396 (Dent ed. 1911) (A. Hamilton).
11. Lusky, *The Unwritten U.S. Constitution,* N.Y.L.J., Aug. 31 and Sept. 1, 1972, at 1, col. 5 (2-part article).
12. Lusky, *Peace ... the Presence of Justice,* 17 THE HUMANIST 195, 201-03, 204 (1957). This article first appeared in THE HUMANIST July/August 1957 issue and is reprinted by permission.
13. A. BICKEL, THE LEAST DANGEROUS BRANCH 31, 105 (1962). Copyright © 1962 by the Bobbs-Merrill Company, Inc., reprinted by permission of the publisher.
14. Chisholm v. Georgia, 2 U.S. (2 Dall.) 419 (1793).
15. Dred Scott v. Sandford, 60 U.S. (19 How.) 393 (1857).
16. Pollock v. Farmers Loan & Trust Co., 157 U.S. 429 (1895).

17. Oregon v. Mitchell, 400 U.S. 112 (1970).
18. Breedlove v. Suttles, 302 U.S. 277 (1937), *overruled in* Harper v. Virginia Bd. of Elections, 383 U.S. 663 (1966).
19. *E.g.,* H.S. COMMAGER, MAJORITY RULE AND MINORITY RIGHTS 40, 79-81 *et passim* (1943).
20. *See* Lusky, *Racial Discrimination and the Federal Law: A Problem in Nullification,* 63 COLUM. L. REV. 1163 (1963); Lusky, *Justice with a Southern Accent,* HARPER'S, March 1964, at 69.
21. U.S. CONST. art. I, § 2, para. 3.
22. *Id.* amend. X.
23. *Id.* art. I, § 9, cl. 1.
24. *E.g.,* L. HACKER, THE TRIUMPH OF AMERICAN CAPITALISM 302-03 (1940).
25. Dred Scott v. Sandford, 60 U.S. (19 How.) 393 (1857).
26. *Id.* at 404-05, 407-08 (1857).

# CHAPTER III

1. 14 Stat. 428 (1867).
2. 297 U.S. 288 (1936).
3. *Id.* at 345-48.
4. *E.g.,* United States v. Miller, 307 U.S. 174 (1939); Slaughter-House Cases, 83 U.S. (16 Wall.) 36 (1873).
5. *E.g.,* Wesberry v. Sanders, 376 U.S. 1 (1964); Civil Rights Cases, 109 U.S. 3 (1883).
6. *E.g.,* United States v. Rumely, 345 U.S. 41 (1953).
7. Lusky, *Invasion of Privacy: A Clarification of Concepts,* 72 COLUM. L. REV. 693 (1972).
8. *E.g.,* Zschernig v. Miller, 389 U.S. 429 (1968); Hammer v. Dagenhart, 247 U.S. 251 (1918), *overruled in* United States v. Darby, 312 U.S. 100 (1941).
9. *E.g.,* Youngstown Sheet & Tube Co. v. Sawyer, 343 U.S. 579 (1952); Myers v. United States, 272 U.S. 52 (1926).
10. Roe v. Wade, 410 U.S. 113 (1973); Stanley v. Georgia, 394 U.S. 557 (1969); Griswold v. Connecticut, 381 U.S. 479 (1965).
11. 322 U.S. 533 (1944).
12. Paul v. Virginia, 75 U.S. (8 Wall.) 168 (1869).
13. Act of March 9, 1945, ch. 20, 59 Stat. 33.
14. 328 U.S. 408 (1946).
15. Paul v. Virginia, 75 U.S. (8 Wall.) 168 (1869).
16. *E.g.,* Hammer v. Dagenhart, 247 U.S. 251 (1918).
17. H. WECHSLER, THE POLITICAL SAFEGUARDS OF FEDERALISM, IN PRINCIPLES, POLITICS AND FUNDAMENTAL LAW 49 (1961).

18. 400 U.S. 112 (1970).
19. The case was decided December 21, 1970. The ratification process was completed June 30, 1971.
20. *E.g.,* United States v. Curtiss-Wright Export Co., 299 U.S. 304 (1936).
21. 343 U.S. 579 (1952).
22. *E.g.,* Omnibus Safe Streets and Crime Control Act, § 701, Act of June 19, 1968, Pub. L. No. 90-351, § 701(a), 82 Stat. 210 (relaxing *Miranda* rule).

## CHAPTER IV

1. Powell v. McCormack, 395 U.S. 486 (1969).
2. U.S. CONST. art. I, § 9.
3. *Id.* § 7.
4. *Id.* § 9.
5. *Id.* amend. IV.
6. *Id.* amend. V.
7. *See* A. GULLIVER, E. CLARK, L. LUSKY & A. MURPHY, CASES AND MATERIALS ON GRATUITOUS TRANSFERS 763 (1967).
8. *See* 1 F. POLLOCK & F. MAITLAND, THE HISTORY OF ENGLISH LAW BEFORE THE TIME OF EDWARD I 467; 2 *id.* at 209 (2d ed. 1923).
9. *See* Dowling, *Interstate Commerce and State Power,* 27 VA. L. REV. 1 (1940), SELECTED ESSAYS 1938-62, at 280 (1963); Powell, *The Still Small Voice of the Commerce Clause,* 3 ASSOCIATION OF AMERICAN LAW SCHOOLS, SELECTED ESSAYS ON CONSTITUTIONAL LAW 931 (1938); *see also* G. GUNTHER & N. DOWLING, CASES AND MATERIALS ON CONSTITUTIONAL LAW 673-78 (8th ed. 1970).
10. 297 U.S. 1 (1936).
11. *Id.* at 62-63.
12. 17 U.S. (4 Wheat.) 316 (1819).
13. *Id.* at 407.
14. 347 U.S. 483 (1954).
15. Brown v. Board of Educ., 349 U.S. 294 (1955).
16. 338 U.S. 25 (1949).
17. *Id.* at 27-28.
18. Mapp v. Ohio, 367 U.S. 643 (1961).
19. *E.g.,* Elkins v. United States, 364 U.S. 206 (1960); Rea v. United States, 350 U.S. 214 (1956).
20. *E.g.,* Pierce v. Society of Sisters, 268 U.S. 510 (1925).
21. Virginian Ry. v. System Fed'n No. 40, 300 U.S. 515 (1937).

## CHAPTER V

1. 401 U.S. 37 (1971).
2. *Id.* at 52.
3. 399 U.S. 1, 12-14 (1970) (concurring opinion).
4. *Id.* at 9, quoting United States v. Wade, 388 U.S. 218, 227 (1967).
5. 399 U.S. at 12.
6. Katz v. United States, 389 U.S. 347 (1967).
7. *Id.* at 364.
8. *Id.* at 364-65.
9. *Id.* at 373.
10. *Id.* at 374.
11. 5 U.S. (1 Cranch) 137 (1803).
12. *Id.* at 175.
13. *Id.* at 178.
14. *Id.*
15. *Id.* at 167-69.
16. *Id.* at 176, 177, 178.
17. *See, e.g.,* Beard, *The Supreme Court — Usurper or Grantee?* 27 POL. SCI. QUAR. 1, 2 (1912); *cf.* CORWIN, THE DOCTRINE OF JUDICIAL REVIEW 62-63 (1914).
18. 1 C. WARREN, THE SUPREME COURT IN UNITED STATES HISTORY 269-73 (1922).
19. THE FEDERALIST No. 78, at 394 (Dent ed. 1911) (A. Hamilton).
20. *Id.* at 395-96.
21. U.S. CONST. art. I, § 9, cl. 5.
22. *Id.* cl. 2.
23. 389 U.S. 347, 364 (1967).
24. H. BLACK, A CONSTITUTIONAL FAITH 20-21 (1968).
25. *Id.* at 10, 14.
26. *E.g.,* Wesberry v. Sanders, 376 U.S. 1 (1964); Sears, Roebuck & Co. v. Stiffel Co., 376 U.S. 225 (1964); Compco Corp. v. Day-Brite Lighting, Inc., 376 U.S. 234 (1964); Marsh v. Alabama, 326 U.S. 501 (1946).
27. *E.g.,* Konigsberg v. State Bar, 366 U.S. 36, 60-80 (1961); Braden v. United States, 365 U.S. 431, 441-46 (1961); Wilkinson v. United States, 365 U.S. 399, 422-23 (1961); Uphaus v. Wyman, 364 U.S. 388, 392-93 (1960); Barenblatt v. United States, 360 U.S. 109, 140-45 (1959); Beauharnais v. Illinois, 343 U.S. 250, 268-70, 274-75 (1952); Dennis v. United States, 341 U.S. 494, 579-81 (1951); American Communications Ass'n v. Douds, 339 U.S. 382, 445-53 (1950).
28. 372 U.S. 335 (1963).
29. *See generally The Supreme Court, 1965 Term,* 80 HARV. L. REV. 91 125-29, 201-07 (1966).
30. 381 U.S. 618 (1965).

NOTES TO PAGES 78-95　　　375

31. 338 U.S. 25 (1949).
32. 367 U.S. 643 (1961).
33. Linkletter v. Walker, 381 U.S. 618, 628 (1965).
34. *Id.* at 629.
35. *Id.*
36. *Id.* at 639.
37. *Id.* at 649.
38. *Id.* at 644, quoting James v. United States, 366 U.S. 213, 225 (1961).
39. Parisi v. Davidson, 405 U.S. 34, 47-48 (1972) (concurring opinion).
40. *See* p. 28 *supra.*
41. *See* G. GUNTHER & N. DOWLING, CASES AND MATERIALS ON CONSTITUTIONAL LAW 285-86 (8th ed. 1970).
42. 17 U.S. (4 Wheat.) 316 (1819).
43. *Id.* at 407-08.
44. Missouri v. Holland, 252 U.S. 416, 433 (1920).
45. 313 U.S. 299 (1941).
46. *Id.* at 316.
47. *E.g.,* Minersville School Dist. v. Gobitis, 310 U.S. 586, 601 (1940) (Stone, J., dissenting).
48. United States v. Butler, 297 U.S. 1, 87 (1936).

## CHAPTER VI

1. *See* p. 81 *supra.*
2. McCulloch v. Maryland, 17 U.S. (4 Wheat.) 316, 421 (1819).
3. *See* pp. 53-54 *supra.*
4. U.S. CONST. art. II, § 2.
5. *Id.* § 3.
6. *Id.* art. I, § 8.
7. L. HENKIN, FOREIGN AFFAIRS AND THE CONSTITUTION 17-23 (1972). Reprinted by permission of The Foundation Press, Inc.
8. *See generally* Levitan, *The Foreign Relations Power: An Analysis of Mr. Justice Sutherland's Theory,* 55 YALE L.J. 467 (1946).
9. 299 U.S. 304 (1936).
10. *Id.* at 319-20.
11. *See* United States v. Nixon, 418 U.S. 683, 708-12 (1974); United States v. United States Dist. Ct., 407 U.S. 297, 321-22 (1972).
12. McCulloch v. Maryland, 17 U.S. (4 Wheat.) 316, 422-23 (1819).
13. 141 U.S. 1, 12, 18 (1892).
14. *See, e.g., In re* Rahrer, 140 U.S. 545 (1891).
15. 41 U.S. (16 Pet.) 539 (1842).
16. L. MILLER, THE PETITIONERS 48-49 (1966). Reprinted by permission of Pantheon Books, a Division of Random House, Inc.
17. *See* p. 21 *supra.*
18. *See* p. 22 *supra.*

## CHAPTER VII
1. 198 U.S. 45 (1905).
2. People v. Defore, 242 N.Y. 13, 21, 150 N.E. 585, 587 (1926).
3. 410 U.S. 113 (1973).
4. 410 U.S. 179 (1973).
5. *See* cases collected in G. GUNTHER & N. DOWLING, CASES AND MATERIALS ON CONSTITUTIONAL LAW 261-85 (8th ed. 1970).
6. *E.g.,* Heiner v. Donnan, 285 U.S. 312 (1932); Senior v. Braden, 295 U.S. 422 (1935); Frick v. Pennsylvania, 268 U.S. 473 (1925).
7. *E.g.,* D. PEARSON & R. ALLEN, THE NINE OLD MEN (1936).
8. 290 U.S. 398 (1934).
9. 291 U.S. 502 (1934).
10. *E.g.,* Carter v. Carter Coal Co., 298 U.S. 238 (1936); United States v. Butler, 297 U.S. 1 (1936); Ashton v. Cameron County Water Improvement Dist., 298 U.S. 513 (1936); Louisville Joint Stock Land Bank v. Radford, 295 U.S. 555 (1935); Schechter Poultry Corp. v. United States, 295 U.S. 495 (1935); Railroad Retirement Bd. v. Alton R.R., 295 U.S. 330 (1935).
11. Morehead v. New York *ex rel.* Tipaldo, 298 U.S. 587 (1936).
12. West Coast Hotel Co. v. Parish, 300 U.S. 379 (1937).
13. NLRB v. Jones & Laughlin Steel Corp., 301 U.S. 1 (1937).
14. Steward Machine Co. v. Davis, 301 U.S. 548 (1937); Helvering v. Davis, 301 U.S. 619 (1937); Carmichael v. Southern Coal & Coke Co., 301 U.S. 495 (1937).
15. *E.g.,* Stern, *The Commerce Clause and the National Economy, 1933-46,* 59 HARV. L. REV. 645 (1946), in SELECTED ESSAYS ON CONSTITUTIONAL LAW 1938-1962, at 218 (1963).
16. Pierce v. Society of Sisters, 268 U.S. 510 (1925).
17. Meyer v. Nebraska, 262 U.S. 390 (1923).
18. Brown v. Mississippi, 297 U.S. 278 (1936); Powell v. Alabama, 287 U.S. 45 (1932).
19. Grosjean v. American Press Co., 297 U.S. 233 (1936); Near v. Minnesota, 283 U.S. 697 (1931).
20. A. MASON, THE SUPREME COURT: PALLADIUM OF FREEDOM 151 (1962). Copyright © by the University of Michigan 1962.
21. 302 U.S. 319 (1937).
22. Fiske v. Kansas, 274 U.S. 380 (1927).
23. Twining v. New Jersey, 211 U.S. 78 (1908); Maxwell v. Dow, 176 U.S. 581 (1900).
24. Palko v. Connecticut, 302 U.S. 319, 324-25 (1937).
25. *Id.* at 328.
26. *Id.*
27. Kepner v. United States, 195 U.S. 100 (1904).

28. Palko v. Connecticut, 302 U.S. at 326-27.
29. 304 U.S. 144 (1938).
30. E. Brown, Harlan Fiske Stone and His Law Clerks, 78 (1965) (unpublished thesis in Butler Library, Columbia University).
31. U.S. CONST. art. I, § 2.
32. *Id.* art. IV, § 4.
33. *See* Lusky, *Minority Rights and the Public Interest,* 52 YALE L.J. 1, 4 (1942); Lusky, *Four Problems in Lawmaking for Peace,* 80 POL. SCI. Q. 341, 347 (1965).
34. A. MASON, HARLAN FISKE STONE: PILLAR OF THE LAW 513 (1956).
35. *See* cases reviewed by Frankfurter, J., concurring in Kovacs v. Cooper, 336 U.S. 77, 90-94 (1949).

## CHAPTER VIII

1. *See* Lusky, *Peace . . . the Presence of Justice,* 17 THE HUMANIST 195 (1957); Lusky, *Four Problems in Lawmaking for Peace,* 80 POL. SCI. Q. 341 (1965); Lusky, *Lawmaking for Peace: The Farther Shore,* 86 POL. SCI. Q. 1 (1971).
2. Lusky, *Minority Rights and the Public Interest,* 52 YALE L.J. 1 (1942).
3. Lusky, *The King Dream: Fantasy or Prophecy?,* 68 COLUM. L. REV. 1029, 1030 (1968).
4. Palko v. Connecticut, 302 U.S. 319, 327 (1937).
5. *E.g.,* Hague v. CIO, 307 U.S. 496 (1939).
6. New York Times Co. v. Sullivan, 376 U.S. 254 (1964).
7. *See* pp. 319-28, 329, 342-43 *infra.*
8. 84 POL. SCI. Q. 169 (1969).
9. *Id.* at 281. Reprinted by permission of the Academy of Political Science.
10. *See* REPORT OF THE NATIONAL ADVISORY COMMISSION ON CIVIL DISORDERS 37-38 (Bantam ed. 1968).
11. Lusky, *Minority Rights and the Public Interest,* 52 YALE L.J. 1, 3-4, 12-13, 21, 38-39 (1942). Reprinted by permission of The Yale Law Journal Company and Fred B. Rothman & Company.
12. G. FERRERO, THE PRINCIPLES OF POWER ch. XI and at 291 (1942).
13. Abrams v. United States, 250 U.S. 616 (1919); Schaefer v. United States, 251 U.S. 466 (1920); Pierce v. United States, 252 U.S. 239 (1920); *cf.* Schenck v. United States, 249 U.S. 47 (1919); Frohwerk v. United States, 249 U.S. 204 (1919); Debs v. United States, 249 U.S. 211 (1919).
14. *Compare* Toledo Newspaper Co. v. United States, 247 U.S. 402, 419 (1918); Minersville School Dist. v. Gobitis, 310 U.S. 586 (1940).
15. *E.g.,* Whitney v. California, 274 U.S. 357 (1927); Gitlow v. New York, 268 U.S. 652 (1925).

## CHAPTER IX

1. 283 U.S. 697 (1931).
2. 297 U.S. 233 (1936).
3. 303 U.S. 444 (1938).
4. 307 U.S. 496 (1939).
5. 167 U.S. 43 (1897).
6. Commonwealth v. Davis, 162 Mass. 510, 511, 39 N.E. 113 (1895).
7. Hague v. CIO, 307 U.S. 496, 515 (1939).
8. Cox v. New Hampshire, 312 U.S. 569 (1941); Kalven, *The Concept of the Public Forum: Cox v. Louisiana,* 1965 SUP. CT. REV. 1.
9. Schneider v. State, Kim Young v. California, Snyder v. Milwaukee, and Nichols v. Massachusetts, 308 U.S. 147 (1939).
10. 308 U.S. at 161.
11. *See* chs. XII and XIII *infra.*
12. *See generally* G. GUNTHER & N. DOWLING, CASES AND MATERIALS ON CONSTITUTIONAL LAW chs. 15-16 (8th ed. 1970).
13. United States v. Carolene Products Co., 304 U.S. 144, 152 n.4 (1938).
14. *E.g.,* Dennis v. United States, 341 U.S. 494 (1951); Braden v. Lady, 276 S.W.2d 664 (Ky. 1955); Braden v. Commonwealth, 277 S.W.2d 7 (Ky. 1955), 291 S.W.2d 843 (Ky. 1956).
15. *E.g.,* Lerner v. Casey, 357 U.S. 468 (1958); Beilan v. Board of Educ., 357 U.S. 399 (1958); Gerende v. Board of Supervisors, 341 U.S. 56 (1951).
16. *See* particularly AMERICAN CIVIL LIBERTIES UNION, ANNUAL REPORTS, 1950-1963.
17. *Id.*
18. *E.g.,* Garner v. Los Angeles Bd. of Pub. Works, 341 U.S. 716 (1951); Gerende v. Board of Supervisors, 341 U.S. 56 (1951).
19. *E.g.,* Konigsberg v. State Bar, 353 U.S. 252 (1957); Barsky v. Board of Regents, 347 U.S. 442 (1954).
20. Communist Control Act of 1954, 68 Stat. 775.
21. 328 U.S. 303 (1946).
22. *Compare* Garner v. Los Angeles Bd. of Pub. Works, 341 U.S. 716 (1951), *with* Wieman v. Updegraff, 344 U.S. 183 (1952).
23. Gerende v. Board of Supervisors, 341 U.S. 56 (1951).
24. *E.g.,* Scales v. United States, 367 U.S. 203 (1961).
25. *E.g.,* Yates v. United States, 354 U.S. 298 (1957); *see* Bond v. Floyd, 385 U.S. 116 (1966).
26. *Compare* Slochower v. Board of Higher Educ., 350 U.S. 551 (1956), *with* Konigsberg v. State Bar, 366 U.S. 36 (1961).
27. 341 U.S. 495 (1951).
28. 354 U.S. 298 (1957).

29. *E.g.,* Slochower v. Board of Higher Educ., 350 U.S. 551 (1956).
30. 354 U.S. 178, 199 (1957).
31. Barenblatt v. United States, 360 U.S. 109, 132 (1959).
32. Wilkinson v. United States, 365 U.S. 399 (1961); Braden v. United States, 365 U.S. 431 (1961).
33. *E.g.,* Deutch v. United States, 367 U.S. 456 (1961); Russell v. United States, 369 U.S. 749 (1962); Yellin v. United States, 374 U.S. 109 (1963); Gojack v. United States, 384 U.S. 702 (1966).
34. Communist Party of United States v. Subversive Activities Control Bd., 367 U.S. 1 (1961).
35. Albertson v. Subversive Activities Control Bd., 382 U.S. 70 (1965).
36. *See* ch. XIII *infra.*
37. *See* pp. 319-28, 329, 342-43 *infra.*
38. *E.g.,* Guinn v. United States, 238 U.S. 347 (1915).
39. Swafford v. Templeton, 185 U.S. 487 (1902); Wiley v. Sinkler, 179 U.S. 58 (1900).
40. 328 U.S. 549 (1946).
41. *Id.* at 556.
42. *Id.* at 566.
43. *See* Baker v. Carr, 369 U.S. 186, 266 (1962) (Frankfurter, J., dissenting); Colegrove v. Green, 328 U.S. 549 (1946) (Frankfurter, J.).
44. *See* Reynolds v. Sims, 377 U.S. 533, 589 (1964) (Harlan, J., dissenting).
45. 369 U.S. 186 (1962).
46. Skinner v. Oklahoma *ex rel.* Williamson, 316 U.S. 535 (1942); *see generally* Karst, *Invidious Discrimination: Justice Douglas and the Return of the "Natural-Law-Due-Process Formula,"* 16 U.C.L.A. L. REV. 716 (1969).
47. Baker v. Carr, 369 U.S. at 226.
48. K. Scott, *Standing in the Supreme Court — A Functional Analysis,* 86 HARV. L. REV. 645 (1973).
49. 367 U.S. 643 (1961).
50. Baker v. Carr, 369 U.S. at 204.
51. *Id.* at 198-99.
52. *Id.* at 217.
53. *Id.* at 208.
54. *See* pp. 151-57 *infra.*
55. 384 U.S. 436 (1966).
56. Baker v. Carr, 369 U.S. 186, 266 (1962).
57. *Id.* at 226.
58. *Id.* at 237.
59. *Id.* at 226.
60. *Id.* at 198.

61. *Id.* at 251.
62. 372 U.S. 368 (1963).
63. *Id.* at 381.
64. 376 U.S. 1 (1964).
65. *Id.* at 7-8.
66. 377 U.S. 533 (1964).
67. *Id.* at 568.
68. *Id.* at 556 n.30 and authorities cited therein.
69. *Id.*
70. Kirkpatrick v. Preisler, 394 U.S. 526 (1969).
71. WMCA, Inc. v. Lomenzo, 377 U.S. 633 (1964).
72. Hadley v. Junior College Dist., 397 U.S. 50 (1970).
73. Kramer v. Union Free School Dist., 395 U.S. 621 (1969).
74. Cipriano v. Houma, 395 U.S. 701 (1969); Phoenix v. Kolodziejski, 399 U.S. 204 (1970).
75. Cardona v. Power, 384 U.S. 672 (1966).
76. Harper v. Virginia Bd. of Elections, 383 U.S. 663 (1966).
77. Oregon v. Mitchell, 400 U.S. 112 (1970).
78. Dunn v. Blumstein, 405 U.S. 330 (1972).
79. Keyishian v. Board of Regents, 385 U.S. 589 (1967).
80. Baggett v. Bullitt, 377 U.S. 360 (1964). *See also* Communist Party v. Whitcomb, 414 U.S. 441 (1974) (loyalty oath for candidates).
81. Tinker v. Des Moines School Dist., 393 U.S. 503 (1969).
82. Healy v. James, 408 U.S. 169 (1972).
83. New York Times Co. v. United States, 403 U.S. 713 (1971).
84. Williams v. Rhodes, 393 U.S. 23 (1968).
85. O'Brien v. Brown, 409 U.S. 1, *dismissed as moot,* 409 U.S. 816 (1972).
86. 395 U.S. 486 (1969).
87. Powell v. McCormack, 266 F. Supp. 354 (D.D.C. 1967), 395 F.2d 577 (D.C. Cir. 1968).
88. *See* 395 U.S. at 571 n.21 (Stewart, J., dissenting).
89. *Id.* at 504-06.
90. *Id.* at 570-72.
91. *Id.* at 548.
92. *Id.* at 549.
93. *Id.*
94. *Id.* at 498.
95. 117 U.S. 697 (1864).
96. 119 U.S. 477 (1886).
97. 277 U.S. 274 (1928).
98. *Id.* at 289.
99. Act of June 14, 1934, ch. 512, 48 Stat. 955.
100. 300 U.S. 227 (1937).

101. *Id.* at 240-41.
102. Powell v. McCormack, 395 U.S. 486, 544 (1969).
103. *Id.* at 545-46.
104. *See* pp. 70-71 *supra.*
105. Powell v. McCormack, 395 U.S. 486, 547 (1969).
106. For a reflection of this movement, *compare* Lusky, *The King Dream: Fantasy or Prophecy?*, 68 COLUM. L. REV. 1029 (1968), *with* Ferry, *The Case for a New Federalism*, SATURDAY REVIEW, June 15, 1968, at 14.

## CHAPTER X

1. *See, e.g.,* Hill, *The Bill of Rights and the Supervisory Power,* 69 COLUM. L. REV. 181 (1969).
2. 295 U.S. 78 (1935).
3. *Id.* at 88.
5. McNabb v. United States, 318 U.S. 332 (1943).
5. Ashcraft v. Tennessee, 322 U.S. 143, 158 (1944) (dissenting opinion).
6. *See* pp. 104-06 *supra.*
7. Barron v. Mayor & City Council of Baltimore, 32 U.S. (7 Pet.) 243 (1833).
8. H. EHRMANN, THE UNTRIED CASE 211-12 (2d ed. 1960); H. EHRMANN, THE CASE THAT WILL NOT DIE 483 (1969); *and see* N. T. DOWLING, CASES ON AMERICAN CONSTITUTIONAL LAW 644 n.3 (1st ed. 1937), quoting statement of Holmes, J., as published in New York Times, Aug. 21, 1927.
9. 261 U.S. 86 (1923).
10. *Id.* at 91.
11. 287 U.S. 45 (1932).
12. 294 U.S. 103 (1935).
13. 297 U.S. 278 (1936).
14. Brown v. State, 173 Miss. 542, 564-65, 161 So. 465, 466-67 (1935).
15. 173 Miss. at 572-76, 161 So. at 470-71.
16. 309 U.S. 227 (1940).
17. *Id.* at 235-36, 241.
18. *Id.* at 236 n.8.
19. 302 U.S. 319 (1937).
20. Adamson v. California, 332 U.S. 46 (1947).
21. Watts v. Indiana, 338 U.S. 49, 60 (1949) (Jackson, J., concurring and dissenting).
22. *Id.*
23. 314 U.S. 219, 235-38 (1941).
24. 322 U.S. 596 (1944).

25. *E.g.,* Brady v. Maryland, 373 U.S. 83 (1963).
26. 338 U.S. 49, 51-52 (1949).
27. 342 U.S. 55 (1951).
28. 346 U.S. 156 (1953).
29. 356 U.S. 390 (1958).
30. Miranda v. Arizona, 384 U.S. 436 (1966); *cf.* McNabb v. United States, 318 U.S. 332 (1943).
31. Jackson v. Denno, 378 U.S. 368 (1964); *cf.* Fay v. Noia, 372 U.S. 391 (1963).
32. 324 U.S. 401 (1945).
33. Chapman v. California, 386 U.S. 18 (1967).
34. 314 U.S. 219 (1941).
35. Watts v. Indiana, 338 U.S. 49, 57 (dissenting opinion).
36. *E.g.,* Rochin v. California, 342 U.S. 165 (1952); Hamilton v. Alabama, 368 U.S. 52 (1961); Pointer v. Texas, 380 U.S. 400 (1965); Duncan v. Louisiana, 391 U.S. 145 (1968).
37. Watts v. Indiana, 338 U.S. 49, 54 (1945).
38. Palko v. Connecticut, 302 U.S. 319, 326 (1937).
39. 342 U.S. 165, 175-76 (1952).
40. 384 U.S. 436 (1966).
41. *E.g.,* Ward v. Texas, 316 U.S. 547 (1942).
42. Chambers v. Florida, 309 U.S. 227, 236-37 (1940).
43. *See* pp. 161-65 *infra.*
44. Malloy v. Hogan, 378 U.S. 1 (1964).
45. Gideon v. Wainwright, 372 U.S. 335 (1963).
46. Mooney v. Holohan, 294 U.S. 103 (1935).
47. Brady v. Maryland, 373 U.S. 83 (1963).
48. Sheppard v. Maxwell, 384 U.S. 333 (1966).
49. Pointer v. Texas, 380 U.S. 400 (1965).
50. Jordan v. De George, 341 U.S. 223, 230-32 (1951).
51. *In re* Oliver, 333 U.S. 257 (1948).
52. Klopfer v. North Carolina, 386 U.S. 213 (1967).
53. Thompson v. Louisville, 362 U.S. 199 (1960).
54. Duncan v. Louisiana, 391 U.S. 145 (1968).
55. *E.g.,* Reid v. Covert, 354 U.S. 1 (1957); United States *ex rel.* Toth v. Quarles, 350 U.S. 11 (1955).
56. 316 U.S. 535 (1942).
57. 274 U.S. 200 (1927).
58. Skinner v. Oklahoma *ex rel.* Williamson, 316 U.S. 535, 541 (1942).
59. 332 U.S. 46 (1947).
60. 338 U.S. 25 (1949).
61. *Id.* at 27-28.
62. 367 U.S. 643 (1961).
63. *E.g.,* Hamilton v. Alabama, 368 U.S. 52 (1961).

64. Haley v. Ohio, 332 U.S. 596 (1948).
65. 319 U.S. 463 (1943).
66. Alcorta v. Texas, 355 U.S. 28 (1957); Napue v. Illinois, 360 U.S. 264 (1959); *cf.* Mesarosh v. United States, 352 U.S. 1 (1956).
67. 333 U.S. 196 (1948).
68. 333 U.S. 257 (1948).
69. 342 U.S. 165 (1952).
70. 349 U.S. 133 (1955).
71. 355 U.S. 225 (1957).
72. 359 U.S. 394 (1959); 366 U.S. 717 (1961).
73. 362 U.S. 199 (1960).
74. 365 U.S. 570 (1961).
75. Mapp v. Ohio, 367 U.S. 643, 674 n.6 (1961) (Harlan, J., dissenting). *Compare* United States v. Calandra, 414 U.S. 338 (1974) (exclusionary rule inapplicable to grand jury evidence obtained through unlawful search and seizure).
76. Mapp v. Ohio, 376 U.S. at 656-57.
77. *See* pp. 77-79 *supra.*
78. 372 U.S. 335 (1963).
79. *Id.* at 342.
80. Adamson v. California, 332 U.S. 46, 89 (1947) (Black, J., dissenting).
81. *See* Fairman, *Does the Fourteenth Amendment Incorporate the Bill of Rights? The Original Understanding,* 2 STAN. L. REV. 5 (1949); *cf.* Duncan v. Louisiana, 391 U.S. 145, 514 n.9 (Harlan, J., dissenting).
82. Adamson v. California, 332 U.S. 46, 89 (1947) (Black, J., dissenting).
83. 316 U.S. 455 (1942).
84. *See* p. 79 *supra.*
85. *See, e.g.,* Duncan v. Louisiana, 391 U.S. 145, 171 (1968) (concurring opinion).
86. 374 U S. 23 (1963).
87. 378 U.S. 1 (1964).
88. 380 U.S. 400 (1965).
89. 381 U.S. 618 (1965).
90. *See* pp. 77-79 *supra.*
91. 386 U.S. 213 (1967).
92. 388 U.S. 14 (1967).
93. 391 U.S. 145 (1968).
94. 333 U.S. 257 (1948).
95. 395 U.S. 784 (1969).
96. 408 U.S. 238 (1972).
97. *E.g.,* Powell v. Texas, 392 U.S. 514 (1968).

98. 377 U.S. 201 (1964).
99. 384 U.S. 436 (1966).
100. 387 U.S. 1 (1967).
101. 388 U.S. 218 (1967); *narrowed in* United States v. Ash, 413 U.S. 300 (1973).
102. 388 U.S. 263 (1967); *narrowed in* Kirby v. Illinois, 406 U.S. 682 (1972).
103. 389 U.S. 347 (1967).
104. 388 U.S. 41 (1967).
105. 394 U.S. 165 (1969).
106. 395 U.S. 258 (1969).
107. 395 U.S. 752 (1969).
108. 407 U.S. 25 (1972). *See also* Berry v. Cincinnati, 414 U.S. 29 (1973) (*Argersinger* rule held retroactive).
109. 407 U.S. 493 (1972).
110. 408 U.S. 238 (1972).

## CHAPTER XI

1. *See, e.g.,* Everson v. Board of Educ., 330 U.S. 1 (1947); Braunfeld v. Brown, 366 U.S. 599 (1961); Sherbert v. Verner, 374 U.S. 398 (1963).
2. Sherbert v. Verner, 374 U.S. 398 (1963).
3. Snee, *Religious Disestablishment and the Fourteenth Amendment,* 1954 WASH. U.L.Q. 378, 385 n.2 (1954); *but cf.* J.H. TRUMBULL, HISTORICAL NOTES ON THE CONSTITUTIONS OF CONNECTICUT, 32-39 (1873) (quasi-establishment of all Christian sects until 1818); Braden & Cahill, *A New Constitution for Connecticut, Part I,* 24 CONN. BAR J. 821, 131 n.14 (1950).
4. Abington School Dist. v. Schempp, 374 U.S. 203, 254 n.19 (1963) (Brennan, J., concurring).
5. Mahoney v. Triner Corp., 304 U.S. 401 (1938).
6. 374 U.S. 203 (1963).
7. *Id.* at 254-55.
8. 330 U.S. 1 (1947).
9. 392 U.S. 236 (1968) (state can provide nonreligious textbooks to all students including those in parochial schools).
10. Norwood v. Harrison, 413 U.S. 455 (1973).
11. Committee for Pub. Educ. v. Nyquist, 413 U.S. 756 (1973).
12. Everson v. Board of Educ., 330 U.S. at 15-16.
13. 323 U.S. 214, 216 (1944).
14. 333 U.S. 203 (1948).
15. 343 U.S. 306 (1952).
16. 366 U.S. 420 (1961).

17. 366 U.S. 582 (1961).
18. 370 U.S. 421 (1962).
19. *See, e.g.,* S. 3981, 93rd Cong. 2d Sess., 1974 (to remove jurisdiction of Federal courts to forbid voluntary prayer in public schools); *see also* H.R. 17147 and 17239 (93rd Cong., 2d Sess.).
20. 374 U.S. 203 (1963).
21. 392 U.S. 236 (1968).
22. *Compare* Committee for Pub. Educ. v. Nyquist, 413 U.S. 756 (1973), *and* Tilton v. Richardson, 403 U.S. 672 (1971), *with* Hunt v. McNair, 413 U.S. 734; *cf.* Wheeler v. Barrera, 417 U.S. 402 (1974).
23. Presbyterian Church v. Hull Church, 393 U.S. 440 (1969).
24. Walz v. Tax Comm'n, 397 U.S. 664 (1970).
25. 397 U.S. 664 (1970).
26. *Id.* at 668-69, 670.
27. *Id.* at 669-74.
28. 403 U.S. 602 (1971).
29. *Id.* at 612-13.
30. 397 U.S. 664 (1970).
31. *Id.* at 695-96.
32. 374 U.S. 203, 307 (1963).
33. 392 U.S. 236, 249 (1968).
34. *See* p. 99 *supra.*
35. *Compare* Doremus v. Board of Educ., 342 U.S. 429 (1952), *with* Everson v. Board of Educ., 330 U.S. 1 (1947).
36. 262 U.S. 447 (1923).
37. 392 U.S. 83 (1968).
38. *E.g.,* United States v. Butler, 297 U.S. 1 (1936).
39. 392 U.S. at 105.
40. *Id.* at 104.
41. *See, e.g.,* United States v. Curtiss-Wright Export Corp., 299 U.S. 304 (1936).
42. 392 U.S. at 98 n.17.
43. *See, e.g.,* Sherbert v. Verner, 374 U.S. 398, 409 (1963).
44. *See* pp. 267-70 *infra.*

# CHAPTER XII

1. 305 U.S. 337 (1938).
2. *E.g.,* Cumming v. Board of Educ., 175 U.S. 528 (1899); Gong Lum v. Rice, 275 U.S. 78 (1927).
3. Mitchell v. United States, 313 U.S. 80 (1941).
4. Steele v. Louisville & N.R.R., 323 U.S. 192 (1944).
5. 321 U.S. 649 (1944).
6. 313 U.S. 299 (1941).

7. 295 U.S. 45 (1935).
8. 334 U.S. 1 (1948).
9. *See, e.g.,* L. HOBSON, GENTLEMAN'S AGREEMENT (1947).
10. *See* 5 POWELL, THE LAW OF REAL PROPERTY para. 671 et seq. (1974 ed.).
11. *See* pp. 210, 235-38 *infra.*
12. *See generally* Henkin, *Shelley v. Kraemer: Notes for a Revised Opinion,* 110 U. PA. L. REV. 473 (1962).
13. 396 U.S. 435 (1970); *see* pp. 230-31 *infra.*
14. 346 U.S. 249 (1953).
15. 384 U.S. 641 (1966).
16. *Cf.* Takahashi v. Fish & Game Comm'n, 334 U.S. 410 (1948) (asserting Congressional power to prescribe regulations for resident aliens and exempt them from discriminatory burdens imposed by states).
17. *See, e.g.,* Clyatt v. United States, 197 U.S. 207, 216 (1905).
18. Ch. 31, 14 Stat. 27; ch. 114, 16 Stat. 140; and ch. 22, 17 Stat. 13.
19. Slaughter-House Cases, 83 U.S. (16 Wall.) 36, 67-72 (1873).
20. Jones v. Alfred H. Mayer Co., 392 U.S. 409 (1968).
21. 17 U.S. (4 Wheat.) 316 (1819).
22. *Id.* at 413-21.
23. *Id.* at 421.
24. *Id.* at 424.
25. 1 Stat. 73, 78.
26. Bank of United States v. Deveaux, 9 U.S. (5 Cranch) 61, 87 (1809).
27. *Cf.* Civil Rights Cases, 109 U.S. 3, 18 (1883).
28. Truax v. Corrigan, 257 U.S. 312 (1921).
29. *E.g.,* Milk Wagon Drivers Union v. Meadowmoor Dairies, 312 U.S. 287 (1941).
30. 83 U.S. (16 Wall.) 36 (1873).
31. *Id.* at 77, 82.
32. 109 U.S. 3 (1883).
33. *See generally* Lusky, *The Stereotype: Hard Core of Racism,* 13 BUFF. L. REV. 450 (1964); G. ALLPORT, THE NATURE OF PREJUDICE (1954).
34. *See, e.g.,* Griffin v. Breckenridge, 403 U.S. 88 (1971); Jones v. Alfred H. Mayer Co., 392 U.S. 409 (1968).
35. U.S. CONST. amend. XIV, § 1.
36. E. ABBOTT, JUSTICE AND THE MODERN LAW 75 (1913).
37. 83 U.S. (16 Wall.) at 79.
38. *Id.* at 77.
39. 6 F. Cas. 546 (C.C.E.D. Pa. 1823).
40. Dred Scott v. Sandford, 60 U.S. (19 How.) 393 (1857).
41. *Id.* at 406.

42. *See* Wechsler, *The Political Safeguards of Federalism: The Role of the States in the Composition and Selection of the National Government,* 54 COLUM. L. REV. 543 (1954).
43. 5 U.S. (1 Cranch) 137 (1803).
44. 83 U.S. (16 Wall.) at 75 (emphasis added).
45. *Id.* at 117-18 (Bradley's emphasis).
46. *Id.* at 76.
47. *Id.* at 117 (emphasis added).
48. 73 U.S. (6 Wall.) 35 (1867) (majority opinion by Miller, J.).
49. 83 U.S. (16 Wall.) at 79.
50. *Id.* at 72.
51. *E.g.,* Whitney v. California, 274 U.S. 357, 373 (1927) (Brandeis, J., concurring); *cf.* Munn v. Illinois, 94 U.S. 113 (1877).
52. *E.g.,* Connecticut Gen. Life Ins. Co. v. Johnson, 303 U.S. 77, 85 (1938) (Black, J., dissenting); *see* Graham, *The "Conspiracy Theory" of the Fourteenth Amendment,* 47 YALE L.J. 371, 48 YALE L.J. 171 (1938) (2-part article).
53. *E.g.,* Duncan v. Louisiana, 391 U.S. 145 (1968); Adamson v. California, 332 U.S. 46 (1947).
54. 347 U.S. 483, 489-90 (1954).
55. C.V. WOODWARD, REUNION AND REACTION 15 (1951).
56. 2 J. DAVIS, THE RISE AND FALL OF THE CONFEDERATE GOVERNMENT 621-22 (1881); L. ORFIELD, THE AMENDING OF THE FEDERAL CONSTITUTION 71, 73-74 (1971); Holifield, *Secession . . . a Right Reserved by the States!,* 18 KY. S.B.J. 160, 171-73 (1954).
57. C.E. HUGHES, THE SUPREME COURT OF THE UNITED STATES 50-54 (1928).
58. 109 U.S. 3 (1883).
59. 94 U.S. 113 (1877).
60. 118 U.S. 394 (1886).
61. 123 U.S. 623 (1887).
62. *See* Colgate v. Harvey, 296 U.S. 404, 436 (1935) (Stone, J., dissenting); Hague v. CIO, 307 U.S. 496, 518 (1939) (Stone, J., concurring); Madden v. Kentucky, 309 U.S. 83 (1940) (Reed, J.).
63. A. MASON, HARLAN FISKE STONE: PILLAR OF THE LAW 399-404 (1956).
64. *E.g.,* Stone's opinions in Hague v. CIO, 307 U.S. 496, 518 (1939); Colgate v. Harvey, 296 U.S. 404, 436 (1935).
65. *E.g.,* Graham v. Richardson, 403 U.S. 365 (1971).
66. *See* pp. 234-38 *infra.*
67. Act of April 9, 1866, ch. 31, 14 Stat. 27; Act of May 31, 1870, ch. 114, 16 Stat. 140; Act of Feb. 28, 1871, ch. 99, 16 Stat. 433; Act of April 20, 1871, ch. 22, 17 Stat. 13; Act of March 1, 1875, ch. 114, 18 Stat. 335.

68. 109 U.S. 3 (1883).
69. Act of March 1, 1875, ch. 114, 18 Stat. 335.
70. 109 U.S. 3, 11 (1883).
71. *Id.* at 17.
72. *Cf.* pp. 187-88 *supra*.
73. 109 U.S. at 11.
74. *Id.*
75. *Id.* at 17.
76. *E.g.*, Strauder v. West Virginia, 100 U.S. 303 (1880).
77. Yick Wo v. Hopkins, 118 U.S. 356 (1886).
78. 163 U.S. 537 (1896).
79. *Id.* at 544.
80. *Id.* at 559, 560.
81. Brown v. Board of Educ., 347 U.S. 483 (1954).
82. *See, e.g.*, C.V. WOODWARD, THE STRANGE CAREER OF JIM CROW (1955), to which a useful bibliography is appended.
83. Lusky, *Minority Rights and the Public Interest,* 52 YALE L.J. 1, 24 (1942); Lusky, *The Stereotype: Hard Core of Racism,* 13 BUFF. L. REV. 450, 452 (1964).
84. Guinn v. United States, 238 U.S. 347 (1915); Lane v. Wilson, 307 U.S. 268 (1939).
85. Lassiter v. Northampton County Bd. of Elections, 360 U.S. 45 (1959).
86. Breedlove v. Suttles, 302 U.S. 277 (1937).
87. Nixon v. Herndon, 273 U.S. 536 (1927).
88. Nixon v. Condon, 286 U.S. 73 (1932).
89. 295 U.S. 45 (1935).
90. Act of May 31, 1870, ch. 114, § 6, 16 Stat. 140.
91. Act of April 20, 1871, ch. 22, 17 Stat. 13.
92. Act of March 1, 1875, ch. 114, 18 Stat. 335.
93. *See, e.g.*, U.S. v. Cruikshank, 92 U.S. 542 (1876); U.S. v. Harris, 106 U.S. 629 (1883). For a review of the post-Civil War laws, and their fate, *see* Gressman, *The Unhappy History of Civil Rights Legislation,* 50 MICH. L. REV. 1323 (1952); CARR, FEDERAL PROTECTION OF CIVIL RIGHTS (1947).

## CHAPTER XIII

1. *See* M. GRODZINS, THE LOYAL AND THE DISLOYAL 105-31 (1956).
2. *See* Korematsu v. United States, 323 U.S. 214, 236 (1944).
3. Korematsu v. United States, 323 U.S. 214 (1944). On this and related cases, *see, e.g.*, Rostow, *The Japanese American Cases — A Disaster,* 54 YALE L.J. 489 (1945); Dembitz, *Racial Discrimination and the Military Judgment,* 45 COLUM. L. REV. 175 (1945); M.

GRODZINS, AMERICANS BETRAYED: POLITICS AND THE JAPANESE EVACUATION (1949).
4. 323 U.S. at 216.
5. 321 U.S. 649 (1944). *See also* Terry v. Adams, 345 U.S. 461 (1953).
6. 334 U.S. 1 (1948). *See also* Barrows v. Jackson, 346 U.S. 249 (1953).
7. *See* pp. 179-80 *supra*.
8. Act of April 9, 1866, ch. 31, 14 Stat. 27.
9. 392 U.S. 409 (1968).
10. 334 U.S. at 11.
11. *E.g.*, Bell v. Maryland, 378 U.S. 226 (1964).
12. *See generally* G. GUNTHER & N. DOWLING, CASES AND MATERIALS ON CONSTITUTIONAL LAW 503-17 (8th ed. 1970), on the background and passage of the Civil Rights Act of 1968.
13. *Cf.* Gilmore v. City of Montgomery, 417 U.S. 556 (1974).
14. 109 U.S. 3 (1883).
15. *Id.* at 25.
16. Brown v. Board of Educ., 347 U.S. 483 (1954) (decided together with Briggs v. Elliott, Davis v. County School Bd., and Gebhart v. Belton).
17. Bolling v. Sharpe, 347 U.S. 497 (1954).
18. Sipuel v. Board of Regents of Univ. of Okla., 332 U.S. 631 (1948); Sweatt v. Painter, 339 U.S. 629 (1950); McLaurin v. Oklahoma State Regents, 339 U.S. 637 (1950).
19. 347 U.S. at 494.
20. *Id.* at 495.
21. *See* Lusky, *The King Dream: Fantasy or Prophecy?*, 68 COLUM. L. REV. 1029, 1033 (1968).
22. *See* pp. 51-52 *supra*.
23. *See* p. 65 *supra*.
24. Brown v. Board of Educ., 349 U.S. 294, 301 (1955).
25. Griffin v. County School Bd., 377 U.S. 218 (1964).
26. MORLAND, SOUTHERN SCHOOLS: TOKEN DESEGREGATION AND BEYOND 4-6 (1963).
27. 349 U.S. at 298-99.
28. Lusky, *Racial Discrimination and the Federal Law: A Problem in Nullification,* 63 COLUM. L. REV. 1163, 1171-72 (1963).
29. *E.g.*, Cooper v. Aaron, 358 U.S. 1 (1958); *see* Lusky, *Racial Discrimination and the Federal Law: A Problem in Nullification,* 63 COLUM. L. REV. 1163, 1167 et seq. (1963).
30. Griffin v. County School Bd., 377 U.S. 218 (1964).
31. Goss v. Board of Educ., 373 U.S. 683, 689 (1963). *See also* Watson v. City of Memphis, 373 U.S. 526, 529-30 (1963).
32. Green v. County School Bd., 391 U.S. 430 (1968).
33. 42 U.S.C. §§ 2000d, 2000d-1 (1970).

34. Jordan, *School Integration Still an Issue Despite Quiet Progress,* N.Y. Times, Jan. 16, 1974, at 75, col. 1.
35. *E.g.,* Mayor and City Council of Baltimore v. Dawson, 350 U.S. 877 (1955) (beaches); Holmes v. City of Atlanta, 350 U.S. 879 (1955) (golf courses); New Orleans Park Improvement Ass'n v. Detiege, 358 U.S. 54 (1958) (parks); Gayle v. Browder, 352 U.S. 903 (1956) (buses); Johnson v. Virginia, 373 U.S. 61 (1963) (courtrooms); Lee v. Washington, 390 U.S. 333 (1968) (prisons).
36. Johnson v. Virginia, 373 U.S. 61, 62 (1963).
37. *See* Lusky, *Justice with a Southern Accent,* HARPER'S, March 1964, at 69, 70.
38. 371 U.S. 415 (1963).
39. *Id.* at 429-30, 431.
40. *E.g.,* Dombrowski v. Pfister, 380 U.S. 479 (1965).
41. 371 U.S. at 444.
42. *E.g.,* United Transp. Union v. State Bar, 401 U.S. 576 (1971); United Mine Workers v. Illinois Bar Ass'n, 389 U.S. 217 (1967); Brotherhood of Railroad Trainmen v. Virginia, 377 U.S. 1 (1964).
43. 372 U.S. 229 (1963).
44. 340 U.S. 315 (1951).
45. 372 U.S. at 236.
46. *Id.* at 243.
47. *Id.* at 244.
48. *Id.* at 237.
49. 357 U.S. 449 (1958).
50. 360 U.S. 72 (1959).
51. 361 U.S. 516 (1960).
52. *Id.* at 523.
53. 364 U.S. 479 (1960).
54. 372 U.S. 539 (1963).
55. *Id.* at 546-48.
56. 376 U.S. 254 (1964).
57. *E.g.,* Garrison v. Louisiana, 379 U.S. 64 (1964).
58. *Cf.* Ocala Star-Banner Co. v. Damron, 401 U.S. 295 (1971); Monitor Patriot Co. v. Roy, 401 U.S. 265 (1971).
59. Time, Inc. v. Hill, 385 U.S. 374 (1967).
60. Rosenbloom v. Metromedia, Inc., 403 U.S. 29 (1971).
61. Gertz v. Robert Welch, Inc., 418 U.S. 323 (1974).
62. *E.g.,* Miami Herald Pub. Co. v. Tornillo, 418 U.S. 241 (1974); *cf.* Gertz v. Welch, Inc., 418 U.S. 323 (1974).
63. Lusky, *Minority Rights and the Public Interest,* 52 YALE L.J. 1, 3-4 (1942); *see also* Adelson & Beall, *Adolescent Perspectives on Law and Government,* 4 LAW & SOC'Y REV. 495, 501-02 (1970).

64. *See* Henkin, *Shelley v. Kraemer: Notes for a Revised Opinion,* 110 U. PA. L. REV. 473, 488 (1962).
65. Naim v. Naim, 350 U.S. 891 (1955), 350 U.S. 985 (1956).
66. McLaughlin v. Florida, 379 U.S. 184 (1964).
67. Loving v. Virginia, 388 U.S. 1 (1967).
68. *See, e.g.,* Moose Lodge v. Irvis, 407 U.S. 163 (1972) (discriminatory private club can be granted state liquor license); *cf.* Gilmore v. City of Montgomery, 417 U.S. 556 (1974).
69. *See* pp. 223-24 *supra.*
70. The closest approach was Bell v. Maryland, 378 U.S. 226 (1964), where the six Justices who reached this issue divided three to three.
71. *E.g.,* Drews v. Maryland, 378 U.S. 547 (1964) (*cert.* petition filed Feb. 23, 1961; *vacated and remanded* June 22, 1964); Fox v. North Carolina, 378 U.S. 587 (*cert.* petition filed May 4, 1961; *cert. granted, vacated and remanded* June 22, 1964). Bell v. Maryland, *supra* note 70, was decided on June 22, 1964.
72. 373 U.S. 267, 270 (1963). *See also* Peterson v. City of Greenville, 373 U.S. 244 (1963).
73. 365 U.S. 715 (1961).
74. 387 U.S. 369 (1967).
75. *Id.* at 371.
76. *Id.* at 376.
77. *Id.* at 387, 390.
78. *See* p. 180 *supra.*
79. Pennsylvania v. Board of Trusts, 353 U.S. 230 (1957).
80. Girard College Trusteeship, 391 Pa. 434, 138 A.2d 844, *cert. denied,* 357 U.S. 570 (1958).
81. Evans v. Newton, 382 U.S. 296 (1966).
82. Evans v. Abney, 396 U.S. 435 (1970).
83. *Id.* at 445.
84. Palmer v. Thompson, 403 U.S. 217 (1971).
85. Green v. County School Bd., 391 U.S. 430 (1968).
86. Swann v. Charlotte-Mecklenburg Bd. of Educ., 402 U.S. 1 (1971); Keyes v. School Dist., 413 U.S. 189 (1973).
87. School Bd. of Richmond v. State Bd. of Educ., 412 U.S. 92 (1973).
88. Milliken v. Bradley, 418 U.S. 717 (1974).
89. 413 U.S. 189 (1973).
90. *Cf.* Norwood v. Harrison, 413 U.S. 455 (1973).
91. Coit v. Green, 404 U.S. 997 (1971), *aff'g mem.* Green v. Connally, 330 F. Supp. 1150 (D.D.C. 1971) (tax benefits); Norwood v. Harrison, 413 U.S. 455 (1973) (textbooks).
92. 347 U.S. 475 (1954).

93. *Id.* at 478.
94. 341 U.S. 651 (1951).
95. *Id.* at 659.
96. Griffin v. Breckenridge, 403 U.S. 88 (1971), *infra* p. 237.
97. 341 U.S. at 664.
98. 378 U.S. 226 (1964).
99. Pub. L. No. 88-352, 78 Stat. 241; *see* pp. 238-40 *infra*.
100. 392 U.S. 409 (1968).
101. *See* p. 212 *supra*.
102. *Id.*
103. Katzenbach v. Morgan, 384 U.S. 641, 651-52 n.10 (1966).
104. 18 U.S.C. § 3501(b) (1968).
105. Act of April 9, 1866, ch. 31, 14 Stat. 27.
106. Act of May 31, 1870, ch. 114, 16 Stat. 140.
107. Act of Feb. 28, 1871, ch. 99, 16 Stat. 433; Act of April 20, 1871, ch. 22, 17 Stat. 13.
108. Act of March 1, 1875, ch. 114, §§ 3-5, 18 Stat. 336, 337.
109. Civil Rights Act of 1866, § 2, 14 Stat. 27, *as amended by* the 1870 Enforcement Act, § 17, 16 Stat. 140.
110. 1870 Enforcement Act, § 6, 16 Stat. 140.
111. 383 U.S. 787 (1966).
112. United States v. Williams, 341 U.S. 70 (1951); Williams v. United States, 341 U.S. 97 (1951).
113. United States v. Williams, 341 U.S. 70 (1951).
114. 383 U.S. 745 (1966).
115. *Id.* at 749-52.
116. Act of April 20, 1871, ch. 22, § 2, 17 Stat. 13.
117. Collins v. Hardyman, 341 U.S. 651 (1951).
118. 403 U.S. 88, 90 (1971).
119. Jones v. Alfred H. Mayer Co., 392 U.S. 409 (1968).
120. *Id.*
121. P. 212 *supra*.
122. Hurd v. Hodge, 334 U.S. 24, 31 (1948).
123. 392 U.S. at 436.
124. *See, e.g.,* Adickes v. S.H. Kress & Co., 398 U.S. 144 (1970); Lynch v. Household Fin. Corp., 405 U.S. 538 (1972).
125. Pub. L. No. 88-352, 78 Stat. 241.
126. 109 U.S. 3 (1883).
127. The relevant provisions in Title II are found in 42 U.S.C. § 2000a (b), (c) (1970).
128. Katzenbach v. McClung, 379 U.S. 294 (1964).
129. Daniel v. Paul, 395 U.S. 298 (1969).
130. Heart of Atlanta Motel, Inc. v. United States, 379 U.S. 241 (1964).
131. *Id.* at 250-52.

NOTES TO PAGES 240-247        393

132. *E.g.,* Phillips v. Martin Marietta Corp., 400 U.S. 542, 544 (1971).
133. Cooper, *Equal Employment Law Today,* 5 COLUM. HUMAN RIGHTS L. REV. 263, 270 (1973); Larson, *Remedies for Racial Discrimination in State and Local Government Employment: A Survey and Analysis,* 5 *id.* 335, 373 (1973).
134. *E.g.,* Griggs v. Duke Power Co., 401 U.S. 424 (1971). *See generally* Rosenthal, *Employment Discrimination and the Law,* 407 ANNALS 91 (1973).
135. Pub. L. No. 89-110, 79 Stat. 437.
136. U.S. CONST. art. I, § 4.
137. *See generally* the House Report on the Voting Rights Act of 1965, H.R. REP. No. 439, 89th Cong., 1st Sess. (1965).
138. *See* South Carolina v. Katzenbach, 383 U.S. 301, 309-10 (1966).
139. Pub. L. No. 85-315, 71 Stat. 634.
140. Pub. L. No. 86-449, 74 Stat. 86.
141. Pub. L. No. 88-352, 78 Stat. 241.
142. Pub. L. No. 89-110, 79 Stat. 437.
143. South Carolina v. Katzenbach, 383 U.S. 301 (1966).
144. Katzenbach v. Morgan, 384 U.S. 641 (1966).
145. Pub. L. No. 91-285, 84 Stat. 314.
146. Oregon v. Mitchell, 400 U.S. 112 (1970).
147. Pub. L. No. 90-284, 82 Stat. 73.
148. 392 U.S. 409 (1968).

## CHAPTER XIV

1. 83 U.S. (16 Wall.) 36 (1873).
2. *Id.* at 67-70.
3. 334 U.S. 1 (1948); *see* pp. 179-80, 212 *supra.*
4. 382 U.S. 296 (1966); *see* pp. 230-31 *supra.*
5. 387 U.S. 369 (1967); *see* pp. 229-30 *supra.*
6. 392 U.S. 409 (1968); *see* pp. 237-38 *supra.*
7. 396 U.S. 435 (1970); *see* p. 231 *supra.*
8. 403 U.S. 217 (1971); *see* p. 231 n.84 *supra.*
9. 407 U.S. 163 (1972); *see* p. 228 n.68 *supra.*
10. Slaughter-House Cases, 83 U.S. (16 Wall.) 36, 72 (1873); Bailey v. Alabama, 219 U.S. 219, 241 (1911).
11. *E.g.,* Yick Wo v. Hopkins, 118 U.S. 356 (1886) (orientals); Hernandez v. Texas, 347 U.S. 475 (1954) (Mexican-Americans).
12. 371 U.S. 415 (1963).
13. 376 U.S. 254 (1964).
14. 372 U.S. 229 (1963).
15. *E.g.,* Cox v. Louisiana, 379 U.S. 536 (1965); Bachellar v. Maryland, 397 U.S. 564 (1970).
16. 364 U.S. 479 (1960).

17. *See* pp. 222-26 *supra.*
18. *See* pp. 226-27 *supra.*
19. Barron v. Mayor & City Council of Baltimore, 32 U.S. (7 Pet.) 243 (1833).
20. Much of the development is reviewed in Duncan v. Louisiana, 391 U.S. 145 (1968).
21. *E.g.,* Miranda v. Arizona, 384 U.S. 436 (1966).
22. 408 U.S. 238 (1972).
23. *Id.* at 245.
24. Railway Express Agency, Inc. v. New York, 336 U.S. 106, 112 (1949) (Jackson, J., concurring).
25. Metropolitan Cas. Ins. Co. v. Brownell, 294 U.S. 580, 584 (1935) (footnote omitted).
26. Korematsu v. United States, 323 U.S. 214 (1944).
27. 316 U.S. 535 (1942).
28. *Id.* at 541.
29. *E.g.,* Kotch v. Board of River Pilot Comm'rs, 330 U.S. 552 (1947); Williamson v. Lee Optical, Inc., 348 U.S. 483 (1955).
30. McLaughlin v. Florida, 379 U.S. 184, 191-92, 194 (1964).
31. *E.g.,* Carrington v. Rash, 380 U.S. 89, 96 (1965); Harper v. Virginia Bd. of Elections, 383 U.S. 663, 668 (1966).
32. Levy v. Louisiana, 391 U.S. 68 (1968).
33. 394 U.S. 618 (1969).
34. *Id.* at 634, 638.
35. *Developments in the Law — Equal Protection,* 82 HARV. L. REV. 1065, 1120-21 (1969) (Copyright 1969 by the Harvard Law Review Association). *See also* Michelman, *The Supreme Court 1968 Term: Forward: On Protecting the Poor Through the Fourteenth Amendment,* 83 HARV. L. REV. 7, 34 (1969); Sager, *Tight Little Islands: Exclusionary Zoning, Equal Protection, and the Indigent,* 21 STAN. L. REV. 767, 779 (1969); Gunther, *The Supreme Court, 1971 Term: Foreword: In Search of Evolving Doctrine on a Changing Court: A Model for a Newer Equal Protection,* 86 HARV. L. REV. 1 (1972).
36. Vlandis v. Kline, 412 U.S. 441, 459 (1973) (concurring opinion). *See also* San Antonio Independent School Dist. v. Rodriguez, 411 U.S. 1, 98-99 (1973) (Marshall, J., dissenting).
37. Powell v. Alabama, 287 U.S. 45 (1932).
38. Gideon v. Wainwright, 372 U.S. 335 (1963).
39. Argersinger v. Hamlin, 407 U.S. 25 (1972); Berry v. City of Cincinnati, 414 U.S. 29 (1973).
40. Griffin v. Illinois, 351 U.S. 12 (1956).

41. Douglas v. California, 372 U.S. 353 (1963). *But see* Ross v. Moffitt, 417 U.S. 600 (1974) (no appointed counsel for discretionary further appeal from appellate decision).
42. Burns v. Ohio, 360 U.S. 252 (1959).
43. James v. Strange, 407 U.S. 128 (1972). *Compare* Fuller v. Oregon, 417 U.S. 40 (1974) (reimbursement statute valid where usual exemptions available).
44. Williams v. Illinois, 399 U.S. 235 (1970).
45. Tate v. Short, 401 U.S. 395 (1971).
46. Boddie v. Connecticut, 401 U.S. 371 (1971).
47. United States v. Kras, 409 U.S. 434 (1973) (bankruptcy); Ortwein v. Schwab, 410 U.S. 656 (1973) (welfare appeal).
48. For analysis of current problems, *see* Botein, *Appointed Counsel for the Indigent Civil Defendant: A Constitutional Right Without a Judicial Remedy?*, 36 BROOKLYN L. REV. 368 (1970); Botein, *The Constitutionality of Restrictions on Poverty Law Firms: A New York Case Study,* 46 N.Y.U.L. REV. 748 (1971). Weinstein, *Delivery of Legal Services Reviewed,* N.Y.L.J., May 2, 1974, at 1, col. 5.
49. 394 U.S. 618, 627 (1969).
50. Dandridge v. Williams, 397 U.S. 471 (1970).
51. Jefferson v. Hackney, 406 U.S. 535 (1972).
52. Richardson v. Belcher, 404 U.S. 78 (1971).
53. United States Dep't of Agriculture v. Moreno, 413 U.S. 528, 535 (1973) (Brennan's emphasis). *See also* Memorial Hosp. v. Maricopa County, 415 U.S. 250 (1974) (durational residence requirement for nonemergency hospitalization and medical care at county expense held invalid as burden on travel).
54. James v. Valtierra, 402 U.S. 137 (1971).
55. Lindsey v. Normet, 405 U.S. 56, 79 (1972).
56. 411 U.S. 1 (1973).
57. Serrano v. Priest, 5 Cal. 3d 584, 487 P.2d 1241, 96 Cal. Rptr. 601 (1971); Governor v. State Treasurer, 389 Mich. 1, 203 N.W.2d 457 (1972); Robinson v. Cahill, 62 N.J. 473, 303 A.2d 273 (1973).
58. 411 U.S. at 28 (footnote omitted).
59. *Id.* at 41, 55.
60. Levy v. Louisiana, 391 U.S. 68 (1968).
61. Glona v. American Guar. & Liab. Ins. Co., 391 U.S. 73 (1968).
62. Weber v. Aetna Cas. & Sur. Co., 406 U.S. 164 (1972).
63. Gomez v. Perez, 409 U.S. 535 (1973).
64. Jimenez v. Weinberger, 417 U.S. 628.
65. Labine v. Vincent, 401 U.S. 532 (1971).
66. Eisenstadt v. Baird, 405 U.S. 438 (1972).
67. Graham v. Richardson, 403 U.S. 365 (1971).

68. *In re* Griffiths, 413 U.S. 717 (1973).
69. Sugarman v. Dougall, 413 U.S. 634 (1973).
70. Espinoza v. Farah Mfg. Co., 414 U.S. 86 (1973).
71. Hampton v. Mow Sun Wong, *cert. granted,* 417 U.S. 944 (1974).
72. 404 U.S. 71 (1971).
73. 411 U.S. 677 (1973).
74. *Id.* at 692 (Powell and Blackmun, JJ., Burger, C.J., concurring).
75. 413 U.S. 376 (1973); *cf.* Cleveland Bd. of Educ. v. La Fleur, 414 U.S. 632 (1974) (mandatory maternity leave for public school teachers several months before confinement held invalid because arbitrary).
76. Geduldig v. Aiello, 417 U.S. 484 (1974). *See also* Kahn v. Shevin, 416 U.S. 351 (1974) ($500 property tax exemption for widows, held not an invalid discrimination against men).
77. *See* p. 138 *supra.*
78. Kramer v. Union Free School Dist., 395 U.S. 621 (1969).
79. Carrington v. Rash, 380 U.S. 89 (1965).
80. Evans v. Cornman, 398 U.S. 419 (1970).
81. *See* p. 138 *supra.*
82. Cipriano v. City of Houma, 395 U.S. 701 (1969); City of Phoenix v. Kolodziejski, 399 U.S. 204 (1970).
83. McDonald v. Board of Election Comm'rs, 394 U.S. 802 (1969).
84. Goosby v. Osser, 409 U.S. 512 (1973).
85. 405 U.S. 330 (1972).
86. Marston v. Lewis, 410 U.S. 679 (1973); Burns v. Fortson, 410 U.S. 686 (1973).
87. Harper v. Virginia Bd. of Elections, 383 U.S. 663 (1966).
88. Breedlove v. Suttles, 302 U.S. 277 (1937).
89. Williams v. Rhodes, 393 U.S. 23 (1968); *cf.* Jenness v. Fortson, 403 U.S. 431 (1971) (milder restrictions upheld).
90. Bullock v. Carter, 405 U.S. 134 (1972). *See also* Lubin v. Panish, 415 U.S. 709 (1974) ($700 filing fee held invalid as to indigent candidate).
91. *See* p. 138 *supra.*
92. Dunn v. Blumstein, 405 U.S. 330 (1972).
93. *See* pp. 138-39 *supra.*
94. Reitman v. Mulkey, 387 U.S. 369 (1967).
95. *See* pp. 251-52, 255 *supra.*
96. 394 U.S. 618 (1969).
97. *Id.* at 662, 677.
98. 410 U.S. 113 (1973).
99. Levy v. Louisiana, 391 U.S. 68 (1968).
100. Sniadach v. Family Fin. Corp., 395 U.S. 337 (1969); Fuentes v. Shevin, 407 U.S. 67 (1972), *limited in* Mitchell v. W.T. Grant Co., 416 U.S. 600 (1974).

101. Brooks v. Tennessee, 406 U.S. 605 (1972).
102. Boddie v. Connecticut, 401 U.S. 371 (1971).
103. Tate v. Short, 401 U.S. 395 (1971); Williams v. Illinois, 399 U.S. 235 (1970); *see* pp. 254-55 *supra.*
104. Cohen v. California, 403 U.S. 15 (1971); Rosenfeld v. New Jersey, 408 U.S. 901 (1972); Brown v. Oklahoma, 408 U.S. 914 (1972); Lewis v. City of New Orleans, 408 U.S. 913 (1972), 415 U.S. 130 (1974); Hess v. Indiana, 414 U.S. 105 (1973); Eaton v. City of Tulsa, 415 U.S. 697 (1974).
105. Groppi v. Leslie, 404 U.S. 496 (1972).
106. *E.g.,* Griswold v. Connecticut, 381 U.S. 479, 507 (Black, J.), 527 (Stewart, J.) (1965).
107. 198 U.S. 45 (1905).
108. *E.g.,* Fuentes v. Shevin, 407 U.S. 67, 97 (1972); Lynch v. Household Fin. Corp., 405 U.S. 538, 556 (1972) (Burger, C.J., White and Blackmun, JJ., dissenting).
109. *See* Frankel, *The New Egalitarianism and the Old,* 56 COMMENTARY, 54, 57 (Sept. 1973).
110. *See* pp. 177-78 *supra.*
111. Hamilton v. Regents of Univ. of Cal., 293 U.S. 245 (1934).
112. 310 U.S. 586 (1940).
113. 319 U.S. 624 (1943).
114. 319 U.S. 105 (1943).
115. Perisich v. Pennsylvania; Mowder v. Pennsylvania; Seders v. Pennsylvania; Lamborn v. Pennsylvania; Maltezos v. Pennsylvania; Anastasia Tzanes v. Pennsylvania; Ellaine Tzanes v. Pennsylvania.
116. 336 U.S. 599 (1961).
117. 374 U.S. 398 (1963).
118. S.C. CODE tit. 68, §§ 68-113, 68-114.
119. 374 U.S. at 422.
120. 398 U.S. 333 (1970).
121. 333 U.S. 203 (1948).
122. 401 U.S. 437 (1971).
123. 406 U.S. 205 (1972).
124. *See* p. 14 *supra.*
125. *See* p. 22 *supra.*
126. *See* pp. 101-02 *supra.*

# CHAPTER XV

1. *See* p. 113 *supra.*
2. 262 U.S. 447 (1923).
3. *Id.* at 488.

4. Barrows v. Jackson, 346 U.S. 249 (1953), *extending* Shelley v. Kraemer, 334 U.S. 1 (1948).
5. Brown v. Board of Educ., 349 U.S. 294 (1955), *implementing* 347 U.S. 483 (1954).
6. *E.g.,* Hannegan v. Esquire, Inc., 327 U.S. 146 (1946).
7. *E.g.,* United States Dep't of Agric. v. Moreno, 413 U.S. 528 (1973).
8. *E.g.,* Griffin v. County School Bd., 377 U.S. 218 (1964); Peterson v. City of Greenville, 373 U.S. 244 (1963).
9. 381 U.S. 618 (1965).
10. *See* pp. 77-79 *supra.*
11. Burnet v. Coronado Oil & Gas Co., 285 U.S. 393, 406-08 (1932) (Brandeis, J., dissenting).
12. *E.g.,* Edelman v. Jordan, 415 U.S. 651, 671 n.14 (1974). Even Justice Black, for all his insistence on literal interpretation of the Constitution (including, surely, Article V) has taken this position. *See* his dissent in Boys Markets, Inc. v. Retail Clerks Union, 398 U.S. 235, 259-60 (1970).
13. 384 U.S. 436 (1966), *limited in* Harris v. New York, 401 U.S. 222 (1971), and Michigan v. Tucker, 417 U.S. 433 (1974).
14. 384 U.S. at 478-79.
15. *Id.* at 479.
16. *Id.* at 442.
17. *Cf. The Supreme Court, 1965 Term,* 80 HARV. L. REV. 91, 141 n.37 (1966).
18. 384 U.S. 719 (1966).
19. Desist v. United States, 394 U.S. 244, 255 (1969) (Douglas, J., dissenting).
20. 395 U.S. 486 (1969).
21. 349 U.S. 294 (1955).
22. *E.g.,* Reynolds v. Sims, 377 U.S. 533 (1964).
23. *See, e.g.,* Hart v. Community School Bd., 497 F.2d 1027, 1030 (2d Cir. 1974).
24. 372 U.S. 391 (1963).
25. *See* p. 104 *supra.*
26. *See* pp. 151-57 *supra.*
27. 372 U.S. 293 (1963).
28. *Id.* at 312.
29. 373 U.S. 1 (1963).
30. 372 U.S. at 430.
31. Published as FRIENDLY, FEDERAL JURISDICTION: A GENERAL VIEW (1973).
32. *Id.* at 16.
33. *Id.* at 17, 32.
34. *See* p. 254 *supra.*

35. Parisi v. Davidson, 405 U.S. 34, 48 (1972) (concurring opinion).
36. 381 U.S. 618 (1965).
37. *See* p. 79 *supra.*
38. *See* pp. 76-77 *supra.*
39. *See* pp. 104-06 *supra.*
40. 342 U.S. 165 (1952).
41. 386 U.S. 18 (1967).
42. *Id.* at 46-47 (1967).
43. 19 U.S. (6 Wheat.) 264 (1821).
44. *Id.* at 404.
45. 312 U.S. 496 (1941).
46. *See, e.g.,* Alabama Pub. Serv. Comm'n v. Southern Ry., 341 U.S. 341, 355-62 (1951).
47. 401 U.S. 37 (1971).
48. *Id.* at 44.
49. 338 U.S. 25 (1949); *see* p. 66 *supra.*
50. 347 U.S. 483 (1954), 349 U.S. 294 (1955).
51. 369 U.S. 186 (1962).
52. 395 U.S. 486 (1969).
53. *See* pp. 132-37, 139-44 *supra.*
54. 392 U.S. 83 (1968); *see* pp. 176-77 *supra.*
55. *See* p. 279 *supra.*
56. 398 U.S. 235 (1970).
57. *Id.* at 259.
58. 403 U.S. 388 (1971).
59. *E.g.,* Barr v. Matteo, 360 U.S. 564 (1959).
60. 392 U.S. 83 (1968); *see* pp. 176-77 *supra.*
61. *See generally,* Hill, *Constitutional Remedies,* 69 COLUM. L. REV. 1109, 1147 (1969).
62. *Cf. id.* at 1145-47.
63. *See* pp. 219-20 *supra.*
64. 390 U.S. 570 (1968).
65. 393 U.S. 483 (1969).
66. 395 U.S. 711 (1969).
67. Act of June 25, 1948, ch. 645, § 1201, 62 Stat. 760.
68. *See* Brady v. United States, 397 U.S. 742 (1970); McMann v. Richardson, 397 U.S. 759 (1970).
69. *See* p. 282 *supra.*
70. *See, e.g.,* Great Northern Ry. v. Sunburst Oil & Ref. Co., 287 U.S. 358 (1932).
71. Stovall v. Denno, 388 U.S. 293, 301 (1967).
72. *See* pp. 65-66 *supra.*
73. Stovall v. Denno, 388 U.S. 293, 301 (1967).
74. 395 U.S. 213 (1969).

75. *Id.* at 217-18.
76. 388 U.S. 293 (1967).
77. United States v. Wade, 388 U.S. 218 (1967); Gilbert v. California, 388 U.S. 263 (1967).
78. 388 U.S. at 301 (1967).
79. 394 U.S. 244, 256 (1969).
80. 389 U.S. 347 (1967).
81. 394 U.S. at 259.
82. Note, *The Guilty Plea as a Waiver of "Present But Unknowable" Constitutional Rights: The Aftermath of the Brady Trilogy,* 74 COLUM. L. REV. 1435 (1974).
83. 390 U.S. 570 (1968); *see* p. 295 *supra.*
84. 168 U.S. 532 (1897).
85. 385 U.S. 493 (1967).
86. 397 U.S. 742 (1970).
87. 397 U.S. 759 (1970).
88. 401 U.S. 646 (1971).
89. *Id.* at 676-77, 697, 698, 701.
90. 338 U.S. 25 (1949); *see* p. 66 *supra.*
91. 373 U.S. 83 (1963).
92. *Id.* at 92.
93. 405 U.S. 645 (1972).
94. *Id.* at 658.
95. *Id.* at 660.
96. 347 U.S. 483 (1954); *see* p. 65 *supra.*
97. 372 U.S. 293, 325 (1963).
98. *Id.* at 327.
99. 384 U.S. 436 (1966).
100. 413 U.S. 15 (1973). *See also* Morrissey v. Brewer, 408 U.S. 471 (1971) (parole revocation procedure; Burger, C.J., for the Court).
101. *See* Wolf v. Colorado (app.), 338 U.S. 25, 33 (1949).
102. People v. Defore, 242 N.Y. 13, 21, 150 N.E. 585, 587, *cert. denied,* 270 U.S. 657 (1926).
103. Wolf v. Colorado, 338 U.S. 25 (1949).
104. 367 U.S. 643 (1961).
105. 277 U.S. 438 (1928).
106. *Id.* at 485.
107. *See, e.g.,* Mapp v. Ohio, 367 U.S. 643, 658 (1961); Bivens v. Six Unknown Named Agents, 403 U.S. 388, 411 (Burger, C.J., dissenting).
108. 369 U.S. 186 (1962).
109. *See* p. 136 *supra.*
110. 367 U.S. 1 (1961).
111. 382 U.S. 70 (1965).

112. 384 U.S. 214 (1966).
113. 402 U.S. 415 (1971).
114. Pub. L. No. 90-40, § 8, 81 Stat. 100 (1967).
115. 393 U.S. 233 (1968).
116. 407 U.S. 225 (1972).
117. See Lusky, *Racial Discrimination and the Federal Law: A Problem in Nullification,* 63 COLUM. L. REV. 1163, 1182 (1963).
118. See pp. 85-91 *supra.*
119. See p. 72 *supra.*
120. 297 U.S. 1 (1936); see p. 62 *supra.*
121. See pp. 161-65 *supra.*
122. See pp. 249-53 *supra.*
123. Sugarman v. Dougall, 413 U.S. 634, 649 (1973) (Rehnquist, J., dissenting).
124. 413 U.S. 508 (1973).
125. 382 U.S. 136 (1965).
126. 319 U.S. 463 (1965).
127. *Id.* at 467-68.
128. 382 U.S. at 144.
129. *See, e.g.,* Mourning v. Family Publications Serv., Inc., 411 U.S. 356 (1973); Marshall v. United States, 414 U.S. 417 (1974).
130. 405 U.S. 645 (1972).
131. See the dissenting opinions in Stanley v. Illinois, *id.* at 659; Vlandis v. Kline, 412 U.S. 441, 459 (1973); United States Dep't of Agric. v. Murry, 413 U.S. 508, 520 (1973); Cleveland Bd. of Educ. v. La Fleur, 414 U.S. 632, 657 (1974).
132. Note, *The Irrebuttable Presumption Doctrine in the Supreme Court,* 87 HARV. L. REV. 1534 (1974); Note, *The Conclusive Presumption Doctrine: Equal Process or Due Protection?,* 72 MICH. L. REV. 800 (1974); Note, *Irrebuttable Presumptions: An Illusory Analysis,* 27 STAN. L. REV. 449 (1975).
133. G. GUNTHER & N. DOWLING, CASES AND MATERIALS ON CONSTITUTIONAL LAW (8th ed. 1970), 1974 Supp. 268.

## CHAPTER XVI

1. See pp. 109-12 *supra.*
2. See pp. 264, 266 *supra.*
3. See pp. 109-10 *supra.*
4. WEBSTER'S NEW INT'L DICTIONARY UNABRIDGED 1019 (2d ed. 1934).
5. Shapiro v. Thompson, 394 U.S. 618 (1969).
6. *E.g.,* Dunn v. Blumstein, 405 U.S. 330 (1972).
7. *E.g.,* Lindsey v. Normet, 405 U.S. 56 (1972); San Antonio Independent School Dist. v. Rodriguez, 411 U.S. 1 (1973); Dandridge v. Williams, 397 U.S. 471, 520 (1970) (Marshall, J., dissenting).

8. Baker v. Carr, 369 U.S. 186, 226, 258 (1962); *see* pp. 132-33 *supra*.
9. 411 U.S. 1 (1973).
10. *Id.* at 28.
11. Jones v. Opelika, 316 U.S. 584, 608 (1942) (dissenting opinion).
12. 336 U.S. 77 (1949).
13. *Id.* at 90, 91.
14. *Id.* at 96.
15. 395 U.S. 486 (1969).
16. *See* pp. 139-44 *supra*.
17. 416 U.S. 312 (1974).
18. *Id.* at 348.
19. 418 U.S. 683 (1974).
20. N.Y. Times, July 2, 1974, at 20, col. 1. Copyright © by The New York Times Company; reprinted by permission.
21. *See* pp. 10, 11-12 *supra*.
22. Lusky, *Censorship,* ENCYCLOPEDIA AMERICANA (1974).
23. Barron v. Mayor & City Council of Baltimore, 32 U.S. (7 Pet.) 243 (1833).
24. Act of March 3, 1865, ch. 89, 13 Stat. 504.
25. Act of March 3, 1873, ch. 258, § 2, 17 Stat. 598.
26. 236 U.S. 230 (1915).
27. 333 U.S. 507 (1948).
28. *Id.* at 510.
29. 334 U.S. 131, 166 (1948).
30. 343 U.S. 495, 501-02 (1952).
31. 323 U.S. 214 (1944); *see* pp. 211-12 *supra*.
32. 338 U.S. 25 (1949); *see* p. 66 *supra*.
33. 354 U.S. 476 (1957).
34. *See* Lusky, *Censorship,* ENCYCLOPEDIA AMERICANA (1974).
35. [1868] L.R. 3 Q.B. 360.
36. Roth v. United States, 354 U.S. at 489 (1957).
37. *Id.* at 484.
38. 383 U.S. 463 (1966).
39. 354 U.S. at 496.
40. 383 U.S. 413 (1966), officially reported as, A Book Named "John Cleland's Memoirs of a Woman of Pleasure" v. Attorney General of Massachusetts; *see* C. REMBAR, THE END OF OBSCENITY 449-90 (1968).
41. 378 U.S. 184 (1964).
42. *Id.* at 197.
43. 383 U.S. at 418.
44. 383 U.S. 502 (1966).
45. 383 U.S. 463 (1966).
46. 390 U.S. 629 (1968).

47. 397 U.S. 728 (1970).
48. Freedman v. Maryland, 380 U.S. 51 (1965).
49. Heller v. New York, 413 U.S. 483 (1973), *modifying* Marcus v. Search Warrants, 367 U.S. 717 (1961), *and* A Quantity of Books v. Kansas, 378 U.S. 205 (1964).
50. *E.g.,* Miller v. California, 413 U.S. 15, 46 (1973); Ginzburg v. United States, 383 U.S. 463, 482-83 (1966).
51. 409 U.S. 109 (1972).
52. *Id.* at 111.
53. 413 U.S. 15 (1973).
54. *Id.* at 24.
55. *Id.* at 25.
56. *See* Leventhal, *The 1973 Round of Obscenity-Pornography Decisions,* 59 A.B.A.J. 1261, 1262 (1973); *see* Jenkins v. Georgia, 418 U.S. 153, 157 (1974).
57. N.Y. Times, June 25, 1974, at 18, col. 3 (copyright © 1974 by The New York Times Company; reprinted by permission); the cases are Hamling v. United States, 418 U.S. 87 (1974), and Jenkins v. Georgia, 418 U.S. 153 (1974).
58. 376 U.S. 254 (1964).
59. *See* the highlights of the 1974 Annual Meeting of the American Law Institute reported in 42 U.S.L.W. 2618, 2620-21 (June 4, 1974), and the subsequent decision in Gertz v. Welch, Inc., 418 U.S. 323 (1974) (limiting damages recoverable).
60. *See* Lusky, *Invasion of Privacy: A Clarification of Concepts,* 72 COLUM. L. REV. 693, 697-99 (1972), criticizing the rationale in Time, Inc. v. Hill, 385 U.S. 374 (1967).
61. 371 U.S. 415 (1963).
62. *See* Brotherhood of Railroad Trainmen v. Virginia *ex rel.* Virginia State Bar, 377 U.S. 1 (1964); United Mine Workers v. Illinois Bar Ass'n, 389 U.S. 217 (1967); United Transp. Union v. State Bar, 401 U.S. 576 (1971).
63. 326 U.S. 501 (1946).
64. *Compare* Amalgamated Food Employees Union v. Logan Valley Plaza, 391 U.S. 308 (1968), *with* Lloyd Corp. v. Tanner, 407 U.S. 551 (1972).
65. 376 U.S. 254, 270 (1964).
66. 337 U.S. 1 (1949).
67. *E.g.,* Gregory v. City of Chicago, 394 U.S. 111 (1969).
68. Cohen v. California, 403 U.S. 15 (1971).
69. Rosenfeld v. New Jersey, 408 U.S. 901 (1972).
70. Brown v. Oklahoma, 408 U.S. 914 (1972).
71. Lewis v. City of New Orleans, 408 U.S. 913 (1972), 415 U.S. 130 (1974).

72. Street v. New York, 394 U.S. 576 (1969); Smith v. Goguen, 415 U.S. 566 (1974); cf. Spence v. Washington, 418 U.S. 405 (1974).
73. Healy v. James, 408 U.S. 169 (1972).
74. *See* Lusky & Lusky, *Columbia 1968: The Wound Unhealed,* 84 POL. SCI. Q. 169 (1969).
75. New York Times Co. v. United States, 403 U.S. 713 (1971).
76. *Id.* at 715, 724-25.
77. 369 U.S. 186 (1962).
78. *E.g.,* Kirkpatrick v. Preisler, 394 U.S. 526 (1969).
79. *E.g.,* Kramer v. Union Free School Dist., 395 U.S. 621 (1969).
80. *See, e.g.,* Gaffney v. Cummings, 412 U.S. 735 (1973); Mahan v. Howell, 410 U.S. 315 (1973); Abate v. Mundt, 403 U.S. 182 (1971).
81. *See* pp. 163-64 *supra.*
82. *See* p. 99 *supra.*
83. 385 U.S. 493 (1967).
84. *See* p. 298 *supra.*
85. 402 U.S. 424 (1971).
86. *See, e.g.,* Hoffman v. United States, 341 U.S. 479 (1951).
87. 397 U.S. 664 (1970); *see* pp. 174-75 *supra.*
88. 403 U.S. 602 (1971); *see* p. 174 *supra.*
89. 396 U.S. 435 (1970).
90. 403 U.S. 217 (1971).
91. 407 U.S. 163 (1972).
92. 83 U.S. (16 Wall.) 36 (1873).
93. 109 U.S. 3 (1883). *See* pp. 203-05 *supra.*
94. *See* pp. 243-46 *supra.*
95. *See* pp. 249-53 *supra.*
96. 198 U.S. 45 (1905).
97. 381 U.S. 479 (1965).
98. *Id.* at 483-84.
99. *Id.* at 485.
100. 357 U.S. 449 (1958).
101. 381 U.S. at 483.
102. *Id.*
103. Meyer v. Nebraska, 262 U.S. 390 (1923).
104. Pierce v. Society of Sisters, 268 U.S. 510 (1925).
105. 394 U.S. 557 (1969).
106. 405 U.S. 438 (1972).
107. *See* pp. 15-19 *supra.*
108. Poe v. Ullman, 367 U.S. 497 (1961) (saying Connecticut statute was apparently dead letter).
109. 405 U.S. 438 (1972).
110. Kingsley Int'l Pictures Corp. v. Regents, 360 U.S. 684 (1959).
111. *See* p. 5 *supra.*

112. 303 U.S. 501 (1938).
113. Act of Feb. 13, 1925, ch. 299, 43 Stat. 936.
114. Davidson v. New Orleans, 96 U.S. 97, 104 (1878).
115. 262 U.S. 447 (1923).
116. *See* Gunther, *The Subtle Vices of the "Passive Virtues" — A Comment on Principle and Expediency in Judicial Review*, 64 COLUM. L. REV. 1, 11-12 (1964).
117. *See, e.g.,* Church of the Holy Trinity v. United States, 143 U.S. 57 (1892).
118. *E.g.,* Johnson v. Zerbst, 304 U.S. 458 (1938).
119. *See, e.g.,* Donnelly v. DeChristoforo, 416 U.S. 637, 648 (1974) (Stewart, J., concurring).
120. Weaver, *The Supreme Court at Work: A Look at the Inner Sanctum*, N.Y. Times, Feb. 6, 1975, at 35, col. 6, at 65, col. 2; Clark, *The Supreme Court Conference*, 19 F.R.D. 303, 306 (1956), quoted in R.L. STERN & E. GRESSMAN, SUPREME COURT PRACTICE 207 (4th ed. 1969).

## CHAPTER XVII

1. Letter to Bishop Mandell Creighton, April 5, 1887, in L. VON G. CREIGHTON, LIFE AND LETTERS OF MANDELL CREIGHTON, vol. I, p. 372 (4th impression 1904).
2. *See* p. 23 *supra.*
3. Decades ago I read that Justice Holmes had said or written this, but I have been unable to locate a citation. I have remembered it because it is so uncharacteristic of him, great clarifier that he was.
4. *See* ch. II *supra.*
5. Printed in 59 A.B.A.J. 1125, 1129 (1973), and reprinted by permission of the American Bar Association Journal.
6. *Id.*
7. *Id.*
8. *See* Tidewater Oil Co. v. United States, 409 U.S. 151, 174-76 (1972) (Douglas, J., dissenting); Justice Brennan's statement to the First Circuit Judicial Conference (1973), partially published in 59 A.B.A.J. 835 (1973).
9. FEDERAL JUDICIAL CENTER, REPORT OF THE STUDY GROUP ON THE CASELOAD OF THE SUPREME COURT (1972).
10. *See* FRIENDLY, FEDERAL JURISDICTION: A GENERAL VIEW (1973) *passim.*
11. ROSENBERG & CARRINGTON, JOINT STATEMENT TO COMMISSION ON REVISION OF THE FEDERAL COURT APPELLATE SYSTEM (April 1, 1974).
12. 308 U.S. 147, 161 (1939).

13. 309 U.S. 227, 236 (1940).
14. 334 U.S. 1 (1948).
15. *See* pp. 294-99 *supra.*
16. *See* p. 297 *supra.*
17. *See* pp. 47-48 *supra.*
18. 22 U.S. (9 Wheat.) 1 (1824).
19. 328 U.S. 408 (1946).
20. Biklé, *The Silence of Congress,* 41 HARV. L. REV. 200 (1927); *see also* authorities cited in ch. IV, note 9 *supra.*
21. 17 U.S. (4 Wheat.) 316 (1819).
22. 304 U.S. 405 (1938).
23. 310 U.S. 296 (1940).
24. *Id.* at 307-08, 311.
25. 378 U.S. 500 (1964).
26. Act of Sept. 23, 1950, ch. 1024, § 6, 64 Stat. 993.
27. *See, e.g.,* Keyishian v. Board of Regents, 385 U.S. 589 (1967).
28. *See* pp. 189-201 *supra.*
29. *See* p. 246 *supra.*
30. 302 U.S. 319 (1937).
31. *Id.* at 328.
32. *See* p. 319 *supra.*
33. 381 U.S. 479 (1965).
34. 410 U.S. 113 (1973).
35. 394 U.S. 618 (1969).
36. Concurring in Railway Express Agency v. New York, 336 U.S. 106, 112 (1949), quoted *supra* in footnote on p. 338.
37. *See* p. 233 *supra.*
38. *See* pp. 280-82 *supra.*

# TABLE OF CASES

Abate v. Mundt, 331n80
Abington School Dist. v. Schempp, 168n4; 169n6; 172n20; 175
Abrams v. United States, 120n13
Adamson v. California, 150n20; 159n59; 162n80, 82; 197n53
Adickes v. S.H. Kress & Co., 194*; 238n124
Aetna Life Ins. Co. v. Haworth, 142n100-101
Alabama Pub. Serv. Comm'n v. Southern Ry., 291n46
Alberts v. California, 320n33
Albertson v. Subversive Activities Control Bd., 128n35; 305n111
Alcorta v. Texas, 160n66
Alderman v. United States, 165n105
Amalgamated Food Employees Union v. Logan Valley Plaza, 329n64
American Communications Ass'n v. Douds, 74n27
Anastasia Tzanes v. Pennsylvania, 268n115
Anderson v. Dunn, 29n9
Apodaca v. Oregon, 14n6, 8; 158*
Aptheker v. Secretary of State, 358n25
Argersinger v. Hamlin, 14n6; 165n108; 254n39
Ashcraft v. Tennessee, 145n5
Ashton v. Cameron County Water Improvement Dist., 102n10
Ashwander v. TVA, 50n2; 52n3
Association of Data Processing Serv. Orgs., Inc. Camp, 13n5

Bachellar v. Maryland, 247n15
Baggett v. Bullitt, 138n80
Bailey v. Alabama, 246n10
Baker v. Carr, 131n43; 132n45; 133; 133n47; 134; 134n50-52; 135n53; 136n56-60; 137n61; 140-41; 292n51; 304n108; 305; 312n8; 330n77
Baldwin v. New York, 14n6
Banco Nacional de Cuba v. Sabbatino, 135*
Bank of United States v. Deveaux, 187n26
Bantam Books, Inc. v. Sullivan, 29n7
Barenblatt v. United States, 74n27; 128n31
Barlow v. Collins, 13n5
Barr v. Matteo, 293n59
Barron v. Mayor & City Council of Baltimore, 146n7; 247n19; 320n23
Barrows v. Jackson, 181n14; 212n6; 275n4
Barsky v. Board of Regents, 29n8; 127n19
Bartels v. Iowa, 108
Bates v. City of Little Rock, 224n51
Beauharnais v. Illinois, 74n27
Beilan v. Board of Educ., 127n15
Bell v. Maryland, 213n11; 228n70-71; 234n98
Benton v. Maryland, 165n95
Berger v. New York, 165n104
Berger v. United States, 145n2-3

# TABLE OF CASES

Berry v. Cincinnati, 165n108; 254n39
Betts v. Brady, 163n83
Bivens v. Six Unknown Named Agents, 144*; 293n58; 304n107
Board of Educ. v. Allen, 170n9; 173n21; 175
Board of Educ. v. Barnette, 2n5
Boddie v. Connecticut, 255n46; 265n102
Bolling v. Sharpe, 214n17
Bond v. Floyd, 127n25
Boys Markets, Inc. v. Retail Clerks Union, 279n12; 292n56
Braden v. Commonwealth, 1n1; 126n14
Braden v. Lady, 1n1; 126n14
Braden v. United States, 74n27; 128n32
Brady v. Maryland, 153n25; 157n47; 301n91
Brady v. United States, 295n68; 298n86
Bram v. United States, 298n84
Braunfeld v. Brown, 168n1; 286n116
Breedlove v. Suttles, 40n18; 209n86; 263n88
Briggs v. Elliott, 214n16
Brooks v. Tennessee, 14n6; 265n101
Brotherhood of Railroad Trainmen v. Virginia, 222n42; 328n62
Brown v. Board of Educ., 65n14-15; 197n54; 207n81; 214n16; 216n24; 218; 275n5; 282n21; 291n50; 302n96
Brown v. Mississippi, 104n18; 146n13; 152; 157
Brown v. Oklahoma, 265n104; 329n70
Brown v. State, 146n14

Buck v. Bell, 158n57
Bullock v. Carter, 14n6; 263n90
Burnet v. Coronado Oil & Gas Co., 279n11
Burns v. Fortson, 263n86
Burns v. Ohio, 254n42
Burton v. Wilmington Parking Authority, 229n73

California v. Byers, 333n85
California v. LaRue, 325n51
Cantwell v. Connecticut, 358n23
Cardona v. Power, 138n75; 194*
Carmichael v. Southern Coal & Coke Co., 103n14
Carrington v. Nash, 251n31; 262n79
Carter v. Carter Coal Co., 102n10
Chambers v. Florida, 149n16; 152; 157n42; 354n13
Chapman v. California, 155n33; 289n41-42
Chicot County Drainage Dist. v. Baxter State Bank, 76*
Chimel v. California, 165n107
Chinese Exclusion Case, 89
Chisholm v. Georgia, 40n14
Church of the Holy Trinity v. United States, 347n117
Cipriano v. Houma, 138n74; 262n82
City of Phoenix v. Kolodziejski, 262n82
Civil Rights Cases, 53n5; 187n27; 189n32; 199n58; 203n68; 213n14; 227; 233; 245
Cleveland Bd. of Educ., v. La Fleur, 261n75; 310n131
Clyatt v. United States, 184n17
Codispoti v. Pennsylvania, 222*

# TABLE OF CASES

Cohen v. California, 265n104; 329n68
Cohens v. Virginia, 290n43
Coit v. Green, 232n91
Cole v. Arkansas, 160n67
Colegrove v. Green, 130n40-42; 131n43; 132
Coleman v. Alabama, 68n3; 69n5
Coleman v. Miller, 260*
Colgate v. Harvey, 201n62; 64
Collins v. Hardyman, 29n6; 234n94; 237n117
Committee for Pub. Educ. v. Nyquist, 170n11; 173n22
Commonwealth v. Davis, 124n6
Communist Party v. Whitcomb, 138n80
Communist Party of United States v. Subversive Activities Control Bd., 128n34; 305n110
Compco Corp. v. Day-Brite Lighting, Inc., 74n26
Connecticut Gen. Life Ins. Co. v. Johnson, 197n52
Cooper v. Aaron, 218n29
Corfield v. Coryell, 191*; 192n39; 194; 195-196
Cox v. New Hampshire, 125n8
Cox v. Louisiana, 125n8; 247n15
Crandall v. Nevada, 196n48
Cumming v. Board of Educ., 179n2

Dandridge v. Williams, 255n50; 312n7
Daniel v. Paul, 239n129
Davidson v. New Orleans, 346n114
Davis v. County School Bd., 214n16
Davis v. Massachusetts, 124n5
Debs v. United States, 120n13
DeFunis v. Odegaard, 314n17

DeJonge v. Oregon, 108
Dellinger, In re, 222*
Dennis v. United States, 40*; 74n27; 126n14; 127n27; 281n19
Desist v. United States, 297n79
Deutch v. United States, 128n33
Doe v. Bolton, 10n4; 13n4; 100n4
Dombrowski v. Pfister, 1n1; 222n40
Donnelly v. DeChristoforo, 348n119
Doremus v. Board of Educ., 176n35
Douglas v. California, 254n41
Dred Scott v. Sandford, 28n3; 40n15; 192n40
Drews v. Maryland, 228n71
Duncan v. Louisiana, 155n36; 157n54; 162n81; 163n85; 164n93; 197n53; 247n20
Dunn v. Blumstein, 14n6; 138n78; 262n85; 263n92; 312n6

Eakin v. Raub, 27*
Eaton v. City of Tulsa, 265n104
Edelman v. Jordan, 279n12
Edwards v. South Carolina, 247n14
Eisenstadt v. Baird, 14n6; 258n66; 341n106; 342n109
Elkins v. United States, 66n19
Ellaine Tzanes v. Pennsylvania, 268n115
Engel v. Vitale, 172n18
Epperson v. Arkansas, 143*
Espinoza v. Farah Mfg. Co., 259n70
Evans v. Abney, 180n13; 231n82; 245n7; 335n89
Evans v. Cornman, 262n80
Evans v. Newton, 231n81; 245n4

Everson v. Board of Educ.,
168n1; 170n8; 171n12; 174;
176n35; 341*

Farrington v. Tokushige, 108
Fay v. Noia, 154n31; 282n24;
284; 288
Feiner v. New York 223n44
Ferguson v. Georgia, 160n74
First Nat'l City Bank v. Banco
Nacional de Cuba, 135*
Fiske v. Kansas, 105n22; 108
Flast v. Cohen, 144*; 176n37;
292n54; 294n60
Fox v. North Carolina, 228n71
Freedman v. Maryland, 324n48
Frick v. Pennsylvania, 102n6
Frontiero v. Richardson, 260n73
Frothingham v. Mellon, 176n36;
274n2-3; 346n115
Frowerk v. United States, 120n13
Fuentes v. Shevin, 265n100;
266n108
Fuller v. Oregon, 254n43
Furman v. Georgia, 14n7;
165n96; 166n110; 248n22

Gaffney v. Cummings, 331n80
Gallegos v. Nebraska, 154n27
Garner v. Los Angeles Bd. of
Pud. Works, 127n18, 22
Garner v. Louisiana, 160*
Garnett, In re, 92n13
Garrison v. Louisiana, 225n57
Garrity v. New Jersey, 298n85;
332n83
Gault, In re, 165n100
Gayle v. Browder, 219n35
Gebhart v. Belton, 214n16
Geduldig v. Aiello, 262n76
Gerende v. Board of Supervisors,
127n15, 18, 23

Gertz v. Robert Welch, Inc.,
225n61-62; 328n59
Gibbons v. Ogden, 357n18
Gideon v. Wainwright, 76n28;
157n45; 161n78; 162n79; 163;
254n38
Gilbert v. California, 17n19;
165n102
Gillette v. United States,
269n122
Gilmore v. City of Montgomery,
213n13; 228n68
Ginsberg v. New York, 323n46
Ginzburg v. United States,
321n38; 323n45; 324n50
Girard College Trusteeship,
230n80
Gitlow v. New York, 108; 120n15
Glona v. American Guar. &
Liab. Ins. Co., 258n61
Gojack v. United States, 128n33
Gomez v. Perez, 258n63
Gong Lum v. Rice, 179n2
Goosby v. Osser, 262n84
Gordon v. United States, 141n95
Goss v. Board of Educ., 218n31
Governor v. State Treasurer,
257n57
Graham v. Richardson, 14n6;
202n65; 259n67
Gray v. Sanders, 137n62-63
Great Northern Ry. v.
Sunburst Oil & Ref. Co., 296n70
Green v. Connally, 232n91
Green v. County School Bd.,
218n32; 231n85
Gregory v. Chicago, 160*;
329n67
Griffin v. Breckenridge, 189n34;
190*; 194*; 237n118; 234n96
Griffin v. County School Bd.,
216n25; 218n30; 279n8
Griffin v. Illinois, 254n40
Griffiths, In re, 259n68

TABLE OF CASES  411

Griggs v. Duke Power Co.,
 3n7; 240n134
Griswold v. Connecticut, 55n10;
 265; 266n106; 364n33; 339n97;
 341
Groppi v. Leslie, 14n6; 265n105
Grosjean v. American Press Co.,
 104n19; 108; 124n2
Grovey v. Townsend, 179n7; 209n89
Guinn v. United States, 130n38;
 208n84

Hadley v. Junior College Dist.,
 138n72
Hague v. CIO, 116n5; 124n4; 124n7;
 201n62, 64
Haley v. Ohio, 160n64
Hamilton v. Alabama, 155n36;
 160n63
Hamilton v. Regents, 267n111
Hamling v. United States,
 328n57
Hammer v. Dagenhart, 55n8;
 56n16; 103*
Hampton v. Mow Sun Wong,
 259n71
Hannegan v. Esquire, Inc.,
 278n6
Harper v. Virginia Bd. of
 Elections, 40n18; 138n76;
 251n31; 263n87
Harris v. New York, 280n13
Hart v. Community School Bd.,
 282n23
Healy v. James, 138n82; 330n73
Heart of Atlanta Motel, Inc. v.
 United States, 22n25; 239n130
Heiner v. Donnan, 102n6
Heller v. New York, 324n49
Helvering v. Davis, 103n14
Helvering v. Gerhardt, 357n22
Hernandez v. Texas, 233n92;
 246n11; 266*

Herndon v. Lowry, 108
Hess v. Indiana, 265n104
Hoffman v. United States,
 334n86
Holmes v. City of Atlanta,
 219n35
Home Building & Loan Ass'n
 v. Blaisdell, 102n8
Hunt v. McNair, 173n22
Hurd v. Hodge, 237n122

Illinois v. Allen, 222*
Irvin v. Dowd, 160n72

Jackson v. Denno, 154n31
Jacobellis v. Ohio, 322n42
James v. Strange, 14n6; 254n43
James v. Valtierra, 256n54
Jefferson v. Hackney, 256n51
Jenkins v. Delaware,
 296n74-75; 297; 299
Jenkins v. Georgia, 326n56-57
Jenness v. Fortson, 263n89
Jimenez v. Weinberger, 258n64
Johnson v. Avery, 295n65
Johnson v. Louisiana, 14n9
Johnson v. New Jersey, 281n18
Johnson v. Virginia, 219n35-36
Johnson v. Zerbst, 347n118
Jones v. Alfred H. Mayer Co.,
 184*; 185n20; 189n34; 190*;
 194*; 212n9; 234n100;
 237n119-120; 241n148; 245n6
Jones v. Opelika, 313n11
Jordan v. De George, 157n50
Joseph Burstyn, Inc. v. Wilson,
 320n30

Kahn v. Shevin, 262n76
Katz v. United States, 69n6-10;
 73n23; 75; 165n103; 297n80

412    TABLE OF CASES

Katzenbach v. McClung, 22n26; 143*; 239n128
Katzenbach v. Morgan, 181n15; 194*; 235n103; 241n144
Kepner v. United States, 106n27
Ker v. California, 164n86
Keyes v. School Dist., 232n89
Keyishian v. Board of Regents, 138n79; 359n127
Kim Young v. California, 125n9
Kingsley Int'l Pictures Corp. v. Regents, 343n110
Kirby v. Illinois, 165n102
Kirkpatrick v. Preisler, 138n70; 331n78
Klopfer v. North Carolina, 157n52; 164n91
Konigsberg v. State Bar, 74n27; 127n19; 127n26
Korematsu v. United States, 171n13; 211n2-3; 212n4; 250n26; 320n31
Kotch v. Board of River Pilot Comm'rs, 3n8; 250n29
Kovacs v. Cooper, 313n12
Kramer v. Union Free School Dist., 138n73; 262n78; 331n79

Labine v. Vincent, 258n65
Laird v. Tatum, 292*
Lambert v. California, 160n71
Lamborn v. Pennsylvania, 268n115
Lane v. Wilson, 208n84
Lassiter v. Northampton County Bd. of Elections, 209n85
Lee v. Washington, 219n35
Lemon v. Kurtzman, 174n28; 334n88
Lerner v. Casey, 127n15
Levy v. Louisiana, 251n32; 258n60; 264n97; 265n99

Lewis v. City of New Orleans, 265n104; 329n71
Lindsey v. Normet, 256n55; 312n7
Linkletter v. Walker, 77n30; 78n33-38; 83; 164n89; 279n9; 288n36; 299
Lisenba v. California, 153n23; 155n34
Lloyd Corp. v. Tanner, 329n64
Lochner v. New York, 98n1; 266n107; 337n96; 340*
Lombard v. Louisiana, 228n72
Louisville Joint Stock Land Bank v. Radford, 102n10
Lovell v. Griffin, 108; 110; 124n3
Loving v. Virginia, 228n67
Lubin v. Panish, 263n90
Luther v. Borden, 120**
Lynch v. Household Fin. Corp., 238n124; 266n108
Lyons v. Oklahoma, 153n24


McCollum v. Board of Educ., 171n14; 269n121
McCulloch v. Maryland, 21n23; 63n12-13; 80n42-43; 83; 85n2; 91n12; 97; 109; 185n21; 186n22-24; 357n21
McDonald v. Board of Election Comm'rs, 262n83
McGowan v. Maryland, 172n16
McLaughlin v. Florida, 228n66; 251n30
McLaurin v. Oklahoma State Regents, 214n18
McMann v. Richardson, 295n68; 298n87
McNabb v. United States, 145n4; 154n30
Madden v. Kentucky, 201n62

## TABLE OF CASES 413

Mahan v. Howell, 331n80
Mahoney v. Triner Corp., 169n5
Malinski v. New York, 154n32
Malloy v. Hogan, 157n44; 164n87
Maltezos v. Pennsylvania, 268n115
Mapp v. Ohio, 66n18; 78n32; 133n49; 159n62; 161; 161n75-76; 303n104; 304n107
Marbury v. Madison, 25; 68n2; 70n11-16; 72-73; 80; 113; 143; 194n43; 217; 273; 280-281; 290; 297; 300*; 307; 314; 349; 351
Marcus v. Search Warrants, 324n49
Marsh v. Alabama, 74n26; 328n63
Marshall v. United States, 310n129
Marston v. Lewis, 263n86
Massiah v. United States, 165n98
Maxwell v. Dow, 105n23
May v. United States, 1n1
Mayberry v. Pennsylvania, 222*
Mayor & City Council of Baltimore v. Dawson, 219n35
Memoirs v. Massachusetts, 322n40
Memorial Hosp. v. Maricopa County, 256n53
Mesarosh v. United States, 160n66
Metropolitan Cas. Ins. Co. v. Brownell, 249n25
Meyer v. Nebraska, 104n17; 108; 340n103
Miami Herald Pub. Co. v. Tornillo, 225n62; 261*
Miller v. California, 324n50; 325n53; 303n100
Milliken v. Bradley, 232n88
Mills v. Alabama, 261*; 306n112
Minersville School Dist. v. Gobitis, 83n47; 120n14; 267n112
Miranda v. Arizona, 135n55; 154n30; 156n40; 165n99; 248n21; 280n13-15; 281n16; 303n99
Mishkin v. New York, 323n44

Missouri ex rel. Gaines v. Canada, 179n1
Missouri v. Holland, 82n44
Mitchell v. United States, 179n3
Mitchell v. W.T. Grant Co., 265n100
Mitchum v. Foster, 306n116
Monaco v. Mississippi, 83*
Monitor Patriot Co. v. Roy, 225n58
Mooney v. Holohan, 146n12; 157n46
Moore v. Dempsey, 146n9-10
Moose Lodge v. Irvis, 228n68; 245n9; 335n91
Morehead v. New York ex rel. Tipaldo, 102n11
Morrissey v. Brewer, 303n100
Mourning v. Family Publications Serv., Inc., 310n129
Mowder v. Pennsylvania, 268n115
Mugler v. Kansas, 201n61
Munn v. Illinois, 197n51; 200n59
Murchison, In re, 160n70
Murdock v. Pennsylvania, 268n114
Mutual Film Corp. v. Industrial Comm'n, 320n26
Myers v. United States, 55n9

NAACP v. Alabama, 340n100; 223n49
NAACP v. Button, 220n38; 247n12; 316*; 328n61
NLRB v. Jones & Laughlin Steel Corp., 102n13
Naim v. Naim, 228n65
Napue v. Illinois, 160n66
Near v. Minnesota, 104n19; 108; 124n1
Nebbia v. New York, 102n9
New Orleans Park Improvement Ass'n v. Detiege, 219n35
New York Times Co. v. Sullivan, 225n56; 247n13; 328n58; 329n65

414 TABLE OF CASES

New York Times Co. v. United
 States, 138n83; 330n75
Nichols v. Massachusetts, 125n9-10
Nixon v. Condon, 108; 209n88
Nixon v. Herndon, 108; 209n87
North Carolina v. Pearce, 295n66
North Dakota State Bd. of
 Pharmacy v. Snyder's Drug
 Stores, Inc., 261*
Norwood v. Harrison, 170n10;
 232n90-91

O'Brien v. Brown, 139n85
O'Brien v. Skinner, 262*
Ocala Star-Banner Co. v. Damron,
 225n58
O'Callahan v. Parker, 165n106
Oestereich v. Selective Serv. Sys.
 Local Bd. No. 11, 306n115
Oliver, In re, 157n51; 160n68;
 165n94
Olmstead v. United States, 303n105
Oregon v. Mitchell, 40n17; 57n18;
 138n77; 241n146
Organization for a Better Austin v.
 Keefe, 14n6; 261*; 306n113
Ortwein v. Schwab, 255n47

Palko v. Connecticut, 104n21;
 105n24-26; 106n28; 116n4; 156n38;
 165; 289n39; 361n30
Palmer v. Thompson, 231n84;
 245n8; 335n90
Paul v. Virginia, 56n12, 15
Pennsylvania v. Board of Trusts,
 230n79
Pennsylvania v. Brown, 230*
People v. Defore, 99n2; 303n102
Perisich v. Pennsylvania, 268n115
Peters v. Kiff, 165n109
Peterson v. City of Greenville,
 228n72

Phillips v. Martin Marietta Corp.,
 240n132
Phoenix v. Kolodziejski, 138n74
Pierce v. Society of Sisters,
 66n20; 104n16; 108; 340n104;
 120n13
Pittsburgh Press Co. v. Pittsburgh
 Comm'n on Human Relations,
 261n75
Plessy v. Ferguson, 206n78; 208; 214
Poe v. Ullman, 342n108
Pointer v. Texas, 155n36; 157n49;
 164n88
Police Dep't of City of Chicago v.
 Mosley, 14n6
Pollock v. Farmers Loan & Trust
 Co., 40n16
Powell v. Alabama, 104n18; 146n11;
 245n37
Powell v. McCormack, 60n1;
 139n86-92; 141n93-94; 143n102-103;
 144*; 144n105; 281n20; 292n52;
 314n15; 315
Powell v. Texas, 165n97
Presbyterian Church v. Hull
 Church, 173n23
Prigg v. Pennsylvania, 93n15
Prudential Ins. Co. v. Benjamin,
 56n14; 357n19
Public Serv. Comm'n v. Wycoff Co.,
 143*

Quantity of Books v. Kansas, 324n49
Queen v. Hicklin, 321n35

Rahrer, In re, 92n14
Railroad Comm'n v. Pullman Co.,
 290n45
Railroad Retirement Bd. v.
 Alton R.R., 102n10
Railway Express Agency, Inc. v.
 New York, 248n24; 338*; 364n36

# TABLE OF CASES

Rea v. United States, 66n19
Reed v. Reed, 260n72
Reid v. Cobert, 158n55
Reitman v. Mulkey, 229n74;
  230n76; 245n5; 264n94
Reynolds v. Sims, 131n44;
  137n66-69; 282n22
Richardson v. Belcher, 256n52
Richardson v. Ramirez, 262*
Roberts v. Noel, 276*
Robinson v. Cahill, 257n57
Rochin v. California, 155n36;
  156n39; 160n69; 289n40
Roe v. Wade, 10n4; 13n4; 14n11;
  15n13-15; 16n17-18; 17n20;
  20*; 55n10; 100n3; 265n98;
  341; 364n34
Rogers v. Bellei, 14n6
Rosenbloom v. Metromedia, Inc.,
  225n60
Rosenfeld v. New Jersey, 265n104;
  329n69
Ross v. Moffitt, 254n41
Roth v. United States, 320n33;
  321n36
Rowan v. United States Post
  Office Dep't, 324n47
Russell v. United States, 128n33

San Antonio Independent
  School Dist. v. Rodriguez,
  253n36; 257n56; 266*; 312n7, 9
Sanders v. United States, 284n29
Santa Clara County v. Southern
  Pac. R.R., 200n60
Scales v. United States, 127n24
Schaefer v. United States, 120n13
Schechter Poultry Corp. v.
  United States, 102n10
Schenck v. United States, 120n13
Schlesinger v. Reservist Comm. to
  Stop the War, 292*

Schneider v. New Jersey, 125;
  345n12
Schneider v. State, 125n9
School Bd. of Richmond v. State
  Bd. of Educ., 232n87
Sears, Roebuck & Co. v. Stiffel
  Co., 74n26
Seders v. Pennsylvania, 268n115
Senior v. Braden, 102n6
Serrano v. Priest, 257n57
Shapiro v. Thompson, 251n33;
  255n49; 264n96; 311n5;
  336n95; 364n35
Shelley v. Kraemer, 179n8;
  184; 212n6; 227; 230; 231; 234;
  245n3; 275n4; 354n14
Shelton v. Tucker, 224n53; 247n16
Sheppard v. Maxwell, 157n48
Sherbert v. Verner, 168n1;
  177n43; 268n117
Sierra Club v. Morton, 13n5; 292*
Sipuel v. Board of Regents of
  Univ. of Okla., 214n18
Skinner v. Oklahoma ex rel.
  Williamson, 133n46; 158n56;
  158n58; 250n27
Slaughter-House Cases, 53n4;
  183*; 184n19; 188n30; 189n31;
  233; 243n1; 245; 246n10; 335n93
Slochower v. Board of Higher
  Educ., 127n26; 128n29
Smith v. Allwright, 179n5; 212n5
South Carolina v. Katzenbach, 30*
Stanley v. Georgia, 55n10;
  341n105; 342
Stanley v. Illinois, 301n93;
  310n130-131
Steele v. Louisville & N.R.R.,
  179n4
Stein v. New York, 154n28
Steward Machine Co. v. Davis,
  103n14
Stovall v. Denno, 76*; 296n71,
  73, 76

Strauder v. West Virginia,
206n76
Street v. New York, 329n72
Stromberg v. California, 108; 110
Sugarman v. Dougall, 259n69;
308n123
Swafford v. Templeton, 130n39
Swann v. Charlotte-Mecklenburg
Bd. of Educ., 231n86
Sweatt v. Painter, 214n18

Takahashi v. Fish & Game
Comm'n, 182n16
Tate v. Short, 14n6; 255n45;
265n103
Taylor v. Hayes, 222*
Terminiello v. Chicago, 329n66
Terry v. Adams, 212n5
Terry v. Ohio, 158*
Thomas v. Arizona, 154n29
Thompson v. Louisville, 1*;
1n1; 157n53; 160n73; 164*
Tidewater Oil Co. v. United
States, 352n8
Tilton v. Richardson, 173n22
Time, Inc. v. Hill, 225n59; 328n60
Tinker v. Des Moines School
Dist., 138n81
Toledo Newspaper Co. v.
United States, 120n14
Tot v. United States, 160n65;
309n126
Townsend v. Sain, 284n27-28;
302n97
Truax v. Corrigan, 187n28
Tumey v. Ohio, 276*
Twining v. New Jersey,
105n23
Two Guys from Harrison-Allentown
Inc. v. McGinley, 172n17

United Mine Workers v. Illinois
Bar Ass'n, 222n42; 328n62
United States v. Ash, 165n101
United States v. Butler, 62n10-11;
83n48; 102n10; 176n38;
308n120
United States v. Calandra,
161n75
United States v. Carolene
Products Co., 108n29; 126n13
United States v. Classic, 82n45-46;
179n6
United States v. Cruikshank,
210n93
United States v. Curtiss-Wright
Export Co., 57n20; 87; 90n9-10;
177n41
United States v. Darby, 55n8; 103*
United States v. Guest, 194*;
236n114
United States v. Harris, 210n93
United States v. Jackson, 295n64;
298n83
United States v. Jones, 141n96
United States v. Kras, 255n47
United States v. Lovett, 127n21
United States v. Miller, 53n4
United States v. Nixon, 28n4;
91n11; 315n19
Unites States v. O'Donnell, 344n112
United States v. Paramount
Pictures, Inc., 320n29
United States v. Price, 194*;
236n111
United States v. Raines, 273*
United States v. Richardson,
292*; 294*
United States v. Romano, 309n125
United States v. Rumely, 53n6
United States v. SCRAP, 292*
United States v. Seale, 222*

United States v. South-Eastern
　Underwriters Ass'n, 56n11
United States v. United States
　Dist. Ct., 91n11
United States v. Vuitch, 17n21
United States v. Wade, 17n19;
　68n4; 165n101; 296n77
United States v. Williams,
　236n112-113
United States Dep't of Agriculture
　v. Moreno, 256n53; 278n7
United States Dep't of Agriculture
　v. Murry, 308n124; 310n131
United States ex rel. Toth v.
　Quarles, 158n55
United Transp. Union v. State
　Bar, 222n42; 328n62
Uphaus v. Wyman, 1n1; 74n27;
　233n50

Virginian Ry. v. System Fed'n
　No. 40, 67n21
Vlandis v. Kline, 253n36; 310n131

WMCA, Inc., v. Lomenzo, 138n71
Walz v. Tax Comm'n, 14n6;
　173n24; 174n25-27; 174-175n30;
　334n87
Ward v. Texas, 157n41
Warden v. Hayden, 158*
Washington v. Texas, 164n92
Watkins v. United States, 128n30
Watson v. City of Memphis,
　218n31
Watts v. Indiana, 152n21-22;
　153n26; 155n35; 156n37
Weber v. Aetna Cas. & Sur. Co.,
　258n62
Welsh v. United States, 269n120
Wesberry v. Sanders, 53n5; 74n26;
　137n64-65

West Coast Hotel Co. v. Parish,
　102n12
West Virginia State Bd. of
　Educ. v. Barnette, 267n113
Wheeler v. Barrera, 173n22
Whitney v. California, 108;
　120n15; 197n51
Wieman v. Updegraff, 127n22
Wiley v. Sinkler, 130n39
Wilkinson v. United States, 74n27;
　128n32
Williams v. Florida, 158*
Williams v. Illinois, 14n6; 254n44;
　265n103
Williams v. Rhodes, 138n84;
　263n89
Williams v. United States,
　236n112; 298n88
Williamson v. Lee Optical, Inc.,
　250n29
Willing v. Chicago Auditorium
　Ass'n, 142n97-98
Winters v. New York, 320n27
Wisconsin v. Yoder, 14n6; 14n10;
　270n123
Wolf v. Colorado, 66n16-17;
　78n31; 159n60-61; 161; 291n49;
　300n90; 303n101; 303n103; 320n32
Worcester v. Georgia, 28*

Yates v. United States, 127n25;
　128n28
Yellin v. United States, 128n33
Yick Wo v. Hopkins, 206n77;
　246n11
Younger v. Harris, 68n1; 291n47
Youngstown Sheet & Tube Co.
　v. Sawyer, 55n9; 57n21

Zorach v. Clauson, 171n15
Zschernig v. Miller, 55n8

# SUBJECT INDEX

Abortion cases
  as judicial legislation, 16-17
  compelling governmental interest test applied, 15
  generally, 15-21
  judicial review and foreign courts, 28
  late pregnancy abortion rule, 17
  post viability examples of justified abortions, 18-19
  premature babies, 17*
  two state interests recognized, 15-16
  unborn child's right to death, 17
  viability as disputable value judgment, 16-17
  what they show, 100

Abstention doctrine
  Black's (Mr. Justice Hugo) refinement, 291

Accusatorial system
  enshrined in the Constitution, 156
  inquisitorial distinguished, 155-156
  self-incrimination privilege as keystone, 333

Adam Smith, 116

Adams, President John
  "midnight appointments", 72

Admiralty
  federal judicial power of, 91-92

Advisory opinions
  adjudication of cases and controversies distinguished, 300
  dicta as moving Court closer to writing, 300-302
  examples, 300-302

Advisory opinions—Cont'd
  primary function of opinions, 299-300
  rule against, 299-300
  rule formulation as tantamount to, 302-303

Agar, Herbert
  peace defined, 115

Aliens
  discrimination against, 201-202

Amendments, Rescission of ratification. *See* Equal Rights Amendment

American Bar Association
  Bill of Rights Committee, x
  citadel of conservatism, ix
  Grenville Clark's address, x

American Civil Liberties Union, 127
  and exclusionary rule, 161

American melting pot, 2

American society
  five major flaws, 98-99, 274

Anarchists
  potential for harm, vii

Appellate jurisdiction
  congressional power to abrogate, 29-30*
  Court's narrow interpretation of statutes limiting, 306-307

Appellate review
  bargained guilty pleas insulated from, 295
  costs waived for indigent defendants, 254

Articles of Confederation
Tenth Amendment contrasted,
94-95

Austin, John
court's creativity as source of law,
78

Avins, Alfred, 200*

Berle, Adolph, 271*

Bickel, Prof. Alexander
on judicial review, 37-38
prudential adjudication, 5, 20
Wechsler-Bickel debate, 4-5, 20

Bill of attainder, 127; 146

Bill of Rights. *See also* Incorporation doctrine
and the state criminal process, 158
complete and literal incorporation into 14th Amendment, 169
expansively interpreted, cases, 165-166
incorporation doctrine questioned, 197
juvenile delinquency proceedings, 165
purpose for which devised, 331

Black Codes
Constitutors intentions, 183-184

Black, Mr. Justice Hugo, 7
and constitution-making, 74
appointment to Court, 103
child benefit theory, 170
constitution as Holy Writ, 74
defense of selective incorporation position, 163
on governmental power, 70
on implied powers of judicial review, 24

Black, Mr. Justice Hugo—Cont'd
on incorporation doctrine, 150, 161-163
on judicial review, 68-71
on lawmaking authority, 70
on "manufactured crime", 150
on pre-1937 substantive due process, 74-75
on superiority of Anglo-American notions of justice, 156
one man, one vote, 137
tyranny defined, 150-151, 157
wall of separation doctrine in Establishment Clause, 170-171, 173, 334

Black Panthers
minority group solidarity, 3-4

Black slavery. *See also* Discrimination, Racial; Minority groups
special constitutional status of problems, 13

Blackstone, Sir William
external sources as court's discovery of law, 78

Boston Tea Party
analogy to Columbia University tenant uprising, 119

Brandeis, Mr. Justice Louis D., 4
jurisdiction of federal courts, 51
on avoiding judicial review, 50-52

Brennan, Mr. Justice William
courtroom as a political forum, 221
Establishment Clause, 169
his "rules of practice", 273*
on legislative reapportionment, 132-138
on political questions, 134
on standing to sue, 134

SUBJECT INDEX 421

Burger, Mr. Chief Justice W. E.
on the two religion clauses, 174
three-part test on Establishment
Clause, 174-175

Capital punishment. *See* Cruel
and unusual punishment—death
penalty

Cardozo, Mr. Justice Benjamin N.
incorporation doctrine, 104-107.
*See also* Incorporation doctrine
"interstitial" lawmaking, 64**

Carolene Products footnote, 121
and "corrective political
processes", 126
and "fundamental rights", 266
constitutional interpretation
theories embodied, 111-112
discussed, 108-112
Frankfurter's (Mr. Justice Felix)
repudiation, 313-314
genesis and development, 108*
subject matter, 108
wording
as amended, 110
as first circulated among
Justices, 108-109

Case or controversy
underlying conception, 304

Center for the Study of
Democratic Institutions, x

Central Intelligence Agency
taxpayer attack denied standing,
294*

Certiorari
neutral principles of granting
or denying, 5

Certiorari—Cont'd
procedures, 355
Rule of Four, 345, 347-348
sanctioned in Judiciary Act of
1925, 290-291, 345
Wechslerian view of grant or
denial, 344

Child benefit theory. *See*
Establishment Clause

Citizenship
"citizens" in the Privileges or
Immunities Clause, 202-203
defined, 196
dual citizenship, 192-193
federal and state distinguished,
191-192
suspect basis of classification,
258-259

Civil disobedience
moral justification, 1

Civil liberties
beautiful mystery explained, 115
concern for as ambivalent
sloppiness, 115

Civil order
key to the problem, 119-120
tension as product of pursuit for,
119

Civil rights
law school grading systems, 3
Louisiana pilotage laws, 3
public accommodations, 22

Civil Rights Acts. *See also*
Voting rights
cited, 203n67
1866 Act
citizenship provision set out,
196*
interpreted, 190*

Civil Rights Acts—Cont'd
1866 Act—Cont'd
  legislative history, 197
  present form set out, 212
  privileges and immunities of federal citizenship, 202
1871 Act
  interpreted, 190*
1875 Act, 204
1964 Act, 22
  employment provisions Title VII, 239-240
  public accommodations Title II
    constitutionality upheld, 239
    provisions, 238-239
    response to Court-to-Congress signal for help, 234
1968 Act
  housing provisions Title VIII, 241-242
old Acts
  civil provisions broadened, 237
  criminal provisions currently, 235-236
  exhumed, 234-238
  new supplemental federal legislation, 238
  prosecution of murders of Mississippi civil rights workers, 236

Civil Rights Cases. See Table of Cases for cites

Civil War amendments. See United States Constitution

Clark, Grenville
  acknowledgment, ix-xi
  and F.D.R., xi
  dedication, iii
  two Supreme Court briefs, x

Clark, Mr. Justice Tom
  Austinian position on law's source, 78
  on exclusionary rule, 161

Classification in statutes. See also Compelling governmental interest test
  all legislation as involving, 249
  compelling governmental interest test applied, 253
  racial classification as inherently suspect, 250-251
  certain classifications of persons, 253
  citizenship, 258-259
  poverty (three dissenting justices), 256
  race, 245-46, 250-51
  sex (four Justices), 260

Collateral attack on convictions. See also Habeas Corpus
  expanded availability on criminal detention, 282-288
  magistrate's fine, 276*
  New York rule, 283

Columbia University
  student rebellion's effect, 116-118
  tenant uprising, 117-118

Columbia University law school
  conceptions of Court and Constitution, 24-25

Commerce Clause. See United States Constitution

Commission on Revision of the Federal Court Appellate System
  correction of Court's caseload situation, 353*

Communist Party
  criminal convictions of organizers, 127-128
  post-World War II fears, 126-128

Compelling governmental interest test. *See also* Classification in statutes
  and right to vote, 251
  and sterilization of habitual criminals, 250
  applied to suspect sex classifications, 261
  applied to voting rights, 262
  device to mask basis of decision, 308
  "fundamental right" terminology used, 252
  fundamental rights branch
    "fundamental" defined, 311
    Harlan's (Mr. Justice John M.) objection to, 264
    substantive due process distinguished verbally only, 266
    wholly subjective, 311-312
  presumption of constitutionality reversed, 265
  strict standard of judicial review, 249-251
  suspect basis of classification traced to Carolene Products footnote, 311-312
  welfare waiting periods, 251-252 invalidated, 264

Conclusive presumptions. *See* Statutory interpretation

Confessions
  admissibility when obtained by torture, 146

Confessions—Cont'd
  and Court's aptitude for factfinding, 152-155
  Court's development of rules, 151
  involuntary
    as dictatorial criminal procedure, 151
    excessive pressure standard, 151-152, 157
    spontaneous distinguished, 151-152
  racial element in Court's criminal process concerns, 247
  reliability approach rejected, 155
  unnecessary delay between arrest and appearance, 145
  voluntary
    as mixed question of law and fact, 153
    trial judge's responsibility to assess, 154

Congressional investigations
  power denied to expose for sake of exposure, 128

Constitutional interpretation. *See also* Statutory interpretation.
  Court's declaration of constitutional rules distinguished, 75-76
  fundamental principle, 111
  implied power doctrine. *See* Judicial power — implied power
  political questions. *See* Political questions
  preferred position theory
    as explanation of Court's decisions, 112
    described, 111-112
    illustrated, 125

Constitutional interpretation—
Cont'd
prospectivity doctrine
as arbitrary discrimination, 297
as exposing judicial
constitution-making, 76-79
Black's (Mr. Justice Hugo)
fears, 79
first ruling discussed, 77-79,
279
illogically limited, 295
limiting the doctrine, 76*
pure and impure, 296-297
purpose, 288
seamy side noted, 298-299
selectively incorporated, 164
retroactivity doctrine
basis for denying, 78
Constitution as neither
prohibiting nor requiring, 78
milestone in development, 299
pandora's box, 76-77
right to counsel, 76-77, 165n108

Constitutional law. *See also* United
States Supreme Court
compelling governmental interest
test, 15, 249-53, 261-62, 264-66
"deliberate speed" doctrine, 65
neutral principles, 4-5
result-oriented adjudication
disapproved, 4-5
"separate but equal" doctrine,
65

Constitutional rules. *See* United
States Constitution; United States
Supreme Court

Constitutors
consistency in imposition of
criminal safeguards, 146
constitutive intent
defined, 45

Constitutors—Cont'd
defined, 46
intentions, 97
judicial review overrides duty to
express will of, 73
legislators compared, 46
national objectives ascribable,
109
view of slavery, 183-185

Court martial jurisdiction
non-service-connected crimes,
165

Court of Claims Act, 141-142

Criminal law administration. *See
also* Criminal procedure
accusatorial and inquisitorial
systems distinguished, 155-156
callous formalism of the 1930's,
146-150
Court's 1937-1961 rulings, cases,
160-161
relaxation of some federal
standards, 158*
state and federal standards
raised, 158

Criminal procedure. *See also*
Criminal law administration
and accusatorial system, 155-156
Court's broad intervention, 159
new safeguards, cases, 157
relaxation of some federal
standards, 158*
revolutionary change documented,
161-166

Cruel and unusual punishment
death penalty, 166
constitutionality, 14
unconstitutional as
administered, 248
unconstitutional per se, 248
selectively incorporated, 165

De facto segregation. *See*
Desegregation, Public schools
de Tocqueville, Alexis
adjudication of political
questions, 28
Death penalty. *See* Cruel and
unusual punishment

Declaratory judgments
as facet of justiciability
question, 141-142
federal courts barred from
entering, 142
Taney's (Mr. Chief Justice
Roger) opinion, 141

Definitions
constitution-making, 59*
constitutive intent, 45
constitutors, 46
definitive judicial review, 50
elected officials, 46-47
governmental powers, 53-54
judicial review
definitive, 50
tentative, 47
large social change, 278*
lawmaking, 59*
legislative history, 45
legislative intent, 45
limitations on governmental
powers, 54
lower courts, 47
ordered liberty, 105-107. *See also*
Ordered liberty
tentative judicial review, 47

Delay in the courts
advantages for convicted clients
after Fay v. Noia, 285-286

Desegregation, Public facilities
cases, 219
Virginia's massive resistance,
220-221

Desegregation, Public schools. *See
also* Schools, Public
all-white private school
movement, 232
busing to accomplish, 231-232
Brown opinion
criticism, 216
deliberate speed doctrine,
216-219
departure from Brandeis's
Ashwander principles, 215
congressional action as decisive
factor, 218
de facto segregation
Court's readiness to provide
judicial remedies, 232
de jure segregation distinguished, 232
defined, 232
deep South states, 217-218
deliberate speed doctrine
abandoned, 219
federal financial assistance, effect
on, 218
form of Court's resistance to
segregationist counterattack,
220
local school boards responsibility,
219

Discrimination, Private
Congress denied power to
prohibit, 193
recent Congressional regulation,
235

Discrimination, Racial. *See also*
Freedom of expression
aberrational decisions, 335
and the Civil Rights Cases,
204-206
anti-Negro as standing in class
by itself, 328
Civil War Amendments as
reflecting national allergy,
246-247

Discrimination, Racial—Cont'd
  Commerce Clause's use to combat, 239
  concept broadened in school cases, 214
  Court's interest in criminal process related, 227
  definitive judicial review recommended, 359-360
  housing, 229
  Japanese evacuation of 1942, 211-212
  privately owned restaurants, 184-88
  racial segregation as a form?, 197
  Slaughter-House Case's effect, 189

Discrimination, Sex
  legal sources, 259

Diversity jurisdiction
  reason for, 187

Double jeopardy
  racial element in Court's criminal process concerns, 247
  selectively incorporated, 165
  strict sixth amendment standard, 145-146

Douglas, Mr. Justice William O.
  impeachment attempts, 9
  one man, one vote, 137
  sterilization of habitual criminals, 158

Dred Scott decision. *See* United States Supreme Court

Due process
  substantive
    Black (Mr. Justice Hugo) on pre-1937 views, 74-75
    framers intentions doubted, 197
    prior to Court's 1937-38 Term, 103*

Due process—Cont'd
  substantive—Cont'd
    reappearance under privacy banner, 337
    use of to justify constitution-making, 98
Due Process Clause
  deactivation as protector of laissez faire, 201
  Equal Protection and Privileges or Immunities clauses compared, 181-182

Eisenhower, Dwight D.
  and the Democratic solid South, 209
Elected officials
  defined, 46-47
Electoral rights. *See* Voting rights
Emancipation Proclamation, 4
Equal Protection Clause
  and legislative reapportionment, 130-138
  discrimination against aliens as presumptive violation, 202
  Due Process and Privileges or Immunities clauses compared, 181-182
  invidious official discrimination, 132-133
  state enforcement of racial covenants, 179-180
Equal Rights Amendment
  effective date, 260
  legality of rescission of ratification, 259*
  states approving, 259-260
  states rescinding, 259*
  wording set out, 259

Equity courts
  discretionary power to shape remedies, 216
Espionage Act cases, 120
Establishment Clause. *See also* Free Exercise Clause
  application to states as judicial constitution-making, 171
  basic thrust as now applied, 177
  Bible reading in public schools, 172
  Black's (Mr. Justice Hugo) reinterpretation, 170-171, 173
  blue laws upheld, 172
  Brennan's (Mr. Justice William) opinion, 169-170
  child benefit theory, 170
  Constitutors' original intent, 168
  Court's intense interest, 176
  Court's rewriting, 167
  establishment defined, 169
  federal taxpayers standing to litigate, 176-178
  function, 167
  grants to religious schools, 176-177
  official interpretaion presently, 170
  original intention, 169
  prayer recitation in schools, 172
  released time program in public schools, 171
  three-part test
    entanglement test
      "entanglement" as fuzzy metaphoric term, 176
      lineage traced, 175-176
      set out, 174
    wall of separation doctrine, 170-171, 173, 334
      strict formulation repudiated, 174
Ex post facto laws, 146

Exclusionary rule, 161
  Cardozo's (Mr. Justice Benjamin N.) maxim, 303
  selective incorporation engenders harmless constitutional error, 289

Fairman, Charles, 197*, 198*, 200*
Federal question
  dismissal of appeals for want of substantiality, 346-347
Federalist Papers
  Hamilton, Alexander in No. 78, 72
  judiciary as least dangerous branch, 72
Federalist Party
  and the Judiciary, 72
Federal Kidnapping Act
  capital punishment authorized, 295
  invalidated, 298
Fee system
  and magistrate's fines, 276*
Felony murder
  and the murder of Wolfgang Friedmann, 286*-287
  New York provisions, 286*-287
Finality of judgment
  concept stretched in recent case, 261*
Flag salute ceremony
  Jehovah's Witnesses, x, 267
Ford Foundation
  Center for the Study of Democratic Institutions, x
Ford, President Gerald R.
  attempt to impeach Justice Douglas, 9

428   SUBJECT INDEX

Foreign affairs
   as example of doctrine of implied power, 85-90
   Henkin, Prof. Louis on, 86-90
   power to regulate
      assumed rather than conferred, 87
      domestic affairs distinguished, 87-89
      resides in the President, 90-91

Fourteenth Amendment. *See* United States Constitution—Amendments

Franchise. *See* Voting rights

Frankfurter, Mr. Justice Felix, 2
   jurors and community standards, 153-154
   on legislative reapportionment, 130

Franklin, Benjamin, 22
   on honesty, 351

Free Exercise Clause. *See also* Establishment Clause
   Constitutors original intent, 168
   Court's rewriting, 167
   function, 167
   primary thrust, 177
   religious hardship cases, 268-270
   super-equal protection clause, 267

Freedom of expression. *See also* Discrimination, Racial
   affected by desegregation obstructionism, 219-220
   and American Civil Liberties Union, 127
   and bills of attainder, 127
   and Communist Party, 126-129
   and League of Women Voters, 127
   and loyalty oaths, 127

Freedom of expression—Cont'd
   and obscenity, 129
   and racial discrimination
      associational privacy case, 224
      courtroom expression as by-product, 221-222*
      illustrative of Court's de-emphasis of race factor, 247
      membership list cases, 223-224
      provocative expression protected, 222-223
      statements about official conduct of public officials, 225
      Virginia's curbing of NAACP, 220-222
   definitive judicial review recommended, 360
   dissident political organizations, 126-129
   election day as giving practical value to, 129
   laissez-faire economics analogized, 115-116
   major cases discussed, 124-130
   obscenity as major aberration, 319
   political, 138
   two conflicting public objectives, 125
   two Hughes (Mr. Chief Justice C. E.) opinions, 111
   vagaries — cases, 328-330

Freedom Rider cases, xi

Freund, Prof. Paul A.
   National Court of Appeals recommended, 352-353

Friedmann, Wolfgang
   trial of alleged murderers described, 286*-287

Friendly, Judge Henry J., ix-x

# SUBJECT INDEX 429

Fund for the Republic, x

Gandhi, Indira
  constitutional crisis in India, 33**-34
Gibson v. Florida Legislative Investigation Committee, 224n54
Gompers, Samuel, 4
Government
  cardinal duty, 122
  services dispensed and regulation by distinguished and described, 277-279
Governmental powers
  Black's (Mr. Justice Hugo) comments, 70
  characterized prior to Court's 1937-38 Term, 102
  defined, 53-54
  lack of powers — cases
    allocation of power to one governmental organ, 55-56
    ante- and post-1937 views, 55-56
    privacy cases, 55-56
  lawmaking and constitution-making
    legislature's primary authority, 61
    nonexclusivity of grant to Congress, 61-62
  lawmaking as one principal power, 59
  Marshall's (Mr. Chief Justice John) comments, 81
  power not granted as power denied, 177
  powers and limitations on powers
    Constitutor's understanding, 55
    definitive judicial review as factor in limitation cases, 57-58

Governmental powers—Cont'd
  powers and limitations on powers —Cont'd
    distinguished, 53-54
    Marshall's (Mr. Chief Justice John) distinction, 85
    reasons for distinguishing, 54-55
    rational relationship test. See Rational relationship test
Great Britain
  constitution
    Britisher's conception, 33
    U. S. Constitution compared, 33-35
    Young's (Prof. W. F., Jr.) comments, 34*
  courts
    lawmaking in opinions, 62
    homogeneity of population, 34
Great Depression
  perceptions of Court's role, 102
Guerrilla warfare
  Symbionese Liberation Army, 4

Habeas Corpus. *See also* Collateral attack on convictions
  caseload results of Fay v. Noia, 285
  1867 Act
    Brennan's (Mr. Justice William) rationale, 284
    main purpose, 284
    newly construed, 283-288
    evidentiary hearings requirement, 284
  federal habeas and jailhouse lawyers, 295
Hague, Mayor Frank, x
Hamilton, Alexander
  on judicial review, 31-32

Handler, Milton, 271*
Harlan, Mr. Justice John M., ix-x
Harmless constitutional error
  Harlan's (Mr. Justice John M.)
    disapproval, 290
  prior to "selective incorporation"
    era, 289
  selective incorporation doctrine's
    effect, 290
Henkin, Prof. Louis
  foreign affairs powers, 86-90
Hitler, Adolf
  American values affected by,
    113-114
Hohfeld, Wesley Newcomb
  eight categories of analytical
    jurisprudence, 113*
Holmes, Mr. Justice Oliver Wendell
  Sacco and Vanzetti case, 146
Hoover, Herbert
  and the Democratic solid South,
    209
House Un-American Activities
  Committee, 128, 294
Housing
  landlord-tenant relationships,
    256-257
Hughes, Mr. Chief Justice Charles
  Evans
  and Carolene Products footnote,
    110-111
Hyphenated Americans, 2


Illegitimate birth
  resultant legal disabilities violate
    equal protection, 258
Impeachment
  Douglas, Justice William O., 9
  Warren, Chief Justice Earl, 9

Implied powers doctrine. See
  Judicial power
Impoundment of funds
  judicial review and foreign courts,
    28
Incorporation doctrine. See also
  Bill of Rights
  and Carolene Products footnote,
    110
  Cardozo's (Mr. Justice Benjamin
    N.) language, 162***
  effects, cases, 165-166
  explained, 104-105
  Fourth Amendment, 159
  full incorporation, 162
  holdings contra, 105
  selective incorporation, 161-166
    Black's (Mr. Justice Hugo)
      defense, 163
    cases, 164-165
    devise to mask basis of decision,
      308
    effect on state prosecutions,
      290
    practical utility, 163-164
    statements of the 1930's, 150
India
  imminence of civil disobedience,
    33**-34
Indigent defendants
  costs of appellate review waived,
    254
  court fees waived in divorce cases,
    255
  right to appointment of defense
    counsel, 254
  working off fines in jail, 254-255
Inquisitorial system
  accusatorial distinguished,
    155-156
Interstate Commerce Act
  racial segregation in interstate
    rail travel, 179

# SUBJECT INDEX 431

Jackson, Andrew
  and Court's constitutional interpretations, 28*
  Arthur Schlesinger, Jr.'s views, 28*

Jackson, Mr. Justice Robert
  on reliability standard in confessions, 155

Jailhouse lawyers, 295

Japanese Americans
  evacuation orders of 1942, 211-212

Jefferson, Thomas, 116
  and Court's constitutional interpretations, 28
  implied Congressional power, 23

Jehovah's Witnesses
  and Free Exercise Clause, 268
  distribution of religious literature, 124
  flag salute case, x, 267

Judicial activism
  debates among Justices, 74-75
  denigrated, 5

Judicial power. *See also* Judicial review
  admiralty, 91-92
  constitution-making power
    abstention doctrine as softening impact, 291
    adjudication subordinated in desegregation case, 216
    application of Establishment Clause to states, 171
    as offending Article V of Constitution, 79
    as offending separation of powers principle, 79
    Black (Mr. Justice Hugo) as participant, 74
    by dictum, 300-302, 320-321

Judicial power—Cont'd
  constitution-making power —Cont'd
    compelling governmental interest test as formula for justifying, 264
    Court's failure to explain source of its authority, 101
    defined, 59*
    example set forth, 67
    existence demonstrated, 73-74
    Hamilton's (Alexander) rejection of idea, 72
    judicial candor in acknowledgment of use, 355-356
    lawmaking power distinguished, 59
    methods for masking the basis, 308-310
    Miranda as illustrative, 280-282
    prospectively applied rulings, 76-79
    prospectivity doctrine as affirming Court's power, 78-79
    selective incorporation doctrine, 163
    Supreme Court refuses to acknowledge engagement in, 74
    two elements, 107
    two principal questions, 97
    use of substantive due process to justify, 98
  Constitution's Art. III, Sec. 2 set out, 133*
  control over legal profession, 280-281
  dangers of usurpation, 24
  implied power
    application of power illustrated, 85-86

Judicial power—Cont'd
  implied power—Cont'd
    as explanation of Court's decisions, 112
    as neutral principle?, 270
    Black's (Mr. Justice Hugo) views, 24
    Carolene Products footnote's effect, 111-112
    classic theory of judicial review superseded, 25
    concept defined, 21
    Court criticized for manner in which assumed, 24
    implications of the concept, 25
    implied Congressional power compared, 23
    interpretation of constitutional text differentiated, 22
    judicial candor in acknowledgment of use, 355-356
    President's powers in foreign affairs, 90-91
    purposes for which used, 97-98
    question on which legitimacy turns, 24
    raison d'etre, 92
    reposes in Supreme Court and Congress, 81-82
    skepticism towards the concept, 25
    Slaughter-House ruling as unwise exercise, 198-200
    source of doctrine, 81
    Stone's (Mr. Justice Harlan) continuance of doctrine, 83
    usefulness in observing constitutional phenomena, 26
    vague and illusory principle?, 22
  Justice's failure to deal with distinctions in, 75
  lawmaking power
    admiralty, 92

Judicial power—Cont'd
  lawmaking power—Cont'd
    as implied beyond powers expressly granted, 92-93
    Black's (Mr. Justice Hugo) comments, 70, 74
    by dictum, 65-66
    Cardozo on "interstitial" lawmaking, 64**
    constitution-making power distinguished, 59
    constitutional controls described, 60
    defined, 59*
    difficulty of courts in fact collecting, 233
    Great Britain's courts, 62
    legislation distinguished, 59*
    narrow vs. broad dispositions of cases, 65
    shift from Congress to Court, 100
    six aspects, 63-67
    two principal questions, 97
    propriety of Court to exert raw power, 75
    unwarranted assumption in some cases, 24
    White's (Justice Byron) remarks, 20*
Judicial review. *See also* Judicial power; United States Supreme Court
  absence as effecting national schemes of other countries, 42
  act of sovereignty, 27*
  ancient litany recited, 62n11
  avoidance
    Brandeis's (Mr. Justice L. D.) seven practices, 50-52
    other techniques, 52-53
    Bickel's (Prof. Alexander) comments, 37-38

SUBJECT INDEX 433

Judicial review—Cont'd
  Black (Mr. Justice Hugo) on, 68-71
  broad categories of constitutional
    cases listed, 53-54
  buttress' failures of majoritarian
    legislation, 38-39
  Constitutors' silence as expanding
    review, 78-79
  "construction" to avoid
    constitutional doubt, 53
  Court's power traced to source,
    27-30
  definitive review
    as implied judicial
      constitution-making, 74-75
    defined and described, 50
    fields in which Court should
      retain, 359-361
    government powers — cases, 57
    limitations on government
      powers — cases, 57-58
    precedent for substitution of
      tentative, 357
    "silence of Congress" cases, 56,
      92
    statutory interpretation
      distinguished, 62
    substantive due process cases,
      98
    Tenth Amendment cases, 56-57
  Dred Scott case, 43
  duty to enforce will of
    Constitutors contrasted, 73
  effect of Palko v. Connecticut,
    106-107
  evaluations of broadened
    conception, 79-81
  existence denied, 130
  Gibson's (Chief Justice,
    Pennsylvania) dissent, 27*
  Hamilton, Alexander in the 78th
    Federalist, 72
  Hamilton's (Alexander) views,
    31-32

Judicial review—Cont'd
  Holmes' (Mr. Justice O. W.)
    comment, 50*
  in heterogeneous cultures
    devices in constitution-making
      which mitigate problems, 36
    heterogeneous defined, 35-36
    homogeneous cultures
      contrasted, 35
  in homogeneous cultures
    homogeneous defined, 35
    necessity negated, 34-35
  Justice's failure to deal with
    distinctions in, 75
  lawmaking in judicial opinions
    distinguished, 62
  Marbury v. Madison conception
    as no longer adequately
      descriptive, 73
    as orthodox conception, 273
    constitution-making by dictum,
      300
    Court's emancipation from,
      illustrated, 280-282
    inverted in Miranda and
      Powell, 281
    Marshall's fundamental point,
      71
    Marshall's (Mr. Chief Justice
      John) position, 73
    source of doctrine, 70-73
    two bodies of pre-existing law
      as controlling decision, 72-73
  Marshall, Mr. Chief Justice John,
    70
  means of keeping peace, 38
  Mill's (John Stuart) observations,
    30**-31
  misuse by Justices and its
    consequences, 39-44
  nature of hazard involved in
    abuse, 13
  new conception, 78
  Nixon appointees, 14

Judicial review—Cont'd
  older conception, 143
  one clear advantage, 34
  passive posture
    abandoned by 1965, 275
    as character of pre-1937
      rulings, 273
  peril inherent in employing, 50
  popular sovereignty as
    dangerous alternative, 41
  post-1937-38 Term applications,
    112-114
  protection of states' rights, 57
  Rehnquist's (Justice W.) position,
    13-14
  Roberts (Mr. Justice Owen J.) on,
    62
  special contribution to feasibility
    of constitutional government,
    32-33
  standards applied
    compelling governmental
      interest test, 249-251
    rational relationship test,
      248-250
  Supreme Court's conception,
    13-20
  Sutherland's (Mr. Justice George)
    narrow framework, 274
  tentative review
    common law adjudication
      differentiated, 49-50
    Congress' power to take away
      what Court has given, 235
    defined and described, 47-50
    fields in which Court should
      employ, 361-366
    foreclosed by Slaughter-House
      decision, 199
    more frequent use suggested,
      356
    net effect, 49
    rationale, 48, 357
    "silence of Congress" cases, 56,
      98

Judicial review—Cont'd
  tentative review—Cont'd
    Slaughter-House and Civil
      Rights Cases as blocking
      Court's access, 233
    statutory interpretation
      compared, 62
    two forms, 47
    two major aspects of drastic
      contraction, 337
    Young's (Prof. W. F. Jr.,)
      comments on American
      experience, 34*
Judiciary Act of 1789
  removal provisions, 187-188
Judiciary Act of 1925
  discretionary denial of certiorari
    sanctioned, 290-291
Juries
  and community standards,
    153-154
  and credibility of witnesses,
    152-154
  and "ought" questions, 153
  discrimination in selection,
    165-166
  federal standards relaxed, 158*
  judges of law and fact, 153
Jurisdiction. See Appellate
  jurisdiction
Jury selection
  discrimination against
    Mexican-Americans, 233
Jury trials
  selective incorporation cases,
    164-165
  unanimous guilty verdicts, 14
Justice
  defined, 1*
Justiciability
  declaratory relief as a facet, 141
  doctrinal morass, 135*
  roots of the notion, 133

Justiciability—Cont'd
  Warren's (Mr. Chief Justice Earl)
    conception, 140-141
Juvenile delinquents
  safeguards for proceedings in re,
    165

Kunstler, William
  comments on the murder of
    Wolfgang Friedmann, 287
Ku Klux Klan
  and private terrorism, 210
  Court's response to violence, 210
  statutory responses to their
    actions, 210

Laissez-faire economics
  analogy to freedom of speech and
    press, 115-116
Law offices. *See also* Wall Street
    law firms
  law school egalitarianism as
    facilitating discrimination, 3
Law schools
  coarsening of grading systems, 3
  egalitarianism, 3
Lawyers
  defense of clients by obstructive
    tactics, 221*
League of Women Voters, 127
Legal rights
  and federal jurisdiction, 133
  and Marbury conception of
    judicial review, 274
  constitutional violation as ipso
    facto violation of, 143*
  violation as essential to existence
    of "case or controversy", 143

Legislative reapportionment. *See
    also* Voting rights
  Black (Mr. Justice Hugo) on one
    man, one vote. 137
  Douglas (Mr. Justice William) on
    one person, one vote, 137
  judicial review and foreign courts,
    28
  malapportionment cases after
    Baker v. Carr, 137-138
  Tennessee constitution, 132
Legislators. *See also* Legislature
  constitutors compared, 46
  legislative intent
    defined, 45
    legislative history as technique
      for determining, 45
Legislature. *See also* Legislators
  defined, 46
  primary authority
    constitution-making power, 61
    lawmaking power, 50, 61
    "silence of Congress" cases, 67
Libel
  statements about official conduct
    of public officials, 225
Lincoln, Abraham
  and Dred Scott decision, 28
  on fooling the people, 351
Literacy tests
  limited then abolished, 240-241
Loyalty oaths, 127

Madison, James, 22
Malcolm X
  minority group solidarity, 3
Mandamus. *See* Judicial review;
  Marbury v. Madison, in Table of
  Cases

## SUBJECT INDEX

Marbury v. Madison. *See* Judicial review; Table of Cases.

Marshall, Louis, 4

Marshall, Mr. Chief Justice John
genesis of judicial review, 70
implied Congressional power, 23
Marbury v. Madison
fundamental point, 71
his position, 73
rejoinder to attack on McCulloch v. Maryland, 23

Marshall, Mr. Justice Thurgood, 4

Martin Luther King, Jr., 4, 116, 225

Mason, Alpheus Thomas, 104, 108*

Maternity Act of 1921
narrow scope of judicial review enunciated, 274

Mill, John Stuart
on Dred Scott decision, 31*
on judicial review, 30**-31

Miller, Mr. Justice Samuel F.
on purpose underlying Civil War Amendments, 243-245
Slaughter-House Cases opinion, 188-202

Minimum wage laws
constitutionality, 102

Minority groups
aid to dependent children benefits, 255-256
aliens, 201-202
Chicanos, 246
Chinese, 206
death penalty as cruel and unusual punishment, 248
elimination as solution to problem, 122
hyphenated Americans, 2-3
Japanese-Americans relocated in 1942, 171, 211-212

Minority groups—Cont'd
Jews, 3
Negroes, 3
disaffection with U.S., 98
qualitative difference in anti-Negro discrimination, 246
Orientals, 246
Puerto Ricans and literacy tests, 241
religious minorities
Jehovah's Witnesses, x, 268
Seventh-Day Adventist, 268
securing their obedience and support, 122
state action doctrine as barrier to integration, 213
step-by-step development of rights as exasperating, 215
women, 3

Miranda warnings
lawyer's main function, 280-281
set out and discussed, 280-282

Miscegenation
Court's early evasion, 227-228

Mootness doctrine
Powell and DeFunis contrasted, 314-315


NAACP organizations
membership list case, 223
purposes, 219-221
state efforts to weaken, 223

National Court of Appeals
as remedy for Court's caseload situation, 352-353

Negligence
finding of as mixed question of law and fact, 153

# SUBJECT INDEX

Negroes
   Constitutors intentions re
      protection, 243
   Court's reversal of southern
      criminal convictions, 146
   devices to frustrate their voting
      rights, 208-210
   disproportionate frequency of
      arrests and prosecutions, 226
   hindrances to interstate travel
      eliminated, 239
   step-by-step development of
      rights as exasperating, 215
   trespass prosecutions for
      "sit-ins", 228

New Deal
   invalidation of its program, 102

Newspapers
   as "forums of the streets", 124, 247
   immunity from official censorship, 124
   right of reply statute invalidated, 261*
   trial by newspaper, 160

Nixon, Richard M., 20
   Court's order to surrender tape recordings, 28, 315-318

Nuremberg trials
   purpose served, 317*


Obscenity. *See* Pornography

Omnibus Safe Streets and Crime Control Act of 1968, 235

One person, one vote. *See* Legislative reapportionment

Opinion writing. *See* Advisory opinions

Ordered liberty
   concept discussed, 105-107
   essentiality of accusatorial system denied, 156
   vagueness of phrase, 107

Orwell, George, 245-246


Parks
   administration as state action if municipal in nature, 231

Plea bargaining
   Habeas Corpus delays as substantial consideration in, 286
   in trial of Wolfgang Friedmann's alleged murderers, 286*-287
   preserved by insulating guilty pleas from attack, 298
   rules favoring, 295

Plurality opinion
   defined, 322

Police
   intrusions upon personal privacy, 98

Political opposition
   main purpose of recognition of right, 120

Political party structure
   judicial review and foreign courts, 28

Political questions
   legislative reapportionment, 130-138. *See also* Legislative reapportionment
   Rhode Island insurrection, 120**
   six characteristics, 134, 140
   state's rescission of ratification of amendment, 260*

Pornography
  Carnal Knowledge case, 326-328
  examples of specific statutory
    definition, 325-326
  Fanny Hill case
    plurality opinion, 322
    redeeming social value test,
      323
    Stewart's (Mr. Justice Potter)
      use of term "hard-core
      pornography", 322
    three rules established, 323-324
  freedom to enjoy in one's home,
    342
  fringe issues in obscenity cases,
    324
  judicial review and foreign
    courts, 28
  redeeming social value test
    as wholly subjective, 323
  semantic accident and obscenity,
    129
  Warren's (Mr. Chief Justice Earl)
    pandering rule, 321, 323

Powell, Adam Clayton, Jr.
  congressional seating, 139-141

Preferred position theory. *See*
  Constitutional interpretation

Preliminary hearings
  right to counsel, 68

Presumptions in statutes. *See*
  Statutory interpretation

Primary and Secondary Education
    Act of 1965
  as violating Establishment
    Clause, 176-177

Privacy
  associational privacy cases,
    223-224
  degradation of term, 336*

Privacy—Cont'd
  Fourth Amendment as covering
    all forms of official intrusion,
    74
  list of Bill of Rights provisions
    which protect, 340
  neo-privacy
    cases, 336-342
    major constitutional doctrine in
      abortion case, 341
    tentative judicial review as
      adequate to enforce, 343-344
  reappearance of substantive due
    process, 337

Privileges or Immunities Clause
  "any law" interpreted, 187-188
  Court's nullification in 1873, 181
  Due Process and Equal Protection
    clauses compared, 181-182
  immunity's meaning, 182
  "make" and "enforce" interpreted,
    182-183
  privilege's meaning, 182
  rationale of Slaughter-House
    decision, 190-202
  seven propositions of the
    Slaughter-House decision,
    191-192
  solidity of Slaughter-House
    interpretation, 201
  terms in which it speaks, 181
  two preliminary questions re
    interpretation, 182-183

Prospectivity. *See* Constitutional
  interpretation

Public school desegregation. *See*
  Desegregation, Public schools

Puerto Ricans
  English-language literacy tests,
    138
  literacy tests, 241

Racial covenants
  and the Civil Rights Act of 1866, 212
  implications of Shelley v. Kraemer, 180-181
  use of house and lot by non-Caucasians, 179-180
  wide use to perpetuate neighborhood segregation, 180

Racial discrimination
  child benefit theory as aiding, 170

Racial segregation
  from Plessy to Brown, 207
  through separate but equal facilities, 206-207

Railway Labor Act
  discriminatory representation in railroad unions, 179

Rational relationship test
  defined and described, 248-250

Reconstruction Act of March 2, 1867, 46

Rehnquist, Mr. Justice William H.
  position on judicial review, 13-14

Released time program. *See* Schools, Public

Rembar, Charles, 322

Remedies
  damages against federal official action, 293-294

Removal statute. *See* Judiciary Act of 1789

Res judicata
  and retroactively applied rulings, 76*

Retroactivity. *See* Constitutional interpretation

Revolution
  method for suppression, 122
  rightness of when corrective political processes fail, 121*

Rhode Island insurrection, 120**

Right to counsel
  and accusatorial system, 155
  at preliminary hearing, 68
  fundamental and essential, 163
  indentification line-ups, 165
  in post-indictment interrogation, 165
  prosecutions leading to jail sentence, 165
  racial element in Court's criminal process concerns, 247
  retroactively applied, 76-77

Roane, Judge Spencer
  attack on McCulloch v. Maryland decision, 23

Roberts, Mr. Justice Owen J.
  on guilty verdicts, 153
  on judicial review, 62

Roman Catholics
  and the Establishment Clause, 170-171
  cost of maintaining separate parochial schools, 98
  financial burden of private education, 173

Roosevelt, Franklin D.
  Court-packing plan, xi, 27*, 80, 102
  on "government by judiciary", 201

Root, Clark, Buckner & Ballantine
  Friendly, Judge Henry J., ix-x
  Harlan, Mr. Justice John M., ix-x

Rosenberg, Prof. Maurice
  modified National Court of Appeals proposal, 353
Rosenwald, Julius, 4
Royall, William L.
  on the Slaughter-House Cases, 198
Rules of law
  law school grading systems, 3
  Louisiana pilotage laws, 3
  objectively knowable rules, 2

Sacco and Vanzetti, 146
Schlesinger, Arthur, Jr.
  on Andrew Jackson, 28*
Schools, Private
  child benefit theory as aiding racial discrimination, 170
  financial burden of Roman Catholics, 173
  municipal administration of segregated facilities as state action, 230-231
Schools, Public. *See also* Desegregation, Public schools
  devotional Bible reading, 172
  federal financial assistance as hastening desegregation, 218
  financing methods, 257
  prayer recitation, 172
  released time program, 171
Search and seizure
  and accusatorial system, 155
  Black (Mr. Justice Hugo) on, 69
  electronic eavesdropping, 69, 165
  federal standards relaxed, 158*
  Fourth amendment as window dressing, 73-74
  racial element in Court's criminal process concerns, 247

Search and seizure—Cont'd
  selectively incorporated, 164
  warrantless searches, 165

Selective Service Act
  conscientious objectors, 269

Self-Incrimination, Privilege against
  custodial interrogation, 165
  selectively incorporated, 164
  two illustrations of extremes in applying, 332-334
  unprotected by Fourteenth Amendment, 156

Separate but equal doctrine
  Harlan's (Mr. Justice John) dissent, 206-207
  violative of Equal Protection Clause, 214

Separation of powers
  doctrine ignored in Nixon tapes case, 315-316
  offended by judicial constitution-making, 79

Sex discrimination. *See* Discrimination, Sex

Sit-in demonstrations, 228
  decisions on as Court's signal to Congress for help, 234

Slaughter-House Cases
  discussed, 189-202
  near-repudiation of rationale, 230
  retraction of rationale preferred to use of old Civil Rights Acts, 234
  seven propositions of the opinion, 191-192
  solidity of interpretation, 201
  soundness of opinion examined, 194-202

Slavery
　as more than mere legal
　　institution, 186
　effect of Whitney's cotton gin,
　　42-43
　judicial review as medium
　　attempting to settle
　　controversy, 43
　original Constitution's failure
　　to resolve, 42
　qualitative difference from
　　discrimination against
　　others, 246, 335

Social change
　large social change's
　　meaning, 278*
　limits on Court's power to
　　institute, 278-279

Speedy trial
　selectively incorporated, 164

Standing to sue
　and the Establishment
　　Clause, 176-178
　Brennan (Mr. Justice William)
　　on, 134
　restoration of vitality in the
　　doctrine, 292*
　roots of the notion, 133
　taxpayers attack on CIA, 294*
　white defendant's complaint of
　　exclusion of Blacks from
　　jury, 166

Stare decisis
　repudiated on constitutional
　　issues, 292

State action
　as barrier to integration of
　　minority groups, 213
　cases eroding the doctrine,
　　228-231
　constitutional restrictions
　　clarified, 121

State action—Cont'd
　discrimination by private lessee
　　of state-owned property, 229
　discrimination in sale of multiple
　　dwelling units, 229
　extensive reconsideration of
　　doctrine, 215
　formalized in Civil Rights Cases,
　　203
　municipal nature of city park, 231
　official aid to private discrimina-
　　tion denied, 180
　power to weaken caste barriers
　　denied Congress, 207-208
　sit-in demonstrations, 228
　state constitutional amendment
　　forbidding legislative action,
　　229-230
　13th Amendment not applicable,
　　237

State churches
　disestablishment, 168n4
　establishment vel non question,
　　168

Statutory interpretation. *See also*
　Constitutional interpretation
　conclusive presumptions
　　as device to mask basis of
　　　Court's decision, 308-310
　　new old equally protective
　　　substantively procedural
　　　due process, 310
　definitive judicial review
　　distinguished, 62
　tentative judicial review
　　compared, 62

Sterilization of habitual criminals
　compelling governmental interest
　　test applied to void, 250
　Douglas' (Mr. Justice William)
　　holding, 158

Stewart, Mr. Justice Potter
　concurring in Baker v. Carr, 136

## 442 SUBJECT INDEX

Stone, Mr. Justice Harlan F., 5
  Carolene Products footnote, 108-112. *See also* Carolene Products footnote
  on implied judicial power, 83
  Sacco and Vanzetti case, 146
  self-restraint philosophy, 83
Stop and frisk
  federal standards relaxed, 158*
Subversive Activities Control Act of 1950
  constitutionality, 128
Sunday observance laws. *See* Blue laws
Supervisory power
  Court's use to control federal police conduct, 145
Supremacy Clause. *See* United States Constitution
Supreme Court. *See* United States Supreme Court
Symbionese Liberation Army, 4

Testamentary trusts
  municipal administration of segregated facility, 230-231
  park for whites only, 231
Thomas, Norman, x
Totalitarians
  potential for harm, vii-viii
Trial de novo
  described, 64*
Tyranny
  Black's (Mr. Justice Hugo) definition, 150-151, 157

Unemployment compensation
  and religious hardship, 268-269
United States Congress
  House of Representatives
    constitutional qualifications, 139*
  implied lawmaking power in admiralty, 91-92
  investigatory power, 128
  naturalization power, 182
  power to prevent private discrimination, 181-182
United States Constitution. *See also* Constitutional interpretation
  allocations of lawmaking power, 60-61
  Amendments. *See also* Civil War Amendments, *infra*
    1st
      Constitutors and pornography, 319-320
      Establishment Clause. *See* Establishment Clause
      Free Exercise Clause. *See* Free Exercise Clause
      freedom of association, 126
      interpretation of religious clauses since 1947, 168
      racial neutrality, 222
    2d
      right to bear arms as dead letter, 307
    4th
      covers all forms of official intrusion, 74
      safeguards extended to state prosecutions, 247
    5th
      double jeopardy clause, 104-105

# SUBJECT INDEX

United States Constitution—Cont'd
Amendments—Cont'd
5th—Cont'd
    privilege against self-incrimination, 128
    safeguards extended to state prosecutions, 247
    set out, 162*
6th, 163
    safeguards extended to state prosecutions, 247
7th
    set out, 162**
8th
    safeguards extended to state prosecutions, 247
10th, 103*
    and federal foreign affairs power, 307
    Articles of Confederation contrasted, 94-95
    set out, 177*
13th
    Court's interpretation, 184-185
    state action doctrine not applicable, 237
14th
    and the Civil Rights Cases, 189, 204-06
    complete and literal incorporation, 169
    constitutors intention, 168-169
    controls gross forms of discrimination, 36
    development had Slaughter-House never occurred, 203
    disputes over exact purposes, 197
    Enforcement Clause set out, 186*

United States Constitution—Cont'd
Amendments—Cont'd
14th—Cont'd
    Equal Protection Clause, 130
    exclusionary rule and state courts, 78
    genesis, 197
    in the Slaughter-House Cases, 183, 188-189
    nullification of Privileges or Immunities Clause, 181
    pornography and the Constitutors, 320
    primary purpose, 184-185
    purpose of first sentence, 193
    race as core, 245
    reshaped national objectives, 45-46
    separate but equal doctrine, 206-207
    three propositions explaining adoption, 199-200
    two-class theory, 233
15th
    nonwhites in party primary elections, 179
24th, 263
26th, 241
27th. *See* Equal Rights Amendment
amendments passed to overrule Court decisions, 40
Art. V amending power usurped, 9
as an outside source of law, 32
as expression of popular will, 32
as pattern of national objectives, 44
Black's (Mr. Justice Hugo) Holy Writ, 74

Civil War Amendments. *See also* Amendments, *supra*

United States Constitution—Cont'd
  Civil War Amendments—Cont'd
    Constitutors intentions, 246
    Court/Congress partnership in implementation, 235
    Court s mutilation (1873-1896), 181
    early interpretations, result, 13
    main purpose underlying, 243-245
    results of delay of the promise, 4
    special constitutional status of anti-Negro discrimination, 335
  colorblind, 207
  Commerce Clause
    discrimination or segregation in public accommodations, 22
    grant of power to Congress, 48
    insurance regulation, 56
    objective, 48
    racial discrimination in restaurants, 239
  conflict with as meaning conflict with language, 69
  constitutional rule-making as offending Article V, 79
  "construction" to avoid constitutional doubt, 53
  Contract Clause
    set out, 182*
  Court's appellate jurisdiction, 29
  dangers of power to interpret beyond plain meaning, 23
  devices mitigating problems of heterogeneity, 36
  focus shifted from text to observed phenomena, 25*
  Founding Fathers
    intentions, 21
    political philosophy, 21-22
    four principles of government embodied in, 122

United States Constitution—Cont'd
  Great Britain's constitution compared, 33-35
  latitudinarian technique of interpretation, 63
  law of superior obligation, 27*
  Necessary and Proper Clause, 86, 91
    set out, 186*
  power to regulate foreign relations assumed, 87-89
  Privileges or Immunities Clause. See Privileges or Immunities Clause
  reflection of consensus of dead supermajorities, 32
  speech or debate clause, 140
  Supreme Court's declaration of rules, 73
  symbol of national unity, 37-38

United States President
  defiance of Court as political suicide, 28
  foreign affairs power as implied power, 85-90

United States Supreme Court. See also Constitutional law; Judicial power; Judicial review; United States Congress; United States Constitution
  abortion rulings (1973), 10
  actions as reflections of actual majority's will?, 39
  appellate jurisdiction. See Appellate jurisdiction
  as continuing constitutional convention, 5, 21, 271*
  broad veto power over government, 27
  caseload
    doctrinal development related, 13, 279
    endangers quality of Court's work, 351-352

SUBJECT INDEX 445

United States Supreme Court—Cont'd
  caseload—Cont'd
    Friendly's (Chief Judge Henry J.) recommendations, 353
    methods to remedy, 352-355
  certiorari petitions, 5
  changes wrought in own role, 273
  constitutional innovation since 1969, 9
  constitutional rules, 73
  cases digested, 265
  Copernican analogy to orthodox constitutional theory, 25, 270*
  Court-packing plan. See Roosevelt, Franklin D.
  criticism of, two dangers, viii
  decisions as usurpations of power, 6
  defiance of orders as political suicide, 28
  Dred Scott decision
    and Abraham Lincoln, 28
    condemned by posterity, 24
    judicial review as attempt to settle slavery problem, 43
    Mill's (John Stuart) comments, 31*
  five-theorem approach to its work, 11-13, 318
  flawed achievement record, vii
  guiding principle, 11
  judicial review. See Judicial review
  judiciary as least dangerous branch, 31-32, 72
  law's servant or master, 1, 19, 58
  liberal bloc, 9*, 132*, 201, 273
  major national interests protected, 11-13
  mandamus writ, authority to issue, 71

United States Supreme Court—Cont'd
  neutral principles of adjudication, 4-6, 20, 22
  1937-38 Term
    judicial review reexamined, 102
    majoritarian philosophy described, 103
    withdrawal from economic regulation, 102
  Nixon appointees, 10*
    on abortion, 14-15. See also Abortion cases
    on compulsory education laws, 14
    on death penalty, 14
    on unanimous guilty verdicts, 14
  objective evaluation, difficulty, 99-100
  observed changes in Justices' role, 9*
  propriety of exerting raw judicial power, 75
  prudential basis of deciding questions, 5, 20
  quo warranto writ defined, 19-20
  refusal to acknowledge constitution-making activities, 74
  signals to Congress for help, 234
  "silence of Congress" cases, 67
  single dominating objective, 11
  state of mind defined, 46
  strategic position in governmental system, 29
  voter's acquiescence in maintenance, 31-32, 80
  Uphaus, Dr. Willard, xi
  vulnerability, 29-30*

Uphaus, Dr. Willard, xi

Use immunity
  court created doctrine, 333

Vinson, Mr. Chief Justice Fred
  on moral obligation to obey the law. 40*-41
Voting rights. *See also* Civil Rights Acts; Legislative Reapportionment
  access to ballot for political parties and candidates, 263
  and compelling governmental interest test, 251
  cases, 130, 262-263
  concept of equal voting power, 131
  convicted felons, 262*
  district lines, three electoral possibilities, 130-131
  grandfather clauses, 208
  literacy tests, 208-209
  nonwhites in party primary elections, 179
  political parties and access to ballot, 138-139
  poll taxes, 209
  practical effect of a vote, 130
  prisoners awaiting trial, 262
  residence requirements, 263
  strict equal protection standards enunciated, 138
  variance ratios in weight of votes, 263
Voting Rights Act Amendments of 1970
  literacy tests abolished. 241
Voting Rights Act of 1965
  provisions and main thrust, 240-241
  white primary, 209-210

Wall Street law firms. *See also* Law offices
  minority group representation, 3
  pro bono practices, ix-x
Warren, Chief Justice Earl
  impeachment attempt, 9

Watts incident, 118
Wechsler, Prof. Herbert. *See also* Constitutional law
  Bickel-Wechsler debate, 4-5, 20
  neutral principles of constitutional law, 4-5, 20, 22
Welfare programs
  aid to dependent children, 255-256
  food stamp program, 256
  subsidized housing, 256
Welfare waiting periods
  and compelling governmental interest test, 251-252
  compelling governmental interest test applied, 264
  discriminates between old and new residents, 251
  four claimed justifications, 252
  violative of constitutional right of unimpeded movement, 251-252
White Citizens Councils
  deliberate speed doctrine as stimulating, 218-219
White, Mr. Justice Byron R.
  dissent in abortion cases, 20*
White primary
  cases, 209-210
  unconstitutional, 212
Wills
  implications of Shelley v. Kraemer, 180
Witnesses, Adverse, Right to Confrontation
  selectively incorporated, 164
Witnesses, Compulsory Process
  selectively incorporated, 164
Wyman, Louis C., xi